GEORGIAN DUBLIN

THE FORCES THAT SHAPED THE CITY

The Hellfire Club, Dublin
(James Worsdale, c. 1735) (NGI)

GEORGIAN DUBLIN

THE FORCES THAT SHAPED THE CITY

DIARMUID Ó GRÁDA

CORK UNIVERSITY PRESS

First published in 2015 by Cork University Press
Youngline Industrial Estate, Pouladuff Road, Togher, Cork, Ireland

Text © Diarmuid Ó Gráda
Images © held by the owners

British Library Cataloguing in Publication Data

A CIP catalogue record for this book is available from the British Library.

ISBN 978-178205-147-3

Book design and typesetting, Anú Design, Tara
Printed by Printer Trento, Italy

If one had any sufficient explanation of this indifference to dirt and odour that are repulsive to many animals, even pigs ... one might also have a clue to the slow and fitful nature of technological improvement itself, in the five millennia that followed the birth of cities.

Lewis Mumford, *The City in History*, 1961

For Celine

Contents

Interpretation

In the Georgian period the pound sterling comprised twenty shillings. There were twelve pence in a shilling. Five shillings made a crown and twenty-one shillings made a guinea. One pound, two shillings and three pennies was written thus: £1 2s 3d. In many cases today's prices would be a hundred times greater than those of the Georgian era.

References to parishes and churches are those of the Established Church or Protestant tradition – that is, the Church of Ireland – unless otherwise stated. This was the body charged with local government and policing during the study period.

Original spelling and punctuation have been retained save for capitalisation. Dates are given in Old Style, as used in Ireland (and England) until the 1752 calendar change, except that the year has been taken to begin on 1 January.

Introduction

Studies of eighteenth-century urban development in Ireland have been greatly neglected, and the prevailing view of Georgian Dublin is unbalanced in many respects. Certain topics have been prominent because of the surviving records that support them. In the sphere of town planning the impact of the Wide Streets Commission is well known on account of the generous archive of maps, drawings and minutes that it left behind. Likewise, the development process within large estates, such as those of the Gardiners and Fitzwilliams, is explained by the documentary evidence, making it easier for us to admire the design and layout of the elegant squares and fine terraced houses that were so carefully coordinated.

It is these features that have attracted the most attention, but it would be incorrect to infer from them that Dublin was amongst the best regulated European capitals during the second half of the eighteenth century. On the contrary, overcrowding and filth reached epic proportions in Dublin, and there were periods when the city was running out of control. This chaos was mainly due to the unrest of the anonymous.

Contemporary sources for the study of eighteenth-century urbanisation are quite plentiful, but they are often intractable, usually partial and sometimes inconsistent. There has been a growing awareness of the value of newspapers as a resource; this study would be a very different one without them. It was during the Georgian era that regular publication of newspapers became established in Dublin. Most of the early papers had their contents copied from English publications, but with each passing decade the proportion of locally derived material increased. They provide insights into those everyday events that cumulatively generated socio-economic responses, and recurring patterns of behaviour can be traced. Digitisation has facilitated access to eighteenth-century newspaper sources.

In this work the use of contemporary newspapers is based on an understanding that the quality and reliability of the accounts is variable. From the outset the city papers followed diverse editorial paths, and there was a considerable variety of emphases placed on the material that appeared. We should consider that scandal and rumour, and the sheer desire to attract readers, could tempt newspapers to distort or even falsify their reports. Each new proprietor was bound to bring his own policy to bear, and that, in turn, was going to be coloured by the search for revenue from sources such as government notices.

This is a reason for consulting several different newspapers, allowing the reader to gauge the weight and frequency attached to both topics and events. Use has been made here of a continuous sequence of Dublin newspapers extending from the 1740s up to the 1810s. The primary sources in this regard are *Faulkner's Dublin Journal* (1743–76), the *Hibernian Journal* (1776–78 and 1780–86) and *The Freeman's Journal* (1779 and 1787–1810). The sequence of the reading was intended to reflect the extent and quality of the accounts. Short runs of supplementary sources were also used to check the balance, namely *The Dublin Evening Post* (1787), the *Dublin Chronicle* (1788) and *The Belfast News-Letter* (1789).

As for the newspapers, so it is with pamphlets. Very many of these publications were advocative or adversarial, and they were usually private publications. For these reasons we should allow for the varying proportions of subjectivity and objectivity. Since so much of the city's everyday administration was based on the parish structure of the established church (Church of Ireland), the surviving vestry records can reveal aspects of local government, policing and social welfare. It is those records of the more affluent parishes that have survived in greatest numbers, and this needs to be borne in mind in assessing the contents.

(From John Carr, *The Stranger in Ireland*, 1806)
(Courtesy of Éamonn de Búrca)

1

Urbanisation in Georgian Dublin

*C'est toujours dans les capitales que le sang humain se vend
à meilleur marché.*

Jean-Jacques Rousseau, 1782[1]

EUROPEAN CITIES SAW GREAT CHANGES during the late seventeenth and early eighteenth
centuries. In Dublin relative peace followed the Glorious Revolution of 1688, and the city
used this opportunity to engage in new development. Its location allowed it to spread out
in many directions. The historic city walls fell into disuse, and, like other European cities,
the sharp distinction between the inside and the outside began to fade away. Suburbia
gradually emerged and the surrounding countryside became safer and within easier reach,
generating a strong attachment to the Romantic idyll that combined rural simplicity with
healthy virtue.

Several factors allowed Georgian Dublin to dominate Irish affairs. It had control over
the progress of the entire island, and over time the great power brought by this pre-
eminence allowed a transformation of the city itself. There were two, distinct, expansion

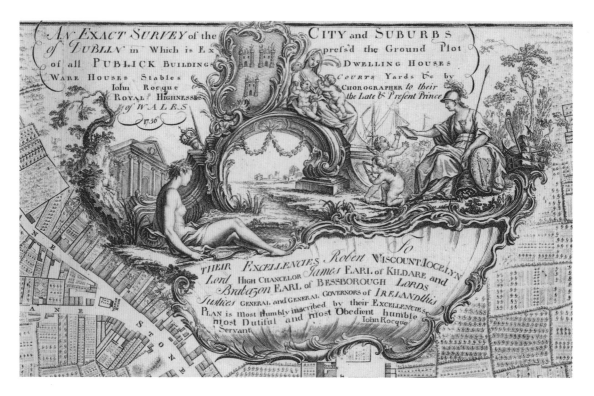

phases. The first occurred during the early decades of the eighteenth century and the second took place between the 1740s and 1760s. Dublin became the second largest city in Britain and Ireland, being superseded only by London, and this distinction was achieved by combining its several roles as a parliamentary, administrative, industrial and commercial centre with that of a major port. Customs duties formed a very important part of government income (far higher than property taxes and excise), and for most of the eighteenth century over half of Irish customs duties were collected in Dublin. It had another advantage in that its function as a colonial capital allowed it to hold a major army garrison.[2]

For the purposes of history, architecture and design, most of the eighteenth century, along with the early decades of the nineteenth century, is identified in Ireland and in the United Kingdom with the Georgian era. It is generally accepted that this period began in 1714 with the coronation of King George I, and ended in 1830 with the death of George IV. Like many such constructs, however, it is more of a notion than a strictly delimited age, as the short reign (1830–37) of William IV intervened prior to the great wave of Victorian urbanisation. The so-called madness of George III adds another dimension to this search for terms; the Regency period extended from 1811 until 1820, but many scholars consider its span to be longer due to the turmoil it brought into several aspects of everyday life. We should also allow that Ireland's peripheral and politically subordinate status, accentuated by linguistic, political and religious divisions, had an impact on the country's engagement with the wider world. These factors could explain some of the time lapse in the adoption of designs and tastes, and this in turn could warp the rigid timeframe imposed by historians.

Everyday life was strongly influenced by the British connection, but until the political union of 1801 Ireland remained merely a colony. London pursued its own interests and sought to impose its will on important aspects of Irish trade and politics. While economic historians now believe that the effects of

Within the sanctuary of the castle, a young boy impresses two ladies by shouldering his toy gun. (From James Malton, *A Picturesque and Descriptive View of the City of Dublin*, 1799)

late seventeenth- and eighteenth-century mercantilist legislation on the Irish economy were exaggerated by nationalist propaganda, the influence of British interests who felt threatened by Irish competition was highlighted by the rejection of Pitt's commercial propositions in the mid-1780s.[3] In particular, its lack of integration with the British economy left Ireland at a disadvantage relative to Scotland, which had been integrated since 1707. Britain itself occupied an exceptional position. It was the most affluent state in the world and was also the most dynamic. Its immense wealth was forged from two sources: the exploited labour force at home and the set-upon Empire abroad. Notable innovations in London usually found their way across the Irish Sea, and this influence was already obvious by the late seventeenth century.

Urban administration took more notice of city planning and urban design. Dublin began to engage with its backdrop of hills, rivers and coastline. In this new era of civic image the River Liffey became a central feature, and quayside buildings started to address the river, thereby opening up expanses of fine architectural expression. This innovation replaced the long-held notion of the river as something to turn your back on – for use merely as a shipping station or to drain away urban waste.

These reforms were to have long-lasting benefits. The government promoted the quality of street architecture. In 1670 the lord lieutenant decreed that all new houses had to be solidly built by using either stone or brick; all thatched roofs were to be replaced with slates or tiles, and any projecting element in the façade had to be removed. This measure coincided with the introduction of fire protection, bringing to Dublin some lessons learned from the Great Fire of London four years previously. Features such as window reveals were widely adopted to control the spread of fire, and innovations such as these facilitated the formation of the elegant streetscapes that we associate with the Georgian era. As the use of brick emerged in the late seventeenth century it allowed greater flexibility in building design, and this was combined with a rapid increase in construction. In public buildings, however, there was still a reliance on stone, especially the calp limestone quarried locally. For many city dwellers, however, these innovations seemed irrelevant. Mud-walled cabins marked the paupers' quarters. These were low dwellings where windows and chimneys were in short supply. As late as the 1780s such hovels occupied most of the outskirts. A step above these were the roadside cottages to be found in places such as the medieval settlement of Kilmainham – small, single-storey buildings with a little window to either side of the front door. Some of the better examples on the south-east side were depicted in the 1760s property inventory of the Pembroke estate.[4]

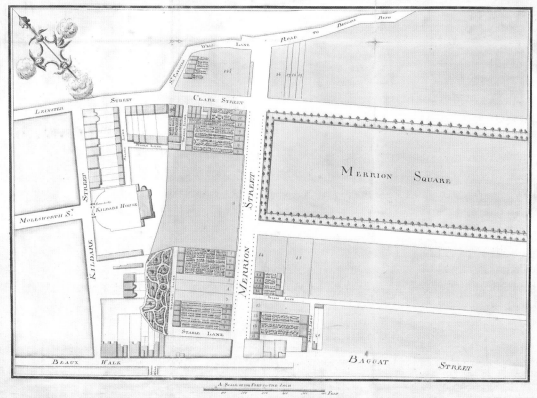

A PLAN OF MERRION STREET AND THE ADJACENT NEIGHBOURHOOD SURVEYED in 1762 by IONATH. BARKER

Merrion Square laid out for development, 1762. Note the adjoining Kildare House (now the parliament house) in an axial relationship with Molesworth Street rather than the new square. (NAI)

There were several factors at work in the expansion of Georgian Dublin, but the foremost influences on the direction and pace of urban growth can be divided into two broad categories. These might be termed the 'push' and 'pull' forces. The push forces were those agencies encouraging the outward spread of expansion, while the pull forces encouraged the concentration and densification of new growth. These forces could by turns be dominant, neutral or subservient. Studies of Dublin have concentrated on the pull forces and this is especially true of the remarkable housing projects carried out within the large private estates of the Fitzwilliams and Gardiners. In this regard, a good topographical source is the *Irish Historic Towns Atlas* published by the Royal Irish Academy; volume 19, Dublin, part ii (2008) dealt with the period 1610–1756, while part iii (2014) brought the work forward from 1756 to 1847.

While housing schemes such as Rutland Square and Merrion Square were undoubtedly significant in transforming the urban landscape, this study will focus more on the push forces that had a greater impact on the daily lives of the ordinary people. Foremost amongst these were the growing tensions within the city that caused it to surge outwards.

※ ※ ※ ※ ※

Urbanisation was part of the socio-economic change spreading across eighteenth-century Europe. National administrations became more centralised and they drew the bureaucrats into the cities. The men of property became increasingly concerned with the management of their environment. In Ireland there was a need to secure the property titles of new proprietors after the Glorious Revolution. In 1707 Ireland's Registry of Deeds was established for this purpose, and its first home in Dublin Castle reflected its colonial role. It remained there until 1805, when it assumed a more mainstream image by moving across the Liffey to Inns Quay. This registry was intended to record all property transactions while at the same time ensuring that no Catholics owned property.

As the main centre of law and learning, Dublin's bureaucracy was bound to expand. Civil servants became more numerous and they were attracted by the salaries as well as the security of tenure. Once inside the system they could see the potential to advance their careers. By the 1760s the city had a thousand attorneys and the number continued to grow. There were half as many again by the end of the century.

Technological innovations helped to transform many aspects of European human relations and public administration. According to Mary Pollard, the printing press was brought to Ireland in the sixteenth century as an instrument of proselytism. It was intended to convert the locals to the Protestant religion by using publications in the Irish language. That initiative failed, but it did show how the Irish press was devoted to the needs of English imperial rule and to the English-speaking Protestant elite.[5] With every passing decade the number of publishers continued to grow, and it also became easier to produce the paper that was the main raw material. This boom in publications was most pronounced between the 1690s and 1760, when the number of booksellers more than trebled and the number of master printers grew more than tenfold.

Dublin's trade in printing and publishing was concentrated within the area bounded by Dame Street and Essex Street, together with the adjoining riverside quarter now known as Temple Bar. Innovation brought more paper mills, printing works and related trades. New possibilities were presented to writers of fiction as the book market emerged. Three editions of Daniel Defoe's *Robinson Crusoe* (1719) were sold within four months, and Jonathan Swift, a Dublin resident,

BLOODY News, laſt Night's Packet.
bloody News—Here's the Monthly
Magazines, and all the neweſt Publications

achieved four editions of *Gulliver's Travels* (1726) in a little over a year. For some this book market turned out to be lucrative, and Dublin editions of both of these bestsellers appeared within their first year. In 1726 Jonathan Swift was paid £200 for *Gulliver's Travels* and in 1772 Oliver Goldsmith received eight hundred guineas for his *History of the Earth*. Many of the Georgian playwrights who achieved enduring popularity had strong Dublin connections – for example, Oliver Goldsmith and Richard Brinsley Sheridan.[6]

Public discourse grew and an expanding volume of printed material brought a revolution in the distribution of information. In these islands there was a demand for the standardisation of the English language so that it could better serve those professions that were becoming more specialised. This need was made more urgent by the emergence of learned journals. Publication of the transactions of London's Royal Society began as early as 1665, and the *Gentleman's Magazine* appeared in 1731. One response to this was the publication of books setting out the rules for writers. Samuel Johnson's dictionary of the English language appeared in 1755, and was followed by a spate of instruction books on both spelling and grammar; more of these guides were issued in England between 1765 and 1800 than during all of the previous century.[7] Ireland was slow to embrace this new dispensation, although the Royal Dublin Society (RDS) was founded in 1731 and the Royal Irish Academy (RIA) was set up in 1785. The capital had been home to the Dublin Philosophical Society from 1683; that organisation had a rather obscure existence, although it did correspond with sister bodies in London and Oxford.[8] Some of these societies were short-

lived – for example, the Physico-Historical Society (1744–52), the Medico-Physical Society (1756–84) and the Hibernian Antiquarian Society (1779–82). Some of them were subsumed into later, more ambitious bodies. The RIA played a part in this process.[9]

Societies such as these had an impact far beyond their modest membership. They became agencies for the circulation of knowledge and part of a network introducing innovation to the workplace. The Royal Dublin Society was very significant in this role as it strived to bring science into the service of the Irish economy. This reform followed an uneven path that reflected a wider debate. There were competing elements within the RDS itself; the members could not agree on whether the rural agricultural sector or the urban industrial sector should get priority. In other words, the elite itself still had misgivings about the urban model of progress.[10]

Trinity College was the only university in Ireland in this period, and it doubled its student intake between 1750 and 1800. This impressive growth matched that of Edinburgh.[11] Nevertheless, education was like so many other elements of city life in retaining rigid social divisions; the city poor were left with

The proximity of the university (right) to parliament (background) made the search for funds a lot easier. College Green and Grafton Street remain public-meeting venues. (Courtesy of Andrew Bonar Law)

a very rudimentary provision that relied heavily on the generosity of benefactors. Education exemplified the great social divide, and affluent families generally kept their children at home to be taught by private tutors. As late as 1805 two city parishes had no school at all and half of those parishes that did possess a school had no playground – the children played in old graveyards that had been condemned as health hazards.[12]

✳ ✳ ✳ ✳ ✳

During the eighteenth century there was a substantial growth in the popularity of art, and this was connected with the fashionable pursuit of good taste. Cheap prints made art available to the general public, and William Hogarth became the best-known artist working with this new form. In 1746 he sold ten thousand copies of his portrait of Lord Lovat, a rebel executed after the Jacobite uprising of the previous year. Versions of Hogarth's work were published in Dublin.[13] The most abiding visual impression of life in the capital is derived from the prints of James Malton. They were issued in the 1790s, and were, in turn, part of an established European tradition. Half a century earlier, Rome's art market saw the publication of printed views called *vedute* that were mainly aimed at the emerging tourist trade. Giovanni Piranesi was the foremost artist of this genre during the 1740s, and over the following decades his work brought the Eternal City into houses all over the Continent; it is no surprise even today to come across examples of them in Irish Georgian houses. Whether fortuitous or otherwise, there is a Dublin link between Hogarth and Piranesi. James Caulfeild, the 1st Earl of Charlemont, was a great patron of the arts; he bought at least two paintings from Hogarth and also had one volume of Piranesi's output dedicated to him. Caulfeild built a large townhouse at Rutland Square, complete with gallery space and a fine library to accommodate his collection.

Pictorial representations of Georgian Dublin are confined to a narrow range – so much so that we find certain images are repeatedly reproduced. It was, therefore, a welcome surprise when an album of street scenes from 1760 was discovered in 2002 and published a year later. This collection of drawings, entitled *The Cries of Dublin*, was the work of the Irish painter Hugh Douglas Hamilton.[14] This again was an international genre, and the London *Cries* of Marcellus Laroon are well known.[15]

✳ ✳ ✳ ✳ ✳

A Tinker

Fresh & Pickled Herrings

Major items of European political news were quick to reach the Irish capital. A notable example of this occurred when the War of the Austrian Succession came to an end. The Treaty of Aix-la-Chapelle was signed on 18 October 1748, and it inspired celebratory firework displays all across Europe. These began in Paris in February 1749; London and Dublin followed within two months, and The Hague joined in two months later. Dublin's show was held in St Stephen's Green, and a print of it appeared immediately afterwards in London's *Universal Magazine* (April 1749). St Stephen's Green acquired an enduring popularity as a venue for fireworks that proclaimed the Protestant city, and there was certain to be a large crowd whenever the show was associated with some aspect of the king's life, whether his coronation (1761) or a respite from madness (1789). City newspapers claimed these gatherings attracted up to fifty thousand people, but such reports were exaggerated for propaganda purposes. The fiery spectacles were combined with musical recitals, and the public was charged for admission. In 1750 the tickets normally cost a shilling, and this ensured a genteel audience, excluding the boisterous hoi polloi.[16]

Left: Ordinary Dubliners relied on menders and fixers to prolong the working life of household utensils. Right: Pickling agents, such as brine or vinegar, prolonged the shelf life of fish. (Both images, Hugh Douglas Hamilton, 1760) (Private collection)

By mid-century the presence of Catholics became more obvious as official enthusiasm for the Penal Laws began to wane. This change clearly emerged in 1744 following a tragic accident when ten people died while attending Mass in an old house in Pill Lane. After this loss, caused by the collapse of the house, the viceroy expressed a preference for services to be held in the regular chapels that had previously been outlawed. Despite this concession, however, the geography of the city's Catholics continued to reflect the lowly status of its members. In 1750 there were nineteen chapels and convents in total, nearly all of them west of Dublin Castle. The main cluster was embedded in the old medieval quarter, with the axis formed by Thomas Street/Cook Street holding almost half of them.[17]

In the broader sense, however, everyday life in Dublin became more secular, and the power of religious institutions began to wane. This was a slow process, but there was a growing belief that the law should operate at a level that was independent of religion. The city's guilds, like their counterparts across western Europe, began to discard their medieval religious trappings. This is certainly true of the so-called miracle plays that had been a central feature of annual guild

Lavish fireworks marked the end of the War of the Austrian Succession, which had lasted eight years. (*Universal Magazine*, 1749)

pageants, the last recorded production being in 1744. Dublin's ecclesiastical courts were defunct by the advent of the Georgian era, and the last convocation took place in 1711. The most public expression of this secularisation occurred in the mid-1780s when it was decided to house the main courts of law in their own purpose-built premises; this meant moving them literally out from under the shadow of the Protestant Church, as these courts had, for most of the previous two centuries, occupied an annex of Christ Church cathedral. Their new home was the splendid Four Courts building designed by James Gandon on the north bank of the Liffey.[18]

Public debate was stimulated by the publication of pamphlets on the controversial topics of the day. Social reformers promoted their ideas by issuing essays, while religious zealots sold tracts offering salvation to lost souls. Doctors peddled booklets promising cures for deadly diseases, and quacks advertised pills for every complaint. These works were intended to encourage people to abandon bad habits and to improve their lives. Dublin took an active part in these debates, and this is reflected today in two of the city's important collections of early pamphlets: the Haliday collection of the Royal Irish Academy and the Gilbert collection of Dublin City Council.

Riverside views became more popular as the quays were opened up by the Wide Streets Commission. (George Petrie, 1821) (UCD)

Conspicuous consumption of fabrics distinguished the wealthy from the poor. (*Walker's Hibernian Magazine*, March 1786) (UCD)

THE MODERN VENUS

Raggs or Old Cloaths

Stockings mended

London saw the blossoming of a popular new artistic medium during the last three decades of the Georgian era. This was the satirical print that gave lasting fame to the likes of James Gillray and Thomas Rowlandson. Here again we find that Dublin was the foremost centre for copying and for pirating these publications. Britain's copyright law of 1709 did not apply to Ireland, and up until the Union in 1801 Dublin printers had plenty of scope to profit from the reproduction of London publications.[19]

Due to a dearth of illustrations, other sources (including newspapers, visitors' accounts and parish records) are needed to reveal details of people's everyday appearance. Ordinary men in the street were plainly dressed. Their outer garment was usually a great coat made of coarse woollen cloth called frieze. This was an adaptable material that allowed for many uses, including the police uniforms issued to the parish watch. In 1724 St John's parish spent almost £5 on eleven uniforms. Each outfit used 3 metres of frieze, with a third of that forming the bright red tunic. A half-century later, the uniforms for St Anne's watch comprised a jacket of thick milled frieze with lapels buttoned across the breast, a pair of trousers made from ticking (tightly woven cotton or linen), a cape fastened under the chin and a leather cap.[20]

During the 1780s Francis Higgins was a well-known city figure, and his nickname of the Sham Squire followed him. His finery marked him out because he wore

> A three cocked hat, fringed with swan's-down, a canary-coloured vest, with breeches to match, a bright green body-coat, with very deep tails, spangled with highly burnished buttons, and he was the only buck in Dublin who carried gold tassels on his Hessian boots; violet gloves concealed his chubby fingers, richly decorated with rings. A stiff stock, fastened by a diamond brooch, elevated still more his already pompous chin.[21]

When newspapers reported thefts, they regularly gave some details of the wrongdoer. Examples from 1770 included one loud suspect clad in a blue cloak and black hat, as well as a pock-marked young woman who wore an old brown gown, a dirty chequer apron, old black shoes and purple stockings. Women who ventured out to the fair at Palmerstown in 1810 were wearing woollen garments known as stuff, frilled linen bonnets called mop caps, and white thread stockings. At the same venue, the men wore blue or brown coarse coats or great coats made of coarse grey frieze.[22]

These newspaper accounts were, however, fairly unrepresentative, and were misleading in that the majority of ordinary people had very little choice in their apparel. Poverty deprived them of discretion, and they picked up the cast-offs of others. Travellers' accounts testify to this array of rags, and the second-hand trade was strong enough to encourage imports from England and Scotland. This tattered aspect of the populace grew more commonplace towards the end of the Georgian era. During the Regency, paupers who raided potato pits on the outskirts of town were entirely naked save for a ragged coat tied around with a hay band. In 1839 a German visitor described those poor souls he came across cowering barefoot in their miserable rags; they wore the shreds of shirts that were at least as old as themselves, and their modesty was barely redeemed by the use of a tattered jacket that was either too big or too small. This impression of the poorest quarters was confirmed a few years later by another German

A Cripple Beggar

A Beggar Woman

visitor; each window facing the street was used to hang out the laundry but he could only make out half-washed shreds – there was seldom an entire garment to be seen.[23]

✳✳✳✳✳

The Georgian era was one of growing international trade. There was mechanisation and innovation in manufacturing. Standardisation came to the fore, and this had a significant impact on the weights and measures used in everyday life. This adoption of more consistent standards was carried into the area of mass production. Probably the most significant innovation for urban living was mechanical timekeeping. Dublin's main civic building was the Tholsel, and it had a public clock as early as the 1660s.[24] Good communications were essential to society and

THE WEAVER.

commerce, and by the 1720s it took about a week for a letter from Dublin to reach London. Connections were made easier by the construction of coaches that were faster and more comfortable. By the end of the eighteenth century, Dublin had more than forty workshops making coaches.

At the advent of the Georgian period, the guilds held control over the manufacture and sale of goods within the city. They regulated the number of apprentices, as well as their working hours and wages. The arms of the individual guilds were prominent features of Charles Brooking's 1728 city map, and this confirms their importance at that time. Membership of the premier guild, the merchants, grew by fifty per cent between 1680 and 1750. Most of Dublin's trades still operated on a small domestic scale. They remained very much family businesses, and it appears that the owner's wife and children were substantially involved. The typical textile unit in the Liberties was probably a small shop of five or six workers. It was headed by the master, who had perhaps two or three journeymen and a few apprentices. It was a close-knit arrangement, with some of the employees living above the workspace along with their boss. The same model prevailed in the trades of printing and publishing. In the early 1760s George Faulkner, Dublin's most famous printer of the age, combined together at Essex Street his printing office, shop and dwelling.[25]

For many apprentices it was a harsh experience, and they had to spend a period of seven years unpaid learning their trade. The wages for an apprentice did not arrive until he qualified as a journeyman, and even then it was a daily rate based on very long hours. It was only the most successful and wealthy journeymen who became masters, allowing them to take on their own apprentices. From the 1720s onwards, there was a growing tension between employers and workers, as journeymen began to form proto-unions known as combinations, thereby exerting their influence on the workplace. There also emerged a clearer distinction between the home and the workshop. At the same time, new industries such as glassmaking were emerging that had much larger workforces – in some cases reaching well over a hundred.

From its foundation in 1731, the Royal Dublin Society sought to make Irish manufacturing more competitive. It spent a decade investigating the opportunities, and then offered premiums to entrepreneurs engaged in invention and innovation. From the early 1740s these initiatives included grants towards machinery for the production of various textiles. The RDS supported the makers of glass, iron, pottery and paper, and these interventions brought the society into direct conflict with the combinations, whose members were strongly opposed to new industrial methods.[26]

The new scale of production was less amenable to guild control, and by the 1780s the guilds had lost their monopoly over Dublin's tradesmen. By the Regency, the decline was reflected in the weaker public profile of the guilds. Their civic ceremonies had become degraded, and they no longer proclaimed their professional pride through pageants of colour. Warburton's *Dublin* (1818) noted that they had even abandoned their annual church service. Factories brought cultural changes to the workplace. There was a colder, impersonal discipline, and the shared interests of employers and staff faded away. This detached profit-driven model was adopted by public institutions to boost their income, and it had government support. A woollen factory was set up at the Foundling Hospital in 1799. Over a hundred boys were employed there to turn out broadcloth, flannel and camlets, while around eighty girls did the spinning, carding and reeling. This might be regarded as child labour as the boys were aged between ten and twelve and the girls aged between seven and ten. It was, moreover, surprisingly productive as the boys turned out 15,624 yards of calico in a single year, while the girls spun 1,606 pairs of stockings.[27]

The intimate connection between the elements of production and consumption was broken; they no longer had to coincide. The retail trade began to intervene as an agent of this change. There was an expanding array of shops that was beyond the control of the guilds. In 1751 *Wilson's Dublin Directory* listed 925 traders, and by 1800 the total reached over five thousand.[28] There was more recourse to the law to regulate both the market and the workplace. The decline of the old guild system could, however, be exaggerated. It was the municipal reform

The most prosperous parishes had the highest proportion of servants, notably St George's and St Anne's. (Map courtesy of Edel Sheridan-Quantz, David Dickson and Matthew Stout)

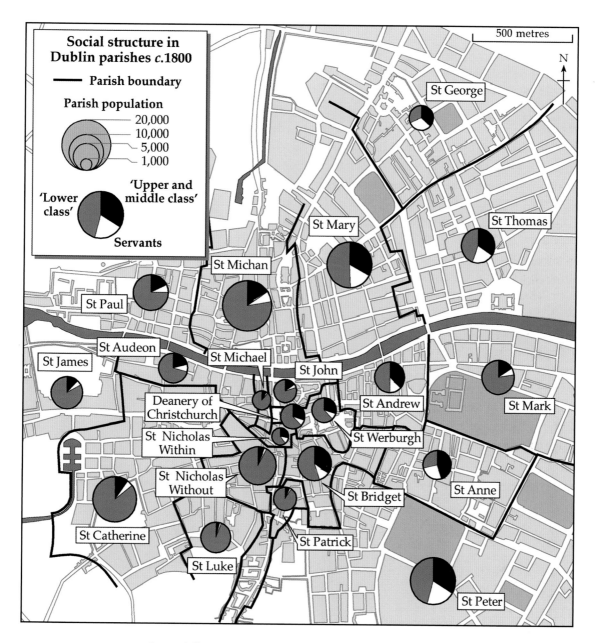

Social structure in Dublin parishes _c._1800

— Parish boundary

Parish population
— 20,000
— 10,000
— 5,000
— 1,000

'Lower class'
'Upper and middle class'
Servants

500 metres

N

St George
St Thomas
St Mary
St Michan
St Paul
St Audeon
St James
St Michael
Deanery of Christchurch
St Nicholas Within
St Nicholas Without
St Catherine
St Luke
St John
St Andrew
St Werburgh
St Bridget
St Patrick
St Anne
St Mark
St Peter

of 1840 (allowing corporation members to be elected by the general public) that finally broke the political power of the guilds.

Men usually held the best jobs and they dominated the workplace. Membership of the guilds was restricted to males. It was only men who were admitted to the army and navy. Women were forced to accept inferior work with lower rewards; it was often menial, seasonal and intermittent. In seventeenth-century London, women replaced men as the majority of domestic servants, and over the following century this pattern was followed in cities such as Paris, Geneva and Madrid. Dublin was no different, and Irish law busied itself in overseeing the movements of these females. Domestic servants within the city led lives that were carefully circumscribed. Their career path was a short cul-de-sac. Households were legally forbidden to hire any servant who did not produce the discharge document given by their previous master. By 1800 the female proportion of domestic servants may have reached twice that of males. When Revd James Whitelaw of St Catherine's parish carried out his own city census in 1798, he found that female servants comprised seven per cent of the total population.[29]

Feminisation of the domestic workplace proceeded alongside other changes in urban life. New domestic tasks were created by modern wooden floors, furniture, fittings and ornaments, each requiring maintenance by washing,

Left: This trader in brushes (1770s) answered the demand of wealthy residents for cleaner homes. Right: Traders in large earthenware, 1770s. (Both images, Anon., The Dublin Cries) (RSAI)

BURCH Brooms, Burch Brooms ;— Here's the cheap Burch Brooms.— Here's the neat Twigging-Whiſks.

WHO buys the Black-Pans? Who buys the Black-Pans? Who buys? —Here's the Earthen-Ware: Here's the China, but where's the Money?

A coin very familiar to ordinary Dubliners (a halfpenny). The scarcity of copper coins encouraged the use of tokens. There was widespread forgery of gold and silver coins.

scrubbing or dusting. Dublin had a vigorous furniture trade, and the names of almost three hundred practitioners have been listed for the period 1752–1800. The output of these workshops went all over the country, but enough stayed within the capital to keep the servants busy cleaning and polishing.[30]

Industrialisation brought household items such as stoves, crockery, kettles and glassware within the reach of more people. As the use of items such as wallpaper expanded, those making it turned to new means of production. Retail outlets began to sell wallpaper in the 1720s, and by 1800 the city had about fifty businesses either making or selling this product; moreover, the larger producers had by then adopted factory production.[31]

Along with the spoils of empire there came new products such as tea, coffee and cocoa. A German visitor to Dublin in 1784 was impressed by the great variety of the retail trade. He found the shop windows in the best streets displayed a wide range of luxury goods, and he noted how fashionable these items were.[32] Items such as hardware and pottery were promoted by the manufacturers' catalogues. The dramatic fall in the price of cotton between 1780 and 1830 made better clothing more widely available.

The mass market was beckoning, and with it came a gradual expansion in the use of paper transactions and, later on, paper money. Pattern books and design guides brought a standardisation to the construction of houses and furniture, and this was accompanied by a growing deference to fashion. Better transport facilities allowed greater mobility and enabled trends to spread more easily. Each year, the Dublin manufacturers of wallpaper went to London to buy the latest patterns so that they could be copied and sold as the fashion for the new season.[33]

✳ ✳ ✳ ✳ ✳

By the 1740s the newspapers were busy promoting the array of attractions available to those seeking entertainment. If we stopped the clock during the early summer of 1744, we could see the variety on offer. Down at College Green, searchers after curiosity could spend time looking at a device called the Microcosm. This spectacle – comprised of a tableau 3 metres high by 2 metres wide – depicted the world on a miniature scale. It was a novelty combining elements of architecture, sculpture and astronomy, along with some music. The admission charge was a shilling. Alongside Dublin Castle at Cork Hill was a three-day cockfighting tournament. A few doors down from the cockpit was a toyshop that boasted a great range of novelties. For those seeking more adult toys there was the Belle-Assembly at Stafford Street – a venue where the select company indulged in card games while drinking cups of tea and coffee. In the background they could hear music played on the lute harp and on glasses. To round off their evening there was a ball and a song recital. For those on a restricted budget there were musical sessions by a military band held each Wednesday in St Stephen's Green.[34]

As early as the 1750s Dublin had acquired the critical mass needed for a lively social scene. From then on, the parliamentary sittings were merely a supplementary feature that added allure to the social round.[35] Dublin society also gained a good deal from the English connection, and it was part of the circuit worked by artists and entertainers. Local performers made this two-way traffic.

Polite conversation in College Green, 1790s. A college student, with a supervisor, addresses a lady. (From James Malton, *A Picturesque and Descriptive View of the City of Dublin*, 1799)

Miscellaneous Characters — A View near Dublin.

If I buy two thousand in the 5 pr Cents.   *I'll sell my Whiskey.*   *I'll buy the Teas.*   *I'll part with the Hides.*   *I'll sell the Wine I think.*
I must buy these Shugars.

Eager merchants
arriving in the city; a
cartoonist's impression,
c. 1810. (Board of
Trinity College, Dublin)

Robert Barker, an artist from County Meath, introduced the panorama format to London. His 1799 depiction of the Battle of the Nile won great admiration, and its accuracy was praised by Lord Nelson himself.[36] At the highest level there was an elite social network that included the Irish and English capitals; candidates who failed in the London marriage market might succeed in the 'second city'.

There was a growing trend for wealthy owners of country estates to spend some of the year mixing with their peers in these livelier cities. It was the landed gentry that dominated Dublin's social life, and this pre-eminence was expressed in the array of monumental town houses occupied by families such as the Kildares, Tyrones and Charlemonts. Their contributions encouraged the growth of urban society, and this, in turn, had implications for those people meeting the needs of wealthy city households. The luxury sought by the gentry attracted craftsmen and artists along with an array of administrators, officials and professionals. As the ranks of the retailers expanded, so did the number of cash transactions.

Family homes became a topic of greater interest and this brought spending on items such as furniture and decoration. These reforms opened up new trades and careers. The amount of silver hallmarked in Dublin trebled between 1700

Beaux and belles promenading in St Stephen's Green, 1790s. (From James Malton, *A Picturesque and Descriptive View of the City of Dublin*, 1799) (DCC)

and 1790. It was this sophistication that left behind the heritage of family group portraits painted by the artists of the period. Women realised they could gain from these changes. Most of the genteel entertainments brought in from England and the Continent encouraged the participation of women. They took advantage of opportunities in art, and especially in music; the arrival of the piano in the 1780s encouraged this.[37]

Along with the growing scale and diversity of urban entertainments, people were offered a wider choice of venues. There were, however, particular forms of recreation that found favour with the arbiters of good taste. Most popular amongst the outdoor activities was the promenade, a French import hardly suited to the vagaries of the Irish weather. However, a casual observer could dismiss these sauntering beaux and belles without seeing their true purpose. Walks of this sort served as social exchanges where deals could be done, where news was circulated, and where intrigues were arranged. Not surprisingly, the foremost promenades adjoined the best housing, namely the Beaux Walk at St Stephen's Green, the Rotunda Gardens at Rutland Square and the Marlborough Green close to Gardiner's Mall. These were all depicted in contemporary prints, and that was a sure sign of their appeal to the affluent. Each of them became a 'Quality Street', the summit for all social climbers.

Assemblies were indoor gatherings for polite conversation, the playing of cards and the drinking of tea. For a while the social round of the golden circle included the theatres at Crow Street and Smock Alley as well as the music hall at

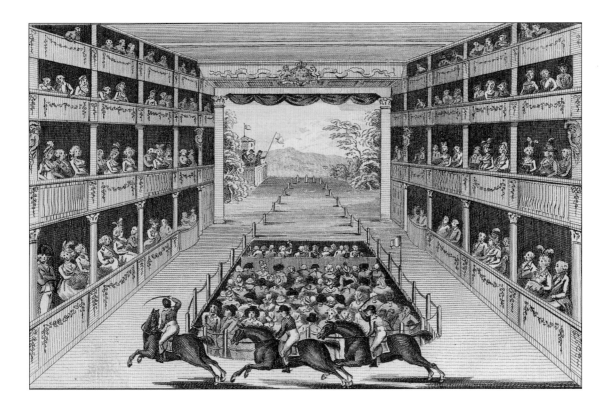

A scene that has echoes of *Ben-Hur* and the Colosseum. Pony races at the Theatre Royal, Crow Street (*Walker's Hibernian Magazine*, November 1795) (Board of Trinity College, Dublin).

Fishamble Street. Later, it was found that suburban villas afforded ample scope for private society, with flower-scented gardens secluded from the riff-raff.

Popular recreation is one of those topics about which our information is limited. For the ordinary people, most recreation was informal and communal. Venues such as the marketplaces and the greens were popular, while at other times it was the churchyards or out in the streets. These diversions were class-responsive, and public places made the activities prominent. When opposition began to emerge, offence was more quickly taken. Insights might only come to light on occasions of outrage, when the common people were condemned for offending their betters.

Many street games had medieval origins and they had a wide circulation. Robert Malcolmson cited a London account of 1720 where the common folk engaged in football, wrestling, cudgels, ninepins, shovelboard, cricket, stow-ball, ringing of bells, quoits, pitching the bar, bull- and bear-baiting, throwing at cocks and lying at alehouses.[38] Most of these events could also be seen in Dublin, and Edward Lloyd, in his 1732 account, listed backsword, cudgels, boxing, wrestling, bull-baiting, cockfighting, hunting, coursing, hawking, setting, fishing, fowling, cards, dice, billiards, tables, draughts, balls, plays, consorts of music, singing, dancing, women and wine.[39] While the modern reader will recognise several of these activities, some of them may seem obscure. In cudgel play, each man was armed with a stout stick and a basket hand-guard, the winner being the first to draw blood from his opponent's head. Backsword fencing was likewise a bloody business that involved weapons with a single cutting edge. It is hardly surprising that these recreations became divisive topics during the second half of the Georgian era, and these are examined in chapter nine.

Historians are divided on the city's status as a cultural centre. Some scholars have argued that Georgian urban life was not notably cultured. Others have contended that, after London, Dublin was the largest centre in these islands for music, theatre and publishing.[40] This divergence of opinion is partly due to much of the artistic endeavour being pursued outside the public realm. Within the great houses, music recitals and theatricals were features of domestic life, especially after the 1770s. Private art collections and libraries were assembled in the city; contributions were made by collectors returning from their European grand tours. Artefacts of this kind were noticed by visitors such as Arthur Young, and their locations were recorded in the sales catalogues prepared for house auctions.[41]

Cultural life was certainly enhanced by the Huguenot craftsmen who settled in the city after 1685. These were refugees from France, and their innovations were reflected in weaving and silverware. Some of the creative writing was in the Irish language and therefore might have gone unnoticed. Recent research has revealed how a French-language culture was more pervasive in the city than had hitherto been believed. By the mid-1760s the middle class had taken up reading as a leisure activity, and its engagement with French extended into economic and educational topics. By 1800 a substantial number of Dublin post-elementary schools offered French as a subject.[42]

These pursuits often had a sectarian element. Religious allegiance played a prominent part in everyday events, and cultural activity had a denominational

A gold freedom box made by Thomas Bolton, who served as lord mayor in 1716. It bears the city arms. The crowned harp (centre) is part of the Dublin hallmark. The box was awarded to John Freeman. (NMI)

aspect. This ever-present religious divide can explain the lacklustre role of Trinity College, where paranoia and distrust effectively subdued new ideas. No significant publication emerged from the university during the four-decade provostship (1717–58) of Richard Baldwin. In the same context, it is notable how many Irish medical students chose to attend courses in Scotland rather than at Trinity. Irish students, including large numbers of Presbyterians and Catholics, comprised a quarter of Edinburgh's medical graduates between 1726 and 1799.[43]

While in the early Georgian era the great majority of Dubliners were Protestants, the balance was reversed around

M.ʳ EDWARD BYRNE,
President of the
Catholic Committee.

Statue of King William III. in College Green.

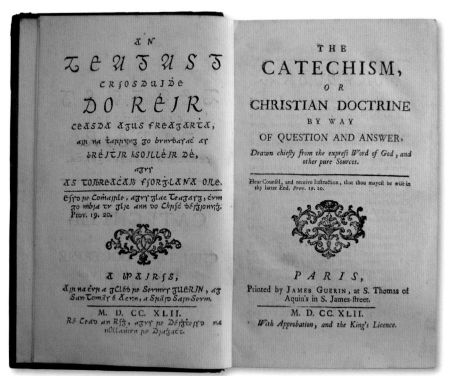

Andrew Donlevy's bilingual (Irish/English) Catholic catechism published in Paris in 1742, contravening Ireland's penal religious laws.

mid-century. There were repeated assaults on the symbols of the Protestant status quo. Little more than a decade after the Glorious Revolution, a very large monument to William III was erected in College Green. This was a triumphal statue that depicted William on horseback as a conquering Roman general. It became an object of abuse but survived into the early nineteenth century. One of the boldest assaults on Protestant triumphalism occurred in 1718 when a group of men broke into the Tholsel. They slashed to shreds the king's portrait that dominated the civic chambers. This attack brought a visceral response from the government: a reward of £1,000 was offered for the culprits. As the Catholic majority grew, so did the tension. An abundance of cheap labour allowed a greater use of domestic servants, and these people were mainly Catholics. Sectarian tension crossed the threshold, and as the household size grew, it was followed by commensurate friction.[44]

Despite all the material and intellectual intercourse between the major cities of western Europe, the Irish capital kept to a cautious path. It remained politically conservative, always wary of any challenge to the status quo arising from the Glorious Revolution. It still deferred to London in its choice of public buildings. Observers of this practice have cited the new Newgate at The Little Green based on Newgate Prison; the Rotunda at the Lying-in Hospital based on the rotunda at

Rare News in the Evening Post.

Ranelagh Gardens; Essex Bridge following Westminster Bridge; St George's Hardwicke Place with a spire adopted from St Martin in the Fields; and Trinity College's Provost House modelled on Lord Burlington's design of General Wade's house.[45]

It was quite safe to embrace neoclassicism in architecture, but Dublin shied away from the unsettling insights of the Enlightenment. This outlook explains why so many authors decided to publish their writings anonymously. Jonathan Swift, the dean of St Patrick's cathedral, used a pseudonym to avoid prosecution for the publication of his pamphlets promoting reform. Political thinkers, such as the apothecary Charles Lucas, who strived to improve the corporation, could be compelled to flee the country. The writings of revolutionaries, such as the Anglo-American Thomas Paine, who challenged the monarchy and all hereditary powers, were strongly condemned. Later again, Daniel O'Connell, who chose the constitutional path to political reform in his search for Catholic emancipation, had his public meetings banned.

✳ ✳ ✳ ✳ ✳

Dublin newspapers had plenty of accounts of foreign wars and political affairs, but they also carried reports and information on entertainments and household matters. There were numerous advertisements, and these testified to the expanding lifestyle choices. Great musical and theatrical personalities came to perform. As early as 1711 the celebrated singer Nicolo Grimaldi Nicolini gave a recital at the Smock Alley Playhouse, and in 1717 Johann Sigismund Kusser became the first master of the state music in Ireland. The first Italian prima donna to perform in the city was Signora Stradiotto, who appeared in 1725.[46]

House entrances
at Merrion Square,
displaying characteristic
period features,
including iron boot
scrapers.

Opposite page:
James Gandon, the
celebrated architect,
with three of his great
works (the Four Courts,
the Rotunda Hospital
and the Custom House)
in the background.
(William Cumming and
Tilly Kettle, 1783) (NGI)

Towards the mid-century, the list of visiting celebrities grew more impressive. George Frideric Handel progressed across Europe from Germany, settling in London under the patronage of the German-speaking George I before he eventually visited Dublin in 1742. Thomas Arne, the most successful English composer of that time, made a trip to Dublin in the same year. A similar progress could be traced for theatre performers. David Garrick, the famous actor, paid two visits to Dublin, firstly in 1742 and again three years later.

Europe revived its interest in the classical art of Greece and Rome, and Dublin's most enduring cultural expression emerged in architecture and civic design. The French kings Louis XIV and XV had a significant influence on the development of European town planning. In this, they were following a tradition begun in the early 1600s. Their forebear Henry IV instigated major Parisian renewal schemes of classical uniformity based on symmetrical streets lined with coordinated and harmonious development. Around 1660 Louis XIV removed Paris' defensive walls and replaced them with a roadway 36 metres wide.[47] This was a harbinger of the great boulevards that became such a distinctive feature of that city.

Successive popes implemented a transformation of Rome, driving long, straight streets through the cluttered quarters to link up the main churches.

Pope Alexander VII (r. 1655–67) was a leading force in this quest for order and harmony. He believed that modern urbanism required spacious squares. An integral feature of this model was the central open area bordered by structures that complemented each other. These squares were arranged in a rectilinear pattern, decorated by well-built palaces.[48] Rome became the source of eighteenth-century neoclassicism, and formed a model for Europe's *ancien régime*. It was at the heart of the grand tour, and these ideas were carried abroad to other cities, such as London and Dublin.

Classical neo-Palladian architecture was adopted as the orthodox standard in Ireland after 1720. Those streetscape elements that are so emblematic of Georgian Dublin began to emerge during the 1730s. Self-confidence was reflected in the new public buildings, such as the Parliament House and the Linen Hall. During the following decades, impressive new streets were laid out. On the north side, these included Henrietta Street and Sackville Mall (otherwise Gardiner's), while on the south side, Grafton Street and Kildare Street were built. The network of imposing structures designed by the foremost architects continued to grow. During the following decades, these additions included Gandon's Custom House (1781-91) and Four Courts (1786–1801), as well as Cooley's Royal Exchange (1769–79) and Castle's Rotunda Hospital (1751–57). By the end of the eighteenth century, Dublin had acquired some of the most splendid public buildings of any European capital.

Covent Garden was London's first classical square, and it provided a template that was widely adopted in Britain and Ireland. It, in turn, had been inspired by the likes of the Place Royale (later renamed the Place des Vosges) in Paris. Changes could be seen in the model that crossed the English Channel. Where the Continental model featured palatial façades addressing formally paved and ornamented open space, London's squares discarded much of the ostentation; most of them comprised restrained brick buildings facing onto a private area of grass and trees. It was this conservative approach that was adopted in Dublin, a model usefully defined as 'a green park formed by architecture'.[49]

Robert Pool and John Cash's catalogue of Dublin buildings appeared in 1780, and it coincided with a high point in the city's progress. It is a skewed portrait of the city because public ornamentation did not reach all parts of the capital; it bypassed the medieval quarter, where narrow alleyways and penthouses prevailed. These trends in urbanisation were repeated across the largest European cities. Commentators such as Rousseau saw little difference between London and Paris. To his eyes they both provided the same features of poverty and oppression. He could have added Dublin to his list when he stated 'Paris et Londres ne sont à mes yeux que la meme ville; toutes les capitals se resemblents, tous les peuples s'y melent, toutes les moeurs s'y confondent' (To my eyes Paris and London are the same town. All the capitals are alike. All people are thrown together and morality is confused).[50]

Paris acquired a population of a half million by 1700, and London's population rose from 575,000 to 900,000 during the eighteenth century. Ireland's largest urban centres, Dublin and Cork, were part of this phenomenon. Dublin's population grew from 60,000 to 180,000 during the eighteenth century. The fastest growth occurred during the first five decades, and by 1750 the city had a population of about 120,000. Yet this extraordinary growth concealed a demographic paradox. None of the population increase could be attributed to the bounty of self-sustaining cities. In reality, these were lethal places where most of the growth could be attributed to the rapid influx of poor families from the countryside. These cities had very high infant mortality, and it was men and women in their late teens and twenties who were more likely to survive in this hostile environment.

Observers in the eighteenth century noticed how the size of a city could determine whether it was a leader or a follower of fashion. Dublin was the capital

State pageantry, 1787. The funeral of the Viceroy Charles Manners, Duke of Rutland. (*Walker's Hibernian Magazine*, November 1787) (UCD)

Representation of the Body of His Grace the late Duke of Rutland lying in STATE in the HOUSE of LORDS.

of England's Irish colony, and this left it in an ambiguous position. It has, at different times, been described as an Augustan capital or the capital of a province of a great monarchy. In some interpretations it has been listed with Edinburgh, Boston, Naples, Bordeaux and Nancy – that is, being the centre for a province's political, legal and administrative life, as well as forming the focal point for its governing elite.[51] Another less favourable interpretation saw it grouped with Edinburgh, Dresden, Geneva, Milan and Bologna, all of them capitals of formerly autonomous areas retaining remnants of independent establishments, but ultimately being assimilated into still not completely unified nation states.[52]

Military review, Dublin Castle, c. 1803. A cartoon view of the gentry lining up for titles, places and pensions. (Courtesy of Andrew Bonar Law)

✳✳✳✳✳

Up to 1801 Dublin's role as the premier Irish city was confirmed by its parliamentary function. By the accession of George II in 1727, the Dublin parliament was allowed a notable degree of legislative initiative, especially with regard to the domestic budget. London nevertheless kept a close eye on Irish affairs, and more than on its other colonies. This was hardly surprising due to its proximity and strategic significance. However, in some important respects the Irish parliament suffered in comparison with other British colonial assemblies. Dublin had a very limited democracy because the electorate comprised only the narrow oligarchy of the minority religion; by the 1740s those people with votes formed about 3 per cent of the entire city population, and this proportion actually declined after mid-century because, notwithstanding the remarkable population growth, the number of electors had not risen, even by the late 1770s. Moreover, general elections were rare events, with none at all between 1727 and 1760.

The status quo was not set in stone, but it was set in statute, and the Irish parliament was firmly under the influence of the Dublin Castle executive. The lord lieutenant and chief secretary were assisted in this work by the 'undertakers', who were long-established landed gentry. This arrangement was intended to secure a government majority whenever it was needed, but reliance on these undertakers came at a high price. Jobbery was rife, and public-spirited individuals, such as Lord Charlemont, took a dim view of all the patronage they saw – 'from education, and from habit, they certainly were well fitted to preside at the funeral of the common weal'.[53]

Big occasions reflected the scale of the vice-regal court. Those seeking favour turned out to express their loyalty. When the French Revolution broke out in 1789, ordinary Dubliners could see about fifteen hundred of their betters gathered at a Dublin Castle ball. Shortly afterwards, the same grandees went praying to celebrate the recovery of George III from his madness. That thanksgiving service at Christ Church drew a procession of three hundred coaches. This expression of loyalty crossed the denominational divide. About three thousand devotees attended a Catholic service held for the same purpose at the Francis Street chapel. The viceroy was a full-time resident from the mid-1760s, and late in that decade legislation was passed limiting the life of parliament to eight years. There were annual parliamentary sessions from the mid-1780s, and by the 1790s about three hundred MPs and over a hundred peers had homes in the city. This proved a boon, and their aggregate annual expenditure is estimated to have reached £700,000, a sum now equivalent to about €70 million.

The main channel for port shipping appears centre left. On either side, the enclosed areas are reclamation schemes that remained inundated. (Charles Brooking's map of Dublin, 1728)

A good indication of Dublin's colonial context was provided by the prominence of the British army. It is hardly ironic that the first great classical building, the Royal Hospital at Kilmainham, was opened in 1684 as a home for old soldiers. After the Williamite settlement, a standing army of twelve thousand men could be maintained in Ireland, and this support for the defence forces may have been Ireland's most significant contribution to the British Empire. There were about a dozen regiments, all paid for by the Irish administration. Dublin's garrison held about seventeen hundred men in 1700, and by the 1770s the barracks had accommodation for three thousand infantry and five hundred cavalry.[54]

＊＊＊＊＊

The social division expressed by architecture. The formal entry to a Merrion Square house (above) and the servants' basement access (below).

Much of the city's early development can be seen in Charles Brooking's 1728 city map. It shows innovations such as the Liffey embankments and the reclaimed areas that were opened up for development. The most extensive reclamation scheme was in the south-east, a district already attracting large-scale development. The impressive rate of progress is confirmed in John Rocque's 1756 map.

Significant social consequences followed the introduction of the formal squares. These places were designed for carriage transport, and the residents were not seen walking about the streets. Any walking was confined to select venues that hosted like-minded and like-moneyed society. The layout of the houses and their relationship with the street reflected the desire of the elite to form separate surroundings for themselves. This model extended the segregation to household functions and to those people who were undertaking them. It brought clarity to household management, with a separation of the employer from his employees in terms of the work area and living space. Segregation within these houses increased with the insertion of features such as the front 'area'. This was the small sunken yard dividing the basement from the street. An entrance was inserted there for domestic servants; these people were to enter the house unseen and unheard. Partitions of this kind brought more rewards when there were unsavoury functions that the residents wanted to avoid. Each side of the square had a corresponding rear access – the stable lane where horses, sewage and dung could be tidied away along with the labourers who were needed to manage them.

Dublin's adoption of these new models came gradually, and it is notable that the earliest of them were promoted by the city council itself. The corporation devised a housing project for the large common called St Stephen's Green, and it soon had a major impact. This was an integrated scheme that occupied a site of 24 hectares, and was based on a rectangular road layout. All ninety-six plots addressed the central green area. Another one of these early schemes undertaken by the corporation was at Smithfield. This likewise comprised a rectangular layout of ninety-six plots, but, unlike St Stephen's Green, it suffered on account of its unfavourable location. By the early eighteenth century, the backyards of the houses were being occupied by workshops. Before long, the tanneries and other smelly trades encouraged families to seek more salubrious surroundings.[55]

Like a great tree, Dublin extended its new branches out over a wide area. Onlookers admired this wave of paving as it moved over fields and waste ground. St Stephen's Green was a great success. In the late 1780s one eyewitness praised the skill of the city surveyor as he laid out a network of new streets between North Strand and Summerhill:

> He found that Mr Byram had staked out a street of eighty feet wide. This will certainly be as elegant a street as any in London, and it is understood the proprietors intend calling it Buckingham Street in complement to our illustrious viceroy … Gloucester Street is to extend to the Circular Road, and between it and Summer Hill there are intervening streets, which are to be called Nugent Street and Grenville Street.[56]
>
> *Dublin Chronicle*, 31 July 1788

Dublin's new prosperity presented opportunities to improve the appearance and layout of the city. There was growing awareness that urban spaces could be enhanced by timely intervention and well-informed management. Older

This Liffeyside view, *c.* 1806, indicates the progress in opening up the new quays to traffic.
(From John Carr, *The Stranger in Ireland*, 1806) (Courtesy of Éamonn de Búrca)

components might be tidied up or rearranged, and at the same time emerging suburbs could be planned. Many of the factors governing Dublin's expansion had previously been seen in London. These included demography (an increase primarily driven by immigration), local circumstances (tenure of land and development of estates), lifestyle (an increasing desire for single-family houses and a quest for social exclusiveness), adaptability (a growing ability and willingness to commute) and finance (availability of capital). Nevertheless, Dublin's growth had aspects that made it different. These included the ever-present sectarian tension and especially the large army garrison.

✳ ✳ ✳ ✳ ✳

During the seventeenth century, individual states got more involved in public administration, and this was extended to the everyday regulation of

A Georgian doorway, Merrion Square. The lamp inset in the fanlight suggests this was a house occupied by an affluent family.

citizens. There was a growing awareness of the power of property. Those who possessed it sought to protect it, and they acquired a whole new legal armoury to assist them. When Blackstone's ground-breaking *Commentaries on English Law* appeared in the 1760s, a quarter of that work dealt with real estate – more than was given over to crime and punishment.[57] Georgian cities saw increasing reliance on the law to keep the men of no property in their place. In Britain and Ireland, this movement began after the Glorious Revolution, and it assumed aspects of a moral crusade in the guise of criminal legislation. In England, the number of offences attracting the death penalty quadrupled between 1688 and 1820, and nearly all of them were related to property.[58] A similar trend could be seen in Ireland. The rule of law became the rule of property.

City councils wanted to tidy up the public realm in order to create formal open spaces and keep nuisances out of sight. These initiatives were intended to add prestige to the property of the power brokers. On the one hand, the surge of rural migrants needed to be addressed, while, on the other, there was a desire to enhance the urban experience for respectable visitors and tax-paying residents. Intervention became more discriminating but less humane. This new bureaucracy circumscribed paupers, criminals, the homeless and the insane, along with anybody else who diminished the pleasure and wealth of the elite. This initiative included reformatories where the idle poor could be chastised and corrected so as to perform a more useful and self-reliant role in the community. There was a rapid expansion of the institutional network, and private bodies were encouraged to join forces in some of these ventures.

Those accustomed to comfort were not prepared to share it with coarse peasants. Much of everyday life was conducted outdoors in the streets and markets, and this made many activities more obvious. In Dublin these activities included offensive begging and Sabbath-breaking. As the city population grew, more penal legislation was enacted to protect the elite. Within the circle of the power brokers there was conflict between the city's mercantile interests and the landed gentry who controlled parliament. This friction was most apparent when major public works were needed. By moving further from the city centre, the elite could distance itself from the hoi polloi in both physical and cultural terms.

These changes were not unique to the Irish capital. What emerges, rather, is how many cities in western Europe were facing similar challenges. Rapid growth in British cities was accompanied by strong social divisions. These did not, however, manifest themselves everywhere at the same rate. In Edinburgh, the aristocracy and the professions made their way from Old Town to New Town in the 1770s and 1780s, and yet the rich and poor of Birmingham were still living quite close together during the 1790s. Mid-eighteenth-century Paris was crowded with vagrants and tinkers selling knick-knacks, lottery tickets and all sorts of second-hand goods. Basic considerations such as air circulation became a priority for Parisians because they had a deep-rooted fear of damp conditions. Rousseau likened the place to a tomb depriving people of their human nature; he advised the citizens to flee from it. Within the older *quartiers*, life expectancy was short, falling as low as twenty-nine years in 1770. Dublin had no monopoly on misery.[59]

Post-Union street life at St Stephen's Green. Note the derelict site adjoining the College of Surgeons. Such views reveal many more people out on the streets. (George Petrie, 1821) (UCD)

2

Conflict and Confrontation

The health and morals of the people ought to be the first care of the legislator.

Edward Wakefield, 1812[1]

EIGHT OR NINE DIFFERENT SOCIAL STRATA were identified in Georgian London, and each of these could be seen in Dublin, albeit in different proportions. They were topped by the aristocracy and gentry, descending through the upper middle class, middle class proper, lower middle class, independent artisans, wage-earning artisans, 'the poor that fare hard' and 'the miserable'. The latter two epithets were borrowed from the accounts of the writer Daniel Defoe.[2]

As we have seen, a person's outward appearance was an important guide to his or her place in the social hierarchy. A select lifestyle was signalled by the dress of the affluent. Those people wearing brocade were not expected to undertake any dirty work, and labouring tasks were left to those wearing either plain cloth or leather aprons. The wealthy people who mattered wore fine garments that were specially made for them. Their neat dress was complemented with impressive accessories such as wigs, jewellery and perfumes. These articles emphasised the good taste of the wearer and secured the *entrée* that was coveted by those who cultivated *le bon gout*. Dublin's social pyramid was a shallow structure, but there were rigid barriers between the layers it contained. Those below deferred to those above

them, while those above adopted a paternal approach to those beneath them. This pyramid also had a very wide base. It followed the profile seen in neighbouring capitals, and it would appear that class consciousness was a predominantly urban phenomenon. Its progress relied on the ongoing urbanisation, and it did not gain widespread currency until the French Revolution.[3]

The top of Dublin's social pyramid was occupied by a small elite that controlled everything that mattered. It was by far the most documented segment of the population. This *beau monde* or *bon ton* could be observed at the Castle and other select venues. Its importance was highlighted by military tattoos or by firework displays, while at other times it observed restraint as it sat listening to charity sermons in church. Up to the 1760s members of the gentry were scattered throughout all sectors of the city, although there were signs that this pattern was weakening some decades before that. Records such as those of craft-guild representation on the corporation indicate growing disparities between certain areas. An absence of political representatives left the poorest parishes at a loss,

Female Curiosity detected.

An eccentric resident of Merrion Square, 1792. Some readers of this magazine were sure to recognise the owner of the man's knee breeches, hat and cane. (*Walker's Hibernian Magazine*, May 1792) (UCD)

and the affluent new suburbs were also under-represented.

Competition between the social climbers extended across the public arenas. Within the Protestant churches, this contest included the acquisition of the best seats for Sunday services. At St Anne's church in Dawson Street, the Earl of Kildare held pride of place during the 1750s. He made a deal with Lord Longford in 1759, exchanging one seat for another. He was then granted permission to join together his two seats to form a fancy wooden closet that was covered over at the top. We can assume this device cut off the offending gazes of the less worthy. This initiative had the desired effect because it was copied by the Earl of Antrim two years later.[4] St Anne's carefully guarded its position at the top of the social ladder. It drew the envy of other parishes because members of neighbouring congregations kept on turning up there. These were people who wished to bring their prayers to the most select venue. It was parishes such as St Andrew's and St Brigid's that lost out as a result.[5]

With the rise of the bureaucracy and the professions there came a growing awareness of an emerging middle class. About a quarter of eighteenth-century Londoners were middle class, but the proportion in Dublin appears to have been a good deal smaller. This remained the case coming into the early nineteenth century, and it was the extreme contrast between rich and poor that surprised English visitors. They could not see the swelling centre ground they saw in London, and how it connected the magnificence with the misery. This middling group always feared its fall from grace, and this brought a constant sensitivity to everyday life, especially where the workplace was concerned. A middle-class family could deem it acceptable for a son to become an apprentice in the printing trade provided he worked as a compositor, because this was a branch of the trade where he would use his literacy.[6]

Middle-class people were often regarded as industrious and thrifty individuals. Their enthusiasm got them involved in philanthropic projects, but it was suggested that their main interest was in creating a better reputation for themselves. Maria Edgeworth, the aristocratic Anglo-Irish novelist, poured scorn on the efforts of the *nouveaux riches*. To her mind they were unlearned schemers who elbowed their way into polite society. Despite these brush-offs, the middle class advanced to the centre of the civic establishment. Their taste in music and theatre brought the arts away from the sanctuary of the court grandees and into the mainstream. This transformation was gradual, and in many respects mirrored the advance of its promoters. Its most rapid progress could be seen during the 1780s and 1790s. Soon after 1800 their ranks had grown to such a point that they were achieving a wider acceptance. It was deemed worthwhile to involve them in charitable ventures, and this was achieved by lowering subscriptions to a level they could afford.[7]

These people believed that a person could claim a stake in society on the basis of wealth, regardless of whether that was inherited property or acquired through trade or industry. Their influence spread, and it began to affect religious pronouncements on the class system itself. Where the Established Church had long held that God's providence determined whether a person was rich or poor, poverty now came to be blamed on idleness.[8] A few surviving diaries from Georgian Dublin offer insights into the city's middle-class families, and these are discussed below in appendix one. What emerges is the regard for conformity in matters of lifestyle and religion.

Stress in the social structure

> Great numbers of idle and vagrant persons do daily resort from the country to the city of Dublin and the suburbs thereof.
>
> 10 Geo. I, c.3 [Ire.] (1723)

> Humanity must shudder at the crowds of petitioning wretches to be met in every corner of the city.
>
> *Hibernian Journal*, 11 June 1783

At the bottom of the social pile were the poor, who accounted for a majority of city dwellers. They had no political role and occupied the penumbra in which it was hard to distinguish between the lowest jobs and mere reliance on charity. This was an area marked by all sorts of casual tasks that put a veneer on begging,

This vendor's licence tag 'Newsman' distinguishes him. (Hugh Douglas Hamilton, 1760) (Private collection)

whether it was singing ballads, washing down doorsteps or selling kindling for fires. Younger people could try their hand as shoe-blacks or link boys. Street corners and other vantage points were keenly contested, and one feature was the prominence of females.

For the increasing numbers of country migrants, contacts within the city were essential. Access to work could depend on connections of culture or religion, as well as any ability or skill. All too often, the newcomers realised their rural skills were not wanted and that there was an extra barrier for those without the English language. This is a factor that is difficult to measure, but it appears, for example, that the Irish language was spoken in the rural parts of Counties Meath and Westmeath throughout the Georgian era. Most of these migrants drifted between subsistence and poverty, and it is not surprising that many of them kept on moving to seek homes abroad. By the 1790s, one-third of London's beggars were Irish, and the squalid parish of St Giles became known as Little Dublin.[9]

In the decades after the Union, the main roads leading to the city carried a heavy volume of struggling paupers. Whenever a new building project started in the capital, large numbers of labourers set out in the hope of getting some work there. They were joined along the way by old people trying to reach the workhouse and unmarried mothers carrying babies to the Foundling Hospital. This was, moreover, two-way traffic, as a significant proportion of it comprised stragglers returning home after giving up on the city. They included elderly labourers, redundant soldiers and those disabled by sickness or work accidents. Western approaches such as Lucan, Clondalkin and Palmerstown offered a respite to these unfortunates. Those lucky enough to have any coins could spend a night in a roadside cabin for a halfpenny or a penny, sharing the heating and food with the owner of the cottage.[10]

HAVE you any old Pots, old Pans, old Kettles or Sauce pans. or any old Brass or Pewter-Pans to mend.—Have you any Work for the Tinker to Day?

BUYE sweet Whey. buye the pure sweet Whey —Hard Cruds here, hard Cruds for the Boys and Girls.

Only those individuals with a well-established residential qualification could expect support from the parish welfare system. The new arrivals were the anonymous poor who occupied an illiterate space outside the statistical world. Most of our insights come from the accounts of public officials and philanthropists or from foreign visitors. What invariably appeared in the newspapers was the unusual, the sensational or the scandalous, and this is what made it newsworthy. It was the sheer number of beggars drawn to opulent passers-by that impressed the Dublin philanthropist Samuel Rosborough: he counted twenty-seven of them buzzing around a single carriage.[11] The denominational divide kept Catholic workers out of most of the skilled trades. This exclusion is suggested by the fact that as late as 1824, ninety-four per cent of labourers' wives admitted to the Rotunda Hospital were Catholics.[12]

By the mid-Georgian years, about a half of the city's workforce was engaged in the textile industry. The urban location put excessive pressure on costs, and an obvious consequence was the setting up of workshops within unwholesome districts, where the workers were forced to accept lower incomes and to live in

Left: A tinker, 1770s. His leather apron offered him protection from hot metal and sharp objects. Right: A woman selling by-products from the dairy, 1770s. She carries two ladles in her belt. (Both images, Anon., The Dublin Cries) (RSAI)

the worst housing. The risks were multiplied by the long working hours, and there was little surprise at accidents such as the loss of limbs.

Remuneration is a topic that reveals aspects of the social gradient. However, those workplaces with details spanning the range of pay scales are largely confined to the public realm. Apart from the army, they are found in bodies such as the civil parishes and the Wide Streets Commission (WSC). The wealthiest parishes provide the best returns, and this is because more of their records have survived. In the case of St Anne's, those posts paying annual salaries during the 1780s included vestry clerk (£45), parish clerk (£20), surgeon (£71), organist (£46), bell-ringer (£12), fire-engine keeper (£20), beadle (£12), organ bellows blower (£4) and sexton's assistant (£6), and to these should be added others, such as the parish watch, where there were four constables, two sub-constables, six corporals (£18) and twenty-four patrolmen (£1 12s each), as well as the watch clerk (£23).[13]

Amongst the lowest-paid agents of the Wide Streets Commission were the watchmen minding their property. The wages paid for this unskilled work hardly changed at all between 1760 and the Union. These men got 1s 2d per day (1766), 7s 6d per week (1792) and 1s 1d per night (1795). Details of the ordinary labourers' wages are also scarce; the WSC paid 15s 2d to a gang of fourteen navvies for digging a cesspit at Merrion Square in 1792 – that is, 13 pence each. During the same period, the officers of the WSC received annual payments. The secretary received £200, as did the surveyor-general, a clerk received £50 and the messenger £10. These pay rates likewise remained unchanged over several decades. It is notable, however, that the salaries (or retainers) of these officials were augmented by productivity bonuses. These top-ups became well established by the 1790s, and they continued even after the government pared back the remit of the WSC. These sweeteners became so large that they made the actual salary pale in comparison. In 1798, for example, the surveyor Thomas Sherrard was paid £150 on top of his £50 annual income, and even the messenger had £20 added to his normal £10. Surveyors in private practice had an average annual income of about £125 during the mid-eighteenth century.[14]

Antagonism and violence

> A number of shoemakers, cobblers, and such like, had contrived to get into authority under the paving laws, and had manifested the most shameful partiality to people of their own class against gentlemen.
>
> Richard Annesley MP, 1782[15]

Friction and faction flowed from the disparity in wealth and prestige. There were plenty of bucks and rakes who flaunted their affluence. Probably the best known of these high rollers was Buck Whaley (1768–1800), a man who served two terms as a member of the Irish parliament. His house at St Stephen's Green has survived, and it remains a very impressive building. Whaley revealed in his memoirs the extent of his frivolous indulgence. He frittered away a fortune of nearly £400,000 and accumulated debts of a further £30,000. This splurge brought him little contentment.[16]

While Dublin's prosperity provided more job opportunities, there was growing tension within the workplace. Wealthy citizens employed large numbers of servants, and this carried the divisions indoors. William Whitelaw's 1798 survey found that the most fashionable districts had an average of three servants per dwelling. Constantia Maxwell stated that even moderately sized households had between ten and fifteen domestics. Whatever the exact figure may have been, servants were essential to the functioning of Dublin society, from the middling ranks upwards. Nevertheless, they were distrusted because they generated concerns over the personal safety of the nobility, as well as the security of its property.[17]

All sorts of undesirables inveigled their way into private dwellings. They included burglars and prostitutes. Servants gave out information about the houses they worked in, and these details were passed on to the opportunists.

Tiger Roche, a notorious buck and adventurer, c. 1765. He was wanted as an outlaw. (Hanlon, from Anon., *Sketches of Ireland Sixty Years Ago*, 1847)

Tiger Roche.

The naming of this musician indicates that he was a familiar figure, and his elegant chair suggests he was a welcome performer. (Hugh Douglas Hamilton, 1760) (Private collection)

Blind Daniel the Piper

Hawkers and servants gathered at street corners exchanging information: 'Molly Gingerbread sits before them as umpire, on a three legged stool, scratching herself with ecstasy at hearing them detract the families with whom they live.' At other times, information was given to burglars befriended by housemaids when they went dancing at the 'hedge ale-houses'.[18]

The *Hibernian Journal* complained that city life made the workers dissipated. It also stated that the bad habits of the rich were multiplied in the poor.[19] Servants expressed their resentment in various ways. Chamber pots were emptied over well-dressed passers-by, and these abuses were copied by the hackney drivers, who delighted in throwing dirt at well-dressed pedestrians.[20] The select walks of St Stephen's Green were disturbed by messengers and footmen playing pitch-and-toss. These people were regarded as 'herds of low ragamuffin vagrants, baskets-boys and servants bellowing forth blasphemy and obscenity'.[21] Homeowners in Merrion Square were angry at the sporting activities of servants within the park. There were violent clashes with groups of stable boys, valets and sedan-chair men, all coming from nearby gentlemen's houses. These scenes were repeated over on the north side of the Liffey. Visitors to Sackville Mall promenade were offended by the gangs of teenagers described as 'puppies' or 'boy-men' who insulted them.[22]

Dublin's expanding middle class felt trapped within the wider upheaval. Coaches and sedan chairs steered the wealthy around the shoddy infrastructure,

Three fishmongers, 1770s. (Anon., The Dublin Cries) (RSAI)

FRESH Herrings, large Dublin-bay Herring alive here'—Here's a large fresh Cod alive here—Here's large Soles or Places alive, or fine Bayn Salmon.

OISTERS! curious Oisters:—Here's the fresh Carlingford Oisters— Who wants the fine Oisters?

BUYE the large black Cockle, fine large black Cockle;—Here's fresh boil'd Crabs or Lobsters, here.

but they were left to stumble over broken pavements or fall into unlit cellars.[23] The elite did not suffer 'porters of all descriptions, barrows, fellows carrying dead carcases and quarters of beef, maliciously and exultingly rubbing the spinal marrow of them against the arms of every decent person they meet, coal porters, and every other nuisance, without meeting the least obstruction or notice'.[24] The increasing influence of the middle class continued to draw ridicule. They were mocked for aping their betters, and in their use of women's fashions they were likened to 'Oonahs and Norahs who had come to town from the bogs in the country'.[25] In the 1780s *The Freeman's Journal* jeered that it had become barely possible to distinguish a shopkeeper's apprentice from a lordling. Two decades later, John Gamble scoffed at shopkeepers who imitated their superiors. He lampooned their indulgence in luxuries and mocked the furniture used to trick out their homes, a folly extended by ostentatious ornaments.[26]

The outrage of the middle class was well founded. Passers-by were assaulted by street traders, and women were shocked by the jarveys who leered at them. Pavements were regularly blocked by beggars, stallholders and pickpockets. During the summer months, the stink of fish on the pavement opposite St Catherine' church was notorious. Street singers occupied prominent corners, and their audiences blocked the footpaths, forcing passers-by to step out into the muck and manure of the carriageways.[27]

> Alas! Poor Stephen's Green! Thy patient earth bears the burden of thousands of unhallowed feet, and thy trees and dykes bear witness to many iniquitous works, the conferences of the sons of rapine and murder and the scenes of lawless love.
>
> Isaac Bickerstaaf, 1763[28]

Promenades for the elite were intended to be sanctuaries for health-giving leisure and sociability. This privilege was challenged by the lower orders, and intruders were a constant source of friction. The promenades were visited by young males seeking jobs as footmen or servants; they confronted prospective employers who were out strolling. These job seekers were often dressed to make an impression on women. At times, they resorted to carrying oak cudgels that might help to persuade would-be employers.[29] The unpleasant throng in places of recreation was also attributed to the growing army of bureaucrats. Everybody was dressing up to look respectable – even the office clerks and professional musicians: 'Francis-street, Bride's-alley, Potatoe-row, and all the scriveners offices in town, vomit

The EARL of WESTMEATH.
In the Character of Father Luke.

Amateur dramatics appealed to the elite. Shows within their own homes allowed private indulgence away from the hoi polloi. (*Walker's Hibernian Magazine*, April 1793) (UCD)

forth their sons and daughters, bedizened to outshine their "equals" in Merrion Square.'[30]

By the 1760s the upper classes were forsaking the city theatres. They preferred their own domestic entertainments, including musical recitals and amateur dramatics. By the 1780s Leinster House and the other select venues were increasingly used for masquerades and balls. Theatre attendance became dominated by the middle class. By the 1790s most of the promenades were abandoned due to their filthy condition. Troublemakers destroyed the reputation of the city's main reservoir, the Basin, which had long been a fashionable resort. In one incident, the offenders were identified as a grocer's apprentice, a parish musician, a carpenter and a waiter. On another occasion, a butcher was prosecuted for relieving himself in the hedgerow that surrounded the site. The perimeter wall of St Stephen's Green was breached by those kept outside. Plans were made in 1792 to upgrade the place, but they were vetoed by the local residents. The inertia was partly due to the lord mayor's personal use of the grazing rights. This was a valuable perk of his office, and in 1803–04, for example, he was paid 150 guineas compensation when the place was occupied by yeomanry.[31] By 1794 the green was allegedly overrun by beggars who threatened to abuse the women there if their demands were not met.[32]

Sackville Mall went into a decline as urban growth altered its surroundings. A new street connected it southwards across the Liffey. This new extension maintained its extraordinary width, but it was degraded by the through traffic trundling over the new Carlisle Bridge (1798). The middle class moved in as their betters moved out, and before long it was attracting 'coxcomical captains, pert coxcombs; ancient beaus; battered belles; bankers clerks; the whole tribe of "pen and ink" and the very dregs and sweepings of the shops at "Merry Eve"'.[33]

These changes redistributed professional services within the city centre. The shift was noted by William Drennan, a city doctor. In 1791 he believed his Gloucester Street home had one of Dublin's best addresses, but over the following years he was very concerned that genteel venues were being overrun by the lower orders. His sister Martha considered the amenity of the Rotunda promenade was fading due to recent 'indelicacy'. Drennan himself was annoyed at the contingents of day trippers he came across; they were venturing too far from home. By the 1790s their presence was even degrading the coach service to County Wicklow; these common sightseers were overcrowding beauty spots such as the Dargle valley. We can see that Drennan's attitude was endorsed

TASTE, A-LA-MODE 1745.

Fashion dictated the transfer of the premier promenade eastwards from the medieval quarter (the Basin) to Rutland Square (Rotunda Gardens). (*Walker's Hibernian Magazine*, July 1790) (UCD)

TASTE, A-LA-MODE 1790.

Rubbish Pickers

by a print of 1815 entitled *A Trip to the Dargle, or the Pleasures of Jaunting*. This unknown artist showed an overloaded jaunting car crashing down a hillside.[34]

Discarded items of all sorts were recycled. Old metal, glass and rags could provide remuneration. (Hugh Douglas Hamilton, 1760) (Private collection)

Pervasive beggary

> Along side of a hedge by the bridge of Drumcondra,
> Poor Murdoch O'Monaghan sat down to beg;
> He brought from the wars, in reward for his bravery,
> A crack in his crown and the loss of a leg.
>
> Pierce Egan, 1821[35]

Debtors came to form the largest category of prisoners in London, and by the 1770s it had reached sixty-five per cent.[36] Dublin was not far behind, acquiring five debtors' prisons. The Four Courts Marshalsea and the City Marshalsea were the main centres, and below them were the marshalseas of St Sepulchre and St Thomas, as well as the dark hole called the Black Dog, where debtors were detained along with dangerous criminals. These were places of predation that accelerated the progress into penury. Those with means could occupy a suite of rooms, while those without shared a cubbyhole with another five or six penniless strangers.

The beggars depicted by Hamilton and Malton wandered all over the city, and their ranks were continually expanded by further contingents from the countryside.[37] Arthur Young disliked walking the streets due to the ever-present *canaille*. According to the minor French aristocrat Jacques-Louis de Latocnaye, these beggars were predatory creatures who exploited the less well-off; they extorted alms from unfortunates living in cellars by hanging their clothes over the railings to cut off the light until they received some payment.[38]

Estimates of the beggar population varied considerably. In 1773 the *Hibernian Journal* claimed there were about two thousand, half of them having recently arrived from the countryside. An enquiry in the previous year found there were about one thousand beggars with official permits. It is unlikely that half of all beggars were licensed; the number was likely to have been lower. By 1786 the same newspaper estimated the total had reached twenty thousand. Later in the same year, however, this paper reduced its estimate to eight thousand. In January 1796 *The Freeman's Journal* claimed there were five thousand beggars, but four months later reduced its estimate to three thousand. Samuel Rosborough, the Dublin philanthropist who paid close attention to prevailing conditions, claimed that there were eight thousand paupers wandering the streets in 1800. Another account, seven years later, put the number at five thousand. There was a relentless trend upwards. A survey published in 1818 stated that the city had thirty thousand indigent people who needed assistance during the Regency. Whatever the exact number, visitors were everywhere presented with the spectacle of weeping sores and ulcers.

> Who has not seen female beggars … extorting from the public a premium for sacrificing the health and lives both of their children, and the persons who support them.
>
> Anon., 1817[39]

In 1810 John Gamble, a well-travelled doctor, noticed how beggars displayed their sores to excite compassion. They walked down the centre of the street in order to be seen from the houses on either side. Spectacles included a half-naked man of a 'most cadaverous, dreadful aspect' and a woman with 'a dropsy, which she nakedly exposes'. Where these tactics brought success, they also brought imitators. A woman pretending to have breast cancer used a cow's bladder covered with a bloody rag. Others feigned insanity to attract contributions. In 1769 a woman set herself up at Ormond Quay pretending to be mad. She tore the clothes off passers-by refusing to give her money. Her business became too offensive, and the parish authorities sent her off to prison.[40]

Valuable impressions of city beggars are given in Hamilton's *Cries of Dublin*. These include Joseph Corrigan, the 'King of the Beggars'. He was depicted in 1760 as an elderly long-haired man nicknamed Hackball who moved about the streets in a throne-like wheelchair pulled by a young boy. He announced his presence by sounding a horn. Other beggars who attracted Hamilton's attention were an elderly blind man with a conspicuous tumour on his nose, and a legless man who shunted himself around in a wooden bowl. Support for blind beggars fell most heavily onto the poorest areas. In one magnanimous moment during 1771, about two hundred blind paupers were given bread in St Werburgh's parish.[41]

Urchins and orphans

> Groups of mere infants in the train of a sturdy mendicant, paddling in dirt, cold, wet, and nakedness; they bring these innocents into the streets to excite compassion.
>
> Joseph Archer, 1801[42]

Children were left struggling in the rising tide of poverty. Dublin did, however, see a rapid increase in the state institutions taking in abandoned children. By the end of the eighteenth century these supposed sanctuaries were overwhelmed. The Foundling Hospital kept on restricting admission, ultimately confining entry to those under one year old. Poverty brought with it a shroud of shame and the majority of foundlings were delivered anonymously. This topic is addressed in chapter seven. Many children were turned away from these institutions, fading away through the dark passages of hunger and disease.[43]

Boys and girls were abducted to accompany beggars, and some of these children were bought (or stolen) from institutions such as the Charter School. Each episode of repression sent more of them into the mendicant ranks. Beggars abused these children, and a favourite ploy was to disfigure them in order to arouse the compassion of almsgivers. In 1768 Esther Whyte, a woman aged about thirty, was arrested for stealing a small boy and blinding him in one eye. By chance, this lad's father on passing by was recognised by his son, who called out to him. After her arrest, Whyte claimed she had borrowed the child from another woman to beg with. In 1797 a city doctor, William Drennan, saw an American merchant taking pity on two young children begging in Abbey Street. He bought them new clothes and sent them home neatly dressed. Their parents' response, however, was one of anger. They told the visitor that since he had clothed them he must now keep them because the parents' profit had all come from their begging.[44]

The trade in abducted children was well known in London. In the 1790s a German visitor claimed that paupers paid between six pence and two shillings to rent a child for a single day's begging – the exact amount depended on the degree of deformity, but a very badly deformed child could attract up to three shillings.[45]

> 'Up to the highest top,' he cries,
> There call out 'chimney sweep!'
> With panting heart and weeping eyes
> Trembling I upwards creep.
>
> Mary Alcock, 1798[46]

Dublin beggars sold young boys to chimney sweeps, and the usual price was a guinea along with a crown's worth of drink. Within the Liberties, destitute mothers sold their emaciated boys to the sweeps, likewise for a guinea. These children were condemned to an ordeal that combined hunger and burning; the tarry smuts brought on a premature death. One of these children, depicted in 1760 by Hugh Douglas Hamilton, can be seen tottering barefoot behind his master, with only a loose sheet to keep out the cold. As the city expanded, so did the number of these 'climbing boys'. According to Warburton, Whitelaw and Walsh in their *History of the City of Dublin* there were up to two hundred of them by 1818. This trade was not confined to Dublin, and the same abuse occurred in Cork. In the years after 1800 the London price for climbing boys ranged from £2 to £5.[47]

Youngsters were imprisoned with hardened criminals. *The Freeman's Journal* asserted that nothing could be more dreadful than throwing children of eight or nine amongst criminal veterans.[48] Great deprivation was caused when the family head went off to fight in foreign battles. During the Napoleonic War, over half

SWEEP, fweep, fweep — Here's the Chimney Doctor! Do you want the Sweep to-Day, Mafter? What Hour fhall I fhall I call to-morrow? Sweep, hot

of those households assisted by the society for distressed room-keepers may have been in this category. The families of soldiers serving abroad often ended up on the streets begging or were forced into prostitution. Women transportees were compelled to leave their families behind. Their children were taken from them as they boarded ship, and left to fend for themselves on the streets.[49]

The Tholsel was the main building occupied by the corporation. This image is misleading as the building had become structurally unsound by the 1790s. (From James Malton, *A Picturesque and Descriptive View of the City of Dublin*, 1799)

3

Municipal Government

A rising sigh, a silent tear declares,
That Dublin has its follies, crimes and cares.

Anon., 1788[1]

EIGHTEENTH-CENTURY DUBLIN HAD A very fragmented administration, and the number of agencies increased with every decade. Each body had its own responsibilities, and all competed against each other to raise money. There was a strong link between religion and local government, and this was expressed through the parish system. Local government based on a proper democratic franchise did not reach the city until the 1840s. During the Georgian era, Dublin Corporation was an unwieldy body with a small exclusive electorate, and was bogged down by procedures retained from the Middle Ages.

The greatest manifestation of these medieval trappings was the pageant called the riding of the franchises – an ostentatious ritual in which the lord mayor and the councillors paraded around the city boundary once every three years in order to assert their authority and delineate the extent of their power. All were colourfully mounted on horseback, with the councillors decked out in costumes representing their individual guilds. This ritual exemplifies the administrative progress made during the Georgian era because the legal boundary of the city became established by a line on a map rather than depending on a motley band of gentlemen trying to recall details of the route taken on previous inebriated excursions.

Law and order, as well as the public health service and the social welfare network, were all managed within the parish structure of the Established Church. Parishes had a variety of responsibilities that extended into tasks such as street lighting and firefighting. These duties placed an onerous burden on the vestry that was charged with getting the work done. Deserving paupers living within the parish were included in the Poor List, and this was a valuable qualification that attracted donations of bread and coal. At the same time, the vestry was determined to drive out undeserving spongers. This system had many facets, of which the most obvious was providing worthy mendicants with licences to beg. St Anne's introduced these badges in 1767 in response to a proclamation from the lord mayor. This was a very ineffective arrangement, and a decade later the parish had failed to implement the scheme.[2]

The eighteenth century saw a move towards the use of paid substitutes to carry out parish work. Good examples occurred in the policing system and in street lighting. Policing acquired its own structures and the men got regular wages. Although more paid jobs became available, the voluntary service of parishioners still remained significant. This gave the force a sectarian taint, but this was bound to happen where policing was carried into the cultural sphere. A position in police politics could attract the attention of the civic powers and lead to progress up the social gradient. Within the rising parishes of St Anne's and St George's, prominent businessmen gave their services, and their reward was extended recognition from customers amongst the city's grandees. As we have seen in chapter two, wealthy parishes built up an extended list of paid positions.[3]

When the Georgian era began, there were twelve Protestant parishes, but it was a very uneven structure due to disparities in size and wealth. There was initially just one parish (St Michan's) lying north of the Liffey. Over the following decades, the number of these civil parishes grew rapidly, and by 1800 there were nineteen. Five of them were situated north of the river. These extra parishes included affluent new suburbs such as St George's, St Peter's and St Anne's.

Some of the new parishes were formed by the subdivision of an old parish that had grown too unwieldy. In 1749, for example, it was found that the population increase within St Mary's made it too large for a single vicar. As a result, the new parish of St Thomas was created on lands where most of the expansion was taking place. Because these parishes were units of local government, these changes were enshrined in law. Such divisions did not always work as planned, and St Mary's was no exception. It was aggrieved at the affluent streets it saw rising within

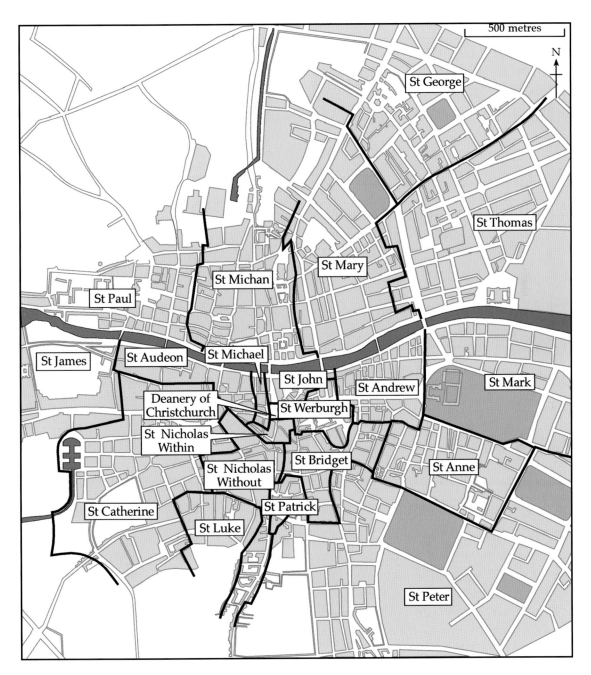

Civil parishes. Their remarkable diversity in size and income weakened the local government system. (Map courtesy of Edel Sheridan-Quantz, David Dickson and Matthew Stout)

PIPEING hot, fmoaking hot, come and buye what I've got, hot Cakes hot: —One a-penny, two a-penny, diddle, diddle Dumpling Cakes

SHOES to mend, Shoes to mend —— Shoes br Boots to mend.— Have you any Work for the Cobler to-Day Madam?

its former territory. There were several court cases about the disputed boundary line, but the real reason was lost revenue. These disagreements had to be resolved through legislation.

The hit-and-miss approach extended to all aspects of the police, even including the uniforms worn by the men. During the 1760s and 1770s new weapons were donated to St Anne's night watch by one of the directors, and they received new caps through the generosity of an army general.[4] These were the lucky parishes, as other areas had to struggle with few resources. There were, in addition, small parcels of land that remained entirely outside the jurisdiction of the civil parishes. These were essentially the old Liberties, and they included manorial properties that were located within the impoverished south-western quarter.

As the number of local government agencies multiplied, their charges and taxes grew more confusing. By the 1780s this muddle was seen in the ways that income was collected. The *Hibernian Journal* listed the main items as follows:

Left: A purveyor of hot cakes and pies, 1770s, offering an early form of takeaway food. Right: A strolling cobbler, 1770s. The majority of Dubliners were pedestrians, creating plenty of work for men repairing shoes. (Both images, Anon., The Dublin Cries) (RSAI)

cleansing, paving and lighting tax was payable on 12 January, pipe-water money on 24 June, metal main rent on 20 May, minister's money on 25 December, watch tax on 25 March and 29 September, and Foundling Hospital tax on 5 January.[5]

Wider powers were gradually acquired by the corporation. Market trading was regulated and tolls were levied on individuals bringing produce into the city. There is not much detailed information available regarding the city budgets. The corporation had a limited role in tax collection, and it left much of this task to the parishes. A notable proportion of the annual budget did, however, come from property rents, tolls and customs, along with charges for specific services such as the water supply. The New Hall Market, for example, yielded almost £240 annually, and this sum was derived from the payments made by upwards of eighty butchers' stalls. For much of the eighteenth century, these sources may have made up half of the total income.

Street traders were amongst those who refused to pay tax, and the police were forced to extract it. In 1789 fifty policemen took part in a raid on the old clothes market at Plunkett Street. They soon found themselves outnumbered, and one of them was left dead. Many comrades of the deceased were wounded in the ensuing riot, and they had to retreat empty-handed.[6]

✳✳✳✳✳

Georgian Dublin saw a slump in the prosperity of its city council. A significant part of the fall-off was due to the decline of the textile industry. It also arose from the outdated basis of local taxation. House valuations, dating from 1716, became skewed in favour of the new squares and streets. Old houses in High Street might pay £2 14s annually, while the best houses in Fitzwilliam Square were only paying a quarter of that. This injustice got a stronger airing after the Union. The grand jury budget grew by twenty-three per cent between 1807 and 1820. After the expansion of the urban boundary in 1808, a growing proportion of houses in the Liberties were shut up in order to avoid their tax liability. This trend accelerated after the Napoleonic Wars, and the number of unoccupied houses in the Liberties grew by over fifty per cent between 1815 and 1821. The property valuations became more uneven, but they were not subsequently revised. Parts of the run-down medieval quarter around High Street ended up paying fifty per cent more local tax than the fine houses around College Green. This withering of the city's wealth reached a crisis during the Regency years. By 1812 the sale of the Mansion House was even being considered, and during the following year the salaries of some city officials were reduced by twenty per cent. Poor administration made matters worse. When the police duty area was extended to the Circular Road in 1808, the extra houses were omitted from the list of taxpayers.[7]

The city's grand jury levied a cess on each of the civil parishes twice each year. Surviving parish records reveal the amounts laid in this way and what proportion of the total was represented by those contributions. This parish cess brought in an average annual income of about £3,000 during the 1770s, and it grew rapidly over the following decades; it had trebled by the 1790s and had grown tenfold by the 1830s. In the case of St Anne's parish – always amongst the most affluent areas – the contribution during those decades varied between nine per cent and eleven per cent of the overall total. It is clear, as well, how the cost of running the city grew very quickly during the eighteenth century; as early as the 1720s gross annual expenditure reached about £8,500, and these outgoings had doubled by the 1780s.[8]

✳ ✳ ✳ ✳ ✳

Parishes were driven by self-interest, and were slow to pay for improvements unless they got enough of the benefits. Even when awareness grew that epidemics crossed the parish boundaries, this did not prevent public benefactors from confining their charity to their own neighbourhoods. When the rising parish of St George opened a dispensary in 1801, the concern of the wealthy for the weak was carefully confined within their own bailiwick. That venture drew over a hundred subscribers, but their addresses were concentrated within the affluent households of Rutland Square, Gardiner Street, Eccles Street and Dorset Street.[9]

As the infrastructure expanded, parishes were forced to compromise. Apportionment was used in projects such as drainage works that served several districts, and the lord mayor was regularly called in to act as the honest broker. In 1761 he coordinated the provision of a trunk sewer at Leinster Street, where four parishes were mired in a dispute. St Peter's ultimately could not pay its share, so the power brokers decreed that it would gain nothing from the project, leaving St Anne's, St Mark's and St Andrew's with all of the sewer capacity. There were also instances where two parishes were at loggerheads over a quite straightforward scheme, causing one of them to seek a legal remedy. In 1773 St Anne's parish sought legal advice when St Brigid's baulked at paying its share for a new sewer in William Street. In 1782 a dispute between St Paul's and St Michan's regarding sewer repairs in the Smithfield area was resolved when St Michan's agreed to pay two thirds of the cost.[10]

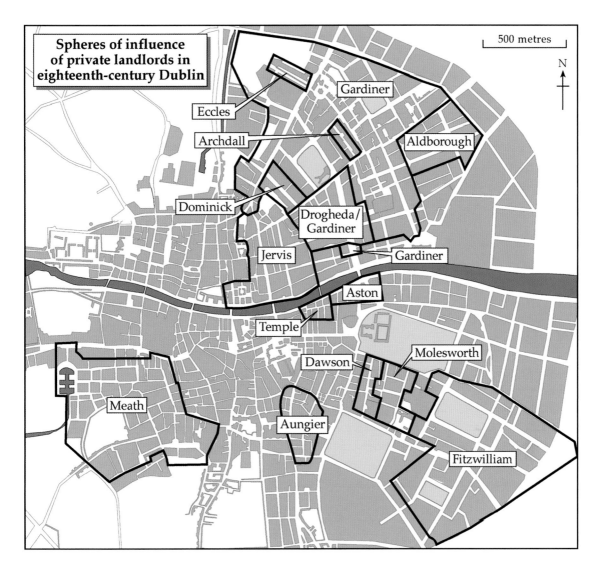

Spheres of influence of private landlords in eighteenth-century Dublin

500 metres

N

Eccles

Gardiner

Archdall

Aldborough

Dominick

Drogheda/ Gardiner

Jervis

Gardiner

Aston

Temple

Molesworth

Dawson

Meath

Aungier

Fitzwilliam

The eastern location of the Gardiner and Fitzwilliam estates are noteworthy. (Map courtesy of Edel Sheridan-Quantz, David Dickson and Matthew Stout)

This parochial self-interest held up necessary works that would benefit the wider community. Examples of this arose at the crossings over the River Liffey. By the 1760s, Ormond Bridge and Essex Bridge were in such a dangerous state that the corporation had to intervene, if only to keep them passable. That involvement continued for several decades because the adjoining parishes kept on bickering. They even refused to install street lighting, and the corporation had to subsidise the malingerers, mainly St Mary's, St John's and St Audoen's. A spur was given to this arrangement in 1763 when crime levels at Essex Bridge prevented the sale of houses within the newly created Parliament Street.[11] Chapter eleven shows how public lighting in each parish was provided by private contractors. There were regular complaints that corrupt management left the entire system neglected.

Dublin's police force, known as the parish watch, was set up by the corporation in 1715. Soon afterwards, its control was handed over to the Protestant authorities. Each Church of Ireland parish had its own constables and watchmen, but in most places the force was under-strength due to the cost. By the 1760s the city had 317 watchmen but only four parishes had a full complement, these being St Andrew's, St Anne's, St Bridget's and St Mary's. Self-interest drove these areas to subsidise their tardy neighbours.[12] It was poor men who were attracted by the low wages and bad conditions. Most servicemen were old and illiterate; in 1750 only four out of twelve recruits at St Thomas' could sign their names.

The lord mayor had a veto on the appointment of constables who supervised the ordinary watchmen. He made good use of that power, and insisted that candidates were householders of the parish. This residential qualification was strictly imposed in St Anne's. He disapproved of persons rising above their station – for instance, a former servant of Lord Kingston was barred in 1768 and a schoolteacher was refused in 1770. It was in 1795 that St Anne's parish first produced a list showing the occupations of constables: they were a grocer, a glazer, a linen draper and a chandler, all with addresses in Grafton Street.[13]

St Thomas' was a north-side parish in the middle range of affluence, and during the 1750s it was divided into seven patrolling routes for police purposes. Each route was short, ranging from 100 to 300 metres. Watchmen occupied small shelters that were constructed by the grand jury. Each shelter was strategically situated within the network, and was identified by the house or business it adjoined. In 1750 St Thomas' listed shelters at Captain King's house in Britain Street, the Earl of Meath's house at Henry Street, Mrs Careless' stall in Abbey Street, and Mr Derby's house at the Ferry Boat in Jervis Street. Two men were assigned to each post, doing consecutive two-hour shifts. Another patrol route was added a decade later to reflect the growing development of the area. This pattern was repeated in St Paul's (in the 1750s), although it boasted eight separate stands.[14]

This system was supposed to provide community support. Patrolling watchmen called out the time and the weather. The watch-house, by default, served as a welfare centre because most of the down-and-outs ended up there. On winter nights, wanderers could benefit from its shelter and its heat. Any drunk encountered by the watch was supposed to be conveyed home; this might mean passing him on to the next watchman along the way, and if necessary into the care of the next parish and so on.

Population growth put pressure on the legal system. As early as 1729 the quarter sessions and the Court of King's Bench were overwhelmed. An additional circuit criminal court, known as Oyer et Terminer, was created, and this sat in the Tholsel, where the lord mayor and aldermen presided as justices. Alongside this system were two independent courts operating in the Liberties.[15]

There were periods in the second half of the eighteenth century when the city appeared to be running out of control. The poorest parishes became dysfunctional, and it was clear that certain people could not pay their taxes. Lord Clonmel revealed that the churchwardens in the most deprived parishes often paid the taxes themselves rather than forcing the local residents to pay them. In 1783 Lord Annaly strongly resisted a tax to expand the Houses of Parliament because it would be an excessive burden on poor people. He argued that such projects conveyed an impression of riches that was altogether illusory.[16]

There was tension between the viceroy and the corporation when their functions overlapped. All too often the army had to maintain public order, and the city council resented the increasing role of the state in law and order. As we have seen, the corporation subsidised poor parishes, and this extended to augmenting watchmen's wages. Sheer frustration drove it to engage more watchmen itself. In 1763 eight men were hired to ensure that people could safely cross Essex Bridge.[17]

Dublin's law courts were modelled on the London system, and this meant certain functions were performed by the lord mayor. He held the position of chief magistrate, and at any time the level of efficiency was related to the zeal of the current office holder. He was given generous allowances, and critics were always ready to deride any overindulgence at the Mansion House. A pamphleteer of 1804 found that year's lord mayor was only remarkable for wearing a tasteless and inconvenient dress with 'a chain like a gilt jack chain round his neck, keeping a number of servants better dressed and better looking than himself, and above all, eating very heartily at certain festivals'.[18]

✳ ✳ ✳ ✳ ✳

There were two parts in the members' assembly of local government. The Upper House comprised the lord mayor and twenty-four aldermen, while the Common Council was made up of forty-eight sheriff's peers and ninety-six guild representatives. Aldermen and the sheriffs were elected for life, but guild representatives only served a three-year term. The aldermen mainly comprised merchants and lawyers, and they also served as magistrates. There were two sheriffs, and they presided over the Common Council. The aldermen held the lucrative positions and made great use of their patronage; they allied themselves with the landed gentry, who had effective control in parliament. This combination gave them great political power, and in the period between 1715 and 1749 they formed all but one of the city's MPs.

Sessions were held at the Tholsel on Skinners' Row, beside Christ Church cathedral. They took place each quarter, but were supplemented by frequent post-assembly meetings. These gatherings set budgets for bridges, drains and other works. Specialist standing committees, such as the Ballast Board (1707) and the Paving Board (1774), dealt with particular functions between the quarterly sessions. In the former case, the duties included maintenance of the harbour, while the latter embraced the public streets, including lighting and sewerage. By the 1790s the Tholsel had become structurally unsound and unsuitable for court cases. Strong evidence of this emerged when a group of eight prisoners escaped through a hole in the floor.[19] Meetings of the corporation were moved to the City Assembly House in South William Street. This was the fine, red-brick building constructed as an art gallery by the Society of Artists in Ireland. In 1797 the court sessions were accommodated in the new Sessions House at Green Street, next door to Newgate Prison.

The merchants provided themselves with facilities in the Royal Exchange. This grand edifice was designed by Thomas Cooley in 1769, and was erected next door to the Castle so that the general public could associate the place with its high status. It was this landmark building that became the City Hall when the corporation moved again in 1852. The inexorable move eastwards reflected the association of power and address.[20]

Although the lord mayor had a wide jurisdiction fighting abuses in market trading, preventing begging, suppressing the sex trade and controlling traffic, he could hardly coordinate the efforts of all twenty-one separate police forces. As happened with other issues of public interest, intervention by the corporation was not solely informed by the highest motives; rather, it was more concerned with suppressing nuisances that discommoded the rising districts. A gradual but continuing loosening of urban networks compromised community organisation and exposed flaws throughout the local government system. Artisan parishes, distinguished by noisy and dirty industries, were fast becoming relict structures.[21]

Social stratification was reinforced by the hierarchical pattern of status, fashion and socio-economic gravity. Disparities in local control of development led to a wider divergence in land use, and this process was facilitated by the unbalanced provision of infrastructure. Efforts at directing growth could only be implemented in a piecemeal fashion. In 1767–68 the city council applied to parliament for more regulatory powers. It sought to follow the precedents set for London and Bristol by including the widening of public streets, the improvement of pavements and the suppression of nuisances. In addition, it wanted to regulate industry (especially the baking trade) and to reform the markets by penalising forestallers, as well as confirming the power of the market jury.[22]

These efforts failed, and the articulate voices left behind by the tide of fashion grew louder. In the 1790s the archbishop of Dublin claimed his great edifice, St Patrick's cathedral, was marooned within the medieval quarter. It was besieged by the forces of destruction and sinful neglect had allowed the sewers to overflow, bringing floods of foul effluent right up to his front door.[23] By that time, however, the religious connection with local government was getting weaker. Wealthy residents were spending more time in their suburban retreats, and this reflected a conscious disengagement with everyday city life. These people were now attending church services in the suburbs, and this had negative repercussions for city-centre parishes.

Map detail: Emerging suburbia beside the Grand Canal reveals the incremental progress of housing development. (F.J. Byrne, 1830) (NAI)

4

Trends in the Pattern of Growth

The western part of this city, consisting of narrow lanes and alleys, has been always unfriendly to the health of the poor, and has become more inimical, in that respect, from the migration of the wealthy inhabitants to the eastern, and modern parts of the city.

Samuel Rosborough, 1801[1]

DIFFERENT INTERESTS GOVERNED THE DIRECTION taken by new building and business activities, and each decade offered more clarification about the forces at work. Eastward expansion was partly a reaction to the condition of the west side. Agricultural merchants were clustered alongside the city approach formed by James Street and Thomas Street, and industrial expressions of the grain trade in breweries and distilleries formed off-putting obstacles close by. Further south lay the troubled workshops of the textile industry. To the north of the Liffey, the cattle market, the hay market and the army barracks discouraged expansion towards Phoenix Park. It became clear that a good location could produce a good address. We have already seen in chapter one how St Stephen's Green fared far better than Smithfield. Those schemes were similar in terms of age, design and even in extent (ninety-six plots), but the green had the cachet of the better address.

The search for a good address

People with large parcels of land were seeking ways to enhance their value. Estate proprietors had a great influence, and within the best-managed landholdings, such as the Fitzwilliam (south-east) and Gardiner (north-east) estates, a strict control was exercised. This power was expressed in the initial planning and layout of streets, and then pursued by close attention to the design of the individual new houses. It should be allowed that these estate developers cultivated exclusivity, and in doing so had a far-reaching impact on the social geography of the city. The tide of fashion worked alongside the attractions of long leases and public amenities. Population growth allowed diversity, but taste could make a place unpopular. One consistent feature was the decline of the medieval Liberties.

A street trader selling his produce to women in the Liberties. (From J. Warburton, Revd J. Whitelaw and Revd R. Walsh, *History of the City of Dublin*, 1818)

Market forces acted to make individual areas advance or fall back, and an example of this transformation was provided by the Aungier estate. This was a late-seventeenth century development undertaken by Francis Aungier, and in keeping with the popular trend was in the south-east quarter. Aungier devised a comprehensive neighbourhood plan that included residential streets, a market and a church. His main elements were Aungier Street and York Street, both of which were broad and airy thoroughfares, 15 metres and 12 metres wide respectively. York Street connected the scheme to St Stephen's Green, and this drew more fashion-conscious traffic. It was seen as a new beginning, turning a fresh face towards the countryside.

The Aungier estate in the 1750s. (John Rocque's map of Dublin, 1756)

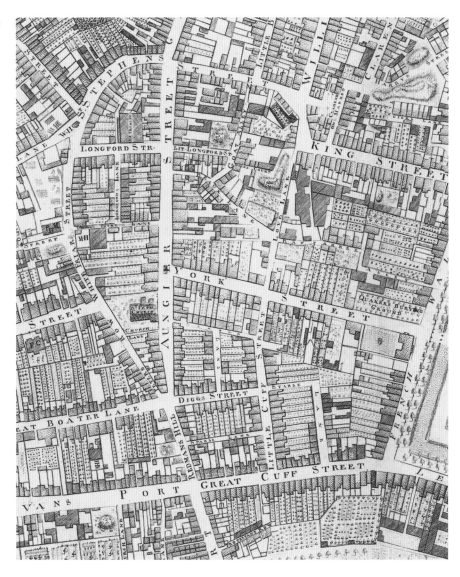

Like its predecessors, Aungier's suburb attracted high-class residents, but that did not last. It was in serious decline by the 1720s as fashion carried the connoisseurs further east. Novelty then favoured the new suburb developed by Joshua Dawson to the north of St Stephen's Green. At its heart was Dawson Street, a wide and straight thoroughfare embellished by the mansion that Dawson built for his own use. In 1715 this fine house was purchased by the city corporation and became the official residence of the lord mayor. It has served that function ever since, and is popularly known as the Mansion House. This put

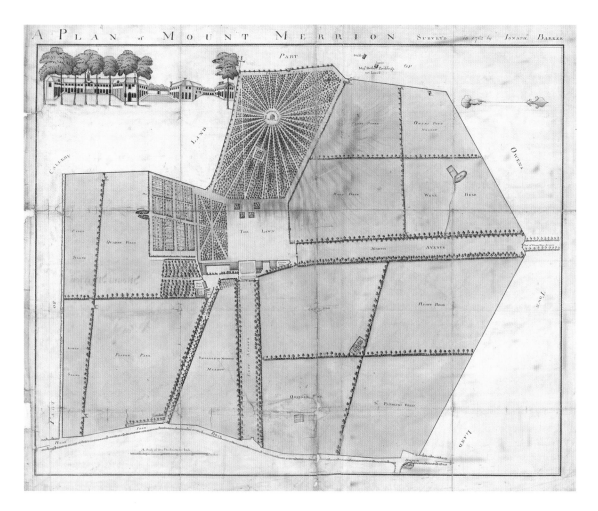

the seal of approval on Dawson's project. Aungier's estate was left behind, and it had to accept lower-class merchants and tradesmen.[2]

Other suburbs saw similar transformations. On the north side, Luke Gardiner's Sackville Mall emerged in the late 1740s. At its heart was a fashionable promenade reserved for the use of elite residents. Gardiner's layout had an unusual elongated configuration, being 350 metres long and 50 metres wide. Modern visitors to O'Connell Street might be unaware of the elegant origins that gave it such a spacious quality. This remarkable width was retained when the street was subsequently extended southwards as far as the Liffey.

> The tawdry fops, with sneering, vain grimace,
> Adorn'd with ignorance – and flimsy lace,

This layout of the Mount Merrion estate, *c.* 1762, reveals European aesthetic influences, with radial tree-lined avenues and axial views focused on the demesne house. (Jonathan Barker, 1762) (NAI)

Strut in mock majesty, and view with scorn
The lower creatures who this scene adorn.

Revd. John Anketell, 1793[3]

Gardiner's Mall attracted the rich and powerful. Its residents included many MPs and peers, and in 1772 this golden circle secured legislation to render the place even more exclusive. This new law prohibited any use of the mall as a marketplace or a cab stand.[4] These initiatives clearly succeeded. For example, ten per cent of the city's private sedan chairs belonged to residents of the mall. That did, however, prove to be the high point, and the grandeur of Sackville Mall peaked a decade later. That great success was followed abruptly by the retreat of the elite. In 1786 a new law allowed the corporation to take over the mall, and during the following years the Wide Streets Commission transformed the place.[5] The street was extended southwards to the Liffey, and construction of Carlisle Bridge began about 1795. This completed the change, turning the quiet cul-de-sac into a busy traffic artery.

Gardiner's Mall, as it appeared during the 1760s and 1770s. The central promenade served the local elite. A few decades later, through traffic degraded the place. (Oliver Grace)

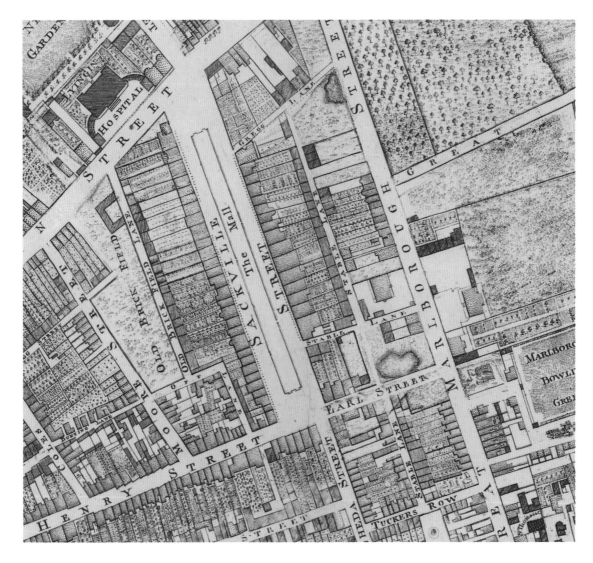

Retail outlets took over the houses, and the social cachet of the mall was destroyed. When the General Post Office was built in 1818, it was given pride of place. Its dominating façade, 56 metres in length, made it clear just how much the street had changed. The domestic scale had been superseded. A great diversity of occupants arrived over the following decades. One English visitor described these newcomers as 'peers, pastry cooks and perfumers, bishops, butchers and brokers in old furniture, together with hotels of the most superb description and a tolerable sprinkling of gin and whiskey shops'.[6] There was also a notable sprinkling of lawyers, no doubt attracted by the proximity of the Four Courts.

Gardiner's Mall, 1750s. The later extension of Sackville Street (now O'Connell Street) southwards as far as the Liffey was a major undertaking for the Wide Streets Commission. (John Rocque's map of Dublin, 1756)

Moving the main street

> The increase of buildings to the east and north-east
> of this city has now become astonishing.
>
> *The Freeman's Journal*, 4 April 1790

Towards the middle of the eighteenth century, property interests decided that intervention was necessary to adapt the city to growth. Old worn-out institutions had to be replaced by better structures set out in brighter positions. One commentator identified those buildings that should be replaced as the Tholsel, Mansion House, Four Courts, Market House, Ormond Bridge, Newgate Prison and the Marshalsea. He also stressed how the new edifices should be arranged along either side of the Liffey.[7] A central tenet was the replacement of the cluttered medieval commercial district with a new, purpose-built business quarter. Dublin was fortunate in having its own development authority, known as the Wide Streets Commission.[8] This agency was established by the Irish parliament in the late 1750s, and it worked to provide broader, healthier thoroughfares – public places enhanced by the harmony of rectilinear streetscapes. There was an ordered elegance in the buildings that lined the streets. The work of the WSC

Beresford Place was amongst the finest streetscapes created by the Wide Streets Commission. The decorative embellishment of its central buildings highlighted the integrated and unified design.

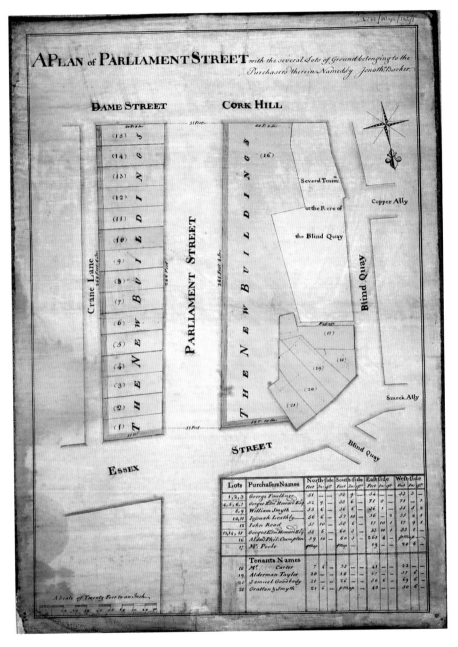

A PLAN of PARLIAMENT STREET *with the several Lots of Ground belonging to the Purchasers therein Named by Jonath. Barker*

DAME STREET   CORK HILL

THE NEW BUILDINGS

PARLIAMENT STREET

Crane Lane

Several Tenem:

at the Rere of

the Blind Quay

Copper Ally

Blind Quay

THE NEW BUILDINGS

Smock Ally

STREET

ESSEX

Blind Quay

A Scale of Twenty Feet to an Inch.

Lots	Purchasers Names	North side		South side		East side		West side	
		Feet	Inc:ff	Feet	Inc:ff	Feet	Inc:ff	Feet	Inc:ff
1,2,3	George Faulkner	51	—	52	9	54	—	53	3
4,5,6,7	Gorges Edw. Howard Esq.	52	9	53	6	71	0	71	—
8,9	William Smyth	55	6	56	6	36	1	35	5
10,11	Iosuah Leathly	56	6	57	10	36	—	35	4
12	John Read	57	10	58	6	17	10	17	9
13,14,15	Gorges Edw. Howard Esq.	58	6	60	3	53	10	53	1
16	Aldm. Phil: Crampton	59	10	60	3	261	4	p.map	
17	Mr. Poole	p.map		p.map		19	—	20	6
	Tenants Names								
18	Mr. — Carter	7	4	33	—	41	—	22	—
19	Alderman Taylor	20	—	18	—	67	—	57	6
20	Samuel Goodbody	21	—	26	—	50	6	69	6
21	Grattan & Smyth	21	6	p.map		43	—	50	6

Parliament Street was the first major work undertaken by the Wide Streets Commission, 1750s. Plots 1–3 were ascribed to George Faulkner, the celebrated printer and publisher. (DCC)

was highlighted by artistic additions to the façades, including balustrades, pedestals, rustic quoins, vases and arms. Parliament provided an ample budget, and, in addition, the WSC had great legal power. It was able to buy the land it needed, even when the owner was reluctant to sell.

ELEVATION of the West Side of WESTMORLAND STREET extending from the Portico of the House of Lords to Fleet Street as approved of by the COMMISSIONERS appointed by ACT of PARLIAMENT for making Wide and Convenient streets in the CITY of DUBLIN.

Thomas Sherrard 1800

Design for the west side of Westmoreland Street, 1800, as constructed. (Wide Streets Commission) (DCC)

Yet the agenda of the WSC was quite selective. It largely avoided the medieval quarter, and there was little concern over the widespread dereliction. Old streets within the Liberties were left to choke; intervention in that area was achieved only by high-placed influence. The crumbling Cornmarket formed a bottleneck that was not cleared away until vehicles found it too hard to squeeze around it. Its ultimate removal was achieved by people who were not easily ignored – the Duke of Leinster and the archbishop of Dublin.

The WSC was a self-perpetuating body, and its members were largely drawn from the ranks of the parliamentary power brokers. Its attention was directed towards satisfying the ambitions of property barons who had speculated on city expansion. This brought a culture of compromise. At times, Lord A could be on the board adjudicating on the interests of Lords B and C, people who were his allies in many aspects of life. Moreover, before long, B and C would be in a position to return any favours when they controlled the traffic of enrichment. Those within this circle who had gambled on eastward expansion of the city could expect a good return. Scholars will find little evidence of a disinterested city-wide strategy in the programme of the WSC.

To enable the capital to expand eastwards, there was a need to extend the arteries of growth. Dame Street was identified as having the greatest potential. It was a place that supported a range of commercial activities, and it connected the Castle with Parliament House. Its narrowness and shabby state needed to be transformed, and this was one of the earliest tasks taken on by the WSC. In 1766 the commission decided on a layout for Dame Street. Both sides were set back and the old buildings were replaced by a classical streetscape. This project was justified on the basis of its role in state occasions, but there was also the simpler acceptance that it comprised the premier business venue: 'in so great and permanent a work as the building the principal street of communication in this city, the Commissioners are fully justifiable in securing and ornamenting the same at the public expense.'[9]

Dublin did, of course, have its own long-established High Street, and that can be seen in John Speed's 1610 map of the city. It was, however, embedded in the medieval quarter, and it fell from grace as the tide of development flowed eastwards. In stark contrast to this, Dame Street was the first street to emerge outside the city wall on the east side. It reached out from the medieval Damas Gate towards the university. Its status rose during the 1730s as the new Parliament House became established. The rise of bureaucracy drove the tavern trade, and Dame Street acquired an array of ale houses with names such as The Sun, The Crown and Punch, The Half-Moon and The Robin Hood.[10]

It took more than three decades to complete Dame Street, and it sapped the energy of the WSC. This delay was partly due to the diversity of property interests. Many of these people remained half hidden within the maze of dark alleys and backyards that stretched out on either side. A valuation jury had to be appointed for each purchase, all complemented with maps, leases and bureaucratic baggage.

Logically enough, work began at the western end leading from the Castle down along the south side towards George's Lane (modern George's Street). The commission's surveys of the late 1770s and early 1780s revealed the range of interests embedded there. At numbers 23 to 49, the shopfronts contained five grocers, two shoemakers, two publicans, two gunmakers, two breeches makers, two apothecaries, a jeweller, a watchmaker, a bookseller, a stationer, a printer, a paper stainer, an instrument maker, a saddler, a tobacconist, a mercer, an optician, a perfumer and a lace man. Close by were three publicans, three booksellers, two printers, two grocers, two mercers, two shoemakers, two watchmakers, a glover, a glass seller and an embroiderer. To the rear, towards the Castle Market, were five butchers along with another publican. As the WSC progressed along Dame Street, it was confronted by the heritage of medieval laxity. There were numerous back alleys where the land uses were heaped together. Any shop space might be shared, subdivided or just casually sublet on a weekly basis. Within the back lands, the owners had individual rooms let out in a random fashion. Rear yards contained a variety of enterprises, some of which reflected their lower rank, such as farriers and brush makers, together with many of the darker drinking dens.

A person's position was dictated by the rent the space attracted. A 1781 survey of the south side of Dame Street revealed three slaughterhouses at Whitmore Alley, and beside them were three chandlers and a substantial sugar factory. There were other sugar factories there also, and at least one of them, belonging appropriately enough to Patrick Sweetman, was quite substantial – it was valued at £497, and the inventory of its fixtures included a mill, metal stoves, cauldrons and iron doors. These secondary streets contained small dwellings, and the residential proportion increased with distance from the main commercial frontages of Dame Street.[11]

The commission's surveys garnered a great deal of information. For example, the front of number 23 Dame Street had a grocery shop held by Martin Richardson; he also had the stable to the rear which he sublet to a butcher named Michael Byrne for £6 per annum; that space may have been used as a slaughterhouse serving the Castle Market nearby. At first-floor level within the same building, Rachel Grogan had a quilting workshop that probably doubled as a dwelling. She also had the room over the workshop, which she sublet to Sophia Thomas for five guineas a year. Next door, at number 24 Dame Street, the ground-floor shop was divided between a tobacconist (Robert Montgomery) and an instrument maker (Joshua Stokes). Montgomery also held the lower part of the house, and he sublet a back room to a Mrs Bushell for £10 per annum.[12]

Tenancies within the back alleys were equally diverse. Chronicle Court lay to the rear of numbers 31–32 Dame Street. It belonged to Lord Bective, but he leased it to Alderman Philip Crampton. A substantial part of Crampton's interest was, in turn, taken up by John Brady, a shoemaker. Brady lived at second-floor level with another shoemaker named William McDonagh. His interests in the premises included a parlour let to Francis Byrne, a bookbinder who paid him £10 per annum. In addition, he had two rooms set to a gunmaker named William Tully for £9 a year, and his garret was occupied by William Chipps for £3 8s 3d per annum. As well as that, Brady let another small part of the building as a dwelling for a widow named Frances Byrne, who paid him £10 a year. These arrangements were not unusual. Many of the cellars and garrets were let to tenants-at-will. At number 39 Dame Street, a garret room was let to a tailor named George Vicar for 2s 6d a week.[13]

By the mid-1780s it was clear that the scale of the project was daunting. There were complaints about the mounds of rubbish behind the new buildings. Despite these problems, the WSC continued to grant Dame Street a key role

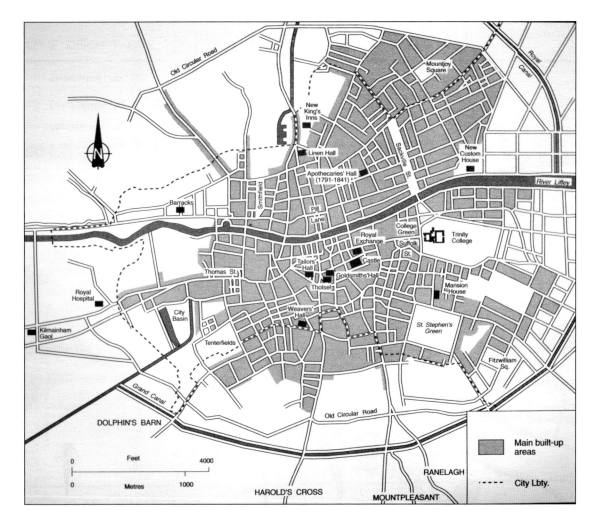

in its overall agenda. The improvements were extended to areas such as road safety, and vehicles were excluded from the pedestrian realm. This was achieved by installing flagged footpaths bounded by kerbside bollards. The scheme also included a sewer, and this was an innovation that presented serious challenges. This topic is addressed in chapter eleven.

What the WSC intended for Dame Street had, in theory, been already tried nearby. A decade earlier, Parliament Street had formed the prototype. That broad, straight thoroughfare leading from the Liffey to the Castle was enhanced by elegant houses; there were no-nonsense specifications and they were consistently applied – for example:

Dublin, c. 1798. It can be seen how growth has surged away from the medieval core towards the north-east and south-east. (After William Wilson) (By kind permission of Jacqueline Hill)

An uniform front to be made by the purchasers and builders throughout the new intended street, as the Commissioners shall direct, and posts and flags to be before the houses; the materials on the said lots and for 25 feet and a half opposite to them to go with the said lots. No projecting window to be to any of the said houses.[14]

This model delivered great benefits to the occupants, but it required the active participation of all the stakeholders. The commission imposed restrictive covenants in order to achieve this outcome. Above all, there was a strict unity within the public realm. In Dame Street, there was a ban on any windows or advertising signs projecting to the front of the buildings. Where departures from this uniformity were found, the WSC acted to correct the situation. In 1783 builders of new houses at Dame Street were forced to correct their work. In one case, the structure was a few inches too low, and in another instance it was 4.5 inches too high. It was this vision, embracing the street as a whole, that brought about the rectilinear vistas that are so closely associated with Georgian Dublin.

Social constraints

> From wicked Dublin happily removed,
> And all its follies (once too dearly lov'd)
>
> John Winstanley, 1742[15]

Some expansion activity was caused by downturns in the city. Deprivation amongst the artisans brought a sudden swelling to the ranks of beggars, making progress through the streets ever more daunting. One such event occurred in the summer of 1782 when a serious epidemic of influenza spread across the city. It brought with it a high death rate because the community-support structure was unable to cope. The parochial welfare system was already in steep decline and unable to meet the demand for accommodation. That autumn the exorbitant price of coal held out an icy prospect. An effort was made by the lord lieutenant to break the cartel amongst the fuel merchants. When this initiative failed, he offered the corporation £3,000 to subsidise coal imports for poor households. In another sign of the catastrophe, two thousand tons of the stuff were donated by the main producer in Cumbria. By the autumn of 1783 one fifth of the city's population was in a distressed state, and this figure rose to one third by the following spring. As the pressure on public institutions grew, a new scheme of outdoor relief was introduced. By February 1784 up to twenty thousand people may have been receiving assistance.

It is clear that the corporation was trying to direct aid towards those people in the greatest need. Thirty-one per cent of the coal bounty went to St Catherine's parish, with another thirteen per cent going to St Michan's. At the other end of the spectrum, affluent parishes, such as St Anne's, St Peter's, St Werburgh's and St Thomas', got no more than two per cent each.[16]

Some factors directing growth operated as silent constraints or as blocking agents. The most obvious was the wall of waste accumulating around the poorest quarters. Garbage strewn across the open end of the city dissuaded property developers. It was another incentive for investors to move out as far as the coastline. By 1800 some efforts were made to move this ordure out beyond the Circular Road. They had little effect, however.[17]

The attractions of the coastline

> From my abode, that lies upon the skirts
> Of the metropolis, with spirits gay
> I take my evening walk, and glad
> Inhale the balmy air.
>
> I.C., 'The suburbean', 1795[18]

Jonathan Swift was a great advocate of seaside recreation. Even on cold days he rode out to Clontarf, and he encouraged others to make similar outings. As early as 1712 he advised a friend to take the sea air at Dunleary, and a decade later one of his friends took lodgings at Blackrock to avail of the local bathing facilities. It was widely held that cold bathing was a great tonic, and it even got clerical endorsement because it was directed by Jesus Christ in baptism ceremonies. Sea bathing offered recreation as well as better health, and this sociability led to the growth in its popularity from the 1720s onwards. Swift boasted to Alexander Pope that Dublin had more convenient year-round seaside places than London. He claimed the long strands at the edge of town were just as firm and dry in winter as they were in summer.[19]

A well-known Dublin figure and one-time lord mayor, Sir Michael Creagh, during the 1720s exhorted his fellow citizens to go bathing in the sea twice a day. Creagh was alarmed that access to beaches was being cut off, and he called on the city magistrates to secure these seaside amenities.[20] As early as the 1720s medical

A romantic view of the scenic landscape around Blackrock, c. 1780. This coastline was transformed by the Victorian railway works associated with later building development. (Anon., engraved by Royce, c. 1780)

publications were promoting seaside living. More of these appeared over the next three decades, culminating in the work of Dr Richard Russell in the 1750s. Russell was a graduate of Trinity College, Dublin, and he had a central role in converting Brighton into Britain's premier seaside resort. A Dublin edition of his main work was advertised in the city newspapers in 1753. Russell's successor at Brighton was another Dublin graduate, Dr Anthony Relham.[21] Lord Charlemont was one of the city's foremost residents, and he took Russell's advice to heart. During the 1750s he left his estate in County Armagh and established himself in the capital. He chose a Marino property as his suburban residence to complement his town house at Rutland Square: 'My health to which sea bathing and the social neighbourhood of a metropolis were absolutely necessary, would not allow me to settle on my estate in the north.'[22]

These initiatives were part of a broader health crusade. Dubliners were told they had to reform their everyday lives. They should turn away from alcohol, drinking nothing but water. This reform could be achieved in a cleaner environment by getting out of the city; the top priority should be trips to the seaside, where they could drink copious amounts of seawater. One pamphlet on this topic became a bestseller and it appeared in several editions.[23] Sea water was sold in city shops during the 1750s and 1760s, and the Howth *appellation* was especially popular.[24] City outlets were quick to see the potential trade in health tonics. An apothecary named Thomas Johnston advertised bottles of the choicest spa water that he imported from Bath.[25]

The household of Lord Kildare (later, Duke of Leinster) was a leader of Dublin fashion, and by the 1770s the family were making trips to the coast for medical and pleasure purposes. These began after English relatives recounted journeys to seaside destinations for cures. Places they mentioned included Brighton and Harwich, and the drinking of seawater was an integral element. The advice was taken seriously because the Kildares were bathing at Blackrock by the 1770s. They were surprised by the novelty of the experience and pleased to see how easy it was to reach the seaside from their city home.[26]

Fashion was a powerful force in ranking the health resorts of western Europe. It was widely accepted that the waters of Lucan and Mallow were just as effective as those of Bath or Spa, but the Irish resorts suffered because they were not 'the ton'. Blackrock, Clontarf and Howth attracted people seeking a respite from tuberculosis and rheumatism. Sober restraint appealed to people such as the archbishop, and he was a regular bather at Blackrock during the mid-1780s.[27]

✳ ✳ ✳ ✳ ✳

Ye females of Dublin make haste and repair
In coach or on carr to Dunlary wash-fair
Pass by the Black-Rocks, you'll quickly be there.

Anon., *c.* 1720[28]

Of exercise, swimming's best,
Strengthens the muscles of the chest,
And all their fleshy parts confirms,
Extends and stretches legs and arms.

Dr Edward Baynard, 1721[29]

These changes coincided with the growing interest in nature that encouraged people to venture into the countryside. By the 1740s outlying areas, some such as Raheny near the coast, were drawing holidaymakers. Kilmore House could be had for the season, and when Raheny House was offered to rent for the summer of 1750, the cognoscenti knew that any recommendation was superfluous – all anybody needed to know was that Mr Cavendish had the place the previous year and Lady Meade had it for two summers prior to that.

A notable proportion of families living in the countryside were summer visitors, but the number spending longer periods grew during the 1760s. The newcomers were aware of the lifestyle choices offered by these surroundings. As early as 1743 an enterprising gardener, Robert Stevenson of Grafton Street, was cultivating new customers who wished to benefit from 'loose and flowing symmetry, lively fancy, neat embellishments and growing beauties'. Any client who found Stevenson unsatisfactory could turn to his rival Thomas Keithly, who boasted about the great garden he had created for Lord Powerscourt.[30]

During the 1750s Dr Charles Lucas, at one time a city MP, strongly advocated resort development on the coastline. This trend united the health and pleasure benefits, but the emphasis remained on the health aspects. In the summer of 1783 the *Hibernian Journal* promoted sea bathing for bronchitis, rheumatism and infertility.

Towards the end of the century, more travel books were aimed at tourists. Visitors were sure to check out the views they saw in these guides, and those pictures reveal their perception of the landscape. Visitors to Blackrock and Clontarf found 'the genteelest society, and the most philosophic retirement may be engaged in pleasing successions, and the valetudinarian of observation will find the work of health go on imperceptibly'.[31] The study of nature was encouraged by the medical profession on the basis that it exalted the human mind, promoting virtue and an appetite for rational entertainment. However, the influence of doctors could be exaggerated and there were other factors involved such as fashionable patronage and better transport. In 1783 the Prince of Wales (later George IV) built a summer residence at Brighton. This had repercussions elsewhere and Dublin was no exception.[32]

✳ ✳ ✳ ✳ ✳

> But not these heaps of brick or stone
> Prove our city richer grown: –
> The frequent street, the sudden square,

The town which seeks the country air;
That town which seems of Dublin weary,
And quickly travels to Dunleary.

J.J. Stockdale, 1812[33]

The Black Rock! Who does not know the Black
Rock that ever has been in Dublin? All the world
goes there on a Sunday to see the other half of it.

Pierce Egan, 1821[34]

Sightseers at Clontarf.
The notorious charter
school appears on the
left. (William Ashford,
1794) (NGI)

Lloyd, in his 1732 description of the city, cited The Strand amongst the best places
frequented by the upper classes for recreation. Its reputation was established prior
to the end of the seventeenth century.[35] Privacy was sought by people who were
unused to making so free out of doors. As early as 1709 a developer at Townsend
Street highlighted the seclusion of his enterprise; he lowered the garden level to
shield his bathing customers from the passing hoi polloi.[36]

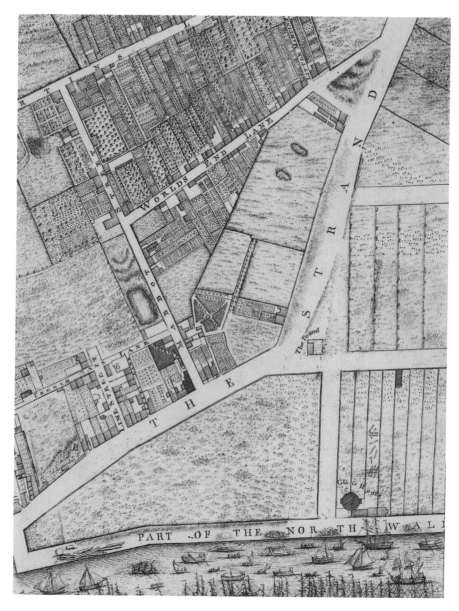

Bathing venues followed urban development out along the bay. They moved eastwards past the North Strand towards Clontarf, while on the south side they stretched from Ringsend out to Blackrock. Old resorts were left behind, and by the end of the century Ringsend was described as a sink of filth. Clontarf acquired an enduring popularity. It greatly appealed to Charles O'Connor, the antiquarian, and in 1757 he encouraged his publisher George Faulkner to take an open carriage out there to avail of the bracing sea air. A half century later, the place was drawing new supporters, such as the family of Daniel O'Connell, the champion of Catholic emancipation. A women's bathing place was established at Blackrock by the 1750s, and visitors were already venturing further south.[37]

The Romantic movement

> The whole rage of building and residence
> tends towards the sea.
>
> *The Freeman's Journal*, 2 June 1789

Nature and the rural environment became topics of conversation. An interest in scenic landscapes was encouraged by the trend towards Romanticism. The concept of the picturesque was promoted – that special type of natural beauty that can be illustrated by artists in their paintings. This was especially attractive to the middle class. For them, unadorned nature came to be viewed as a symbol of eternity. This trend accelerated in the late 1760s.

A taste for country life was generated by several forces. It might be attributed to the likes of William Wordsworth for his imaginative poetry or to the artist Claude Lorrain for his dreamlike landscapes or, yet again, to the philosophical musings of Edmund Burke on the interpretation of scenic landscapes. Whatever source inspired it, it was deemed to be a simple station where joy was drawn from the superior pleasures of the countryside. The appeal of occasional solitude spread across Europe, and quiet rural retreats brought connoisseurs seeking spiritual renewal. The visitor's gaze might follow the grazing sheep moving over the pastures or the cattle meandering across the meadows. Any cottage was sure to contain a family that was free and happy. In all of this, however, there was another agenda. Aficionados of the picturesque stressed it was not a topic for frivolous minds distracted by the vulgar indulgence of the city. It was only the great who could gain the benefit, and their nobility proved they were predisposed to benefit from the experience. One of the foremost connoisseurs was Revd William Gilpin, and he made it clear that the observer needed to be educated to appreciate the picturesque.[38]

A separation from neighbours was a feature of this emerging suburbia, and this gave it a strong contrast with rural living. There was a desire to set one's household apart, and this appealed to individuals such as Mary Delany, the artist who was a member of Jonathan Swift's circle. She savoured the isolation of her detached house on five hectares:

A 1744 view from 'Delville', Glasnevin, the home of Mary Delany, looking south towards the city. Note the windmills, centre right. (NGI)

I am very happy that I have no dangling neighbours. I may be thought too reserved in our village, but I choose to be censured for that, than to expose myself to the interruption and tittle-tattle of a country neighbourhood; my acquaintance is large in Dublin and I never want company. [39]

Romanticism accelerated suburban living and popularised forms of leisure that had hitherto been mainly the preserve of the elite. This was especially true of sea bathing. Jane Austen, in her novel *Sanditon* (1819), claimed marine air and bathing cured disorders of the lungs, the blood and the stomach. [40] Like all fashions and lifestyles, there were negative reactions to the Romantic movement. It was seen as anti-urban, and Charles Morris (*c.* 1797) was not alone when he mused:

A house is much more to my mind than a tree,
And for groves, O! a fine grove of chimneys for me. [41]

Along with the Romantic movement and the Enlightenment came a change in family life. Children came to the fore, and this consideration by parents extended to meeting their needs. A logical extension of this would be the acquisition of a larger home complete with enough garden space for the children's pony.

Patronage

> The two health-giving and rival villages have long contested for superiority; but if we may judge from the number and elegance of the villas, some of which are indeed magnificent edifices, with the prodigious concourse of nobility and gentry resorting there in the summer season for the benefit of bathing, the Black-rock seems to claim the pre-eminence.
>
> *Hibernian Journal*, 30 June 1783

Royal patronage was greatly beneficial to England's coastal resorts. Brighton gave the best example and it was there the Royal Pavilion was constructed. In Ireland, vice-regal favour encouraged Blackrock. As early as the mid-1770s the lord lieutenant was taking holidays at Frescati, the summer house of the Duke of Leinster. He even expressed an interest in buying the place. Blackrock served as the summer residence for the king's deputy during the remaining years of the century, and great benefits flowed from this patronage. By the late 1780s the environs of Blackrock provided summer homes for many of Dublin's top lawyers. These included the lord chancellor, two lords chief justice, a justice of the King's Bench and another of Common Pleas.[42]

The 'Rock, however, became a victim of its own success, and questions were asked about the lewd behaviour of new visitors. Its social cachet began to fade in the early 1790s as modest women complained they were harassed by naked men prancing around them. This behaviour prompted the trendsetters to retreat. The Duke of Leinster resolved to sell Frescati when his family made it clear they no longer wished to use it.[43]

Infrastructural expansion

> [Dublin] being as closely or perhaps closer built than any other great city in Europe, there being no squares to convey goods to, or many large streets to receive them.
>
> *Faulkner's Dublin Journal*, 5 November 1748

Demands for better infrastructure followed the urban growth of the 1760s. There were calls for radial routes marked out with milestones, and some property

A prospect of the bay, including Irishtown and Ringsend, with Clontarf in the background, c. 1780. Prominent features include the two quay walls constructed to assist shipping. (Anon., engraved by Royce, c. 1780)

developers speeded up access to the coastline. Clontarf and Blackrock kept competing for customers, and throughout the 1780s their two roads were substantially improved. By 1786 Clontarf had gained a lot from the efforts of a developer named Weekes. His attractions for bathers included shelters and a water supply. Blackrock was not to be outdone, and two years later it was promoting its own advances; these included the opening of Strand Road, connecting Ringsend along the Sandymount shoreline with the Blackrock road. This new artery made the journey 'perfectly commodious'.[44]

The Dublin Journal listed improvements that the city needed for safety and convenience. These included better street lighting, effective fire escapes, reliable public clocks and the fixing of number plates on all front doors. However, these reforms were slow and piecemeal. There were, nevertheless, some new services that did facilitate suburban growth. In 1773 the Post Office promised that letters within the Circular Road would be delivered the next day. Within a year this service was extended four miles out from the GPO, and by 1819 it went two miles further.[45]

✳ ✳ ✳ ✳ ✳

Tis at the Black Rock, where all parties combine
To tipple the whiskey or generous wine
Through the day, and as night settles dark on the scene,
Mirth ends with shillelagh, and wigs on the green.

Pierce Egan, 1821[46]

The Freeman's Journal advised landlords to cater for the changing market. They should provide those facilities enjoyed by middle-class bathers at English resorts.

Blackrock should have a hotel, fitted with compartments for breakfast parties. It required a spacious coffee house supplied with foreign and domestic newspapers to amuse the customers. Improvements came quickly. Assembly rooms were opened for the 1791 season, and a more comfortable coach service arrived a year later. This bigger coach carried sixteen passengers. Visitors were soon willing to venture out further, and by 1796 another coast road was running southwards from Dunleary through the estates of the earls de Vesci, Longford and Carysfort. This reduced the journey to Dalkey by a mile. As the exclusive edge crept out, Blackrock became more commonplace. In 1819 John Gamble remarked on its appeal to noisy day trippers.[47]

The south side of the capital was twice blest. Along with the seaside there was the lure of the foothills. Better roads and more settled conditions encouraged traffic where fresh air was combined with fine views of the city. Hely Dutton (1802) saw how these foothills were wasted on the sportsmen who went there just to shoot game. He encouraged city gentlemen to set up their villas on this higher ground to avail of the urban panorama below.[48]

There was a strong contrast between the scenic seaside roads and the other outlets. This was not merely a matter of amenity. Arterial connections to rural Ireland had long suffered from being turnpikes (roads on which a toll had to be paid at a toll gate). This was a burden that checked the advance of new resorts. Places like Lucan and Milltown were held back. There were, however, some promoters who defied the odds. Lord Powerscourt developed services on his estate in north County Wicklow. His splendid waterfall drew discerning travellers, and he widened the approach road to make it suitable for coaches. He also provided an inn for his customers. As early as the 1750s he cleared away enough trees to make his landscape features stand out impressively. Powerscourt's success was reflected in the published views of his untamed waterfall, and culminated in the visit to the estate by George IV in 1821.[49]

Resurgent urbanity

> Walk around this capital and behold. See the difference between the old and new houses. Examine the increase.
>
> Anon., 1760[50]

John Rocque's 1756 map coincided with a threshold in development. Suburban expansion was becoming more apparent, and there was a need to address the decline of the established quarters. By the early 1770s St Catherine's parish was brimfull of 'tottering wretched habitations', and the streets off High Street were described as one continuous mass of ruin. This decay spread out from the Liberties. In Smithfield, fourteen people died in 1783 when a garret floor gave way together with each successive floor underneath, right down to the cellar. In the 1790s several houses in the infamous Copper Alley collapsed onto the street.[51]

Hawkin's Street with the Theatre Royal, *c.* 1820. (George Petrie, 1821) (UCD)

It was not just low rents that kept the poor in their place. Poverty brought an insecurity that might only be relieved by the parish officers. This compelled people to acquire rights of entitlement, known as settlement of the parish, in order to gain relief from sickness and want. It was only the men who acquired this status, although a wife could share it and it was inherited by their children. There were specific qualifications, including the serving of an apprenticeship, working as a domestic servant for a year or renting a property for a year. These tests made a person inclined to stay put within the parish.

By the late 1780s the geography of social status was finding more expression in the commercial life of the city. Five of the thirty licensed pawnbrokers were clustered together in Skinners' Row. In contrast to this, the lottery offices had gathered within the central business district; eight of the thirteen that were licensed were in Dame Street. The pace of change could be exaggerated, and there were forces counteracting the outward movement. In 1786 a petition was sent to parliament to control urban sprawl. This was an anonymous pamphlet that argued that existing areas such as Temple Bar should be improved rather than promoting expansion out towards Ringsend, Donnybrook or Ballybough. The writer believed the city could satisfy the demand for new housing once those streets already planned were completed. It is notable that some of the city's most iconic housing and streetscapes date from the same period.[52]

There was advice available for those households considering suburbia. Savings included the escape from city taxes. Peripheral parishes, such as Donnybrook, gained substantial infrastructure without contributing towards the cost; by the 1820s this had become a contentious issue. While the annual cost of a carriage could run to £2, this was recouped by avoiding expensive entertainment. Suburban households were not expected to host costly social gatherings. Another option was to combine the best of both worlds; a city house could serve for the winter season with an escape to suburban lodgings for the summer. It was claimed this arrangement combined great savings with fashionable rewards.[53]

✳ ✳ ✳ ✳ ✳

These early suburban homesteads could convey a sense of isolation. Dublin's coastline still retained a rural aspect throughout the Georgian era. Dr John Rutty, a naturalist, wrote in the 1750s that wild birds such as gannets frequented the southern shore of the bay, and the playwright John O'Keeffe described the great popularity of stag hunting between Dunleary and Bray during the 1770s.[54]

Gent. Mag. Octo.r 1789. Plate III. p.897.

View of the Hill of Howth, Irelands Eye, & Lambay, taken from Killonacud, 1788.

It would appear that early suburban villas had a low profile and were well spread out. These villas were situated both north and south of the city, some of them within reach of healthful sea breezes and with distant views of the bay, but virtually all with some sort of private garden.

Romanticism encouraged the retention of trees. Landscape paintings and prints show pastures bounded by tall hedgerows. On the north side, the prospect from Mary Delany's retreat at Glasnevin (about 5 kilometres from the city centre) was still dominated by greenery in 1744; the exceptions were the windmills on the fringe of the built-up area. On the south side, the remarkable number of thatched cottages listed in the Pembroke estate inventory of 1762 shows how the vernacular architecture still dominated the environs of the city even as new villas were built. They stretched out towards Ringsend, Blackrock

Ringsend and Irishtown form a strong contrast with the surrounding countryside south of the city, c. 1800. A glass factory belching smoke is centre left. (John Henry Campbell, 1809) (NGI)

and Donnybrook. Two decades later a dainty house at Kilmacud, aptly named Wholesome Hill, was sold along with 20 acres set in meadow 'well divided by good quickset ditches … in a fine sporting country'. That kind of landscape was illustrated in a 1788 print of the same area. As late as 1809 this open greenery appeared in the view of Ringsend and Irishtown painted by John Henry Campbell.[55]

Peripheral growth was continuous but unevenly spread. During the 1790s fears of a French invasion checked the growth of English coastal resorts such as Brighton, and had a similar impact on Dublin Bay. A military survey of 1794–95 revealed the vulnerability of the southern shore. Tension within the affluent urban areas was reflected in the precautions taken against any incursion by 'Johnny Foreigner'. St Anne's parish paid to augment the city militia. In 1795 it raised money for an extra ten men, and more contributions followed. The government response included the establishment of an army camp at Loughlinstown, 10 kilometres south of the city. It remained until 1799, and the troop numbers reached 5,300.[56] Movement within the city was restricted during the 1798 rebellion, and the names of house occupants were posted on each front door. When the emergency passed, however, greater numbers of summer lodgers reappeared in Blackrock and Clontarf, with some now going as far as Leixlip and Lucan.[57]

This army camp at Lehaunstown (1796) was a reaction to the fear of a French invasion. (*Walker's Hibernian Magazine,* October 1796) (UCD)

AN Accurate VIEW of the ENCAMPMENT at LEHAUNSTOWN.

One of the defensive Martello towers built around Dublin Bay in response to a threatened French invasion in the 1790s. (From J. Warburton, Revd J. Whitelaw and Revd R. Walsh, *History of the City of Dublin*, 1818)

✳ ✳ ✳ ✳ ✳

Many of the most valuable houses and streets of the city of Dublin, as it stood in the reign of George I, have fallen into decay, and are now inhabited either by the most abject poor, or at least by the humblest traders and the poorest description of mechanics and artisans.

Select Committee on Dublin Taxation, 1822[58]

Scholars are divided over the impact of the Union in 1801. There were diverse factors involved and some of them were not readily apparent. Even before the Union was rushed through, the Wide Streets Commission was in trouble. In 1793 it was instructed not to get involved in any new projects. Its work had been directed towards the east of the city, and the change was keenly felt there. Amongst the flagship projects was the connection from the Castle to the city's northern approach at Dorset Street, and this decree halted the last link between

Rutland Square and Dorset Street. The WSC attributed this hold-up to 'the times'. The largest developer in the north-east was Henry Ottiwell, and he grumbled that improvements were 'at a stand'. The situation got worse, and by 1797 the WSC was seeking relief from the lord lieutenant.[59]

With the reduction of political power, the splendour of the viceroy's court was bound to be diminished after the Union. This, in turn, reduced the demand for goods and services. Some historians doubt that the Union can be blamed for subsequent economic setbacks as the departure of the gentry was gradual and this allowed their places to be filled by the professional classes. Others have pointed to the growth in bureaucracy and the professions, both of them compensating for the depletion of rich landowners.[60]

> In Dublin, thoughtless speculation in the building trade, for some years back, attracted vast multitudes of young artisans, who were tempted by large earnings to raise large families.
>
> British House of Commons report, 1820[61]

There was a post-Union upheaval in Dublin's housing market. Many large houses on the urban fringe were offered for sale, and these properties attracted the attention of city businessmen. John Carr, an English lawyer, noticed how the

One of the newly emerging hotels, 1820s. (From John James McGregor, *New Picture of Dublin*, 1821)

MORRISSON'S HOTEL, DAWSON STREET.

price of middling houses had increased considerably, but he added that this was matched inversely by the fall in the value of the larger ones. William Drennan, a city doctor, described other aspects of this change. He claimed his 'first rate' practice declined sharply for two years after the Union, and he ascribed this to the departure of many great families. Drennan nevertheless found the city was as prosperous as ever – rents and wages had not fallen due to the influx of country folk, and fortunes were still being made by merchants from the ongoing war. However, two years later he was surprised how many great houses had been converted into either hotels or barracks. In 1810 another doctor, John Gamble, asserted that the aristocracy was now formed by the professions, namely law, medicine and the clergy, in that order.[62]

This was also a topic addressed by the aristocratic author Maria Edgeworth. To her eyes, wealth had replaced birth as the measure of social standing. She ridiculed the vulgar ostentation of the newcomers, but also allowed that they might serve a function, albeit a temporary one. Convention made these interim occupants of noble places a necessity because the lord lieutenant and his wife would otherwise have to perform their parts to empty benches.[63]

Civic amenities and the benefits of planning

> When any ruinous, old houses are pulled down, they rebuild them on the same spots, and instead of building them further back, they rather encroach on the public streets.
>
> *Faulkner's Dublin Journal*, 7 August 1756

> Amongst a refined and civilised people, in great and opulent cities, all improvements and alterations should be carried with a view towards something more extensive on a future day.
>
> *The Freeman's Journal*, 17 January 1769

A new urbanity was emerging by the mid-1780s. The Wide Streets Commission brought an interest in streetscapes, and the *Hibernian Journal* claimed Dublin was fast becoming one of Europe's most beautiful capitals because of its 'ornamental progress'. However, it advised the adoption of a system of uniformity because notable improvement opportunities had already been lost: the Lying-in Hospital (Rotunda) should have closed off Sackville Street, and the Royal Exchange should have directly faced Parliament Street. One place where the city could still make amends was at Blackhall Place. This was where a new street ran west from Queen Street, allowing Bluecoat School to terminate the view. That potential was only partly realised, but where better results were achieved they proved to be influential. There was an enduring outcome when Sackville Street was stretched southwards to the Liffey while retaining its remarkable width.[64]

Innovations in the public realm enhanced street frontages. There were more sidewalks, combined with lighter, transparent boundary fencing. This trend began in the 1750s as high masonry walls yielded to shop fronts, brighter windows and iron railings. There was some unease at the loss of security, and this concern was heightened by reports of criminals arriving from London. *The Dublin Journal* advised readers that letterboxes would prevent robberies by predators posing as either messengers or postmen. Theft of boundary railings became a serious issue for the suburbs in the 1780s. St Anne's parish offered a £10 reward for anyone convicted of stealing iron fencing.[65]

The glazing used to brighten up interiors could expose the occupants to nuisance or worse. A gun was fired at Lord Kingsborough as he relaxed in his house at Henrietta Street. The shot lodged in the wainscot directly beside him. His servants ran out immediately, but the attacker escaped unseen. Incidents such as this unnerved others who were exposed to the gaze of passers-by. Significant advances were nevertheless made during the 1780s. In some places these improvements were encouraged by better street lighting. In 1784 Rutland Square was transformed by removing the boundary wall around the Rotunda Gardens. The old wall was replaced by a railing, and this new fashion was followed elsewhere. Substantial changes were discussed for St Stephen's Green, and the improvements to Merrion Square were held out as a model for other areas; the new features included gravel walks, extensive planting and an 'iron balustrade'. It was argued that the university should follow suit, to open up the views of College Park. However, the residents of Kildare Street blocked that plan, and the college wall was not lowered until the 1840s.[66]

Industrial development and residential amenity

A few years ago, there was scarcely a steam engine in Ireland; recently a manufactory for their construction has been established in Dublin.

J.C. Curwen, 1818[67]

Tolls and customs were levied on certain goods entering the city. Toll gates were let out annually by public auction, and the income could therefore reflect the level of commercial activity and where the heaviest goods traffic occurred. There were ten gates, divided into four lots that were situated in the south-west, north-west, north-east and south-east, respectively. Lot 1 comprised James Street, Park Gate and Dolphin's Barn, lot 2 included Stoneybatter and Glassmanoge, lot 3 comprised Drumcondra Lane and Ballybough Bridge, with lot 4 covering St Stephen's Green, Ballsbridge and Kevin's Port. From the 1760s onwards virtually all this traffic arrived on the western approaches, and the high proportion of commercial traffic was reflected in the rents paid for lots 1 and 2. During the first half of the 1760s the south-west brought in sixty-four per cent of the total income and the north-west yielded twenty-seven per cent. Compared to that, the north-east and the south-east only produced seven per cent and two per cent, respectively. During the second half of the 1760s the three busiest lots (1, 2 and 3) yielded over ninety-eight per cent of the tolls.[68]

Dublin's emergence as a significant industrial location was based on the processing of raw materials. These were basic goods that were either processed or assembled for the Irish market. Industries using foreign materials included iron founding, metal finishing, sugar baking, furniture production, glassmaking and silk weaving. By 1750 the capital dominated half of the country's overseas trade, and its most valuable export was linen. This was sourced outside the city, but the added income included the substantial sales of soap to bleachers, and, as with other exports, there were transport and handling jobs. A substantial part of the port's development arose from the coal trade. High canal tolls discouraged the trade in native turf, and Dubliners became reliant on British coal.[69]

By the 1760s the scale of the city's industrial development and its unregulated behaviour were causing great harm. Within the Liberties and down along the quays, factories were emitting large volumes of smoke and dust. Glass factories, brickworks and limekilns were the worst offenders. In the late 1760s calls were made to expel the wrongdoers. As the pollution spread it was contended that wealthy people would leave the city.[70] There was a cluster of glass factories beside the Sackville Mall, and local residents identified the main offenders:

> The inhabitants of Sackville-street present their most respectful compliments to the proprietors of the sugar house in Greg-lane, and acknowledge with gratitude the great advantage their situation has received since the commencement of trade in said house, but more particularly, for the late odoriferous effluvia, which so generously

extended itself to the most distant parts of the neighbourhood ...
They also have another advantage which few others can boast of;
that when the wind is easterly, they can regale their noses with the
cephalic fumes of the glass-houses ... Nor can we omit our thanks to
our neighbouring brick-burners, who take such pains, to oblige us by
burning their bricks within view of our bedchambers.

Faulkner's Dublin Journal, 7 August 1770

Parliament conceded that pollution had killed city dwellers, and brick-making
was prohibited within two miles of the street lamps. Compliance with these
regulations was patchy. Those fortunate enough to live in the suburbs could see
the contribution clean air made to good health. When an academy for boys was
opened to the south at Rathmines in the 1790s it boasted about its benevolent
situation. This village was a retreat for tuberculosis patients because it combined
the fresh air flowing in from the mountains and from the sea.[71]

Dublin had an extensive textile industry. There was a move towards the
factory system during the 1750s as masters began to employ more journeymen
and apprentices within their own premises rather than giving out raw material
for workers to weave within their own homes. It grew rapidly up to the 1770s,
by which time it may have supported half of the population of the city and
surrounding villages. Factories producing printed fabrics of linen and cotton
were set up beside convenient sources of water power, including the riverbanks
at Lucan, Palmerstown, Chapelizod, Islandbridge, Rathfarnham, Milltown,
Ballsbridge, Donnybrook and Drumcondra.[72] Silk weaving became an important
source of employment, and it was concentrated within that part of the Liberties
known as The Coombe.[73]

Mairéad Dunlevy described the progress of one silk manufacturer named
Edward Hamsley, who operated from Church Street during the 1790s. His
employees included throwsters, who prepared yarn, as well as spinners and
weavers, but he also engaged subcontractors, including one at Meath Street and
another at Skinner's Alley. His machinery was made on-site, and his equipment
included weighing scales and copper pans for dyeing. Hamsley sold a varied
stock, but he specialised in the less-expensive silks. He supplied local weavers
with spun silk (warps) wound on bobbins, as well as hanks and assorted weft
threads.[74]

By the 1780s Dublin had accumulated about a hundred breweries, distilleries
and refineries. Paper mills, tanneries, breweries and tuck mills spread along the

This view from the south-west, *c.* 1820, includes two glass factories – the conical structures belching smoke, centre right.
(Anon., *c.* 1820) (NGI)

rivers Liffey, Dodder and Camac. Some of these processes were attracted by the ready market and easy source of raw materials. Dublin had a concentration of paper mills because the rags that formed the main raw material were easily sourced.[75]

Landlords within the Liberties let matters run free as long as the rent rolled in. When the intensity of manufacturing expanded, so did the pall of smoke. By the early Victorian period a cloud of grey was fixed over the Liberties. That is how the area was depicted in the 1854 Dublin panorama published by *The Illustrated London News*.

Diminishing urban space

> Mid trees of stunted growth, unequal roes,
> On the coarse gravel, trip the belles and beaus.
>
> Thomas Newburgh, 1758[76]

> When city belles in Sunday's pomp are seen,
> And gilded chariots troll round Stephen's Green.
>
> Anon., 1771[77]

Sectarian division reached the select promenades of St Stephen's Green. From the outset the park was surrounded by a high wall, and rangers kept out undesirables. Each religious group followed its own path, and when seats arrived in the 1730s everyone knew where to sit. The Protestant elite kept the 'court' bench and the Catholics kept to themselves; they knew they were not welcome on the most fashionable walks.[78] After the Act of Union, religion and recreation were more closely tied together, and this coloured everyday city life:

> Within a few years some of the gayest resorts of fashion and dissipation have been transformed into edifices of devotion and charity: Ranelagh has become a convent, Smock Alley playhouse a parochial chapel, and Ostley's Amphitheatre a house of worship for blind females.[79]

Something akin to a caste system governed the city's parks. Spaces reserved for the elite were carefully tended. At the top of the tree were the Rotunda Gardens, and they even got legal protection: an act of 1775 cited their health-giving benefits

and barred new buildings within the pleasure grounds.[80] Amongst the common people the streets served as venues for leisure activity, but development absorbed open spaces that could provide recreation. Rocque's 1756 map shows a considerable amount of open ground, but telltale mounds indicate they were dunghills. A good example could be seen near Thomas Street, bounded appropriately enough by Dunghill Lane and Dirty Lane.[81] Any open space that remained free of this nuisance was likely to be invaded by new buildings. That is what happened at Oxmantown Green and also at The Little Green. At Oxmantown Green the incursion began as early as the 1740s. The army barracks moved in from the west side, while the Bluecoat School came in from the east. Rocque's 1756 map shows the artillery set up behind the brothels of Barrack Street. In 1767 the army cornered more of the green in order to build extra accommodation. On market days Barrack Street was a very disturbed area. These nuisances drove away developers, and the area remained rundown.[82]

In the mid-1770s the corporation began cleaning up Oxmantown Green. It filled in the craters left by illegal gravel extraction. Anybody taking a lease was allowed the first seven years rent-free. In 1780 the Bluecoat School moved over from Queen Street, and its new building became a central feature of the renewal. The scheme included Blackhall Place, linking Stoneybatter with Barrack Street, while Blackhall Street connected the development eastwards with Queen Street. Despite these efforts, developers remained cautious, and building lots were left unsold until the 1790s.[83]

A similar chain of events could be seen at The Little Green. In 1759 the place was described as a receptacle of filth, and the construction of a market was delayed by large dunghills. The corporation offered incentives to developers, including three years rent-free, but not much happened. A decade later the corporation chose The Little Green for a jail but the new building (Newgate) was not opened until 1780. In the late 1780s part of the green was designated for private development, and the sale of lots began in 1790. However, the prison kept the area very depressed. Soon after the Union one foreign visitor stated the place resembled the environs of many other jails, being distinguished only for its infamy and dirt.[84]

Sectional interests drove the corporation to control the pace of city growth. There was a desire to retain business within the medieval core, and this was reflected in the campaign to halt downriver growth. The corporation opposed the eastward move of the Custom House (1781–91), just as it later fought against the Liffey crossing at Carlisle Bridge (1794–98). It warned that this downriver bridge would cut off shipping from the old quays. However, the corporation undermined its own efforts by, for example, removing public administration from old quarters down to the Liffey quays, and by moving the Main Guard from Werburgh Street in 1789 and transferring the Tholsel from Patrick Street in 1790.[85]

✳ ✳ ✳ ✳ ✳

The rage for building towards the sea has arrived to such a degree of ardour that even the marshy and swampy grounds near the North Wall are reclaiming.

The Freeman's Journal, 26 June 1791

Extensions of the Liffey quays made reclamation easier, and schemes were carried out along both sides of the channel. This work had some influence on property development because the foul smell and flooding discouraged visitors.

The most comprehensive scheme, called the North Lotts (on 100 hectares), was devised in 1717. It included 266 plots, served by a rectilinear road layout. All the best plots faced the quayside, and a second row, comprised of larger plots, lay behind them. The size of the parcels grew as distance increased away from the city centre.[86] There was less scope for reclamation on the south side and there was also less enthusiasm for it. The promontory formed by Ringsend screened the genteel areas further south, and the prevailing south-west wind kept away the offensive smell.

✳ ✳ ✳ ✳ ✳

The south now opens! Clad in various green
Embattled groves, o'er groves embattled rise;
Villas over villas, verdant lawns between,
And lofty mountains reach the distant skies.

Abraham Bosquet, *Howth, a Descriptive Poem*, 1787[87]

Out beyond the city boundary, urban sprawl was taking shape, 'rising palaces, the projectors of which, after running up the shell, advertise for purchasers possessing more cash than prudence, to finish and occupy them'.[88] Their success was reflected in the publicity they received. In the north-east, a bright terrace of twenty-six houses called Marino Crescent appeared near milestone 2 as early as 1792. It occupied a scenic location, facing the bay to the front of Lord

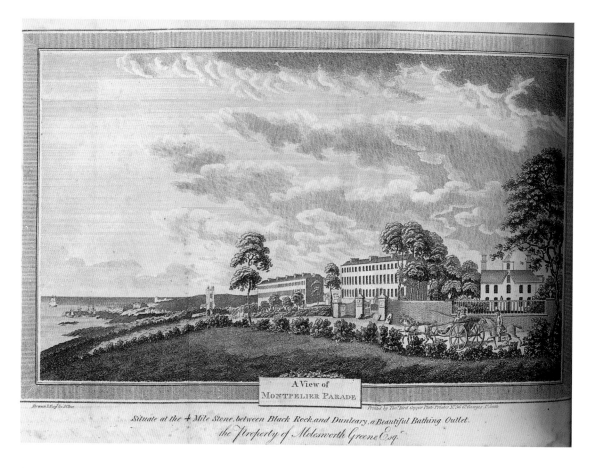

A View of
MONTPELIER PARADE

*Situate at the 4 Mile Stone, between Black Rock and Dunleary, a Beautiful Bathing Outlet.
the Property of Molesworth Greene Esq.*

Charlemont's demesne. On the south side, speculative ventures spread even further out. Terraces of stuccoed houses appeared beside the 4-mile stone in 1797. These twin terraces, named Mount Pelier Parade, rose from the green fields beyond Blackrock.

English visitors noted how the north side of the bay was dotted with a growing number of gentlemen's seats, while the south side formed a rich carpet adorned with villas.[89] There was a spread of smaller villas on reduced holdings and, eventually, semi-detached cottages on even smaller plots. In many instances the latest arrivals were accommodated along the road frontages, leaving the older demesnes concealed behind them. The most telling attribute was a verdant curtilage, as gardens held a special appeal for those people leaving the city behind.

It is ironic that the city's most influential clergyman joined the exodus. By the 1830s Archbishop Richard Whately had found his urban residence too oppressive and he decamped to Kilmacud, 7 kilometres to the south. Whately's new home,

Montpelier Parade, Monkstown was amongst the earliest suburban speculative housing schemes. (*Walker's Hibernian Magazine*, March 1802) (Board of Trinity College, Dublin)

called 'Redesdale', provided the repose he sought. It contained a spacious garden where he loved to consider aspects of his work while

> he was budding, pruning, turning up the earth with his spade, or making some novel experiment on tree or shrub. The easy distance from Dublin enabled him to be at the Palace for transacting business between breakfast and dinner; and he always returned home with a holiday feeling.
>
> E. Jane Whately[90]

There was a great expansion of road transport. People now made their way individually from their household to the workplace. Carriage transport began to open its doors to those lower down the social ladder. It was notable how the cartouche seen in William Duncan's 1821 map of Dublin depicted the affluent new

A housing layout beside the new Kingstown Harbour, early 1820s. (J. Cooke, 1823) (NAI)

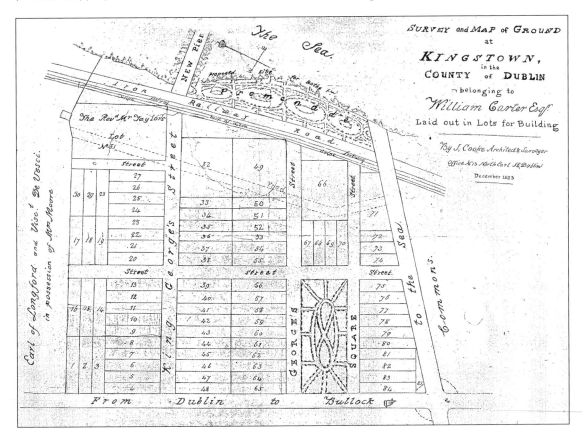

town of Kingstown (Dún Laoghaire); that was now the destination of aspiration.[91] Kingstown benefitted from the difficulties of the city port. A safer approach to the cross-channel shipping terminal was made more pressing by the rising loss of life during bad weather. A severe storm in 1807 claimed 385 lives, and this tragedy led directly to the formation of an asylum harbour at Dunleary, comprising two long, curved piers with a combined length of 2,650 metres. This decentralisation of strategic port activity coincided with the renaming of Dunleary as Kingstown during the visit of George IV in 1821.[92]

If the gathering of manufacturing within the Liberties formed the basis for an industrial zone, those features had come about by default rather than design.[93] The quarter around St Patrick's cathedral was described in 1809 as a cluster of filthy, wretched-looking streets, while the notorious Barrack Street almost defied description. These were places crowded with redundant artisans. Visitors saw the streets lined with 'deranged fabrics tottering to their ruin'.[94] The crime wave that followed the Napoleonic Wars accelerated the exodus from the city. There was a twenty per cent population increase in the suburbs between 1820 and 1840. This change was most apparent in the south-east, where the coastline reaching towards Kingstown grew by forty-four per cent. In strong contrast, the south-west quarter dominated by the Liberties fell further behind, losing almost one fifth of its people.[95]

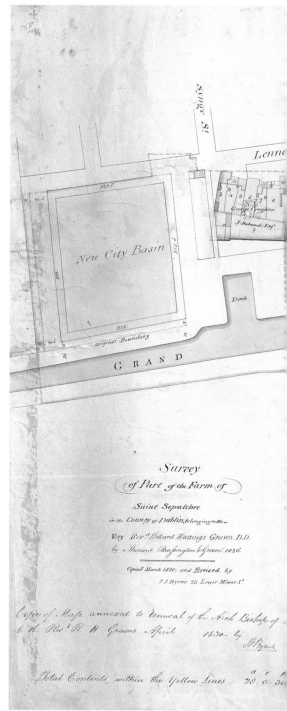

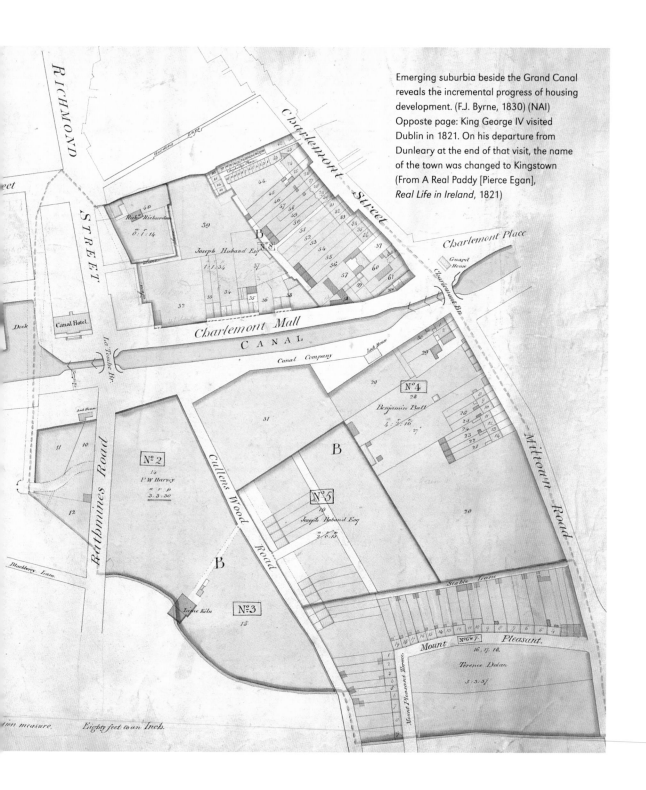

Emerging suburbia beside the Grand Canal reveals the incremental progress of housing development. (F.J. Byrne, 1830) (NAI) Opposte page: King George IV visited Dublin in 1821. On his departure from Dunleary at the end of that visit, the name of the town was changed to Kingstown (From A Real Paddy [Pierce Egan], *Real Life in Ireland*, 1821)

The ascendancy used public occasions to express its political power. (Irish School, 1784) (NGI)

5

Crime and the Failure of
the Legal System

EUROPEAN CITIES WERE SLOW TO react to the crime wave that followed the surge of migration from the countryside. Georgian London had a rotten police force, and only one in ten of that city's crimes resulted in prosecutions. This corruption was epitomised by the infamous Jonathan Wild, who was officially employed as a magistrate but whose large income actually came from trading in stolen goods. Unease spread across the cities of Europe, and it brought great confusion and uncertainty. In Paris the crowd that was busy attempting to lynch a thief might also prevent the arrest of a beggar. Edinburgh saw a crime wave between 1760 and 1790. There was a vast surge in burglaries, church collections fell by a third, whiskey replaced beer, and brothels grew twentyfold.[1] Rome's police force was ineffectual; the ordinary police – the sbirri – were so rotten that the general public often sided with the criminals. In 1778 the Vatican police chief was convicted for stealing his men's wages and giving jobs to his cronies.[2]

In Ireland it was not until the nineteenth century that the state assumed its place in ordinary prosecutions of the criminal law. Prior to that, nearly all cases of theft or violence required the aggrieved individual to take the initiative. This meant he or she had to bring the offence to the notice of the authorities, assemble witnesses and present the evidence in

Three Papist Criminals going to Execution.

court. This procedure might require the individual to engage counsel for the court appearance, but all the trouble and expense were borne by the victim. It is easy to see how people might be put off by a system that made them so unwelcome.

These convicts were restrained with ropes and handcuffs. (Hugh Douglas Hamilton, 1760) (Private collection)

The weakness of the parish watch

> Our parish beadles, heretofore,
> Were beggars, now they're men in pow'r,
> Are made illit'rate constables,
> Who with their mercenary staves
> Protect night-walking sluts and knaves,
> For bribes, and always are as ready,
> T'oppress the honest and the needy.
>
> Anon., 1725[3]

A parish watchman doing his nightly rounds in the 1770s. He carried a halberd and a lantern. His alarm rattler is tied to his waist belt. (Anon., The Dublin Cries) (RSAI)

NINE o'Clock! Nine o'Clock! past Nine o'Clock, and a dark cloudy Night.

Amongst the largest categories within Dublin's workforce were labourers who depended on casual employment. They had no political rights and politicians regarded them as a threat. This may explain why the government introduced greater repression into the law. Anger and despair could, however, be dangerous emotions when combined with cold and hunger. Along with the remarkable rise in the city population, large crowds gathered in the streets and rioting was an obvious expression of their grievances. Violence was a feature of everyday life, and the readiness of bystanders to join the rioting groups suggested a toleration of brute force. Prisons were used as places of detention rather that as penal institutions, so the modern forms of custodial sentences were largely absent. The official deterrents for criminals included the pillory and the scaffold, but there were also floggings and burnings, as well as transportation to some far-off land.

Eighteenth-century Ireland was a dangerous place; the murder rate may have been four times higher than in England. Dublin had its own speciality crimes, and robberies attracted most of the death sentences. Thieves comprised the greatest proportion of the 242 people hanged in the city between 1780 and 1795. These included ninety-four street robbers and seventy-seven burglars, together with twenty-six others who had stolen items such as animals or clothes.[4]

By the early eighteenth century civilian parish peacekeeping had been devolved to paid substitutes, but this force was unable to cope with the surge of urbanisation. The watch was badly managed and the men could just as easily be reprimanded for leaving their shelters to quell a riot as for not leaving their stand at all to assist the victim of a robbery.[5]

Within the poorest districts the watchmen were a seasonal workforce hired to protect residents on winter nights. They were hired for a six-month term stretching from autumn to spring. Two men shared each of the small shelters that were dotted about the street corners. Every man in turn did a two-hour stint patrolling a short, well-defined walking route. They were paid between £2 and £3 for the contract period, but they rarely received that amount because of substantial deductions for absences and breaches of discipline. These watchmen were overseen by constables and deputy constables, above all of which were the directors. As stated in chapter one, the ordinary watchman was easily recognised by his cape, lantern and halberd; the latter was his duty weapon, and its design combined a spear with a battleaxe. Although these men were employed on a temporary basis, it appears that some of them tried to make a career of it. During the 1770s about twenty per cent of those in St Thomas' parish stayed in the service for five years, with a few of them serving as long as eight years.[6]

Because this was a parish-based system, it formed an uneven network, and impoverished localities were unable to cope with rural migration. At the same time the affluent parishes realised that their own security could be at stake if trouble came spreading in across their boundary. By the 1760s there were only four parishes that were able to raise adequate funds (St Andrew's, St Anne's, St Bridget's and St Mary's), and these areas found themselves subsidising their less-well-off neighbours.

Excerpts from the parish records reveal how arbitrary the process was; for example, the log book for St James' parish for the night of 30 October 1765 contains the following entries:

> About the hour of eleven o'clock, Hugh Owens, Sarah Owens and Elizabeth Harrison charged John Christian Rhule for abusing them in their room. But they took bail for him.

> Between the hours of 12 & 1 o'clock Jas Mulhall was struck at his door by one Mce Keegan living in Nicholas Street but sd Mulhall took bail for him & discharged him.

Parliament exposed extensive corruption in the watch system as early as 1729. Constables were involved in extortion and false imprisonment, as well as stirring up riots in order to claim the reward for catching troublemakers. It would appear that a lot of ordinary watchmen were parish dependants. Feeble old men were given this work to prevent them from being a burden on the relief funds of the parish. Many of them were illiterate; during the 1720s and 1730s half the watchmen of St John's parish signed their names with an x. In 1750 only four out of twelve recruits at St Thomas' could sign their names. Many were ex-soldiers and this made it difficult to deal with army crime. Soldiers prevented the detention of their comrades and in many cases forcibly released their mates from jail. In one breakout during 1765 soldiers set free seventy-seven prisoners from Newgate Prison. The corporation could only look on and offer rewards for their capture.[7]

✳ ✳ ✳ ✳ ✳

Confusion and fear came with arbitrary implementation of the so-called Bloody Code. Sanctions were very unevenly applied and a person could be executed for a minor offence. In 1769, for example, a man was hanged for stealing clothes in Parliament Street.[8] The parish watch took part in all sorts of crime, but robbery was most favoured. Even the city executioner was convicted of armed robbery. Yet few watchmen paid for their crimes because they were soon released by their comrades. In 1754 sixteen constables wanted for murder had all absconded. By the late 1770s it was alleged that convicted constables had become prosperous businessmen operating public houses and brothels. Watchmen connived with criminals and refused to testify against them, even when they had seen them commit serious offences.[9] A newspaper account described the haphazard situation:

> Between eleven and twelve at night, as Mr Wallace of Essex Street, peruke-maker, was passing through Pill Lane, he was accosted opposite to the Fishmarket Gate by a lusty fellow, who asked him for charity, when he gave him a penny, upon which the villain immediately collared him, drew out a long knife, and with the most dreadful imprecations demanded his money; but Mr Wallace tripped up his heels, and got the knife from him, when two of the associates coming to his assistance, Wallace pulled out his curling irons, and assured them if they came any nearer he would blow their brains out, which irons the rogues imagined to be a pistol, took to their heels and made off. He then conducted the first villain to St Mary's watch-house, but as the attempt was made in St Michan's parish, he was obliged to take him to the watch-house on the Inns Quay, where he gave him in charge to the constable of the night, and while the wig-maker was writing his name and where he lived, in order to be found to prosecute, the villain was suffered to escape.

> *Faulkner's Dublin Journal*, 5 September 1769

It was easy for wrongdoers to profit. A good example of this occurred in St Thomas' parish during the winter of 1771. Two watchmen were taking a woman to Newgate Prison when they were attacked in Castle Street by a local resident. This man, named John Armstrong, tried to free the prisoner. When he was restrained he charged both of the watchmen who were, in turn, detained by the St Werburgh's watchmen and duly sent off to Newgate. They remained in prison until their own parish arranged bail four days later. They had to stand trial, and the legal bill for St Thomas' parish ran to almost £23.[10]

It was common for the perpetrator to lodge a sworn statement prior to the quarter sessions, anticipating that the victim would pay to have the charge withdrawn. Timid individuals were targeted in the belief that they would buy their way to peace and quiet. This could be appreciated because the perpetrator of the least crime had to abide in jail until the court sessions. In 1790 a Plunkett Street sharper by the name of Bridget Moore took a case against an innocent old woman named Sarah McManus. Moore charged her victim with robbery, but her scheme backfired. On the day of the hearing she was castigated by the recorder and then hooted out of the courtroom. That evening the respectable residents of Plunkett Street lit a bonfire to celebrate the failure of the false prosecution.[11]

Parish beadles were used to control vagrancy and begging. Anybody who was poorly dressed might be taken in, and this zeal was prompted by the reward of a shilling for each beggar they caught. Hatred of the black cart remained a feature of city life, and its appearance led to running battles. Onlookers, including street traders, threw stones at beadles driving beggars through the streets. During one attack at Merrion Square in 1783 the assailants were identified as servants and porters. Most confrontations occurred between the 1770s and the 1790s. In one episode a beadle was killed and several rioters were badly injured. In another episode the guards retaliated by opening fire, killing two men and wounding two more. Brutal behaviour by the beadles forced the authorities to withdraw them from the streets. After one clash they were grounded for a year.[12]

By the early 1780s street crime had become so common that there were suggestions it was quietly tolerated. Soldiers and sailors carried out robberies without any fear of arrest. Their haunts near the barracks and along the quays were out of bounds for the general public. Yet the same troops were relied upon to supplement the watchmen in any emergency.[13] As the city expanded, law enforcement based on community involvement withered, and by the time of the Union voluntary participation by private individuals had all but disappeared.

Street crime

> If one or two street robbers were stoutly opposed, it would contribute much to the safety of the citizens this next winter.

Hibernian Journal, 8 September 1780

By the 1730s the prevailing morality was muddled. A crowd was just as likely to agitate against prostitution as it was to prevent the arrest of a bawd. A decade later the city had a higher rate of rioting than London. Much of this was attributed to distressed migrants from rural Ireland.[14] Their need for support set them at odds with the law. Affluent children and their mothers were targeted, with some thefts leading on to murder in order to hide the identity of the perpetrator. Well-dressed people walking the streets risked having their clothes robbed. A stolen shirt could feed a family. Women from the Liberties stole garments and sold them in the Plunkett Street Market. Those robbers unlucky enough to get caught were roughly treated. The crowd pelted them with stones or dumped them in the Liffey. Those arrested by the police might be hanged or severely whipped.[15]

Pickpockets used several ploys. They were drawn to street gatherings along the quays, and other black spots included Capel Street, Dame Street, Essex Street and Parliament Street. At street corners they mingled in audiences listening to ballad singers, and their tactics were similar at the Smock Alley Playhouse. Sometimes they started fights in order to gather a crowd, but more often they acted one-to-one. Farmers were popular targets. Pickpockets in the Liberties taunted their victims by pretending to run away; they then returned to throw stones and broken bottles at their victims, and this mayhem made it easier to prise their booty.[16]

Pickpockets followed prostitutes and robbed distracted customers. Some 'dippers' were actually prostitutes themselves. On Saturdays they attended the public executions, which attracted large crowds. They were particularly active amongst church congregations, and St Patrick's cathedral was a popular haunt. In 1757 two worshippers were trampled to death in St Mary's church. This happened after pickpockets had raised a false alarm that the galleries were collapsing. During the 1770s Parliament Street and Dame Street were overrun by pickpockets and the local residents were kept awake by the screams of victims. Many operators were elegantly dressed. It was claimed they were clerks, apprentice boys, journeymen barbers and hairdressers.[17] During the summer months they turned their attention to race meetings and fairs. English pickpockets on the run from London were frequently active in the city. Older women who had retired from prostitution organised young boys to pick pockets. In 1783 one of these groups was very busy in the area between High Street and the Castle. Any lads who got caught were sent off to the Marine School for service in the navy.[18]

Nocturnal predators known as footpads pounced on people that passed their way. On moonlit nights they lurked in overcast alleys and their strategy was straightforward: an initial blow served to distract the victim, putting him off guard and making it easy to grab valuables. Sometimes, however, another ploy might be used:

> A cord was provided with a loop at the end of it. The loop was laid on the pavement, and the thieves watched the approach of a passenger. If he put his foot in the loop, it was immediately chucked. The man fell prostrate, and was dragged rapidly up the entry to some cellar or waste yard where he was robbed, and sometimes murdered. The stun received by the fall usually prevented the victim from ever recognizing the robbers.[19]

By the early 1780s street crime had become so serious that gentlemen venturing out after dark were advised to go well armed. Housekeepers were encouraged to keep a blunderbuss handy. One newspaper reported that Temple Bar's most notorious offender, known as Blind Peter, had been breaking the law with impunity for two decades.[20]

On winter nights the neglect of public lighting brought total darkness to the streets by 4 p.m. Residents within the Temple Bar area responded by forming groups called prosecution associations. These neighbourhood organisations rounded up undesirables from brothels and gambling dens, and consigned them to the House of Industry.[21] Another initiative came from St Anne's parish in 1777 when gentlemen were invited to assist in suppressing robberies and burglaries. Nineteen volunteers turned up for the inaugural meeting and set out to patrol the streets. They brought bodyguards to secure their own safety, and at the same time offered rewards for the arrest of offenders: £20 for a first-time arrest, £10 for the second and £5 for the third.[22]

These protection associations were following a precedent set in London a few decades earlier. In that city they were parochial, middle-class bodies that arose from anger and frustration. These associations were usually short-lived. The Dublin version was a hit-and-miss venture, mainly because it relied too much on voluntary service. In St Anne's parish the protection association soon lost its impetus, and by 1784 the lord mayor was requesting the gentlemen to stir themselves again, this time to suppress riots. Wealthy residents looked to these associations for security, and there was particular concern over the safety of the gentry arriving for winter parliamentary sessions.[23] The Attorney General acknowledged there were periods when anarchy prevailed:

> Was any man safe in his bed? Was any man safe in his house? Were not gangs of ruffians going about, ready to carry to the tenter-fields, and subject to the American patriotic discipline of tar and feathers, any man who had the misfortune to fall under their displeasure.[24]

❋ ❋ ❋ ❋ ❋

From the 1780s onwards there was a growing emphasis on public-sector law enforcement. In 1786 a citywide police force was installed, and its work included

Robert Emmet's execution in Thomas Street in 1803 following his involvement in the unsuccessful insurrection. (F.W. Byrne, 1877) (Private collection)

traffic regulation and the licensing of trade. It had powers of social control, rounding up beggars, prostitutes, errant servants and apprentices. It also arrested people engaged in drunken carousing and illegal gambling. This repression created antagonism because it was a Protestant force and usually dealt with Catholics. However, reaction to these policemen was part of the wider resistance to the centralisation of authority. The police were likened to the hated French gendarmerie – men who were salaried, well armed and wearing a military-style uniform that was the hallmark of oppression.

More urban agencies were taken under the control of parliament. The Paving Board and the Ballast Office were singled out as offensive examples of government interference in local affairs. Opposition hardened when little improvement could be seen to public security. Newspapers complained that the police force remained unchanged. There were some early signs of reform, but the respectable men soon deserted. Speaking in the House of Lords in 1788 Lord Mountgarret compared the new men to a regular military force. He saw something sinister in their looks as they swaggered about the environs of parliament. It is not surprising that the protection associations remained busy and that new ones were formed.[25]

The official response to these charges was to treble the number of police. While the enlarged force had some early success, recruits were still deserting. Bounties of £20 encouraged many of them to join the army. Nathaniel Warren, the police commissioner, explained how thirty men absconded in a single night. They had sneaked off, taking with them all their uniforms and equipment.[26]

Public anxiety remained, and even those areas with established defence associations were regarded as hazardous. Henry Grattan, the statesman who gave his name to the parliament of the 1780s, described some of the abuses he saw: payments were extorted from innocent detainees and lost children were locked up with prostitutes. A Commons inquiry in 1791 found senior police officers guilty of the greatest abuses, and four years later the corporation condemned the police for being absolutely useless. Francis Higgins, a government spy, informed Dublin Castle in 1796 that the managers were preoccupied with bureaucracy and rarely did their duty. According to the writer John Ferrar, who visited the city in the same year, what began as an armed force had become a band of decrepit invalids.[27] When a change eventually came it was merely a better paid version of the doddering watch. Within months the old complaints were repeated and bad management was blamed. It was easy to see why few of the men had overcoats, and even on the coldest nights their watch-houses had no fires. It emerged in 1797

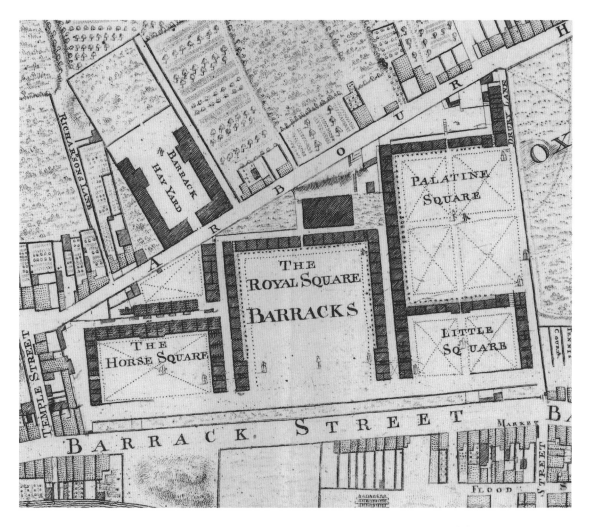

Royal barracks, 1750s. This view includes the notorious Barrack Street. (John Rocque's map of Dublin, 1756)

that the patrolmen had not been paid for almost two years. The men's reaction to this abuse was an extended strike.[28]

Prosecution associations were still being formed, and those already in existence intensified their patrols. Martial law was introduced during the 1798 rebellion. There was a curfew and the cavalry patrolled the streets. As the century closed the lord mayor arranged a public review of the entire watch at St Stephen's Green. One parish corps of thirty men shared fifteen ragged coats between them, and they also had to share fifteen weapons. The watchmen argued that they were owed £3,763 in wages, and the constables claimed they were owed a great deal more.[29]

The impact of the armed forces

> The outrage and misconduct of the soldiery has been long a subject of melancholy complaint.
>
> *Hibernian Journal*, 8 January 1781

Dublin had a large garrison and the Royal Barracks dominated the northern bank of the Liffey. This stronghold was designed to hold five thousand men. It was built in 1706 and was extended soon afterwards.

During the Georgian era the British army was marked by a mercenary culture. Each regiment had great independence, with the colonel essentially acting as a proprietor. In the same way the captain was the proprietor of his company, and this system survived up to the 1870s. Friction between these fiefdoms was a feature of army life. Regiments fought each other, and when this became tiresome they sought opponents outside the parade ground. Faction fights with the butchers of the Ormond Market led to many deaths. Bands of soldiers carried out gang rapes: fourteen men of the Newgate guard were indicted in 1772 for the rape of a servant girl. In 1779 a woman was dragged into the barracks' guardroom and raped by several soldiers; they then placed gunpowder on her breasts and set it alight.[30]

Residents around the barracks loudly complained of the damage caused by training exercises. There was a real peril alongside the Ringsend artillery firing range as cannon balls occasionally landed beside the houses. Throughout the 1760s and 1770s the corporation called for the army to be entirely removed from the city. These appeals were ignored by the government, but when new barracks were added later, they were located out on the periphery, with the Richmond infantry barracks at Kilmainham and the cavalry barracks at Portobello.

Harsh discipline brutalised the men, the accommodation was rough and the pay was low. There was a perceived bloodlust amongst the common soldiery, and those people bold enough to protect their victims were cruelly abused. It was accepted that the army had a coercive discipline: 'the fear of sure and immediate punishment dreadfully inflicted are prevailing incitements to truth and honour.' In 1784 a soldier died after receiving three hundred lashes, and in the same year another soldier barely survived five hundred lashes. The soldiers found the service hard to bear, and deserters added to the street violence. Runaways banded together in order to avoid apprehension, and this strength of numbers turned them into bolder criminals. In the winter of 1789 nine deserters formed a gang that plagued the North Circular Road.[31]

Soldiers of all ranks engaged in crime during the 1770s. The *Hibernian Journal* blamed them for most of the city robberies. It was claimed there were three or four army thefts each night, with up to eight soldiers involved in each incident. Army curfews were announced, but they were brief and ineffective. In 1783 the viceroy set up a tribunal to try those soldiers accused of numerous attacks on women in the Parliament Street area, but fear of retaliation discouraged witnesses from coming forward.

Great numbers of army dependants appeared on the streets when family breadwinners were away on active service. They cornered passers-by and pressed them for money. Carriages were besieged by mothers trying to feed their children. In 1771 *The Freeman's Journal* sought contributions for families left destitute by the absence of soldiers quelling disturbances in the north of Ireland. This appeal cited seventy-one soldiers' wives, many of them with large families. During the Napoleonic Wars, over half the families supported by the society for distressed room-keepers were in this category. Some army officers also assisted those left behind. In 1795 Colonel Doyle of the 87th Regiment gave three hundred guineas to female dependants of his troops, who were serving in the Netherlands.[32]

The temptation for soldiers to turn to crime was heightened when large numbers were made redundant. After major campaigns, men were discarded with little welfare provision. This is what happened in 1714, 1748, 1763, 1783 and again in 1815. During the winter of 1783–84 there was a clamour over the demobilisation following the American Revolution. Great numbers of soldiers were left idle, and they soon turned to crime because there was no work available. During Christmas 1790 about four hundred sailors were made redundant with £1 severance pay. Many of these men turned to highway robbery, and travellers on the Blackrock road were warned not to venture out at night unless they were well armed.[33] At the end of the Napoleonic Wars large contingents of men were cast off. Between 1815 and 1820 the prison population rose by 110 per cent.[34]

Military recruiting and the press gangs

> Dreadful apprehensions are entertained of the violence, robberies, and murders, which the disbanding of the army must produce the ensuing winter.
>
> *Hibernian Journal*, 8 October 1783

It was Samuel Johnson who pointed out that being in the navy was like being in jail except that it brought the added hazard of being drowned. British navy ships rarely had more than fifteen per cent volunteer crew members. Press gangs had a legal authority to compel men to enlist, and in his celebrated commentaries on English law, William Blackstone explained that this tradition was part of

A request for recruitment of a twelve-year-old boy by the navy, 1822. This petition was made by the secretary of the Kingstown Harbour Commissioners, the boy's father. (NAI)

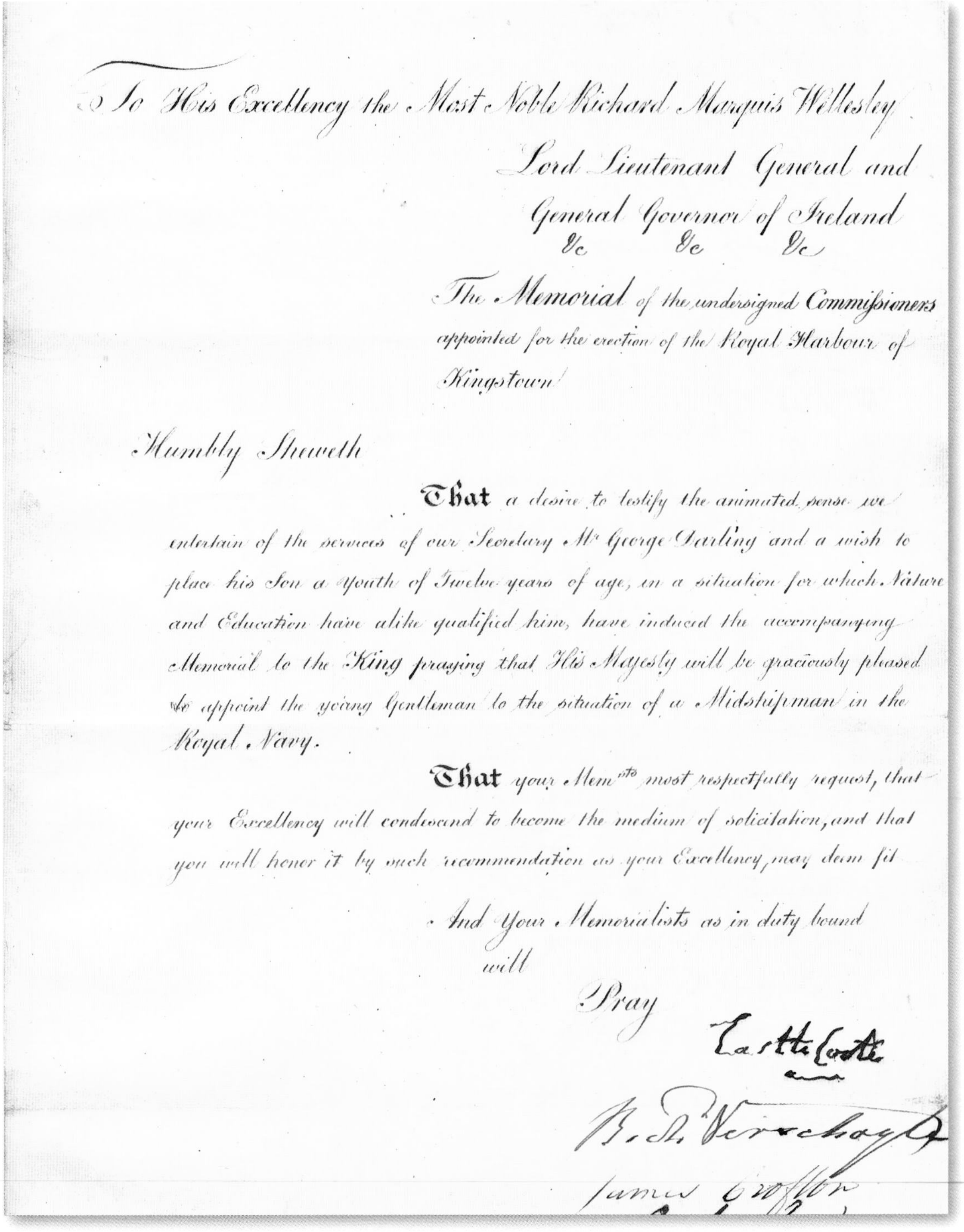

To His Excellency the Most Noble Richard Marquis Wellesley,

Lord Lieutenant General and

General Governor of Ireland

&c &c &c

The Memorial of the undersigned Commissioners appointed for the erection of the Royal Harbour of Kingstown

Humbly Sheweth

That a desire to testify the animated sense we entertain of the services of our Secretary Mr George Darling and a wish to place his Son a Youth of Twelve years of age, in a situation for which Nature and Education have alike qualified him, have induced the accompanying Memorial to the King praying that His Majesty will be graciously pleased to appoint the young Gentleman to the situation of a Midshipman in the Royal Navy.

That your Mem[to] most respectfully request, that your Excellency will condescend to become the medium of solicitation, and that you will honor it by such recommendation as your Excellency may deem fit

And Your Memorialists as in duty bound will

Pray

Castle Coote

B. S. Verschoyle

James Crofton

the common law. Press gangs were a threat to the working population, and they concentrated on the Liffey quays, where the crews of coal boats and trawlers were the main victims. Entire crews could be seen jumping overboard to escape from their grasp. Farm labourers on seasonal migration to England were captured. In one account from around 1780 a pitched battle was fought at George's Quay when a group of about forty haymakers repulsed the press gang. They used their pitchforks and reaping hooks, together with bricks and stones taken from the ship's ballast. Press gangs within the Temple Bar area rounded up customers from taverns and brothels. Porters and messengers feared to venture near the quays. Wealthy people complained that recruiting parties took away their domestic servants. Antagonism towards the press gangs intensified during the 1770s. Women formed defence groups, pelting recruiters with stones and driving them into the river. Members of the raiding parties were killed.[35]

Some of this recruiting work was organised by high-ranking volunteers. In 1782 Thomas Connolly of Castletown House rounded up men on the city streets and dispatched them to navy vessels. Each man was given six guineas and an outfit of clothes. These efforts had considerable success, and about two hundred men were rounded up on the best nights. As we have seen, the bounties offered to military recruits enticed policemen to switch jobs. The number pressed in any single night varied considerably: the crews of twenty coal boats in April 1756, thirty men in December 1770, 258 men (mainly from colliers) in March 1778, forty-five sailors in April 1779, two hundred sailors in July 1790, and about two hundred fishermen from trawlers in April 1791. This pattern of violent recruiting was also seen in Cork; press-gang activity in the 1770s caused such widespread disturbances that city workshops were closed for the duration of each 'hot press'.[36]

Hired thugs called crimpers were also used by the press gangs, and their tactics caused even more unrest. Their quayside hangouts were ransacked. Five crimpers were drowned in one battle with passing fishermen. This problem escalated further when criminals posed as press gangs. The object of these thugs was ransom, and they only released their captives when they received large sums of money.[37]

Recruiting within the port had wider repercussions. It affected the price of coal, and severe shortages sometimes put heating beyond the reach of the poor. Legislation passed in 1761 and 1763 provided for public coal yards that sold the fuel at moderate prices. This initiative offered a respite, but forestallers intervened and raised the price again. A very heavy 'press' during March 1778 almost doubled the price of coal. That was a turbulent episode, with 258 men press ganged in a single night.[38]

Infanticide

> Some bastard by a barb'rous mother kill'd
> To hide the sinful shame of being defil'd.
>
> John Winstanley, 1742[39]

It was accepted by parliament that many infants born outside of marriage were killed. As early as 1707 a law was passed to curb infanticide and punish it with the death penalty (6 Anne, c.4 [Ire.]). This stricture hardly proved effective, but it did lead to more children being put on the parish.

Newspaper reports leave us in little doubt about the circumstances. When a newborn infant was found in St Patrick's churchyard in 1774, its head injuries indicated infanticide. According to *The Freeman's Journal*, this supposition was reasonable because frequent incidents had already occurred there. Newspapers carried reports of newborn infants found drowned in the Liffey. Brian Henry has claimed that there were thirty-four infanticides in the city between 1780 and 1795, but, like many crimes, there were probably a lot more that went unreported.

When the Foundling Hospital halted admissions in 1830, alarm spread because babies were dumped throughout the city. A growing number of infants were drowned in the Grand Canal. A lot of these unfortunates did not even reach the water, and were left to perish on the canal bank. It was the poorest districts that suffered the most, and the churchwardens of these put-upon parishes expressed their alarm to the lord lieutenant.[40]

Kidnappers

> A poor creature, in the greatest distress, whose wretched family may be starving for want of food, is oftentimes hanged for stealing a sheep or lamb. And, shall a villain escape who stealeth a child?
>
> *Faulkner's Dublin Journal*, 11 June 1751

Kidnapping, in its original sense of stealing children to work on American plantations, was actively practised in Dublin. There were several episodes in the decades after 1750, and it continued beyond 1800. Victims were as young as four and as old as nineteen. Old women lured the children with gingerbread, gagging them and covering them with their cloak. Teenagers were abducted by people wearing disguises, and were forced to sign agreements with the captains of ships bound for Philadelphia. These indentures allowed the captains to sell them as servants in America.[41]

At least sixty-five children were taken during one severe episode in 1781. On one ship they were found packed into barrels. One kidnapper confessed that she had taken thirty-two children during the previous fortnight. They were all later rescued from houses along the quays. She divulged their whereabouts after the crowd had cut off her ears and hauled her naked through the streets. When another woman was caught stealing two children beside Dame Street, she revealed the location of another eighteen hidden in a Barrack Street cellar. These women were part of a wider network. A woman arrested at George's Quay explained how a ship's captain paid her £30 for eight children. Merchants and state officials were involved, and the police allowed kidnappers to use official places of detention.

Severe punishment was inflicted on these abductors. In 1767 a woman stealing three children in Francis Street was killed, and a year later another offender was pelted with stones after two children were found in a vessel at Sir John Rogerson's Quay. Following the severe episode of 1781 some innocent women were terribly abused. The ears were cut off one woman in Mary's Lane, while another was left for dead in Winetavern Street. Others were thrown into the Liffey. There was another severe episode in 1794. *The Freeman's Journal* warned that mob law was rampant and that it was only necessary to point a finger at someone as a kidnapper before the crowd was bent on killing that person. Four kidnappers were savagely attacked in Winetavern Street and Merchants' Quay. When one of them sought refuge in a grocer's shop, the owner was threatened with destruction of his premises, and he handed over the woman to the police. A week later a man stealing a child in Exchequer Street was severely injured by the crowd, and the police had to rescue him.[42]

Private initiatives

> How many wretches must fall, to secure the safety and quiet of the endangered public?
>
> *Hibernian Journal*, 9 February 1784

The number of crimes attracting the death penalty grew rapidly during the eighteenth century.[43] This followed the London pattern, where there was a fivefold rise in hangings during the second half of the eighteenth century. Dublin's scaffold was situated on the south-east just beyond St Stephen's Green. Executions took place on Saturdays, and those put to death were as young as fourteen. There were 242 hangings during the period 1780–95. London had over a hundred nicknames for the gallows, and many of them sounded familiar to Dubliners.[44]

As discussed in chapter nine, there were growing doubts by the 1770s that public executions were a real deterrent for criminals: 'even human dissolution loses the effect of being no more.'[45] The public gallows near St Stephen's Green was replaced by Newgate in 1783. It is notable that Dublin closely followed the London pattern – in the same year the Tyburn scaffold was moved indoors.

✳✳✳✳✳

From poverty a man's dress, from accident his behaviour, or from nature his look may offend the delicacy, caprice, or sagacity of gentlemen condescending for the public safety to act as constables, beadles, watchmen, etc.

Faulkner's Dublin Journal, 31 October 1769

As we have seen, the initiatives of citizens' protection associations emerged around 1760, and residents paid for the arrest of transgressors. Parishes such as St Werburgh's made some progress in catching criminals, but this success proved illusory.[46] By the early 1770s these associations had reached the suburbs. Patrols were intensified during 'chalking' outbreaks when soldiers had to be kept off the streets. In 1773 the Leeson Street gentlemen followed the example set on the Milltown road and at Kevin's Port. They patrolled between 9 and 11 p.m. each night, and had some success. Robbers were rounded up on the Donnybrook road, and the following year the residents of Summerhill and the North Strand raided houses frequented by robbers. The St Stephen's Green association adopted the same approach, conducting patrols by night and prosecuting shoplifters by day. Later in the 1770s, the Clontarf association erected alarm bells on rooftops and posted rewards for raparees. A similar scheme was employed by the Ranelagh association.[47]

At times the zeal of the associations spurred the parish watch to try harder. In 1776 St Paul's watch began patrolling five hours each night. This brought arrests but ended badly. A brothel keeper near the army barracks took legal action,

Elite Dublin Volunteers parading at King William III's monument in College Green, 1779. It was a show of strength and a commemoration of the royal birthday. (Francis Wheatley, 1779) (NGI)

turning the tables on his tormentors by suing them for false imprisonment. It was the parish directors who were sent for trial. The *Hibernian Journal* expressed its despair of the legal system:

> If gentlemen of character and reputation are to be open to every litigious prosecution which may be commenced against them for doing their duty, the streets of this city will soon be infested with swarms of rogues, robbers, thieves, etc.[48]

The Volunteer movement was prompted by fears of a French invasion during the American Revolutionary War. It reached Dublin in 1778 and continued until the mid-1780s. For about a decade it was an important body that combined military, political and social roles. Its members performed military revues of the kind depicted in Wheatley's College Green tableau. In addition, they formed press gangs and took control of several protection associations. They raided night houses in the parishes of St Thomas', St Michael's, St Mary's and St Paul's. The St Mary's group had 237 members, armed with carbines and bayonets. These initiatives brought results, such as the arrest of over a hundred criminals in December 1780.[49] Offenders reacted by moving to the countryside. Perhaps they included the thieves who raided Lord Charlemont's fine Marino retreat four times between 1774 and 1789; these episodes included being robbed at gunpoint in his garden and having a ton of his roofing lead stolen.[50]

The fervour of the volunteers faded away. Their patrols began later each evening until they were eventually reduced to just one night each week. Criminals resumed their old ways, and over the following years the Essex Street and Fishamble Street associations renewed their raids on brothels and gambling dens. The most influential associations were formed in the early 1780s. One of the best was the St Mary's association, and amongst its targets were people stealing boundary railings. During 1783 the patrols went into decline, but were replaced by a band of ex-soldiers. This patrol did not last long because the troops extorted money from the residents they were supposed to protect. By late 1784 the local people complained that they were living under martial law.[51]

The strongest organisation on the south side was the Blackrock association. It was founded in 1782 and had an average membership of around fifty. It covered an extensive area stretching southwards along the bay from Merrion to Dalkey and inland around the foothills to Cabinteely, Stillorgan and Kilmacud. It was an elite body, including peers and knights, which expressed a disdain for 'various vagrant people come within the limits of this Association on pretence of bathing etc.'. It maintained a private jail at Blackrock, and the rewards it offered succeeded in bringing in highway robbers. In 1787 it sought permission from the government to carry out executions, and it remained active up to the end of the century.[52]

The fruit market at the Coal Quay,
on the south bank of the Liffey, c. 1805.
(From a print published by R. Ackerman)
(Courtesy of Andrew Bonar Law)

6

Public Health

Coughs and consumptions, pleurisies and agues in spring, the cholera in summer, the dysentery in summer and autumn, the diarrhoea in autumn; to which add the returns of cutaneous and of scrophulous disorders in spring and summer, and the regular gout in January or February.

Dr John Rutty, 1770[1]

GEORGIAN DUBLIN DID NOT UNDERSTAND the germs that spread fevers through the population. A bath even every few months was considered an excessive indulgence, and this mentality could explain why the flamboyant beaux were considered eccentric because they insisted on washing themselves daily. This muddled attitude to hygiene might also reveal why sea bathing was regarded as such a novel idea. Rutty (quoted above) was not alone in associating some illnesses with particular times of the year. Over a half century later Dr William Stoker related influenza to spring, pestilential diseases to midsummer, and dysentery and cholera to autumn, with typhus fever and malignant cholera occurring during both summer and autumn.[2]

Doctors kept floundering in this environment of ignorance, and were willing to attempt cures by eccentric means that had no basis in science. Many illnesses were simply attributed to the local climate that caused the soil to discharge some peculiar destructive

A surgical operation in a city house, 1817. It was a primitive procedure, relying on daylight shining through the drawing-room window. This patient died shortly afterwards. (Meath Foundation)

agent; the remedy lay in taming this uncultivated land. Dry, gravelly ground, for example, was blamed for tuberculosis. Altitude was reckoned to be a factor in bringing on skin disorders, and could also cause cancer and rheumatism. Those people stricken by tuberculosis considered it a hereditary condition, and this explanation was promoted by the medical profession.

Blood was at the heart of the health conundrum; it was essential to keep it in good order if the body was to function properly. Personal neglect allowed the blood to get too thick, to slow down or to clot. Everyone should start the day by swallowing several pints of water to ensure the blood was thin enough to circulate with ease.[3]

Urban ailments

It was realised that lifestyle and longevity were closely related, but this connection was explained in terms of private morality. In one version, each person's lifespan was limited to a predetermined number of heartbeats, and temperance was therefore essential in securing a slower pulse. During the 1780s the *Hibernian Journal* announced that the main cause of illness was obstructed perspiration, and the best remedy for this was a warm bath. It then went on to advise its readers that a cold bath was also a great tonic because it could brace the system when a person suffered from a weak constitution. Strange medical techniques accordingly came and went as either utility or popularity warranted. Publishers made money by promoting all these fads. By the time of the Regency there was a strong reliance on bloodletting to cure dreaded fevers. A city doctor named John Brennan summed up these treatments in the pamphlet he published in 1813:

> Bleeding is now the rage, purging was lately the go, sweating yielded its place to both. Vomits are expected to be the next favourite panacea.[4]

Places within Dublin's casualty hospitals were at a premium. These were infirmaries where the main function related to accidents and emergencies. The nature of cases might be suggested by some admissions at Jervis Street during the late 1780s, where the name, occupation and illness were given:

- John Roe (a labourer), seriously injured in a fall at a house in Henrietta Street;
- Thomas Sullivan (a tailor), received serious head injuries from falling bricks at a building in Dame Street;
- Thomas Conroy (a boy), desperately burnt by a fall into a limekiln at Raheny;
- John Kilchinan (a sawyer), had his skull fractured by a falling brick in North Great George's Street;
- Margaret Holiday (a poor woman), broke her leg from falling down a stairs at Newmarket in The Coombe;
- William Brown (a painter), got severe head injuries after falling off a ladder at Capel Street.[5]

Various quack remedies were used on women suffering from puerperal fever. There were regular outbreaks at the Rotunda Hospital during the early nineteenth century. The treatment made affected women sweat profusely in the belief that this would drive away the fever. Plenty of hot packs called fomentations were applied, and these were combined with large numbers of leeches – a treatment that could render the patient unconscious and quite unprepared for the challenge of childbirth.[6]

There was, in the middle of this muddle, some inkling of immunology, and this was coming forward in regard to the most disabling diseases. A city consultant named William Turton saw how a sheltered lifestyle could leave a person less able to fight infections. He cited the daughters of respectable squires and clergymen: their clean habits, neat dress and retiring orthodoxy left them prone to tuberculosis. Quite simply, they needed more exposure to everyday life. In professing these ideas, Dr Turton was echoing the thoughts of colleagues such as Dr Henry Kennedy and Dr Martin Twomy, who argued that there was a lower mortality from typhus fever amongst the poor. While these observers could not explain why this happened, they did express a belief that there was an elevated and unacceptable death rate from fevers amongst the middle and upper classes.[7]

> The western part of this city, consisting of narrow lanes and alleys [is] full of neglected, and ruined habitations which have been, for the most part, converted into cow-houses, pigstyes and dung yards, where fordes of every kind, the source of infection, accumulates …
>
> Samuel Rosborough, 1801[8]

Mounds of muck filled up backyards and alleyways. Congested districts had no sewerage system and their water supply was rotten. A severe epidemic in 1791 was blamed for thirty deaths a day.[9]

Dubliners were not alone in misunderstanding this contagion. People believed that it arose from dead-animal matter that formed an invisible malignant cloud called the miasma. A sudden change in the weather, such as increased humidity, made people very apprehensive. Each summer revived concerns because it was believed that warm weather gave people cancer. Any cooling off was hardly reassuring either because the advent of rain after a long dry spell brought on 'anguish fever'. Public entertainments spread epidemics; several fatalities followed the 1742 visit of David Garrick, the celebrated English actor. These deaths were attributed to 'Garrick Fever', and it is likely that such incidents hastened the move towards private theatricals. Affluent residents were inclined to remain indoors in order to avoid the evening damp and the night dew, both of which might 'corrupt

A Blind Beggar remarkable for a large Wen on his No.

the blood and prepare the body to receive every infection that offers'.[10] At that time the term 'fever' actually embraced two deadly conditions: typhus fever and relapsing fever. The former was the most prevalent disease in Dublin. Relapsing fever was, as the name suggests, characterised by recurrent fever. These illnesses were transmitted by the lice that thrived in dirty living spaces, and the dysentery that followed these diseases was spread by flies, either through direct contact or from polluted water supplies.

For poor people arriving from the countryside, vagrancy followed the progress from rural poverty towards urban beggary. There were two categories of supplicants: the local vagrants, who were entitled to parish permits, and the unwholesome beggars who were mere blow-ins and therefore should be run out of town. Affluent areas shunned new migrants for fear of catching infectious diseases. Epidemics were made worse by the quacks selling dubious remedies to keep illness at bay. An example of this was the 'pestilential preservative', a concoction of herbs and vinegar that had to be inhaled near any infection.[11]

Poverty and disease

> And whereas great quantities of ashes, dirt, rubbish, dung, and other
> filth are frequently laid in the waste ground on the back of Capel

Street, known by the name of the Little Green, and on the waste ground at the end of Aungier Street, known by the name of the Dunghills, next adjoining St Peter's Church and in divers other parts of the said city and Liberties …

6 Geo. I, c.15 [Ire.], cl.3 (1719)

Reformers allowed that the health of the poor was the security of the rich, and motives of self-preservation reinforced their benevolence. Insofar as the government had any health policy, it coincided with its agenda of social control. There was a desire to confine the poorest people to identified quarters so as to contain epidemics. This complemented the security motive to suppress threats to law and order. It was supposed that fever hospitals within the poorest districts would save lives and contain illness. When rich benefactors acquired a house in Basin Lane in 1745 to accommodate smallpox patients, they were supported by generous citizens. The contributors were specifically asked not to give alms in the streets because this accelerated the spread of a great nuisance.[12]

A high price was paid for poverty. In 1788 Lord Earlsfort claimed that a quarter of the debtors locked up in the City Marshalsea hardly owed two guineas each. He blamed their predicament for the suffering of entire households. Lord Clonmel described the consequences for these men: 'They were debauched with liquor, were addicted to tobacco, or whatever had a tendency to divert thought, and had an extreme aversion to labour.'[13]

The living quarters of the poor continued to deteriorate. Street lighting was inadequate and was subject to constant vandalism. This added to the tension after dark, when rubbish was casually thrown from windows. Passers-by had 'butter-milk, oyle, excrements and dirt thrown over their cloaths and spaw-water flasks and bottles broke upon them'. A window tax implemented in 1799 caused a further deterioration in living conditions. The philanthropist Samuel Rosborough claimed that this tax had caused the rents of paupers' lodgings to rise by a quarter in little over a year.[14]

As the city expanded so did the mounds of manure. Rocque's 1756 map depicts several dunghills on Dunghill Lane, off Bridgefoot Street, and nearby Dirty Lane, part of Thomas Street. By the end of the century the Liffey was likened to a gutter struggling between two dunghills. These dumps drew discarded items of all sorts, and local patterns could be seen. Trinity College adjoined the Townsend Street dunghill, and this was where numerous corpses ended up after they had been dissected by medical students. In 1787 the naked, rotten corpses of an entire

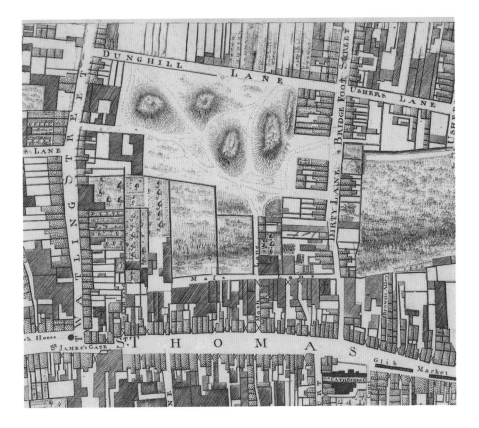

Dunghills partly bounded by the aptly named Dunghill Lane and Dirty Lane, 1750s. (John Rocque's map of Dublin, 1756)

family were found on the Townsend Street dump – they 'had passed under the hands of chirurgical professors'.[15]

> Most infections, malignant fevers and plagues have been brought into cities and great towns by beggars, who convey the infection in their cloathes, which, as well as their bodies, smell most offensively by their dirt and vermin.
>
> *Faulkner's Dublin Journal*, 17 June 1749

Such was the view of those concerned at the poor state of public health and they also noticed how fevers spread more quickly between dirty, congested houses. Narrow streets with no sanitation were recognised as a health hazard, even when the reason could not be given. Many believed it was a fortuitous combination of good situation and benign air that prevented plagues. In such circumstances wealthy residents were unlikely to leave their own well-being to mere chance, and Samuel Rosborough said that doctors did not dare to visit any patients within the distressed areas for fear of the health hazard. By the 1790s advocates of health reform were writing that diseases such as typhus were caused by poor infrastructure, and the evidence for this assertion became evermore widespread. By 1805 the houses of Ringsend had acquired a reputation for great stinking heaps of muck blocking the doorways. In 1818 St Mark's parish was condemned for a cluster of ten dairy yards that had accumulated over seven hundred tons of dung. Rotting garbage blocked the drains in Dorset Street, and sewage flowed down into the basements.

A 1790s shopkeeper displays a hat to a genteel customer. She does not deign to step out of her carriage. (From James Malton, *A Picturesque and Descriptive View of the City of Dublin*, 1799)

There were occasional interventions by the grand jury, but its concern was confined to the public realm: it removed waste that blocked traffic. There were regular demands to remove the ordure from the city; people believed this manure could be sold in Wales and the west of Ireland.[16]

＊＊＊＊＊

A society for the formation of cleanliness would at the same time be one for the suppression of vice. Those who could introduce among the poor here a taste for cleanliness would not be more their benefactors than of the city at large.

John Gamble, 1819[17]

Dublin's business community grew weary of all the dirt. By the 1770s wealthy customers were discouraged from entering their shops; they insisted on doing business from their coaches and sedan chairs. This practice was greatly resented by shopkeepers, who had to stand in the streets in all weathers. They complained that staff had died from fevers caught serving customers outdoors on winter days.[18] New hazards emerged as building activity accelerated. Fatalities followed malpractice, and more workers were killed by collapsing structures; in 1766, for example, eight men died during the construction of two houses at Merrion Square. There were constant complaints about passers-by falling into excavations, and during the 1750s it was estimated that a thousand pedestrians fell into unprotected cellars each year.[19]

Manifestations of the miasma

If our streets are not kept cleaner it is very probable that we shall have more sudden deaths, spotted, putrid, epidemical and other infectious fevers, small pox and variety of sickness to sweep away our miserable inhabitants.

Faulkner's Dublin Journal, 31 August 1754

In this cluttered city it was hard to find a place to bury the dead. Graveyards attached to the old churches became overcrowded. In 1758 the chaplain of the House of Industry described the precautions he took at the funerals of paupers.

When the graveyard overflowed with rotten corpses his solution was to stand outside and conduct funerals from the gateway. His situation was made worse when the place was flooded and the channel carrying the city's water supply regularly spilled out over the burial ground.[20] New development put great pressure on graveyards; in the late 1780s local residents were horrified to see corpses dug up at The Little Green, and cartloads of putrid limbs carried away.[21]

There was a rapid increase in the number of hospitals after 1750. The city directory listed seven in 1749, and the total had doubled three decades later. Philanthropists joined together in these ventures, and funds were raised to treat particular diseases. Cork Street Fever Hospital (1803) was opened in response to the high death rate of the previous years. One charity took an innovative approach to fund-raising for the House of Industry: in 1818 it organised a public procession of beggars through the streets in order to stimulate subscriptions. This enlightened self-interest was endorsed by John McGregor; as a doctor he saw how various charities addressed the suffering of the poor while bringing benefits to 'the higher orders of society'. While the bonus from dedicated accommodation for infectious patients was exaggerated, it did provide some protection for residents within poorer districts. These various hospitals also extended medical education. It is clear that the House of Industry formed part of that agenda: it was a teaching centre for doctors serving in the army and navy.[22]

The role of hospitals in Georgian civic government deserves more investigation. They were agencies of social control where entry, confinement and discharge were enforced through a quasi-penal regime. A parallel might be drawn with the security arrangements at the jails. The security force at the Lock Hospital comprised army men, and this continued until 1809. It only ended because too many soldiers were having sex with the female venereal patients. The House of Industry had a large security force, which by the Regency period comprised sixteen beadles; so many men were hardly needed to subdue frail or elderly inmates, and it is more likely that they were used to control the mentally ill patients.[23] It would be wrong, however, to consign all these enterprises to sanitary utilitarianism. There were less-clamorous places that supported the quiet and the retiring, and therefore often went unnoticed. Amongst these places was the Molyneux Asylum for Blind Females (1814). It was set up in an old house at Peter Street, and its emergence might be attributed to the evangelical crusade. The Molyneux was under pressure right from the start: there was no government grant and by the mid-1820s over eighty per cent of its income came from private donations. It was laid out to receive fifty females, but it normally had to restrict its capacity to just twenty-six occupants.[24]

Traffic hazards

Many complaints are come to hand against hackney coachmen carrying the bodies of people who have died of spotted fever, measles, small pox, and other malignant disorders, which must render it unsafe for the publick to go in such carriages.

Faulkner's Dublin Journal, 6 August 1754

The drivers of cars, after having sold their goods at the markets in Dublin, on their return home drove their cars diagonally along the road, and often injured the passengers, and if they were remonstrated with, they generally answered with a lash of their whip, or with a curse.

Lord Clonmel, 1793[25]

The road network did not keep up with the growth of traffic, and many accidents arose from overcrowded wagons speeding out of control along narrow streets. There was hardly any regulation of public transport. These vehicles were notorious … and so were the drivers who worked them. During the 1780s and 1790s hackney coaches on the Blackrock road were carrying ten passengers where the regulations allowed only four. Onlookers were upset to see a horse pulling so much weight – it was 'sweating blood from every pore, and his eyes ready to start from their sockets'.[26]

Public vehicles carried dubious loads. Hackney coaches were used by grave robbers to carry corpses, to bring infectious patients to the fever hospital, and to carry convicts to jail. Hamilton's *Cries of Dublin* illustrates a poor man's funeral where the coffin can be seen protruding through the front window of the hired coach. In 1758 a sealed coffin with a rotten corpse burst open in the street.[27] Regulation of these hackneys was passed to the police commissioner in the late 1780s, and he condemned most of them. A lot of the coaches and sedan chairs were declared totally unfit for use. Newspapers warned the public and published the registration numbers of the worst offenders. Some institutions, such as the Cork Street Fever Hospital, began taking their own precautions: they only admitted patients who arrived in the hospital's private carriage.[28]

Alcohol abuse

> Low tippling houses, an evil great and multiplied where wretched men and women pass entire nights and days, pipers and fiddlers are heard mingling with the roar of intemperance.
>
> *The Freeman's Journal*, 16 September 1797

Hogarth's *Gin Lane* was played out in Dublin. Richard Twiss, in his tour of 1766, was shocked at all the drunkenness he saw. It was clearly well established because he was able to recall how Dr John Rutty recorded 3,500 drinking venues in the city in 1749.[29] During his visit John Carr (1806) came to the conclusion that every second house in Thomas Street, in the Liberties, was a dram shop. He drily declared that one of these shops saw a surge in profits when the owner offered a free funeral to anyone who died of drink there. Edward Wakefield (1812) followed in the same vein, but his ire was directed at the producers. He believed that cheap whiskey left the labourers too weak to work. It corrupted the people and men lost their sense of moral obligation. This theme was repeated afterwards in Warburton, Whitelaw and Walsh's *History of the City of Dublin*. The authors

One of the drinkers has attacked the parish watchman (centre right, holding rattler), whose halberd lies on the ground. (Courtesy of Andrew Bonar Law)

THE HUMOURS of WHISKEY

Temperance campaign, 1750s. (From Anon., *A Dram For Drunkards: A Funeral Sermon, on the Death of James Buchanan and Robert Port, Who Killed Themselves by Drinking Whiskey*, 1759) (RIA)

were hardly surprised at that area being a centre of the 1798 rebellion because it had so little regard for the rule of law: the dram shops never shut. By the 1810s the reform crusade had been extended to temperance, and Wakefield claimed that the city was consuming less alcohol, although the lower orders still drank far too much whiskey. The teetotaling crusade of Father Theobald Mathew was, of course, still to come (1830s and 1840s).[30]

Many drinking venues were low-grade hovels. Ructions spilled out onto the streets, where the fisticuffs and loud singing drew in an audience. Those living nearby protested that 'the polluted stuff is distinctly heard in whatever part of a house a company happens to be'. According to Warburton, Whitelaw and Walsh, a quarter of the 190 dram shops in Thomas Street had no licence. *The Freeman's Journal* railed at the frightening number of shebeens; a quarter of the houses in some parishes sold alcohol, and this evil was now spreading into the refined parish of St Mary's, which already had 190 public houses. In 1785 the grand jury denounced the sale of whiskey in every street and asked parliament to take decisive action against it.[31]

Towards the close of the century stronger efforts were made to deal with licensing. About two hundred tippling houses were closed down in March–April 1791, and it was expected a further five hundred closures would follow. These campaigns only served to drive the problem underground. Soon afterwards more gingerbread hawkers and other street traders were selling whiskey. These pedlars were, of course, always careful not to offer the stuff to well-dressed passers-by in case they turned out to be revenue officers.[32]

Mental illness

He gave the little wealth he had,
To build a house for fools and mad:
And showed with one satiric touch,
No nation needed it so much.

Jonathan Swift, 1731[33]

Modern psychiatry evolved during the nineteenth century. A new outlook encouraged socially aware treatments that responded more closely to human emotions. In these islands the innovations may have been spurred by the evangelical zeal. Around 1800 there were hardly a few thousand people confined as lunatics in English institutions. A century later there were about one hundred thousand. It is likely that a parallel trend occurred in Ireland. Some of those people considered to be mad were cared for within their families, but most were left to wander abroad. The stigma attached to mental illness drove the wealthy to conceal sick members of their families in order to safeguard the marriage prospects of siblings.

Of those wandering the streets, a significant number were either mentally ill or physically disabled. When those meandering abroad became an offensive spectacle they were liable to be taken into custody. Out of sight was out of mind, and the out-of-mind had to be kept out of sight. Prison keepers were quick to punish those who could not contribute towards their keep, and the mentally disturbed prisoners were therefore consigned to the darkest corners; Dublin was no exception in this regard. Even in a city like Rome, the epitome of neoclassical urban Europe, the facilities for the insane were overwhelmed. The main establishment, Santa Maria della Pietà de Povere Pazzi, was forced to take in drunkards, malingerers, epileptics and the mentally handicapped. In this competition for shelter it was the most severely disturbed who were squeezed out or dispatched to prison.[34] A substantial proportion of the insane ended up in institutions such as the House of Industry. It was pressure on penal institutions that ultimately led to the opening of purpose-built hospitals such as Swift's charity, St Patrick's Hospital and, later, the Richmond Lunatic Asylum. Treatment within these hospitals consisted of close confinement, and most patients remained there until they died. They were locked up in cells, and heavy, iron fetters were used to restrain the more boisterous ones. A high-level window allowed in some daylight, but cells were left entirely unheated. Deranged patients provided a freak show

An early cell door at St Patrick's Hospital exemplifies the severe restraints imposed on patients. Food was delivered through the upper aperture, and chamber pots were passed through the lower opening.

for voyeurs, who were charged a shilling entrance fee. William Hogarth depicted such a (London) spectacle in one of his popular prints of the 1730s.[35]

Dublin's House of Industry had to take the most troublesome lunatics because neighbouring counties failed to provide places for their own people. In the post-Union decades the House of Industry admitted lunatics from all over the country. This topic is more closely treated in chapter seven.

✳✳✳✳✳

Dublin's response to the mentally ill was seen in the opening of St Patrick's Hospital in 1757. Jonathan Swift left funds to establish it. He was aware of the appalling conditions of London's Bedlam, and wanted to provide a more humane regime. His hospital was purposely located on the outskirts in order to shield the genteel from the screams of disturbed patients. Most of those admitted were from the city, and by 1817 it had room for 150 patients. The early records are incomplete but suggest there were almost equal numbers of male and female sufferers. Where a diagnosis was made, it cited either mania or melancholy (depression). When a profession was stated for those patients prior to 1840, and invariably this was for men, eighty per cent were either lawyers, army and navy officers, clergymen, teachers, physicians, college students, artisans, engineers, shopkeepers or government officials. What stands out is the high number of clergymen. There would presumably have been a desire to avoid any spectacle of dishevelled and disoriented priests wandering the streets.

Those statistics that survive cast doubt on the assertion that St Patrick's took in the deranged poor of the capital. It is not reflected in the occupations of those admitted, and it was clearly an impossible task. Some entries appear for poor lunatics who roamed abroad, but in the main these unfortunates were not accommodated. Exceptions appear where the wider issue of public safety arose, thereby bringing the burden of legally imposed detentions to bear on St Patrick's. This problem came to a head in 1783–84 when excessive congestion within the jails caused nineteen lunatics to be transferred from the House of Industry and the Bridewell. These people were clearly unwelcome at St Patrick's, and, reflecting this, none of their names are given in the records.[36]

St Patrick's followed its own path, and by the 1830s the accommodation was sharply segregated. Fee-paying patients were allocated suites within the bright, southern end of the building. First-class boarders paid over £100 per annum, and their quarters were compared to a *maison de santé*. Genteel patients could bring their own servants with them. Some even brought their own hens to provide them with fresh eggs every morning. The sickest paupers were locked away in a damp basement that received no sunlight or ventilation. They were supposed to have access to two small yards, but this space, including the toilets, was taken over by the elite patients for the use of their hens.[37]

Dublin acquired a second, even larger, mental hospital in 1815, with accommodation for 228 patients. This was the Richmond Lunatic Asylum, and its methods were not much different from St Patrick's. It employed physical restraints such as straitjackets and solitary confinement in dark cells. In 1821 John McGregor found it a gloomy place – half of its patients were deemed incurable, and these unfortunates were classed as reprobates who could be dispatched to the House of Industry.[38]

> The want of work causes much more mental and corporeal disease among the poor operatives of Dublin than the manner or materials in which they were employed.
>
> Dr William Stoker, 1835[39]

During the early nineteenth century the emergence of larger mental institutions was matched by a growing demand for places. It became a game of 'pass the parcel' as the House of Industry sent its inmates to the Richmond Asylum only to have them returned again when they were found to be an incurable burden. By the 1830s the Richmond was under great pressure, with a continual stream of patients coming from country jails. The Richmond and St Patrick's could only take about four hundred people, but a rural patient's prospect of admittance was enhanced if he or she was referred by a gentleman or a Protestant clergyman. Overcrowding led to considerable numbers of disturbed people being detained within their local rural jail for several years, with many of them never going any further.[40]

Burial grounds

> A corpse can seldom rest above three or four years before it is dispossessed of its place to make room for another, and I have seen bones thrown up with great quantities of flesh adhering to them.
>
> Charles Topham Bowden, 1791[41]

As the demand for graves increased, the demand for burial places became more selective. Some parishes paid for paupers' coffins, if only to prevent the random disposal of corpses. Where this service was provided it was increasingly relied upon by the poorest families; for example, St Paul's gave out seventy-seven coffins in 1740. This figure grew to 109 in 1783, and reached 278 in 1801.[42]

In 1761 St Anne's parish decided that its poorest parishioners could no longer use the burial ground beside the church; instead, five shillings would be given to their friends to take them elsewhere.[43] This put extra pressure on those parishes that were already hard-pressed. The nuisance brought legislation in the early 1770s prohibiting burials within 12 feet of any church. This remedy was widely ignored, especially where important church patrons were involved. Yet as late as 1818 this was a matter of great concern for wealthy parishes such as St Anne's and St Mary's. In the latter case there were only 2 square feet left for each burial.[44]

> Our ideas are now, I trust, too much enlarged, to permit a veneration for old bones to counteract a proposal for the general health of the inhabitants.
>
> Hely Dutton, 1802[45]

Bully's Acre, beside Kilmainham, was the last resort of the poor. It was overloaded with corpses, and as late as 1810 John Gamble, an army doctor, was nauseated by the sight of decaying bodies 'in every progressive state of putrefaction, and in some the knees were falling from the sockets, and the eyes melting in their eyeballs, the worms crept along their fingers'. This site was outside the city boundary and was therefore unregulated.[46] As the nuisance grew, the government applied more restraints, including a ban on any new burial grounds within the city limits.

Hely Dutton (1802) included graveyards in the list of nuisances to be banished beyond the Circular Road. The sharp increase in demand for graves gave rise to new crimes; at the Garden Lane Market, off Francis Street, poor people from the Liberties bought second-hand coffins robbed from fresh burials.[47]

Unlike either London or Paris, Dublin retained a sectarian regime of cemeteries. Permission had to be obtained from the Protestant authorities before prayers could be said at Catholic funerals, and this frequently led to confrontation and sometimes violence. In 1828 the Catholic Association bought its own land for burials. Its first purchase was on the southern outskirts beside the Grand Canal at Golden Bridge, and three years later it began a more ambitious project on the northern perimeter at Glasnevin. This extensive scheme, under the title of Prospect Cemetery, marked the arrival of a new model based on airy, green spaces. This fashion emerged in 1804 at the Père Lachaise cemetery in Paris. Thus Dublin acquired its iconic cemetery, laid out on the new European rectilinear landscaped model, complemented with riverside vistas and yew-lined walks.[48] The strong religious affiliation might explain why later ventures by the Catholic Association were not welcome. Local residents frustrated the opening of a south-side equivalent of Prospect Cemetery at Milltown. They got a legal injunction blocking development of the site beside the River Dodder. Thus the geography of poverty was confirmed by a denominational post-mortem.[49]

Abuse of animals

Animals in Georgian Dublin served as beasts of burden, while others were a source of food. Some were used for security, sporting activity or merely for companionship, and most were badly treated. Animal-baiting was popular amongst poor people, and there were riots when the army tried to stop bull-baiting. Thieves attacked flocks of sheep, cutting the fat from live animals so that it could be sold to local chandlers. This became such a regular outrage that it was specifically outlawed in the 1740s. Millers bringing flour to city markets hoisted it onto the bare backs of horses. This left the flour fouled with sweat and blood, giving some people a dislike for bread. Calves coming to the market were forced into tiny carts, with their heads stuck against the wheels; onlookers were shocked by the injuries this caused.[50]

Dublin, like English and US cities, allowed pigs to augment the street cleaning. These roaming animals were a traffic hazard, and pedestrians were kept at bay by their aggressive behaviour. They were drawn to the food markets and attacked children, occasionally with fatal results. The Liberties contained an area called Pigtown; it adjoined the City Basin and was a byword for stench. This

Two pigs lie undisturbed near St Patrick's cathedral, *c.* 1810. The ground-floor window shutter of the house suggests that security was a concern for the occupants. (From J. Warburton, Revd J. Whitelaw and Revd R. Walsh, *History of the City of Dublin*, 1818)

reputation was confirmed by Warburton, Whitelaw and Walsh in their *History of the City of Dublin* (1818); it showed two well-fed swine lounging in the shadow of St Patrick's cathedral. Malton's painting of Parliament House in the 1790s showed a swineherd driving his animals along the street, and Stockdale showed pigs near the same spot a decade later.[51]

The law allowed people to slaughter wandering pigs so that poor people might have free pork. In 1793 the lord mayor's men caught five of them to feed paupers. In 1795–96 the lord mayor personally led search parties made up of parish constables armed with spears. On one day seventeen animals were taken and dispatched to city charities. These initiatives were followed elsewhere in Ireland. Cork's mayor made use of a special pig trap; this was a horse-drawn device, and it was used in the post-Union years.[52]

There was a widespread fear of being bitten by mad dogs, and calls were made to license them. Modern readers might wonder at the number of stray dogs shown in street scenes; Malton's *Dublin* featured thirty-four. Tudor's 1749 view of fashionable St Stephen's Green included five dogs, while the 1780 view of College Green by Pool and Cash showed a fight between two more.[53]

The Georgian city had numerous horses. They were everywhere, and this was made clear by all their public noises and waste products. Each of these animals deposited about 10 kilograms of dung daily – that is, about 3.5 tons each year. Disposal of horse carcasses created a nuisance, and it was advised that those animals dying of infectious distemper should be buried deep underground. During the severe flooding of 1726 at least thirty-seven horses belonging to the city scavenger were destroyed. By mid-century the army barracks had accommodation for five hundred horses, the corporation owned over sixty horses, and there was a stable lane behind each new fashionable street. These animals had to be trained, and there was little space to prepare them for coach service. They were broken in on the streets, inevitably leading to accidents. The threat of a public whipping did not deter the offenders, and in 1760 a substantial reward was offered for those taming horses near Leinster House in Kildare Street.[54]

Venereal disease

> With gentlest touch, she next explores
> Her chancres, issues, running sores,
> Effects of many a sad disaster,
> And then to each applies a plaster.
>
> Jonathan Swift, A Beautiful Young Nymph Going to Bed, 1730

Venereal disease (VD) was rampant in Dublin, and there was ample evidence of the problem.[55] However, the official response was muted. VD was viewed as a foreign product imported into Ireland by sinners. When Richard Twiss inserted a short list of common Irish words into his 1776 tour, he included this disease, calling it *An Bolgach Francach* (the French disease).[56]

Advertising campaigns by city doctors suggest there was a strong demand for venereal treatments. Doctors looking for VD patients were bold enough to stick their posters onto the front of the Royal Exchange. The owners of this building were grossly offended and threatened to prosecute those who disfigured their fine façade. The aim of the government was to get the nuisance off the streets. Various institutions were used, but there was little treatment available and it was confined to adults. In 1779 *The Freeman's Journal* claimed there were innumerable sufferers and made an appeal for funds to set up a VD hospital.[57]

From time to time initiatives were taken to reduce the impact of the disease. McGregor (1821) claimed the incidence of VD in Dublin's foundlings was over ninety-nine per cent during the period 1775–1796, while Robins (1980) put the incidence at about forty per cent in 1790. These figures appear to be exaggerated. In reality the shocking mortality within the Foundling Hospital was due to poor administration.[58] This topic is more closely examined in chapter seven.

The Lock Hospital, dedicated to treating VD, was established in 1755. It was set up in a building previously occupied by the Lying-in Hospital at George's Lane. In the following decade it transferred to Clarendon Street, and subsequently moved out to the Donnybrook road. On a smaller scale, the Charitable Venereal Hospital operated in North King Street from 1758. It treated over 560 patients in its first seven years. The hospital offered male patients to the navy, but that offer was declined because enough healthy recruits were available.

Quacks and fake medicines accelerated the disease. Legislation was introduced in 1761 to control the trade in drugs, but there was little evidence of meaningful reform during the following decades. The main aim of hospitals was to treat married women. With such a narrow agenda, deadly medicine (mercury) and

The Lock Hospital being demolished in the 1950s. (*Irish Press*)

a constant shortage of funds, they could hardly succeed. One approach used by doctors was a generous application of laxatives to remove the offending matter. In order to remove callouses from a woman's urethra, a wax candle was inserted to lop off the offending growth. If that failed, some burning acid was applied through a cannula. In cases of a deeply embedded caruncle, a metal probe was inserted to break off the growth by sheer force.[59]

> Next Miss o' the Town, on a cull will not frown,
> For a trifle will turn up her skirt.
> At length her pretender, she fires him like tender
> Till the trifle in Lock must be put.
>
> Anon., *c.*1784[60]

By 1770 the Lock Hospital had become the main centre for venereal patients, and the Charitable was no longer listed in city directories.[61] In its first eight years, the Lock treated 11,386 patients and also dealt with 16,934 outpatients. The normal treatment was administered over ten weeks, but this action only suppressed the symptoms. A remarkably low mortality (two per cent) was achieved in two ways: firstly, by discharging women before the terminal symptoms appeared, and, secondly, by getting rid of the male patients. In 1792 the Lock moved to Townsend Street, where it took over the building vacated by the Hospital for Incurables.[62]

During the 1780s one in ten of the Bridewell's female prisoners were kept in the infirmary due to their venereal disorders. Yet this figure masks the real extent of the problem. An investigation found that six terminally ill women were confined together in a cell of less than 5 square metres. They received no treatment and were forced to huddle together, lying naked on the stone floor until they died.[63]

From the start, the Lock's dockland location was condemned. It was a place where 'marsh and animal miasmata of every species of malignity must be concentrated by a swamp on one side, the reliques of every tide on the other, the offals of an adjoining market, the effluvia of three hundred patients … and the filth and contamination of numberless inhabitants of the most licentious habit in surrounding and dirty lanes'.[64] This location reflected the downstream expansion of the sex trade. It also expressed the policy of keeping the sufferers out of sight – something that was understandable because patients were often distressed at having to leave the place. They lingered outside on the pavement, sometimes for weeks, begging for a place in some asylum. The moral mission of the Lock was kept to the fore, and the management boasted that the character of the place had

A Funeral procession of the Lower Rank

a particular significance. Wards were classified according to the profligacy of the
patients they contained.

There was an abrupt change at the Lock in 1820, prompted by public outrage
at the unrestricted intercourse between male and female wards. All the men
were moved to other institutions, including Dr Steevens' Hospital, where thirty
beds were set aside for male paupers. Many of the men ended up in prison when
they could find no other refuge. Some treatment was provided for those held in
Newgate; they were given mercury together with bandages for open sores, but
anyone refusing treatment was thrown out onto the streets.[65] (See appendix four
for details of Lock Hospital admissions for the period 1793–1823.)

Jail fever

> Our prisons are dreadful: cast your eyes into the chief receptacle in
> Green Street for cowardly villainy and slavish crime; there the voice
> of applause is never heard, the hope of future fame never enters; the
> mind expiates on a life to come with gloomy despondency, and the
> barriers erected by virtue before a weak understanding are instantly
> broken down, or so shattered by the persevering assaults of vice in

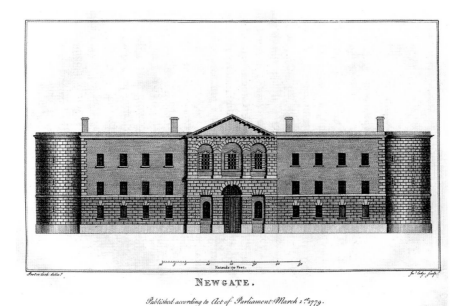

NEWGATE.

Published according to Act of Parliament March 1st 1779.

this den of infamy, that when freed from durance they are easily carried by the next corrupt invader.

Pierce Egan, 1821[66]

Early eighteenth-century prisons functioned as holding centres for people awaiting trial. Other institutions known as houses of industry and houses of correction were charged with reforming wrongdoers. There were also debtors' prisons (often called marshalseas), and all of these became places of custodial punishment. Each centre had its own agenda and did not distinguish between hardened criminals, paupers, children and lunatics. Managers ran their prisons as private enterprises, selling necessities and luxuries to inmates.

Newgate occupied a filthy site on the northern periphery. It had no outdoor yard and there was no sewer. Black Dog Prison, located near the medieval quarter, was allegedly situated within the dirtiest meat market in Europe; during the summer stinking garbage made the situation of the prisoners unbearable. A law of 1763 required the grand jury to provide jails with primitive toilets while simultaneously expelling all the cows and pigs. Jailers were directed to get rid of their breweries. After a severe outbreak of jail fever a few years later, further legislation required the jails to install sickbays and each cell had to be whitewashed annually.[67] Sponging houses were used to relieve overcrowding in prisons. These were small, private detention places, but they became even more notorious. At Angel Alley (off High Street) there were ten prisoners squeezed into each cell; four men shared the same bed. These inmates paid over three shillings per night although they had no heating, lighting, water or food.

James Dexter controlled the Four Courts Marshalsea in the 1780s. He had an annual income of £2,000, combined with the use of an elegant house. Dexter gave suites of five or six rooms to his favourite prisoners – wealthy usurers and receivers of stolen goods. They were allowed to keep dogs, pigs and poultry. At the opposite end of the spectrum, the poorest prisoners were confined to the common hall. That was a space containing eighty people lying on dirty straw 'without a staunch window to keep out the inclemency of the weather, or perhaps a fire to give the air of their damp prison a due degree of action to prevent diseases'. By the 1790s the disorder of the Four Courts Marshalsea made it very risky for court officers to serve summonses there.[68]

Nearby residents were always on the alert for the dreaded jail fever. This was a typhus spread from the keepers and prisoners by all the toing and froing. An estimated four hundred inmates of the House of Industry died from an outbreak in 1788.[69] An episode of disease could bring court sittings to a halt. Lawyers were loath to approach clients, and any prisoner who was injured might be denied hospital treatment. A severe outbreak spread through the jails in 1807, causing several fatalities amongst barristers and jurors.[70]

It was often self-interest that spurred concern over the welfare of prisoners. Following a large breakout from Newgate in 1776, calls were made for medical staff to treat the fever inside the jail. It was soon realised that nothing less than the entire replacement of the building itself would bring any lasting relief. Four years later, when Newgate was being demolished, the roof was first removed to disperse the noxious stink. The prison reformer John Howard went to inspect the new building after it opened; he paid dearly for his concern as inmates stole his watch and his money.[71]

The new jail had many admirers. It was portrayed by Pool and Cash (1780) in their catalogue of Dublin's best architecture. It received praise for security and convenience based on an improved design of single-cell occupancy that checked the dreaded distemper. These claims were, however, premature, and within a few years the new jail had gained the same reputation as its predecessor. The executioner was selling whiskey and prostitutes were doing business in the men's quarters.[72]

Breakouts remained commonplace. In 1790 forty-six prisoners escaped through a sewer. Reformers wanted to remove the prison away from the city. In 1820 the Richmond General Penitentiary was established on the northern

A Newgate Prison account for several prisoners, dated 1803. It includes a subsistence bill for Robert Emmet (for one night), the patriot hanged at Thomas Street. The entry for 30 gallons of whiskey for prisoners is notable. (Private collection)

periphery at Grangegorman. It was intended to function within a wider reform of the Irish penal system wherein those liable for transportation to Australia might instead be detained locally. A spacious site complete with exercise yards would allow reform through hard labour, solitary confinement and religious instruction. This new prison was imposing: over 200 metres long and occupying over a hectare. However, the old prisons were not closed. The notorious Newgate remained, and in 1827 the penal reformers Elizabeth Fry and Joseph Gurney said it was worse than having no prison at all.[73]

Mountjoy Jail, Dublin's landmark of law enforcement, was not opened until 1850. It is noteworthy how its peripheral location on the North Circular Road was chosen: it is complemented on two sides by the security barriers offered by the Royal Canal. Over time an array of public health and penal institutions moved away from the confined streets to spacious properties. A good example of this was the House of Recovery at Cork Street. This hospital occupied a sloping site separated from other buildings and busy roads, and the site was chosen because a small watercourse supported a wholesome environment endowed with fresh air and gardens. Even then, the governors took one more step to secure the desired reform. They built a solid boundary wall to prevent inmates trading their daily bread for whiskey and tobacco.[74]

Reformers were getting a grasp of the wider context, but a fear of social upheaval was still forcing the deepest of thinkers to hesitate. In 1800 a good example of muddled assessment could be seen in the analysis undertaken by a city charity. On the positive side were counted the advantages that should allay disease, such as the reliable and plentiful supply of provisions. Along with these came temperate climate, as well as proximity to the sea and the airy position of several elevated streets. Against these positives were listed the closeness and dirt of those quarters occupied by the lower orders of humanity, the streets without sewers and the substantial number of houses falling into decay. However, the greatest drawback identified in this study was the supine improvidence of the poorest residents.[75]

In 1800 the Fever Hospital at Smithfield was set up at the suggestion of the philanthropist Samuel Rosborough. During the following decades health reformers became bolder. One of the most notable was Edwin Chadwick, whose 1842 *Report on the Sanitary Condition of the Labouring Population of Great Britain* made it clear that radical engineering solutions were required. Chadwick's ideas found supporters in Dublin, and one of these was Thomas Willis, a doctor working in the poverty-stricken parish of St Michan's. In 1845 Willis published a pamphlet on the health regime serving Dublin's poor. Like Chadwick, he stressed the need for a clean, reliable water supply complemented by a waterborne sewerage system.[76]

Clontarf's Charter School (1748) was set up to immerse poor Catholic children in the Protestant religion and the English language. It gained a notorious reputation for its workhouse ethic. (From J. Warburton, Revd J. Whitelaw and Revd R. Walsh, *History of the City of Dublin*, 1818)

7

Responses to Deprivation

But slaves and beggars always must
Be wrong'd by those they're forced to trust.
In hospitals, if well endow'd,
The stewards all go rich and proud,
Whilst the poor pensioners are fed,
With half their due of flesh and bread.

Anon., 1725[1]

DUBLIN BECAME THE SUPPORT CENTRE for the nation's down-and-outs. Every time rural Ireland saw severe shortages, such as during the famines of the early 1740s, the hungry poor came pouring into the city. Each wave of migration made vagrancy more apparent, and surges often coincided with economic downturns within the city itself. There were serious bouts of unemployment in key industries, and trouble associated with the textile trade of the Liberties forced entire families out onto the streets. There was growing tension between local mendicants and the burly strangers who were trying to oust them.

Public initiatives

With each passing decade the number of workhouses in Europe spread further across the urban fabric. Dublin's first workhouse was established in James' Street in 1706, and in keeping with the prevailing ethos was called the House of Industry. Little is known about its inmates. Like so many other aspects of Georgian poverty, what we know has largely come from events concerning people who got into trouble with the law. One such incident provides us with an image of two young men who absconded in 1747: 'Dennis Roan, a boy about 17 years of age, five feet high, marked with the small-pox, wears a dark brown wig, a brown and sometimes a blue coat with a white clothserge waistcoat; and one John Bryan about 20 years of age, five feet and a half high, marked with the small-pox, somewhat freckled in the face, of a brown complection, and wears his own short brown hair, and brown and sometimes a blue coat with a green waistcoat, speaks a little Irish, and hangs his head as he walks.'[2]

These challenges came to the city fathers at a time when social attitudes were changing. Poverty was losing its medieval meaning of a holy state attracting works of charity. The public perception of paupers became more detached, and this, in turn, was associated with the declining status of religion. The term 'hospital' still retained its meaning as a sanctuary that offered support to the suffering; it catered for vulnerable people who were also sick, but it was not restricted to them alone. Christian teaching, whatever the denomination, had long promoted specific works of corporal mercy, namely to feed the hungry, give drink to the thirsty, to clothe the naked, shelter the homeless, minister to the sick, visit those in prison and bury the dead. Alms-giving was the main expression of private charity up to the mid-eighteenth century, and people saw it had two aims: discharging a religious duty and reducing those threats to society that arose from poverty and criminality.

Rural life also changed a great deal during the eighteenth century. Agricultural productivity grew substantially. Crop yields rose, as did the acreage under cultivation. Innovations such as the change from the sickle to the scythe left less work for women, but the demand for rural male labour was rising. Still, country people were tempted to try their luck in the burgeoning urban centres, and Dublin played a significant role in this transformation of the settlement pattern.

The surge of migration was unsettling, and those who opposed it sought to prevent it from growing any further. Apart from the competition for jobs, there was a clash of cultures that brought local officials to resent these newcomers. In 1727 Sir Michael Creagh, one of the capital's grandees, condemned the

The DISTRESSED MANUFACTURER.

destructive impact of the rural influx. He called on the corporation to drive out
these strangers because of their sinful ways and their bad influence. He accused
them of setting up taverns and brothels instead of engaging in good, honest
labour – 'they walk the whole day with their hands in their pockets in lieu of
handling the spade, or the plow, so as the first man Adam was obliged to do.'[3]

Efforts to tackle this issue began as early as the 1720s, but they were bound
to fail as the population of the city kept on growing too rapidly. During the
second half of the eighteenth century Ireland's population doubled, increasing
from around two million to five million by 1800. This growth put an enormous
strain on the resources of the countryside. Unskilled workers were paid less, and
at the same time there was less land available to rent. As the lot of the poorest
people declined, they were forced to consider alternatives.[4]

Throughout this period, alms-giving still went on, but along with casual
contributions there were individuals who believed that poverty might be relieved
by more substantial and targeted donations to local charities. This altruism could
be expressed in legacies, and some bequests were sizeable. In 1727, for example, a
benefactor from St Brigid's parish named William Howard left £100 in this way.
We can see where Howard's money was spent: just £10 of it went directly to the
paupers, £70 was put into a trust to provide weekly bread for the parish poor, and
the remaining £20 went to the Charity School. Another example of disinterested
donations was inspired by the Liberties Dispensary. This facility was opened in
Meath Street in 1794, and most of the funds were given by former local residents
who had moved out to more desirable addresses.[5]

Some benefactors had done well in business, and they may have included
Catholics who wanted to help others of their own religion. In 1764, for example,
a Mr Lynch (a merchant) and a Mr McManus (described as a gentleman)
combined to contribute £500 to three institutions treating venereal disease. A
few years later, the Committee of Merchants donated a further £700 to the same
charities. During the 1770s the private contributions to the House of Industry
amounted annually to around £3,000. According to Samuel Rosborough, private
donations to the public soup kitchens exceeded £1,000 per week at the time of
the Union. These contributions regularly exceeded those of the government.[6]

Notable gestures were also made by parishes. In 1792 St Anne's church sold
the rights to one of its most prestigious pews in order to support the poor. That
auction brought in twenty-six guineas. St Peter's established a charitable fund in
1812 to give loans to deserving parishioners: the sums did not exceed £5, and each
candidate had to be honest and industrious. A remarkable source of funds was
the so-called charity sermon, when a fashionable congregation gathered to hear

some celebrity preacher. Dublin's star performer was Revd Walter Blake Kirwan, who perfected his skills during the 1790s. According to the republican activist John Binns, each of Kirwan's blasts could raise £1,000. There may be some exaggeration in this claim, but there is a record from 1760 of a charity sermon bringing over £712 to the Foundling Hospital. In order to stir his listeners' response, Revd Kirwan gathered around him a circle of the hungriest orphans he could find. This tactic never failed, and the plates filled up with rings, watches and all sorts of jewellery. Charity sermons made a significant contribution to public institutions. They were undertaken by County Dublin parishes during 1773 in order to provide accommodation for vagabonds and beggars; this initiative brought in a total of £3,045, an impressive sum that was put towards the construction of the new House of Industry at Channel Row.[7]

Revd Walter Blake Kirwan, a celebrated charity sermon preacher, 1780s. (*Walker's Hibernian Magazine*, December 1789) (UCD)

The Rev.d WALTER BLAKE KIRWAN

*****

Great numbers of idle vagabonds of both sexes, strole about the city, some through necessity, and others under a pretence of it, to the great annoyance of the inhabitants thereof.

Faulkner's Dublin Journal, 18 November 1746

Humanity must shudder at the crowds of petitioning wretches to be met with in every corner of the city.

Hibernian Journal, 11 June 1783

This benefactress was the wife of a wealthy banker and part of the Huguenot Protestant refugee group that fled France to avoid religious persecution. (*Walker's Hibernian Magazine*, February 1796) (UCD)

While richer parishes such as St Anne's and St Andrew's could offer relief to local residents, there were too many other districts with no funds to do so. This was the problem that confronted parishes such as St John's and St James'. By the late 1750s they were operating an onerous support network for paupers. A few thousand people relied on the free meals available three days each week. This became an emergency where the lord mayor felt compelled to intervene and donate 1.5 tons of oatmeal.[8]

Better-off parishes tried to control the number of beggars by only granting licences to worthy locals. In the 1770s parishes such as St Anne's and St Werburgh's restricted permits to their own candidates. These paupers were given brass badges to wear publicly on their right arm, and harsh measures were used to enforce the rules.[9] Most beggars refused to wear badges, and struggles between the paupers themselves went on as before. Weaker individuals were pushed aside by competitors, and those at the back were left hungry.[10]

As the pressure grew, something better was needed to bring the beggars under control. Several agencies were drawn into this agenda, and the aim was to place them in an institution where they would be converted into more useful members of the community. A renewal of each individual was to be brought about by getting them to do useful tasks within a securely enclosed establishment. They were to be committed to manual labour in order to pay for their keep. According to this model they would return to everyday life as better people making a useful contribution to mankind. There was, however, little consistency in the application of the policy.

Children's institutions

> While a revolution of religious impressions has converted on the continent houses consecrated to pious purposes to scenes of pleasure, the feelings of the metropolis of Ireland seem to have taken an opposite direction, and within a few years some of the gayest resorts of fashion and dissipation have been transformed into edifices of devotion and charity.
>
> Warburton, Whitelaw and Walsh, 1818[11]

A network was formed to manage abandoned babies, and it became a feature of everyday life in Dublin. There were, on the one hand, those who quietly sought out a corner to 'drop' the infant. On the other hand, there were those people who were hired to act like human cuckoos, surreptitiously disposing of these dropped babies by passing them onto another location where they might be supported by somebody else. In the 1720s parishes employed women of this kind, called 'lifters' – officially described as parish nurses – to discard infants in some adjoining parish. In a single year there were seventy-three babies dropped in St Michan's parish, and two fifths of them died within the following year. In 1730 Elizabeth Hyland was the lifter working in St John's parish. During the previous year she handled twenty-seven children, and seven of these died in her care. She encountered great problems with her opposite number at St Paul's, who was ever-vigilant, and promptly returned infants she had dumped there. This was an expanding business, and officially a blind eye was turned to it.[12]

Those institutions dealing with children included the Charter Schools founded in the 1730s and the Marine School set up in the 1760s. The main object of the Charter Schools was to immerse young Catholic boys and girls in both the Protestant religion and the English language. One such school, set up to the north-east of the city, at Clontarf, gained a notorious reputation. These schools were imbued with aspects of the workhouse ethos and took in youngsters from very poor families. They only served small numbers of young people, but were resented on account of the tactics they used. The children were sent to the most remote schools in order to defeat any attempt they might make to return home. Anybody who obstructed the removal of children from their parents was liable to six months' imprisonment with hard labour. The system became corrupt, and the youngsters were essentially used to generate an income. Employers were reluctant to take on these children because they were so rowdy and unskilled. Sexual molestation of girls was a concern, and public whipping was the prescribed sanction for any school employee who was caught out.[13]

The Hibernian Marine Society was set up to save poor boys from a life of crime by sending them away to sea. Dublin's Marine School was founded in 1766 and followed the London template created by Jonas Hanway a decade earlier. It had a very modest beginning at Ringsend, but then moved into more central premises. An elegant building was constructed on the south quays in 1773 and it appears prominently in Malton's *A Picturesque and Descriptive View of the City of Dublin*.[14]

The Foundling Hospital

There were so many abandoned infants that the authorities struggled to deal with the issue. By far the greatest proportion of the women concerned were unmarried mothers – often domestic servants or manual labourers who had been violated. The House of Industry was obliged to take in abandoned babies without asking questions. It was unprepared for this task, and foundlings arrived in ever-increasing numbers during the 1720s. As early as 1725 half the occupants were very young children, and this proportion kept growing. This new role increased the running costs because the babies were obviously unable to work for their keep. By the end of that decade the place had effectively been converted from a workhouse to a foundling hospital.[15] Mothers who brought their offspring there believed they had some prospect of getting them back at a future date. (See appendix five for details of petitions from mothers who wanted to retrieve their children.)

Admissions rose as knowledge of the place spread. The annual intake trebled between 1730 and 1830, with most coming from the eastern, northern and western counties. There were women who worked as couriers, carrying five, six or even more infants packed together in a basket. William Dudley Wodsworth related how some babies were sent to the Foundling Hospital because of multiple births or some physical defect. Many failed to reach the place, having died in transit or – in the final decades – being abandoned nearby at the Grand Canal when they were refused admission. In the three decades after 1730 at least four fifths of the infants died soon after entry. The death rate reached nearly ninety per cent during the 1780s. In reality, mortality was even higher, and the hospital records were falsified. Pressure on space built up rapidly during the 1770s, and the governors tightened the rules. Entry was confined to infants under one year old,

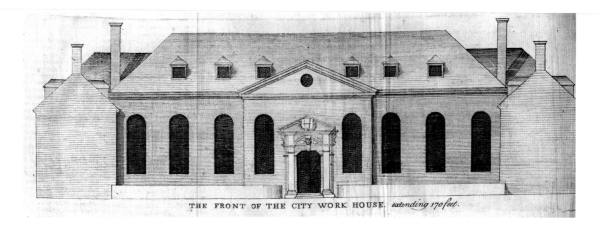

THE FRONT OF THE CITY WORK HOUSE, *extending 170 feet*.

and during the 1780s over two thousand of these children were taken in annually – that is, about six every day.

The Foundling Hospital. (*Dublin Magazine*, July 1762) (DCC)

It would appear that the number of infants received at the hospital during the Georgian era exceeded two hundred thousand. The food was bad and the sanitary accommodation was primitive. On arrival the children were branded and consigned to dark cellars where the only light came through a shaft. The general public could only see them when they were allowed out for church services. Onlookers at St Thomas' church were appalled at their condition. They angrily berated the minders, directing outrage at the supervisor who rode a horse 'more like a Negro-driver than one to take care of the children of charity'.[16]

The 'reasonable punishment' allowed by law against recalcitrant foundlings included a beating by birch or cane and being placed in the black hole. During the 1730s the punishment for runaways was whipping over several days followed by confinement in the dungeon chained to a wooden block. Children sent out to work did not escape this climate of fear, and there were frequent records of apprentices escaping due to the abuse. Wodsworth found that a substantial number of the young lads later died in the service of the British army.[17]

During the second half of the eighteenth century it was widely believed that most infants left in anonymously were tainted with syphilis. This attitude made it difficult to find foster parents because of the widespread belief that venereal disease was transmitted to any wet nurse who fed them. Yet up to five infants were farmed out to each wet nurse, who often was already undernourished. In its desperation the hospital considered options such as killing those infants who arrived with suspected VD; there was an attitude towards 'sinful' diseases like syphilis that allowed this approach. The children concerned got no medicines save for a tranquilliser called diacodium that allowed them to die quietly. In the period

1810–16 well over five thousand children were killed in this way. The hospital surgeon told an inquiry in 1813 that wet nurses refused to take the mercury that was necessary to cure the infants. He added that even if the children recovered, they would remain an excessive burden on the state.[18] Thousands of children suffering from smallpox were likewise dispatched to the infirmary and left there to die. This approach inevitably attracted political attention. The mercy killing of sick children was endorsed by Lord Altamont. When he addressed the House of Lords in 1797 the expression he used was 'to put an end to whose experience with pistol shot would be a humane act.' It is clear that Altamont's view was endorsed by the executive because he was appointed as a governor of the place.[19]

Such a sensitive agenda was sure to leave little commitment to an official record, but when allowance is made for the great mortality it can be seen how this institution became an agent in curbing population growth. When we add to the number of officially admitted infants all the others who were dumped around the city, we can see the scale of the problem. Wodsworth cited several comparable European establishments operating in Spain, Russia and elsewhere, but what marked out the Dublin hospital for him was its selective treatment of

This view of the Foundling Hospital does not betray the appalling conditions inside. (From J. Warburton, Revd J. Whitelaw and Revd R. Walsh, *History of the City of Dublin*, 1818)

Catholics. There were two official objectives: to take in the unwanted illegitimate children and to raise them in the Protestant religion. It soon became clear that it was unable to achieve this. When Protestant wet nurses could not be found, Catholic women had to be employed, and this undermined the process. Efforts were made by the hospital to prevent foster children becoming too attached to their Catholic nurses, and sanctions awaited those who did not bend to the rules. A survivor of the regime told Wodsworth how, on Fridays, children were force-fed with meat-based broth. Those refusing to practise the official religion were struck off the books – that is to say, they were left to starve or to fend for themselves elsewhere.

At the same time, these youngsters were outcasts in the eyes of the city's Catholics, who feared that proselytism had damaged them. When they were brought to the lord mayor for inspection, they needed protection from irate Catholic bystanders. Religious bigotry remained a feature of the post-Union capital. From 1801 it was decreed that charity children were to be apprenticed to good Protestant employers. Threats were then made against anyone taking on these youngsters.

In the post-Union decades there was a rapid growth in the proportion of foundlings surviving the regime. By then the vast majority were living long enough to be boarded out to Catholic wet nurses. When hospital funds ran low, the governors sought assistance to take more of the children into Protestant care. Their petition cited their mission of promoting the Protestant interest in a city abounding with papists of the lowest rank. In the mid-1820s, when the improving health of children became an excessive burden for the hospital, over six hundred of them were sent to the Charter Schools for a Protestant formation. Of course, the improving lot of those resident foundlings had terrible implications for those excluded. It is impossible to gauge the number of young children who died outside.[20]

Support for adult paupers

As the pressure on institutional space built up, the authorities considered other options. Certain beggars were allowed to remain on the streets provided they were better disciplined. As we have seen, this included the granting of permits, and from the 1750s onwards messengers and porters were added to those required to have a licence. This law was later extended to those selling newspapers and to boys cleaning shoes or carrying baskets from the markets. Hamilton's *Cries of Dublin* shows a newspaper seller wearing one of these badges.[21]

The poverty and distress of the people surpass all description. If something is not speedily done for their relief, 'tis hard to say what may be the consequences.

Henry Ellis, 1773[22]

Over time the range of places taking in the needy was expanded. Amongst the new venues was the Hospital for Incurables, an institution set up as an almshouse due to overcrowding at the House of Industry. It had a riverside location at Townsend Street. In 1744 the Incurables gave notice that all the city's mendicants had to enter the place without delay. The reason given was the same as before: these people were an offensive spectacle. This policy arose from public frustration, but the challenge for the Incurables got worse. It is not clear how the institution tended its hopeless patients, but twenty years later it was caring for vagrants who were 'disgusting to all, and dangerous in their effects to many beholders'.[23]

The Incurables made an impressive start, but it became so overcrowded that admission was restricted to the most offensive spectacles. These included prostitutes in the terminal stages of VD. These women were disturbed, and the hospital could not cope with their behaviour. In 1792 there was a big surge in the number of sick females arriving from the House of Industry. This proved to be a breaking point as this new contingent of 120 women overwhelmed the place. The Incurables had to admit failure, and the manager rendered up the establishment.[24]

In 1803 Cork Street Fever Hospital was opened, and in reality served as an asylum that took in allcomers, including expectant mothers when there were spare beds. In times of emergency, such as 1818–19 and 1826, there were almost five hundred patients. On those occasions overcrowding was so severe that half the inmates were kept in tents spread over the adjoining grounds.[25]

Wandering waifs were regularly banished to the countryside, where there was supposed to be plenty of seasonal work. These efforts failed because the down-and-outs refused to budge. Beggars got louder and bolder, and, seeing strength in numbers, quickly surrounded any passing coach that held out the prospect of a reward. They harassed pedestrians and rounded on vulnerable women or elderly men. Most Catholics lived in back streets and found it difficult to go to Mass on Sunday without passing through hordes of pleading beggars. The possibility of being committed to an institution no longer had much effect when there was hardly any place to put them. It was conceded that mere punishment was no longer enough. One proposed alternative was to round up the sturdiest male offenders and enlist them in the navy.[26] Affluent parishes took their own initiatives, and these were encouraged by proclamations from the lord mayor. St Anne's set up a special fund to assist those paupers included in the Poor List; bread was distributed and coal was supplied at reasonable prices. These schemes were, however, part of a carrot-and-stick approach. During the 1770s St Anne's hired beadles to round up vagrant sturdy beggars and dispatch them to the House of Industry.[27]

> If the offspring of these wretches were obliged to weed, pick up stones, card and spin, we need not have any idle hands in the kingdom ... Blind people may turn many kinds of mills, play on musick, card, spin, weave, row in boats, and carry burthens.
>
> *Faulkner's Dublin Journal*, 20 October 1747

As early as the 1760s some observers accepted that poverty could be due to factors outside an individual's control, and that victims of misfortune should have some call on assistance. The north–south division in the city's social gradient was carried over into this sphere. As the burden of social welfare increased, more agencies were transferred north across the Liffey. In 1772 legislation was brought in to implement these policies. At its heart was the setting up of a new House of Industry. It set out four distinct categories of entry: poor helpless adults, male and female; adult males classed as either vagabonds or sturdy beggars; and street prostitutes in need of medical care but who were still fit enough for manual labour. In reality, a policy of indiscriminate admission was followed.

This new workhouse provided support services, including three hospitals: the Hardwicke (1803), the Richmond (1811) and the Whitworth (1817), which became known collectively as the Richmond. This regime reflected the public opinion that laid more emphasis on individual discipline and personal reform. It was a repressive system and punishment was inflicted on those people who refused to work. More emphasis was placed on personal hygiene; no pauper with a 'squalid' appearance was given leave of absence, and women who did not comb their hair were liable to have it all cut off. This crusade singled out streetwalkers for severe sanction. Sentences for them began with two months' hard labour for the first offence, this being doubled for each subsequent infringement, so that a fifth offence attracted four years' detention. Youngsters accompanying unlicensed beggars could also be taken into custody; those under eight could be dispatched to the Charter Schools, while the rest could be apprenticed to some trade.[28]

This regime reflected the underlying centralisation of social control. In 1773 the policing of poverty was transferred from the parishes to the corporation. The regime spread its net wider and tightened the definition of offences. These campaigns were aimed at people regarded as fraudsters – beggars who pretended to be dealers hawking goods about the streets. They were seen as unlicensed mendicants who should be treated as vagabonds. Parliament took the view that there were too many young people doing outdoor tasks that could be done by inmates of the House of Industry, and disabled individuals were substituted for the able-bodied to reduce costs. Those inmates who got clothing had to pay for it through extra work.[29]

✳ ✳ ✳ ✳ ✳

By the late 1780s the homes of the poorest residents in the Liberties were likened to fever hospitals occupied by ghost-like figures. Some well-off families responded to this catastrophe with donations of food. The Pauper Soup given to distressed households was made from leftover beef, vegetables and stale bread. By the time Samuel Rosborough published his observations in 1801, conditions were much worse. Of the eight thousand poor people he saw in the streets, nearly three thousand were begging children, while another two thousand had arrived from the countryside. He claimed Dublin's attractions for newcomers included greater personal security and several sources of charity. John Gamble (1810) agreed that public charity could explain the extraordinary number of beggars. He was a well-travelled observer and believed London was less crowded with beggars on account of the absence of public charity.[30]

Mothers were blamed for the misfortunes of their children. Women were singled out by the evangelists for the worst tongue-lashing. They were scolded for being idle and lazy when they should be at useful tasks such as knitting and spinning. In 1789 one newspaper asserted there were twenty thousand female layabouts in the city. In reality, men were forcing women out of the workplace. During the mid-1760s at least four hundred women silk weavers were expelled from their looms by male colleagues. These females had very little bargaining power. Over the following decades they turned to the leading ladies of society for help. In one plea, dated 1794, a group of unemployed women explained that men had taken a thousand of their jobs and that these included linen drapers, mercers, milliners, haberdashers, perfumers and toy sellers.[31]

Statistics indicate the House of Industry had a rapid turnover of inmates, and there could be several reasons for this. For the able-bodied the novelty wore off when the tedium of grinding work set in. Frequent escapes and high mortality left plenty of beds empty. Between 1775 and 1820 the average annual intake was almost 7,400, but the usual stay was just two months. The average number of inmates during the 1780s was about 1,540, but this increased to about 1,700 in the late 1790s. There was a spike in 1800, a year of near-famine, when the number reached 8,020. This surge overwhelmed the place because there were only 772 beds available. Despite the terrible mortality, the authorities felt the regime was drawing in too many undeserving individuals. In 1800 the feeding regime and medical services were severely cut back. In order to discourage idlers the diet was reduced to below what an industrious labourer could obtain on the lowest wages. There was to be no place for people who could be maintained outside by friends. More of those now admitted were labouring under the pressure of age and destitution.

The House of Industry set up a public soup kitchen to cater for two categories of people: the employed identified as industrious mechanics and the unemployed categorised as the impotent poor. Price reductions were offered to the usefully employed, and it is clear that this initiative had an immediate impact because the soup kitchen served 6,431 people in its first three weeks.[32]

> In Dublin, laziness in filth and rags, squanders away time till want comes on, and then setting up its pride against the mean pursuits of honest industry, prefers the genteeler occupation of begging, and exhibits a reproach to the folly of benevolence, by carrying on that bounty which the aged or the orphan should only enjoy.
>
> *The Freeman's Journal*, 21 November 1793

The House of Industry played an important role, but some of its supporters were too easily impressed. Pool and Cash, in their study of Dublin architecture (1780), lauded the place for saving the public from rude impostors. George Faulkner, the famous printer and publisher, believed it had banished ninety per cent of the beggars from the streets, thereby allowing householders to remove security devices. R. Lewis (1787) was more accurate when he stated the House of Industry was set up to relieve wealthy citizens from the demands of beggars who besieged them at every turn.[33]

A substantial number of those in the House of Industry were helpless creatures. In 1782 forty-five per cent were classified as sick or injured, and of the rest two per cent were blind and twelve per cent were children. Yet these statistics should be treated with caution. A majority of inmates was officially deemed unemployed, but this figure hardly allowed for the growing proportion of lunatics and feeble

The seal of the workhouse attested to its purported reforming function, 1749. (From *By-laws, Rules and Orders Made by the Governors*, 1749) (DCC)

old people. The records also suggest that the proportion forcibly detained was small: only fourteen per cent were compelled to stay. This figure is probably too low. In 1819, for example, about one third of patients were so weak that they had to be fed in their beds. Any interpretation should also allow for the desire of the operators to maximise the number of workers.

Funding for the House of Industry was provided from the grand jury presentments, with state grants and private subscriptions making up the remainder. In 1778 there was much controversy over the local tax. It was argued that it should be levied nationally because half the beggars came from the country. Moreover, the system penalised commuters renting a house in the outskirts because they were taxed twice. This remained a contentious issue, and it was eventually conceded by the government that entry should be limited to the people of Dublin, the only exception being lunatics.[34]

The House of Industry was subject to numerous allegations of mismanagement. Where conditions were so precarious it was easy for the manager to increase his income, and he extorted large sums from beggars who were blind and lame. There were eight parliamentary inquiries in the half-century following 1725, and it is clear the manager adopted various stratagems to secure public funds. He doubled the number of inmates during parliamentary sittings by rounding up the noisiest offenders, while at the same time threatening to release them again if public funding did not increase.[35]

During the 1770s around one thousand street beggars had permits – for example, 1,200 in 1772 and 980 in 1773; each badge cost five shillings and expired after six months. There was a growing belief that this system was getting out of hand, with too many disparate authorities granting licences. In 1773 the badging function passed from the parishes to the city corporation; this was intended to control all beggars within two miles of the Castle.[36]

By 1800 the House of Industry was advancing 'social tranquillity' as a major element of its mission. It used more female labour and claimed this would undermine the workers' combinations that were exclusively operated by men. Moreover, women were paid much less and their employment would remove the temptation for them to enter prostitution. It would also reduce public drunkenness. The jobs given to girls included frame hosiery and shoemaking, while the boys were put to weaving, carpentry and wood turning.[37] After the Union, allegations of corruption about the House of Industry persisted, and it was asserted that the governors covered up these offences. One doctor blew the whistle on a colleague who never turned up for work.[38] For its part the institution defended its reputation, stating it had to deal with distressed people from wretched backgrounds. It claimed to have great success, curing eighty-five per cent of fever patients and seventy per cent of the lunatics.

In 1812 work began on a new penitentiary in a greenfield site at Grangegorman. It was designed on the model advocated by John Howard, providing solitary confinement (see chapter nine). By the 1820s the reforming function of the House of Industry was abandoned and it became a receptacle for dependent people of all sorts. Warburton, Whitelaw and Walsh's *History of the City of Dublin* (1818) described the residents as 'the compelled and the profligate'. Half the occupants were old and infirm, and the other half comprised orphans and lunatics.[39]

Unemployment and distress

> There is no man who wears the least appearance of ability for alms giving, who can walk the streets of Dublin, without being importuned by two hundred beggars per day.
>
> *The Freeman's Journal*, 5 September 1793

Businessmen were upset by the beggars who swarmed between the Castle and Trinity College, concentrating on College Green, Dame Street and Capel Street, as well as the Temple Bar area. Traders argued that the middle class suffered the most as the paupers crowded about their doors, refusing to go away without a payment. Shopkeepers' families were especially vulnerable; a man's pregnant wife was shocked by the diseases and deformities, while his sister or daughter could not leave home without being pursued by mendicants. Within the affluent areas of Merrion Square, St Stephen's Green, Sackville Street and Rutland Square, the beggars were compared to a mosquito infestation. Those offenders entering

St Stephen's Green were described as lusty fellows, pursuing passers-by with blasphemous imprecations, 'idle and sturdy beggarwomen too, with their faces daubed with oaker, or exhibiting some filthy cancer to public view, which must attend with dangerous consequences to so many of the fair sex, as well as cause their feelings to shudder'.[40] As early as 1752 it was claimed that the licensed beggars of St Mary's parish were so successful that their badges were traded at high prices. Some licences were withdrawn.[41]

> Will not the collected numbers, that are promiscuously crowded together for the purposes of manufacture, engender contagion, not less fatal to the morals, than that which their unwholesome haunts daily send forth, is found to be to the health of the lower classes of the community?
>
> Revd William Magee, 1796[42]

Distress was associated with industrial recessions, and severe unrest became an established feature of city life by the 1750s.[43] Conditions in 1757, a near-famine year, were alarming, and it was claimed that twenty thousand people were suffering. A fund was set up to relieve unemployed weavers, and the threat of starvation led some of them to collect waste from slaughterhouses. The desperate search for morsels was noticed by visitors in crisis years; in 1839 a German visitor saw poor people at the markets devouring the half-eaten vegetables dropped by cattle.[44]

During the 1760s imports of English cloth put pressure on Irish products, and this came at a time when rising prices were causing great stress in the Liberties. By 1771 the corporation was giving a bounty to men enlisting in the navy. It was argued that the labour-intensive textile industry was unsuited to an urban location; it should be transferred to a rural situation, where living costs were lower. This initiative was supported by the *Hibernian Journal*. It stressed that intensive, low-paid production had no place in the city; the comfort and cleanliness of the countryside were much preferable to the squalid misery of the Liberties.[45]

The government gave subsidies to out-of-town initiatives. In the early 1780s distressed families were told about ventures such as Robert Brooke's new mill at Prosperous, County Kildare. Brooke got strong support from the state for his factory-scale production (23 & 24 Geo. III, c.12 [Ire.]), and built houses and shops for his workers. Brooke's efforts had an early success, and 224 persons moved from Dublin during November 1783. These arrivals included sixty-five weavers. Total employment may have reached two thousand that year. In 1786 Brooke boasted that his new arrivals included over three hundred families, along with a notable number of single men. His success was not as strong as it appeared, and he had to concede the people coming to his factory were desperate individuals. Many of them arrived in the depth of winter with just the clothes they wore.[46]

Workers who remained behind in the Liberties strongly resented Brooke's methods, and violently attacked any weavers from Prosperous who did business in the city. The Earl of Meath was concerned at the growing number of vacant houses within his Liberty estate, and considered clearing the entire area for redevelopment. As conditions continued to deteriorate in the early 1790s groups of journeymen could be seen begging for the price of a passage to England.[47] A vivid account of this degradation coincided with the Union of 1801:

> In those parts of the city where a house is so far fallen into decay as to be unfit for the habitation of any decent family, the lower floor is generally let to a publican or huxter, and the remainder in separate apartments. In these wretched tenements from six to ten persons are not infrequently crowded into one room; the house undergoes no repair, no provision is made for cleaning.[48]

As we have seen in chapter four, the post-1800 accounts of physical disintegration might be too easily attributed to the Union. The calamity was coming in any event. Dr William Drennan, the city doctor already mentioned, saw some benefit in the various relief schemes, but thought they merely provided a temporary respite. He believed wider reforms were needed, including a tax on English fabrics that were being dumped on the Irish market.[49]

The contribution made by the parishes to social welfare was hit hard by their declining fortunes. St Anne's found its Poor Fund was in arrears: the seventy-six families on the Poor List in 1800 could no longer expect the same support. The vestry blamed this setback on the fall-off in subscriptions, the sharp rise in dependants and a spike in the price of bread (1800 being a near-famine year). Over the following decades the situation got much worse, and by the 1830s St Anne's was spending two fifths of the parish dues on deserted children. In light of the relative wealth of St Anne's, there must be questions about the plight of other parishes. The national system of poor relief did not arrive until 1838.[50]

Rehabilitation

> Be vile and vicious if you please,
> But why communicate disease?
> Or if you must extend the evil
> Why lead your children to the devil?
>
> Anon., 1805[51]

Public concern about brothels included consideration of a location policy, and potential areas included the urban fringe and back alleys away from main streets. One campaigner called for a designated quarter, as in Italian cities, where brothels would pay an annual £50 licence, and where the working women would wear distinguishing outfits, like uniforms. The opening of the Lock Hospital in 1755 coincided with a moral crusade drawing attention to female victims of the sex business. Its leaders were public figures who took a different view of the working women, and they offered support to those leaving the trade. Over the following decades several safe havens were founded, and these places catered mainly for younger females. In exchange for shelter, these women had to work in the workshops and laundry. Rehabilitation typically lasted two or three years, and it had a strong religious aspect.[52]

A public meeting at Fishamble Street Music Hall in 1766 led to the foundation of the Magdalen Asylum. It received government support and opened two years later in Leeson Street. The Magdalen catered for young women (under twenty) and had places for fifty residents. Over the following five decades it admitted a total of eight hundred females. By 1790 it was overwhelmed by the demand, and made a public appeal for help. It sought a new secluded situation out on the urban fringe and away from all main roads. This location policy was supported by some city doctors who proposed that all medical hospitals should be excluded from the city; they claimed that a rural setting was an essential element of the cure.[53] Female reformatories took account of that advice. The Lock Penitentiary (1794) chose a peripheral site at Dorset Street, taking in three hundred women during its first decade. It functioned as a workhouse and was also known as the Bethesda. Similarly peripheral was the Dublin Female Penitentiary (c. 1811) on the North Circular Road, where 175 women were admitted in the first decade. By 1821 accommodation was also provided by the Female Penitents Asylum in Bow Street (thirty-four residents) and the General Asylum in Townsend Street (thirty-seven residents).[54]

McGregor's New Picture of Dublin (1821) devoted an entire section to institutions for the reformation of manners. These were places for former prostitutes, accommodating about 220 females. It is likely that a proportion of these females were seeking a respite, while others considered acquiring a skill in craftwork or domestic service. The demand for places was always unsatisfied, and in the post-Union decade there were over ten candidates for each vacancy at the Lock Penitentiary.[55]

There was also a demand for female orphanages to keep girls away from prostitution, and these places likewise favoured peripheral locations. In 1790 an orphanage was founded in Prussia Street and three years later it moved to the North Circular Road. It was intended that the girls, on reaching sixteen years of age, would find employment as servants or apprentices. There were other proposals to reform the youngest females (under thirteen), including spinning schools where the remedies would include hard labour. In 1786 a detention centre opened at the Bridewell to accommodate prostitutes and vagrants. It was given a strict regime, not releasing any prostitute until she had two respectable housekeepers to vouch for her. *The Freeman's Journal* asked the government to divert one third of the city jails budget to the promotion of religion amongst poor children.[56]

THE
STATUTES
AT LARGE,

PASSED IN THE

PARLIAMENTS

HELD IN

IRELAND.

VOL. VII.

Containing from the Twenty-third Year of GEORGE the
Second, A. D. 1749, to the Firſt Year of GEORGE the
Third, A. D. 1761 incluſive.

PUBLISHED BY AUTHORITY.

DUBLIN:

Printed by BOULTER GRIERSON, Printer to the King's Moſt Excellent
Majeſty. MDCCLXV.

Dublin's parliamentary function created jobs for many tradesmen, including printers.

8

The Interface of Criminality and Immorality

The growing licentiousness of the times, especially with respect to matrimonial infidelity, is so alarming …

The Freeman's Journal, 19 October 1771

THE DEFECTIVE LEGAL SYSTEM MADE urban reform difficult. The carriage of justice was easily overturned. In Dublin, as in London, ordinary householders found it difficult to get reliable legal advice; solicitors were more interested in working for wealthy clients who would retain their services in the future. Anybody making an official complaint about an assault was detained along with the attacker, and both parties were locked up overnight. Many offences went unreported as the legal process was far too cumbersome.

> The custom of mutual charges and detention though well designed, is converted to the worst purposes, and often becomes an instrument of peculation, or illegal imprisonment, as it is in the power of a common thief or prostitute to confine an honest person for the night, whose only mode of expiring such indignity and inconvenience, is a bribe, or perhaps forgiveness of an insult or attack.[1]

Urban dissolution

Streetwalkers were regarded as agents of crime. In one of the worst incidents five men were killed in a Copper Alley brothel and the madam later paid with her life. Brothels attracted customers who traded stolen goods for favours. Highwaymen shared their booty with these women, and prostitutes collaborated in serious crimes, including highway robbery. Manifestations of this 'entente' increased after the mid-1780s, with more brothels harbouring criminal gangs. Prostitutes joined offenders at the shelters of the sedan chairmen in order to learn about new victims. In 1791 an inquiry by Justice Walsh attributed the crime wave to brothels, night houses and smoking clubs. He described these venues as dealing houses for lawbreakers. Dorset Street had a particular notoriety, and other black spots included Essex Street and Great Strand Street.[2]

> Prostitutes emerged from the stews of King's Head Court [...] through the filthy nuisance of a passage that leads into George's Street, and these meeting their robbing associates of all distinctions, they retire to two famous whiskey-forges upon the same spot and after maddening themselves with liquid poison, sally forth, committing every depredation and insult they can.
>
> *The Freeman's Journal*, 26 November 1795

Prostitutes attacked people passing through their soliciting places. During the mid-1790s the Dame Street/George's Street corner had a bad reputation – even worse than the infamous Blind Quay. Every night prostitutes and footpads emerged from King's Head Court to block Dame Street. *The Freeman's Journal* called for the closure of the offending public houses. The parish watch raided one of them, detaining fifteen women, who were sent off to the House of Correction.[3] More raids followed in Exchequer Street, Cope Street and Sycamore Alley. Residents of Cope Street expressed relief when a tottering bawdy house was boarded up by the sheriff. The trouble spread, however, and one woman was killed during a melee at Trinity Street. Disturbances continued at King's Head Court, and passers-by were jostled to provoke quarrels so that they might be robbed.[4]

Margaret McClean was possibly the most successful bawd in Georgian Dublin, and she amassed a fortune from the 'plunder by apprentices, shop-men, clerks, and others entrusted with property'. In 1780 the *Hibernian Journal* blamed the rampant crime on the multitude of brothels in which bawds enticed young

A cartoon view of a notorious night house on the Liffey quays, c. 1820. The pipe-smoking harridan is in charge. (From A Real Paddy [Pierce Egan], *Real Life in Ireland*, 1821)

men to cohabit with a doxy, and where these men, aged between fifteen and twenty-five, were inveigled into the gambling dens, where the toughest criminals led them further astray.[5] This period was recalled by the rake Buck Whaley (1768–1800) when he described how he set up a woman named Courtney:

> I hired her a magnificent house, suitably furnished, and settled an allowance of five hundred a year on her: this was merely pro forma, for she cost me upwards of five thousand. At her house I kept my midnight orgies, and saw my friends, according to the fashionable acceptation of the word.[6]

According to the *Hibernian Journal*, ballad singers hastened the growth in crime: street songsters drew innocents into the school of infamy, where the prostitutes completed the infernal science. The *Dublin Journal* proposed a novel solution, calling for these women to be rounded up and sent to the US and the West Indies, where white women were urgently needed.[7] The women sometimes retaliated against the hypocrisy. One episode from 1795 stood out on account of the unusual details. When a prostitute gave birth to a baby boy, the father wanted nothing to do with her. The spurned mother then went around to the home of the old codger at Granby Row and left the infant at his door. The child was found with a message pinned to his clothing:

" The Night before Larry was ftretch'd," &c.

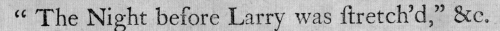

An Irifh Slang Song ;   to be pronounced as fpelled.

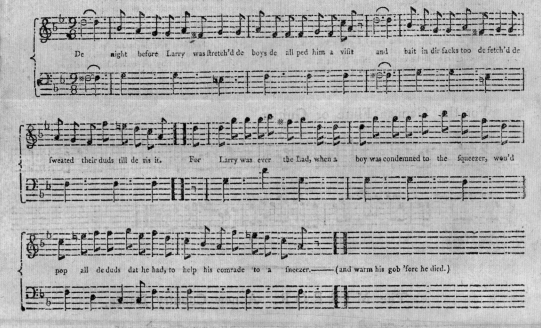

De   night   before   Larry   was ftretch'd de   boys de   all ped him a   visit   and   bait in dir facks too   de fetch'd de

fweated   their duds till de ris it.   For   Larry   was   ever   the Lad, when a   boy was condemned to   the   squeezer,   wou'd

pop   all   de duds   dat   he had,   to   help   his   comrade   to   a   fneezer.———(and warm his gob 'fore he died.)

II.

De Boys de came crowding in faft,
De drew all their Stools round about him,
Nine Glims round his Trapcase were plac'd,
  Oh ! he cou'd not be well wak'd widout dem ;
When one of us ax'd " cou'd he die
  Widout having truly repented ?"
Says Larry, " dat's all in my eye,"
  And fut by de clergy invented
    (To fatten dir gobs wid a bit.)

III.

I'm sorry, dear Larry, says I,
  To see you in dis Sittiation,
And blifter my limbs if I lie,
  But Id's liff it had been my own ftation ;
Oghone ! its all over, faid he,
  For de neck-cloth I'll be forc'd to put on,
And by dis time to-morrow you'll see
  Your poor Larry as dead as a mutton,
    (Bekaife why my caufe it was good.)

IV.

De Clargy ftep'd up wid his book,
  And fpoke him fo nate and fo civil,
Larry tip'd him a Kilmainham look,
  And pitch'd his big wig to de Devil ;
Den gently raifing his head
  He took a fup out of de Bottle,
And fighing moft bitterly faid,
  Oh ! de Hemp will be foon round my trottle.
    (And fqueeze my poor windpipe to death.)

Note—The Words between Parenthefis to be fpoken in the Slang Stile.

Dear Sir,

Though I am not quite sure you are the father of this little one, I am certain you had a finger in the 'pie' – and very sure I am, you can better afford to father it than any of your 'assistants' on the occasion. So, presenting you the babe, as a monument of your 'vigour', a surety for the continuance of your race, an heir for your fortune, and a diverting companion for your declining years,

I remain,
Your unfortunate,
Incognita[8]

✳ ✳ ✳ ✳ ✳

Besides constant abuse from bawds and bullies, prostitutes were also attacked by fellow workers. In 1780 a streetwalker in South King Street was severely injured by butcher boys hired by a rival to kill her. In Capel Street a battle between rival brothels lasted four hours. The crowd joined in, throwing stones and breaking windows before order was restored by the parish watch. Students from Trinity College regarded these women as fair game for their own pranks, and assaulted streetwalkers who came too close to the campus. Attacks by students were regularly followed by wider disturbances.[9]

Some of the bodies taken from the Liffey were victims of erotic misadventure. These deaths were supposed to go unnoticed but sometimes turned up in the newspapers. In one episode during 1785 two bodies were thrown into the river beside Capel Street Bridge, and in 1788 the mutilated body of a prostitute was lifted from the Liffey at George's Quay. In another incident during the mid-1790s two women were found drowned after soliciting the crews of several vessels. Some of the women found in the river were suicide victims. In 1790, for example, a woman who was prevented from drowning herself explained that a man tricked her into prostitution and then abandoned her.[10] Newborn babies from riverside brothels were suffocated and thrown into the Liffey or dumped in graveyards and dunghills. There must, however, be uncertainty about the circumstances of infanticide. There were procurers who could be hired to carry out the work. When a young woman in Kevin's Port was accused of this crime, her defence was that she had been specifically hired to kill the baby.[11]

Homosexuality was a topic that the newspapers largely avoided. Where it did receive attention the incident was reported in an obscure manner. In 1792, for example, *The Freeman's Journal* described how an adult male propositioned a young man in Essex Street. The instigator, who was dressed as a clergyman, made 'an indecent attempt'. He was stoutly resisted and beaten up. According to the newspaper, this punishment was richly deserved because any such 'detestable attempt' required a stiffer sanction.[12]

Collusion by the police

> If a knot of prostitutes be seen in consultation, a watchman is sure to be in the midst of them.
>
> *The Freeman's Journal*, 16 March 1797

There were persistent claims that public houses and brothels were set up by constables who had been convicted of theft. Members of the watch were easily bribed: they got alcohol from soliciting women, and douceurs of any kind were tempting because they were so badly paid.[13] In the early 1790s the grand jury found that prostitutes in Newgate had ready access to the male prisoners. At the Four Courts Marshalsea the governor increased his income by renting apartments to bullies keeping their prostitutes there. Some reforms were made to the watch, and several notorious brothels were cleared of customers. Before long, however, the newspapers renewed their condemnation. They claimed the officers had turned their own jobs into sinecures – they had abandoned their posts and gone off to the seaside to spend their ill-gotten gains. It was claimed that any females being detained were released the following morning.[14]

> Surely no watchman acquits his duty who suffers such women to roam the streets at unreasonable hours of the night, and disturb whole neighbourhoods by their hideous screams, and drunken gambols.
>
> *The Freeman's Journal*, 10 October 1795

Some watchmen were charged with extortion from brothels, others with falsely imprisoning prostitutes who refused to pay. By the mid-1790s it was argued that these women formed the watch's main source of income. The force was described as 'the accomplice of riot, the assaulter of defenceless institutions, the advance guard of the night-house, and the bully of the brothel'. The inactivity of the magistrates was attributed to most of them being merchants. Bawds bought their wine from

those merchants currently in office, and if that failed the magistrates were bribed.[15]

Prostitution was blamed for many army crimes. Soldiers broke open the jails to release their favourite women, and in one incident the troops set free sixty females from the House of Industry. All ranks were involved in extortion from brothels, and those refusing payment were ransacked. A riot erupted in 1778 when soldiers tried to force their way into a Ross Lane brothel to 'levy' a contribution. They fired on two passers-by who tried to stop them, seriously wounding one man. That incident caused soldiers to be confined to barracks for a while.

Soldiers themselves were often beaten up and robbed in the riverside brothels. That was the fate of four troops who spent time in a Lazer's Hill bordello in 1777. In 1780 a soldier was seriously wounded as he left an Essex Street brothel; he was attacked by the women, and his comrades retaliated violently. A passing sedan-chair man was killed in the riot that followed.[16]

Connections between prostitution and gambling

> We see beardless boys turning their backs on modesty, ridiculing the admonitions of grand-sires, and aping all the ridiculous extravagance of dress, and all the profligacy of the brothel, the gaming house and the tavern.
>
> *The Freeman's Journal*, 2 January 1796

The association between prostitution and gaming brought certain night houses to the attention of the police. These venues were concentrated within the Temple

Bar area and extended up towards the Castle. During the 1760s there were several hotspots in Cork Hill, and Swan Alley was a notorious resort of gamblers. There were numerous stamps (gambling houses) in Smock Alley; they included Madden's at the Globe, Reilly's in an adjoining tavern and another at Ben Johnson's Head, also a tavern. These places did well until the arrival of the Royal Exchange in 1779. That development raised the tone of the area, and many gaming warrens were cleared out to make way for the finer engines of finance.[17]

An example of the corruption around gaming houses was provided by Francis Higgins, the man contemptuously described as the 'Sham Squire'. In the 1780s he operated a large gaming centre near the Castle, fronting onto Parliament Street, Essex Street and Crane Lane. Following complaints from neighbours it was eventually raided by the magistrates. Higgins, however, had enough influence to overcome all opposition:

> When lo! A wonder 'midst the noisy crew,
> Came bailiffs, aldermen and sheriffs too:
> But when they came within my powerful reign
> Down dropt the mace, the ermine and the chain.
> They came in magistrates and went out men.
> Such was the influence of the magic wand
> That great Shamado wielded in his hand.[18]

Dublin was hardly exceptional in this regard. Extortion from London brothels took a similar form: watchmen received payments from soliciting women, and lawmen helped them to plunder the customers. Officials investigating public houses accepted bribes from the publicans, and magistrates collaborated with the brewers to prevent brothel closures.[19]

The alleged motive in raiding premises was moralistic: to save young men from ruin. It was claimed that late-night gambling interfered with work performance. There was concern, too, at the substantial amounts spent by apprentices and servants. However, repressive methods were used to enforce the law, especially when the activity breached the Sabbath. The lord mayor organised several raids, demolishing gambling tables and arresting participants.[20] Like the brothels, many gambling dens were in houses let out by magistrates because these uses attracted higher rents. Magistrates were casual in giving out public-house permits. In 1793 504 licences were issued for the city and county, but less than ten per cent of the applicants had the necessary certificate of fitness.[21]

This culture of equivocation survived up to the end of the Georgian era.

In 1812 a group of concerned citizens complained to the viceroy that police corruption reached right up to the highest levels. Their petition claimed the magistrates colluded with the gambling dens, and it named those senior officials who took backhanders. A detective named John O'Neill was cited as one of the most bent officials: he owned two gambling houses in Essex Street. Similarly, a magistrate named Joshua Dixon received backhanders from the most lucrative casinos. It was claimed that six gambling houses operated within a few hundred metres of the police headquarters. The worst offender was identified as Daly's of College Green, and others included M'Coen's (Exchequer Street), Molloy's (Crow Street), Dowling's (Palace Street), Byrne's (Essex Street) and Thornton's (Crow Street) – all Catholic surnames.[22]

Initiatives in controlling the sex trade

> I pray keep good hours, don't be a disgrace,
> To be taken at night by a guard of Police:
> You know the Commissioner's ordered the same,
> To take up all vagrants and girls of game.
>
> Anon., 'A New Song on the Police Guards', *c.* 1786

From time to time efforts were made to suppress prostitution. In 1765–66 the lord mayor cleared out several brothels in St John's parish, and the women were committed to hard labour. During 1770 the constable of St Andrew's helped the residents of Dame Street and Essex Street to banish notorious streetwalkers. Another campaign was undertaken in 1796 by one of the sheriffs; he encouraged the magistrates to control those brothels and gambling dens that were attracting young people. When his call went unheeded he acted with the lord mayor to close down brothels selling spirits without a licence. He also rounded up all the prostitutes and pickpockets he came across.[23]

These campaigns could only reflect the zeal of the participants. In many cases prostitutes were driven from one parish into another, usually where the local residents were too lazy to control them. In 1781 the *Hibernian Journal* assured its readers that the notorious Essex Street had assumed a tranquil atmosphere, yet eight months later it had to concede it was so crowded with streetwalkers that normal traffic could not pass through. By the late 1790s it was claimed that Dame Street had more soliciting women than London's Strand. In 1799 fifty-seven prostitutes were detained by St Stephen's watchmen in a single night.[24]

Guests on their way to Dublin Castle, *c.* 1820. Note the mitred bishops in the background, also hoping for patronage. (From A Real Paddy [Pierce Egan], *Real Life in Ireland*, 1821)

9

Public Opinion and the Prevailing Ethos

THE GEORGIAN ERA WITNESSED PROFOUND social change. A new template was created for each person's dealings with the wider community.[1] Change was driven by a secular form of puritanism that placed a high value on self-discipline in order to counter the moral decay perceived as prevailing in the cities. Such condemnation was taken up by Dublin's medical community, which saw the tradesmen indulging in orgies of intoxication that consigned their families to a brief existence marked by poverty and disease. This invective took on a raw, anti-urban bias.[2]

Industrial progress and workplace innovation became central to the reforming philosophy. At its core was a credo that the national strength should be built on purified foundations of religion and morality. Enterprise acquired a quasi-religious value and idleness became a major sin. This outlook held that progress was to be derived from the workforce, and that far too many people were withholding their labour by reason of indolence and immorality. Dublin took steps to render the lazy and work-shy more amenable to their duty. These initiatives were expressed in government policy, and were accompanied by different supports for the sick and the weak. There was a rise in institutions with titles such as the House of Correction, the House of Industry and the House of Recovery.

The burden of medieval morality

Attitudes towards crime and punishment in the eighteenth century still incorporated much of the savagery of earlier periods. There was a tolerance of cruel violence. Husbands could bend their wives to their will by beating them. Mortal duels might end men's disputes. Corporal punishment was taken for granted by both domestic servants and school pupils. Popular pastimes saw cruelty caused to participants and to animals, and that indulgence reached all social levels. The gentry had a tolerant attitude towards public recreation and this even extended to blood sports such as bull-baiting and cockfighting. This forbearance may have been informed by both self-interest and paternalism.[3]

The criminal law was intended to secure the advance of the political elite. Legal power became concentrated in the highest levels, and there was a reduction in the role played by the general public. In 1763 a law was passed (3 Geo III, c.19 [Ire.]) to indemnify people who broke up gatherings of the lower orders, and this protection even extended to the killing of transgressors. Those indemnified included the lord mayor and his sheriffs. This distasteful work was soon passed to hired men. As the police became a remunerated force there was less enthusiasm for their role as moral guardians.

The intention of the government was to allow enough discretion to the elite to

Drunken grandees attacking the parish watch in Dame Street. This was a regular occurrence. (From A Real Paddy [Pierce Egan], *Real Life in Ireland*, 1821)

demonstrate their influence, thereby securing and enhancing their own authority, but this was to be achieved without alienating too many ordinary people. It was a system that marked out the place of the accused in the social hierarchy, and it is no surprise that certain sanctions were not applied to the elite themselves. Gentlemen (and, by extension, their ladies) were exempt from the humiliation of whippings and pillories; that degree of ignominy exceeded what the legal culture intended for the chosen few.[4]

The expanding prosperity of the elite and the consequent spread of affluence to the middling sort provided more possibilities for criminals. The official response was to adopt punishments that would deter the wrongdoers. It was supposed that offenders would be put off by having the sanction executed in public, thereby bringing together the pain and the shame. It was held that potential criminals would be converted by the sight of convicts being whipped, pilloried or burned. Where those sanctions were insufficient the ultimate deterrent was the scaffold. Hanging had two purposes: it removed from society those wicked people who were incorrigible, and it showed the working poor where disobedience could lead them.

This penal code reflected the willingness of the general public to take part in its rituals. Bystanders were prepared to get involved when they thought the culprit had sinned against the community. The procedure known as the hue and cry was an age-old one where volunteers gathered to pursue a felon. It was best suited to urban locations because it depended on the presence of enough pursuers who could be quickly summoned by a loud outcry. The pillory allowed the community to vent its anger against wrongdoers, and it was a dangerous place for anyone who offended public opinion. In 1789 a man named Robert Edgeworth was so severely injured at the pillory that his life was put in danger. He had bribed a witness in a notorious rape case. The missiles used against him included stones, potatoes and rotten eggs.[5] Most cases of physical abuse were privately revenged. Where there was any retaliation on behalf of the victim it did not normally end up in court, and this was particularly so in cases of rape, where the shame forced the victim to shun publicity.

Punishing the sinners

> As America and the West Indies want white women so much, it is a pity every prostitute is not sent there after a third commitment to Bridewell, or any other prison.
>
> *Faulkner's Dublin Journal*, 13 September 1770

Across Europe, reformatories were set up to correct the able-bodied poor who refused to work. In Dublin, anybody found begging was liable to be put to hard work in order to deter others. These sanctions were extended to the workplace and used against apprentices who disobeyed their masters.

By the 1750s the relaxed attitude was being questioned. A decade later the nobility was becoming suspicious that assembled crowds fortified by alcohol might challenge its authority and pose a threat to the social order. Those engaging in discredited activities could pay a high price. City hospitals might refuse to treat them. This happened after a boxing match at George's Quay when there were several fatalities after part of the platform collapsed; the injured spectators were turned away from the hospitals because they had not suffered in a 'natural or accidental way'. Such pursuits were regarded as elements of a debauched lifestyle that sprang from European Catholicism. Not alone did blood sports destroy the compassion of the individual, they also removed people from productive labour.

Members of the Hellfire Club, a group of self-indulgent gentlemen, most active during the 1730s. (James Worsdale, c. 1735) (NGI)

There was a friction attached to Sabbath observance and it had a sectarian edge. Sabbatarianism was based on the Protestant precept that recreation should contribute to human health in order to enhance a person's ability to work. Sunday activities such as walking or swimming were acceptable, but pursuits that allowed gambling or drinking were abhorrent because they promoted immorality and idleness. Sunday was the main day for sporting pursuits for the growing ranks of Catholics, and betting was an integral element. In 1766 *Faulkner's Dublin Journal* reported how a football match at Milltown attracted a very large gathering 'to the great scandal of religion and this metropolis'.[6] Reformers were unremitting in their attempts to suppress these seminaries of vice that they saw corrupting the younger generation. All those people found at a ball court, including the spectators, were liable to be carried off to jail.

Hurling and football matches were held at several venues on the outskirts, notably Phoenix Park, Drumcondra, Summerhill and Milltown. They attracted fruit and cake sellers as well as whiskey dealers. During the late 1770s hurling matches in Phoenix Park were allegedly drawing crowds of up to ten thousand people, and great violence was used to suppress them. The Irish love of horses was seen in the races held at Crumlin, Kilmainham, Ringsend and Booterstown. Wealthy neighbours condemned these meetings, and the army was regularly called out to disperse the punters. Irate land owners welcomed a 1773 bill to ban horse racing within twenty-five miles of the city. That, however, turned out to be a non-runner as it remained only a bill. Boxing contests were confined to poorer districts such as George's Quay, Oxmantown Green and Blackpits (in The Coombe). For the elite, these places were out of the way and consequently drew less criticism.[7] Animal-baiting took various forms, often using bulls stolen from the markets. These events were badly organised, and participants were left open to attack when crazed animals tried to escape. The most offensive form of cockfighting was known as the Welsh Main – a tournament of thirty-two cocks, with the last surviving bird declared the winner. Such contests were popular, and tournaments at the Essex Street cockpit beside the Castle sometimes lasted five days. Close by, the cockpit at Cork Hill was notorious for violence and debauchery.[8]

Bustling street life brought out entertainers. The competition for coins forced these players to work hard to draw in an audience, and there were constant complaints about indecency. Balled singers who gathered around public houses were regarded as lewd and scandalous. As early as 1770 a group of gentlemen committed themselves to the suppression of obscene street singing.[9]

Efforts were made to promote polite activities. There was a tennis club for gentlemen at Townsend Street as early as 1750, and Blackrock had a swimming club in 1771. These were respectable pursuits that allowed polite socialising. Each club had its own tavern where the members met together. Dublin had several commercial baths and washhouses, but most of them were notorious. Those few actually used for health-giving purposes were supported by a respectable clientele. One of these was Dr Achmet's Royal Patent Baths at Bachelor's Walk, where the customers included John Beresford (Chancellor of the Exchequer) and Lord Charlemont.[10]

Reform and regulation

> The visible great returns and extraordinary blessings, which, for the most part, attend the industrious man's labour, cannot fail of having such an effect upon his mind, as may make him truly sensible of the great Author and Giver of them.
>
> Revd Thomas McDonnell, 1760[11]

The crusade for moral reform began by identifying the repugnant activities. That was followed by active engagement when the full force of the state was used to apprehend the scandal-givers. By the 1760s calls for Sabbath observance was getting stronger, and reflected concern at the impact of Catholics on everyday life. New laws were made to impose good sense on the populace. There was more control over public houses, and laws banned the sale of alcohol in prisons and workhouses.[12]

During the 1770s there was more suppression of public sports. Hurling games at Marlborough Green and football matches at Milltown were singled out for censure. Remedies included the arrest of all participants and confiscation of the Sabbath-breaking hurleys. The campaign spread to entertainments such as throwing at cocks. This game was offensive because of its association with the religiously significant Shrove Tuesday. Oxmantown Green was a popular venue for it, and the sheriff was kept busy breaking up sessions there. The denominational dragnet reached ever further, and venues out as far as Ringsend and Phoenix Park were raided.[13]

Sabbatarians allowed strange distinctions between these activities. Servants playing pitch and toss for halfpennies were hunted down, while their employers betting sovereigns on cockfights went undisturbed. This differentiation between rich and poor was based on the attitude that distinguished their places in the world. The elite was afforded a life of leisure as a perk, and the poor could only expect a life of toil. Cultural expressions explained the pattern. Even simple things such as everyday humour came to be condemned. Straightforward laughter was a taboo in polite society. Decorum allowed a modest smile so long as it did not cause the face to wrinkle. Relaxed laughter was left to the poor because it made the perpetrator appear both loud and unseemly. This area of manners allowed the middling sort to advance. Their beliefs bolstered their restraint, and they were quick to acquire the correct responses.

The task of reform became more pressing as the number of Catholic revellers increased. The men of property felt that further reforms were required to keep the attention of the ordinary people fixed on workplace discipline. In such circumstances necessity could sharpen the instruments of social control. Low wages and high prices could discourage idleness and, consequently, raise productivity. It was hardly coincidental that workshops were increasing in size, diversity and mechanisation. The devotees of Saint Monday were put under pressure. However, all this evangelical zeal was ultimately in vain. The crowds at hurling matches in Phoenix Park kept on growing, and by the late 1770s they were supposed to contain around five per cent of the entire city population. By the 1790s these sportsmen were using central venues such as St Stephen's Green.

This challenge brought a brutal response from defenders of the status quo. Violence was used to suppress boxing matches and animal-baiting. Participants and bystanders were killed. Animal-baiting was seen as a pastime of the poor, the idle and the disorderly – people who should be doing some useful work. Towards the end of the century there was a move away from barbaric pastimes, a shift promoted by the middle class. John Gamble, who was a keen observer of Irish life, saw a significant decline in everyday violence by 1810.[14] Legislation to control blood sports was introduced in 1822 by the Irish MP Richard Martin, and comprehensive reform followed in 1835. These initiatives reflected a compassion for animals, but their main purpose was a broader social change.

Puritanism, prudery and penal reform

> Do you envy the rich? – Don't mind what they do,
> But mind with what labour, they now excel you,
> Their fathers, like some, once worked at the door;
> If idle, like some, we shall ever be poor.
> Mind the lark and the cock, who go with the sun,
> Keep their hours, be sober, and our business is done.
>
> T.B., 'Journeyman Weaver', 1759[15]

Reform reached the wider aspects of everyday life and had cultural manifestations. In music, for example, composers in the classical sphere were drawn closer to religion. Handel's oratorios were dramatic musical expressions of religious themes. They were intended to replace the European opera that was now regarded as debased and popish. By the 1770s the London magistrate Sir John Fielding was suppressing operas because the city had excessive entertainment. He even blocked a revival of John Gay's highly popular *Beggar's Opera* on the basis that it encouraged crime.[16]

Handel's *Messiah* (1742) was first performed in Dublin, thereby securing for the city a place in musical history. These oratorios appealed to reformers because they drew a parallel between the righteous English and God's chosen people of the Old Testament. They espoused modesty, and to achieve this even dispensed with stage sets and costumes.[17] This self-censorship reached other art forms; bowdlerisation reached its high point with the expurgation of Shakespeare's works in 1818.[18]

As the moral crusade became more strident it put greater emphasis on self-discipline. Domestic life had to receive more priority than any commitment to the wider community. The family home was seen as a refuge from the sinful world outside, and domestic recreation was favoured over public assemblies. This reform appealed to the middle class, and it supported the trend towards a more insular family unit, particularly where it placed greater emphasis on respectability.

✳✳✳✳✳

John Wesley, the Methodist evangelist, made his first visit to Ireland in 1747. He found the Irish far too feckless, and felt compelled to make twenty more trips to cure or convert them. Wesley looked to the elite to provide a good example for everyone else. This could explain why evangelists took time to denounce the laxity they saw in high society. Their pronouncements were aimed at the moral welfare of each household, and sexual licence was singled out for rebuke. There was great indignation when high-class prostitutes were allowed within the most elevated social circle. These females turned up at promenades in the Rotunda Gardens and at celebrity concerts, and even made their way into Castle balls. They were regarded as being worse than robbers because they destroyed the reputation of entire families.[19] There were, however, some double standards, and high society was willing to tolerate transgressions provided there was no scandal.

Up to the mid-eighteenth century the terms 'family' and 'household' were synonymous, embracing all those within the home, including close relations, servants and even lodgers. Subsequently, however, the definition of family was narrowed down and reserved for the nuclear family. This arrangement opened up a gap between the householder and his servants. As we have seen, there was a growing edginess over the presence of Catholic staff. English visitors were suspicious, and some of them concluded that Irish domestics were not trustworthy: these servants saw no sin in stealing from wealthy employers. There may have been additional factors at work. There was, for example, a growing friction over the money paid to servants, and this came to a head in regard to the payments called vails – servants' gratuities paid by visiting grandees on departing the house. When these perks were slow to appear, the servants could use delaying tactics. By the 1750s these payments formed a major proportion of some servants' incomes. They could make visiting too expensive and, moreover, the ritual caused embarrassment to both the host and his guests. A London initiative to ban vails began in 1764, and it was repeated in Dublin. During the following year the Marquess of Kildare banned them, and compensated his staff with a wage increase. The payment of higher wages emphasised the commercial status of the servants.[20]

✳ ✳ ✳ ✳ ✳

But there certainly exist many degrees of deviation from perfect cleanliness, which, if not sensibly injurious to health, are extremely offensive to delicacy.

'A Physician', 1777[21]

After 1750 a greater emphasis was put on the domestic role of women. They were perceived to be more morally robust than men, and the home, the family and religion were all deemed to be appropriate interests for them. This reduced the latitude allowed to women in the male domain of business. Men were to concentrate on concerns such as status and politics. Social pressure was becoming the main agent of moral control, and it was especially active in securing the chastity of women.[22]

More-loving relationships emerged between spouses and also between the parents and their children. Domestic recreation lured the elite towards private theatricals, retreating from the playhouses of the city. St Stephen's Green held a measure of the prevailing ethos. It was a venue that retained its cachet until the 1780s, although its social glow had already begun to fade. Public recreation by the aristocracy was pared back and frivolity was confined indoors: it might be seen at Castle balls or other gatherings well away from the prying eyes of the hoi polloi. Those who moved beyond these mores were open to condemnation. The finger of rebuke could reach right up the social scale, and not even the lord lieutenant was exempt. Edward Wakefield, in his account of Regency Ireland, castigated the Duke of Rutland for the poor example he set in his vice-regal court: his dissipation had spread down into the lower ranks. Rutland died in office, of syphilis.

For the elite, Sunday drives along the Circular Road offered a novel attraction, and it was one that could be family-based. The Circular Road was a turnpike, and the proprietors encouraged leisure traffic by halving the Sunday toll. This lower price drew in the affluent and discouraged the riff-raff. At the same time the middle class made more use of the green but these new promenaders were more restrained. Desmond McCabe suspects that Malton's well-known print of the late 1790s, *Beaux Walk*, is misleading because it shows the place as it appeared some years earlier. During the 1790s the green was invaded by trespassers of all sorts. On Sundays, hurling and football matches brought confrontations with the guardians of the Sabbath.[23]

Pressure from the Sunday enforcers encouraged pleasure-seekers to venture beyond their reach. This partly explains the success of Donnybrook Fair, which built up its reputation for debauchery over many decades. By the 1790s it was drawing crowds estimated at fifty thousand. These revellers were working people, and for them the highpoint of the week was Sunday.[24] As the leisure of the elite

Charles Duke of Rutland appointed LORD LIEUTENANT *and Governor General of the Kingdom of Ireland Feb? 1784 Died there Oct? 24th 1787 Universally Lamented.*

Charles Manners, Duke of Rutland, viceroy 1784–87, a notable client of the exclusive brothel operated by Margaret Leeson. He died in Dublin of syphilis. (*Walker's Hibernian Magazine*, February 1790) (UCD)

Above: This view of
Donnybrook Fair
is more sober and
restrained than that
depicted by the written
accounts. (Francis
Wheatley, 1752) (NGI)
Right: Donnybrook Fair,
notorious for drunken
debauchery. This view
was inspired by the
earlier work of William
Hogarth depicting the
decadence of London.
(Courtesy of Andrew
Bonar Law)

inclined more towards the coastline it was followed by the hectoring moralists. Bawdy indulgence was associated with Blackrock and Seapoint during the Regency. A baronet's wife, possibly Lady Antrim, was at the seaside because her constitution needed frequent saltwater immersion. However, she was christened the 'Mermaid of Seapoint' on account of infamous amours with several army officers. Even worse was the clergyman who glorified in his shame; this voluptuary could no longer be trusted with the reclamation of souls: 'Why should the lips of pollution be permitted to preach virtuous sentiments?'[25] For those at the lowest levels of city life the castigation was complete. Fallen females had forsaken their claim on humanity. By the 1790s reforming prostitutes were regarded as less than human. The hymns sung at the Lock Penitentiary left them in no doubt:

> We too, poor worms of earth, would join
> In work and worship so divine.
>
> Poor, guilty, and helpless worms,
> Into thine hands we fall.[26]

✳ ✳ ✳ ✳ ✳

Amongst the foremost social reformers to make an impact were Jonas Hanway and John Howard. Hanway was driven by a religious conviction that saw ignorance of the Christian faith amongst the lower classes as the main reason for London's social disintegration. He blamed this ignorance for the presence of so many abandoned women and children. Hanway took an active part in setting up several institutions in the English capital. He founded the Marine Society in 1756, and was a board member of the Foundling Hospital for almost two decades, ultimately becoming its governor in 1771. Later in the 1770s he campaigned for the young chimney sweeps called climbing boys and supported charities trying to reform young prostitutes. However, he avoided any wider change that could challenge the social structure. He held that only ten per cent of charity children should be taught to read and write. During the 1780s Hanway's tracts examined the wider context of crime and punishment. He advocated solitary confinement for criminals to shield them from the corrupting influence of other convicts.

John Howard published an account of England's prisons in 1770. He advocated the building of new jails that would take account of the latest medical knowledge. He urged better ventilation and cleanliness, along with nutritious food and fresh water. Spiritual reform was his main purpose, however, and, like

This barefoot little chimney sweep is a distracted soul. His master looks surprisingly clean and pert. (Hugh Douglas Hamilton, 1760) (Private collection)

Hanway, he argued that this should be achieved by isolating prisoners, particularly at night. These calls for improvement of the penal regime found favour in Dublin. During the 1780s it was claimed that city criminals had become more cruel and callous, and that this behaviour needed a firm response. After execution these miscreants should be hung on the gibbet, so as to expose the body to birds and flies in order to reduce it to a skeleton. This was seen as an effective deterrent because even the most hardened villains cared about the destination of their remains after death. *The Freeman's Journal* supported the isolation of all prisoners, complemented by hard work, a meagre diet and no whiskey.

Some Irish benefactors sought a better outcome for the beleaguered. The literature contains frequent references to individuals such as Lady Arabella Denny and Samuel Rosborough. Lady Denny supported asylums for prostitutes, and garnered support from like-minded women (her Leeson Street refuge is discussed in chapter twelve). After her death in 1792 an elegy recalled how she had turned many fallen females onto a virtuous path.[27]

※ ※ ※ ※ ※

We are regulated by a police which stands in the highest degree of reprehension.

Hibernian Journal, 4 July 1781

By the 1750s the growing criticism of urban life made a connection between health and religion. To be clean became a moral duty. It was feared that the

city had a debilitating impact on people and that working-class immorality was damaging the country's welfare. An early response was the establishment of more hospitals, and these care centres had a dual function: they were intended to fortify the population by removing disease, but were also agencies of social control, removing offensive objects off the streets. This hectoring was not all confined to Protestant zealots; there were publications directed at Catholic malingerers, but these were bound to be less visible. An example dating from 1760 condemned Sunday excesses: it railed at the concupiscence of the common people who came together to talk, joke, dance and drink; human passions had to be kept in check through daily exertion in the workforce.[28]

A charity sermon for a city orphanage, 1806. The preacher was Revd Walter Blake Kirwan. (Hugh Douglas Hamilton) (Courtesy of Andrew Bonar Law)

This movement for spiritual renewal was carried into the early decades of the nineteenth century. Its later phase coincided with the despondency of post-Union Dublin, and its expression could be confused with the political upheaval; it would appear that these two trends proceeded side by side. An engaging view of the evangelical crusade emerges from the accounts of Edward Wakefield and John McGregor. There was a surge in the formation of charities after 1780 which accelerated during the 1790s and went on until 1820. These reforms, therefore, were under way prior to the Union. This crusade took on a fashionable aspect: as we have seen, charity sermons became features of the social calendar. Wealthy residents were willing to donate money on these occasions as this could be an ostentatious gesture and much preferable to paying taxes to the parish. Preachers such as Dean Walter Kirwan were in great demand because they could draw large audiences, and charities vied to secure their services.[29]

John Binns, the republican activist, was twenty years old when he heard one of Kirwan's sermons around 1792. When Binns arrived at the church he found that extensive security was installed to keep out the riff-raff. Fences were erected beside the entrance to ensure grandees alighting from their carriages could not be accosted by beggars. Policemen and ushers safeguarded the visitors. Lesser mortals

These fashion-conscious ladies carried ostentatious watches, 1790s. (*Walker's Hibernian Magazine*, September 1795) (Board of Trinity College, Dublin)

A Bundle of Straw.   A Scaramouch.   A Scare Crow.

THE FASHIONABLES, 1795.

did, however, get to hear the sermon from the street outside; they squeezed up to the highest windows, even using ladders to peer inside. These church gatherings added to the social latitude allowed to women. Aspiring socialites used these occasions to introduce their daughters into fashionable society. Collections were undertaken by women of the foremost rank: 'On man, the fascinating influence of the beauty, pleading, with a look of compassion, for the unfortunate, must have a powerful effect, and those insensible to female charms may be induced to be liberal, from an apprehension of the satire of a dashing belle.'[30]

The aura of fashion reached into organisations supported by these occasions. In describing a refuge for blind females at Peter Street, John McGregor revealed the change in public opinion. This property had previously been occupied by a playhouse and circus, but the taste for such frivolous entertainments had now been replaced by a thirst for more noble pleasures, and the theatre was converted into the chapel of the Molyneaux Asylum, a place that drew devout worshippers. The promoters of this blind asylum saw the change as a conversion from licentiousness to redemption. Profanity had given way to the support of helpless females; it was 'one among the many signs of the times which declare that the witnesses of the Lord's side are fast multiplying in these favoured islands'.[31]

Missionary organisations were a response to the moral decline that Protestants perceived in papist Europe. Bodies described as societies for the reformation of manners concentrated on evangelical and charitable works. They dispensed Bibles and tracts, and people were willing to contribute to these causes. About £2,000 was raised in 1795 to purchase Bibles for the poor; remarkably, this sum of money was collected within a few months. This feat was achieved by the Association for Discountenancing Vice, an organisation that found support in select quarters. During the 1790s its influence secured the suppression of the Dublin lottery as well as the Sunday sale of alcohol. In 1803 its condemnation brought an end to Sunday promenades at the Rotunda Hospital.[32]

Many of these devil-defying organisations were directly inspired by London counterparts: one obvious example was the Irish Auxiliary to the London Society for Promoting Christianity Among the Jews, founded in 1819. The Society for Promoting the Comforts of the Poor was founded in 1799, just three years after a similar group in England. In 1814 the Hibernian Bible Society amalgamated with its British counterpart. These societies clustered together; by 1821 there were seven of them located side by side at numbers 12 to 16 Upper Sackville Street.

Ultimately, this crusade failed and the biblical battalions faded away. Dublin was left divided along religious lines. The Protestant elite was at odds with the mainstream population. This division gave cohesion to the Catholic majority,

Premises of the
Education Society,
Kildare Place. (M.H. and
J.W. Allen, 1825) (RIA)

resulting in the formation of organisations such as the Catholic Bible Society
(1813) and the Irish Catholic Society for the Diffusion of Religious Knowledge
(1823). The foundation of the Catholic Association in 1823 widened the gap
even more. This was the body associated with Daniel O'Connell, who led the
Catholic-emancipation movement, culminating in the legal reform of 1829.[33]

Private punishment and public sobriety

> Salutary regulations for preventing evil prove more effectual in
> rendering men good citizens, than the severest code of penal laws
> that can be framed.
>
> Edward Wakefield, 1812[34]

> The general character of the inhabitants, which was once gay and
> dissipated, has now become more serious and religious, and those
> sums formerly lavished on expensive pleasures, are now happily
> converted to a much more exalted motive.
>
> John James McGregor, 1821[35]

This improvement programme spread its influence into law and order – a sphere where it had a lasting impact. The criminal code fostered a strong alliance between religion and retribution. The state Church did not question the death penalty, and members of the judiciary were willing to lend their support. England's premier dispenser of punishment was amongst the campaigners for reform: Chief Justice Hale was a strong advocate of Sabbath observance. He allowed that some bodily exercise was desirable, but it should not be undertaken too often; what was needed, above all, was restraint and sobriety.[36]

As the opposition to public violence gained ground, it raised questions over those punishments used by the state itself. Britain and Ireland saw a widening range of secondary punishments and this softened the desire for the death sentence. Sanctions such as transportation were either introduced or revived. Banishment of convicts to the American colonies had been introduced in 1718 for non-capital offences, and was at its height during the 1750s and 1760s, before being suspended when the American Revolution broke out in 1775. The figures for 1763–64 reveal that there were 189 transportations compared to eleven hangings. Banishment to some far-off place could really terrify those people who were bound up in it. Contingents were assembled for dispatch and onlookers watched as convicts were brought down to the prison ships. In 1789, for example, there was a procession of thirteen carriages conveying 127 convicts bound for the US.[37]

Many legal sanctions introduced in the eighteenth century were driven by moral reform rather than as a response to crime. This could explain why some of the capital offences were not rigidly implemented. Considerable discretion was used where crimes were perceived to arise from the broader decline in public morality. By the 1780s the destructive force of whiskey received more prominence in the campaign: 'The air of this country is infected by the poisonous vapour; a residence in it is destructive of manners and morals.'[38]

This agenda was pursued at parish level. St Anne's denounced the pernicious effects of alcohol, and was keen to lead the charge against the soaks. During the 1790s it employed sixteen inspectors to suppress speakeasies, and cooperated with adjoining parishes to bring about reform. This crusading fervour waned after the Union and funds became scarcer. The bootleggers got bolder, and in 1809 St Anne's had to face the ignominy of a £10 fine when an unlicensed still was discovered right beside the Mansion House in Dawson Street.[39]

Law enforcement and public disorder

The vice of a capital city, with its numberless train of incentives to drunkenness, idleness and debauchery, must always produce a languor in the industry, and a gangrene in the morals of the lower class of people.

Hibernian Journal, 28 September 1778

Public hangings were supposed to be a deterrent that inspired deference and reverence in the giddy multitude. For this reason hangings were sometimes carried out at the scene of the crime. In 1777 four robbers were hanged in Meath Street, and in 1797 two men who plotted to kill Lord Carhampton were executed at the junction of Jervis Street and Strand Street. This latter spectacle had a celebrity aspect and drew an immense crowd. The most famous crime-scene execution was that of Robert Emmet, the patriot hanged at Thomas Street in 1803. Hanging declined in London during the late eighteenth and early nineteenth centuries because middle-class businessmen were reluctant to bring charges that attracted the death penalty. This change was also seen in Dublin.[40]

Henry Luttrell, Lord Carhampton, a notorious army officer. He raped a young girl but was not charged (1784). A decade later, two men were executed for trying to kill him. (*Walker's Hibernian Magazine*, December 1797) (UCD)

Public executions attracted large crowds, and the number of onlookers increased in accordance with the criminal's infamy. That was certainly the case when Terence Lawless, an aptly named street robber, was hanged in 1771; thousands of spectators blocked the surrounding streets for several hours. This gallows celebrity grew to such an extent that some men expressed disappointment at the lack of observers turning up for their turning off.[41]

Convicts were dispatched with great brutality. After the hanging of James Ennis in 1785 the corpse was disembowelled: 'his entrails were thrown among the people, which a ravenous bull-dog devoured, to the terror of many hundreds then present.' Many onlookers were seriously injured as panic spread through the crowd. Women were strangled rather than hanged, and their bodies were then burned; such was the case with a coiner's wife in 1786. Two years later a murderous brothel keeper was barely dead when her body was burned in front of the horrified onlookers.[42] Such horrors were captured in verse:

His pendant form with pungent pain
Convulsive writhes, and wildly throes.
Heav'ns! See him struggle, spring, and stretch,
Now swell, now sink, now scarcely shake.

James Orr, 'The Execution', 1798[43]

There was a gruesome anticipation as the ramshackle machinery often failed to operate properly. Even when it did work the hanged were left suffocating, surrounded by distressed relatives and friends. In several cases it was found that the hanged person had not actually expired, and the body was quickly removed to be resuscitated. In 1789 *The Freeman's Journal* castigated the city executioner; his incompetence stretched executions over half an hour, while the county hangman at Kilmainham dispatched his victims much more rapidly. As late as 1805 John Carr, an English barrister, found convicts were frequently flung onto the pavement through mismanagement of the rope. They ended up torn and mangled before they were finally dispatched. An incident of that kind occurred in 1792 – the rope broke and the victim was stunned in his fall. The crowd panicked, thinking it was an escape attempt and that soldiers would open fire. One onlooker was killed in the crush and many more were seriously injured. Some convicts speeded up their exit by paying for a longer rope to provide a fatal shock. One price quoted for this was five guineas.[44]

The presence of the gallows at Lower Baggot Street created great unease in the vicinity, and residents agitated to have it moved elsewhere. This pressure grew as new housing reached out in that direction. They clamoured for hangings to be carried out early in the morning to deter city workers from attending. It was not just the hanging itself that upset them. Poor families collected door-to-door to raise money for the wake. The corpse was left at the gallows until the following day. This happened to the body of a horse thief in May 1789; his remains were left overnight, to the great annoyance of neighbours.[45]

In criminal cases the corpse might be removed by the crowd and laid at the accuser's door. In 1747 this occurred to William Lefanu, a merchant in St Stephen's

Green. Over five hundred people turned up at his house with the corpse of a man named Deacon who had been hanged that day. After laying down the body they smashed all of Lefanu's windows and threatened to demolish his house. One of the ringleaders was John Deacon, a butcher from the Ormond Market and a brother of the deceased man. Further violence was only prevented by the arrival of the army.[46]

Calls were made for the suppression of such practices by taking the corpses to the university medical school for dissection. It was announced in 1780 that any corpse involved in these outrages would be sent off to the college, but the law allowing dissection of criminals was not provided until 1791.[47] In 1783 the scaffold was moved to Newgate Prison, purportedly to provide a greater deterrent. In the same year London saw a similar change when the gallows was moved from Tyburn to Newgate.

> It is to no purpose to hang up some scores of villains every year, while thousands more roam at large.
>
> R. Lewis, 1787[48]

It was argued that there should be more respect for the condemned men, with hangings carried out inside the jail so that criminals could die with dignity. Others advocated alternative proportionate punishment, such as whipping offenders through the streets in order to humiliate them. Removal of the gallows to the north side of the city did not satisfy everyone. In 1785 the residents of Green Street petitioned parliament to move all executions inside the jail. For a while executions were again carried out at Lower Baggot Street, but that ended quickly after the locals used their influence to have them shifted once and for all to the north side.[49]

✳ ✳ ✳ ✳ ✳

Medieval sentences such as burning, scourging and the pillory remained popular up to the 1750s. Whippings reached a peak during the 1780s, and like other punishments the maximum public exposure was sought to deter wrongdoers. Scourging took place at the whipping post or at the cart's tail; in the latter case the victim was tied to a wagon and trailed through the streets. The course taken was supposed to attract as many observers as possible. A similar attitude applied to the pillory. The desired humiliation relied on communal acquiescence, and where this was absent the outcome could be counterproductive. There were instances when onlookers strongly objected to a perceived innocent being put into the stocks. This occurred, for example, when a couple named Cullen were pilloried near George's Street in 1777; they were accused of brothel-keeping, but the spectators reacted by throwing missiles at the executioner.[50]

The pillory was used for offences that drew public hostility, such as fraud, extortion, sodomy and child molestation. This might explain why a man named John McKenna was pilloried for perjury in 1778. According to the *Hibernian Journal*, his ears were nailed to the post, but it is not clear whether this was done literally or metaphorically. The crowd was actively encouraged to condemn the culprit. An example of this was seen in the pillorying of a man who displayed obscene prints in 1791; he was identified as an Englishman named William Aldrige.

Whipping followed the general trend, and after 1750 this punishment tended to be privately administered; it ended up indoors by 1800. A similar policy was followed for the pillory, although there were exceptions; St Paul's parish acquired two new pairs of stocks as late as 1815. Other more obscure punishments petered out in the same way. An example of this was the sanction known as 'burned in the hand'. In this very public spectacle the offender was marked by the application of a red-hot branding iron. This practice had fallen out of favour by the early 1790s when *The Freeman's Journal* stated that it was discontinued some decades before that.[51]

During the 1770s imprisonment came to be seen as a useful method of punishment in its own right. Prior to that, incarceration was a side effect of other punishments, usually where someone was either whipped or pilloried. Use of prison as a custodial sanction proved an alternative to transportation, which, as we have seen, was made more difficult by the American Revolution.

> Our system has been rather to prevent crimes by punishment, than to encourage virtue and industry by reward.
>
> Society for Increasing the Comforts of the Poor, 1800[52]

Following the campaigns of Jonas Hanway and John Howard, penitentiaries were set up as places of hard labour to enforce discipline and to inspire reform. The old houses of correction essentially became penitentiaries that might promote a religious awakening. Dublin embraced this change, and the Richmond General Penitentiary was built on the northern perimeter at Grangegorman; it opened in

1821. Reform was to be inculcated through a combination of solitary confinement, hard labour and religious instruction. There was a rigid classification of prisoners based on Howard's model, and this was reflected in the use of eight strictly segregated exercise yards. The Richmond recognised stages in the healing progress as each individual moved from communal work by day and solitary confinement by night towards eventual sharing of a cell with somebody making similar progress. The place had hardly got off to a start, however, before state interference frustrated its plans. It was forced to take in boys from the Smithfield House of Correction, and it became a fever hospital in 1832.[53]

The progress sought by religious reformers was rendered more precarious by the widening gap between the social classes. Paupers could not comply with the law until they were fed and clothed. Hungry Dubliners who ventured out into the countryside to rob potato pits were doing so without any sense of shame, and they were not put off by the fear of being caught; rather, they thought that arrest would bring them a respite. It could deliver them to where they would get food to eat and garments to wear.

Transgressions were categorised and allocated to the appropriate social class, and penalties grew as one descended the social ladder. Dissipation within the elite might bring embarrassment, but for the middle class it could attract family distress or even bankruptcy. At the bottom of the scale, however, there was no salvation because the outcome for the lower orders was presumed to be violence and insurrection. Some of those engaged in Dublin charities sensed that moral reform would require an entirely new paradigm. They acknowledged that there had to be intercourse between the different classes. This would require access to education because the poor needed incentives to bind them into society at large.[54]

Hawkin's Street with the
Theatre Royal, *c.* 1820.
(George Petrie, 1821) (UCD)

10

Factions and Combinations

A reprehensible propensity to inflict summary justice ... without any just consideration, actuates in general the lower classes of the people.

The Freeman's Journal, 3 June 1794

As GREATER RESPONSIBILITY WAS ASSIGNED to each individual in his or her dealings with the wider community, many questions arose about law and order, as well as the moral authority that supported them. Religious institutions began to lose their influence over everyday life, and this, in turn, tended to loosen the bonds of social behaviour. In England and in Ireland the archaic religious courts had already lost their power, and this weakness came at a time when urban growth needed better management. There was uncertainty over many aspects of everyday life, and those making the rules were getting more hostile towards those who had to obey them. Londoners reacted by trying to take more power into their own hands, and by the 1720s there was a prosecution for rioting every second day. Those familiar with London's street violence could see it repeated in Dublin. Nevertheless, the battle lines kept moving, and the cause of the unrest could be industrial, sectarian, political or even mere mischief.

Industrial agitation

Women and children formed a substantial proportion of the workforce. In the reign of George I working women had very little security. Those females engaged in domestic service were not much removed from slavery. They had to get a formal discharge when moving from one employer to another. Children fared even worse. Waifs were seen to be a burden on the community, and it was therefore incumbent on each parish to take them off the streets. They were to be bound out and made to work for good Protestants. For girls in service this indentured confinement continued up to the age of twenty-one, and for young men in the trades it ended at twenty-four. In theory, parental consent was needed for these interventions.[1]

Most of the city's industry and commerce were controlled by the guilds, and they operated a regime that had hardly changed since the Middle Ages. It was a culture based on exclusivity, and only guild members could practise the organised crafts. It was a system that nurtured a dense framework of small workshops. There were many categories of crafts; for example, wood carvers were split between those men who worked on chairs and those who made picture frames. Each workshop was headed by a master, who had one or more apprentices and a similar number of journeymen. The workplace was subject to harsh discipline. There was usually a seven-year apprenticeship, and this began early in the teenage years. Trainees might spend a year or more gaining a grasp of reading and writing; this was obviously a necessity in trades such as printing.

Apprentices were prohibited to marry. They were also forbidden to gamble, to enter public houses or to visit theatres. Those who took part in the 1771 riot at the Crow Street theatre were horsewhipped by their masters. In most cases the workshop formed part of the master's house, often occupying the ground floor, with his own family living overhead and the other workers sleeping wherever a space could be found on hall floors or above in the attic. This arrangement forced all the participants into an intimacy that was bound to bring tension. For Dublin weavers crowded into the Liberties the threat of disease was always close at hand. Households in that area commonly shared a single apartment, with the loom occupying the whole central area and family beds arranged within surrounding corners. In his memoir, John Binns recalled the conditions of his apprenticeship to a soap-maker during the 1780s; he counted himself fortunate as he was allowed to spend one or two evenings each week with relations.[2]

A distinction was made between indoor and outdoor apprentices, with the former receiving bed and board from the master. This subsistence had to be paid for by parents, along with a substantial indenture fee. Sums paid to masters varied according to the potential earnings to be derived from the career. In 1786 John Binns got his soap-making apprenticeship for thirty-five guineas, and in 1813 the indenture fee for a printer's apprentice was £100.[3] These are exceptional accounts, however, because of the paucity of surviving records. This silence is surprising when trades such as surveying are considered because that was work that found an enduring expression in estate records and maps. This silence has been attributed to a lack of regulation within the profession. The surveyor Samuel Byron was admitted to the guild of cutlers, painter-stainers and stationers. He appears, moreover, to have been the only member of his profession allowed into that organisation.[4]

The merchants formed the dominating guild, and effectively controlled the city's wholesale and retail trade. They monopolised the importation and distribution of goods, and extended their influence into several other activities. The carrying trade was a substantial source of work, and the merchants controlled the election of twelve master porters, each of whom was allowed ten assistants.[5]

※ ※ ※ ※

As early as 1700 there was a weakening in the guild structure. This decline accelerated during the Georgian era, and there were several reasons for this. Firstly, the guilds were exclusively Protestant, and Catholic apprentices were expressly forbidden. Some Catholic merchants were admitted on lesser terms that deprived them of any voting rights. Although each master was formally restricted to two apprentices, this regulation was widely disregarded in order to reduce costs. In 1765 the printers' guild claimed that there were 116 apprentices but only 70 journeymen. Some printers had six or seven trainees, and this became an abiding feature. In 1835 the proportion in printing was 200 apprentices and 150 journeymen.[6] Thirdly, the guilds admitted unqualified individuals who were non-practitioners – men who were merely looking for the political influence that came with membership. By the 1830s municipal reform was in the air, and it revealed how far the dissolution had advanced. Amongst the bricklayers and plasterers only thirty-eight per cent were qualified, and within the merchants' guild the majority comprised lawyers, clerks and suchlike.

By this time there was an added factor in the workplace. There was official endorsement of larger production units, and this was encouraged by the Royal Dublin Society. By the early 1730s this organisation gave financial assistance to expanding industries. The scheme was an effort to promote import substitution;

those items identified for support included glass bottles, earthenware, cutlery, paper, sugar and farm implements. One of the early suggestions was to set up a prototype – that is, that the society would engage a Birmingham manufacturer to undertake hardware production in order to provide a useful example for local enterprises. The work of the RDS gained the support of parliament, and in the early 1760s £10,000 was provided in grants for suitable individuals. The worthy candidates were mainly engaged in linen production, glass (bottles and windows), paper and carpets. Several aspects of linen production were included, such as damask, dowlas (coarse fabric), bleaching, calendaring (smoothing), tapes and thread. Many of these manufactures were located in and around the city.

Petitions to the RDS reveal the increasing scale of production. One delftware maker had twenty employees, while a linen printer employed eighty people and a carpet weaver operated five looms. This move towards larger production units suited certain types of manufacturing. One of these was glass bottles, a trade that made use of incentives such as staff housing. When Deane's glass factory was opened in 1793 near the end of the North Wall, it included twenty-one houses for workers. In 1806 the Flint Glass Manufactory at Lower Abbey Street accommodated 120 workers in thirty houses.[7]

These changes had dire consequences for traditional sources of employment. Foremost amongst these were the small workshops that employed weavers and tailors. It was claimed that the Liberties lost seventy per cent of its plain-cloth weavers during the 1780s. Moreover, those who remained were kept on half-time. Speciality crafts suffered most from mechanisation. The carving of picture frames was killed off soon after 1800 by the arrival of moulded composition and machined decoration. The post-Union decline in the luxury market put specialist trades such as plastering under great pressure. Up to the 1790s leading firms of plasterers had employed ten full-time workers, with smaller ones having about five employees.[8]

Workshops merged into factories, and this weakened the paternalistic structure, especially where money transactions were involved. Cachet lost out to cash. Every decade reduced the hegemony of the Protestant power brokers, and this was unsettling for those with privileges based on religious affiliation. By 1831 the Protestant proportion of the capital's population had fallen to twenty-seven per cent, but, more significantly, the non-Catholic part of the city's artisans was as low as three per cent. The fatal blow came with the municipal reform of 1840. That greatly widened the franchise, breaking the political power of the guilds.[9]

✳ ✳ ✳ ✳ ✳

New workers' organisations began to emerge, and they were determined to loosen the bonds between the masters, journeymen and apprentices. In Dublin covert groups called combinations may have been formed as early as the 1720s. They replaced the journeymen's clubs that had enjoyed guild acceptance because their main objective was to organise welfare support for workers who had fallen ill or had died. With the expansion of capitalism the workers' interests broadened, and they were no longer assured of guild support. What did remain, however, was a rigid system that effectively made the journeymen dependants of their masters. Any employer who deemed himself offended by one of his men could withhold his discharge papers. The cost of redeeming this freedom was £50, a sum beyond the reach of those concerned.

In the 1750s journeymen barber-surgeons were obliged to work from 6 a.m. to 9 p.m. during the summer, and from 7 a.m. to 9 p.m. in winter. Combinations for carpenters emerged about 1761 at a time when the journeymen worked a thirteen-hour day. Dublin combinations became a potent agent of industrial change. Three decades later the carpenters' wages had doubled, with their working day reduced by an hour.[10]

Throughout the Georgian age violence was used by weavers to secure better terms for their members. This agitation normally began fairly suddenly, and went unreported when it occurred in the Liberties. Published accounts reflect the reaction to prominent episodes. In 1749 the weavers confronted masters who refused to recruit combination members. They singled out bosses taking on female workers. One group attacked the premises of the weaver John Lee in a back street called Tripilo. In order to avoid detection they dressed themselves as sailors and carried swords. They erected a mock gallows at Braithwaite Street to show Lee what he could expect. In another skirmish a weaver named William Whelling had his stock of fabrics destroyed after he showed spirited opposition to the combinations. Whelling's produce had been hanging out on tenters. These incidents led to the posting of substantial rewards, but the inducements failed to quell the violence.

The number of agitators continued to grow. In 1762 over two hundred workers attacked the homes of journeymen linen weavers who had refused to accept minimum wages. One victim was taken to the dunghills at Dirty Lane, where he was badly beaten up before being removed to the Liffey, and was only saved from drowning when a sheriff intervened. This assault was viewed by officialdom as a very serious matter because a reward of £100 was offered for the ringleader, John Farrelly. The upheaval spread outwards from the Liberties. When the hatters' apprentices joined the journeymen's campaign they attacked employers who opposed their cause. In 1765 they ransacked the house of William Parvisol in

G. II. R.

BY THE
LORD LIEUTENANT *and* COUNCIL
OF
IRELAND,
A
PROCLAMATION.

HARRINGTON.

WHEREAS it appears to Us by several Examinations taken upon Oath, that the Journeymen Broad-Weavers and other Workmen in the Cloathing Trade, have Entred into a Combination not to Work with any Master-Workman, who should for Seven Years to come, take an Apprentice or Employ a Woman at Weaving, and that *William Whelling*, Master of the Corporation of Weavers, called an Hall in order to apply to Parliament to provide a Remedy against such Combinations.

That about the latter End of *September*, or the beginning of *October* last, *John Sherry*, and *Michael Shaw*, Broad-Weavers, with several other Persons Dressed like Sailors, and Armed with a Sword and Sticks, Entred the Room of *John Lee* of *Tripiloe*, in the Earl of *Meath's* Liberty Broad-Weaver, and Dragged him thereout to the *Comb*, and from thence to *Crookedstaff*, under pretence that he had been a Sailor, and forced him to Swear by a Book, not to Work with an Apprentice that should be taken after the said Journeymen Broad-Weavers Association, or where Women were Employed in Weaving, and that, in some time after, there was a Piece of Wood Erected in *Braithwaite-Street*, in the said Liberty, which as the said *John Lee* was informed, was to Hang the said *John Lee* upon, in order as he believed, to Deter him from Prosecuting the Persons who abused him as aforesaid.

That on the Twenty Fifth Day of *October* last, there were Two Pieces of Broad-Cloth belonging to the said *William Whelling*, and One Piece of Broad-Cloth belonging to *Valentine Codd*, on *Tenters*, in a Field called *Gibton's* Field, in the Liberty of *Donore* and County of *Dublin*, and that, in the Night between the Twenty fifth and Twenty sixth Days of *October* last, the said Three Pieces were Cutt in several places from End to End, except about One Yard and a Quarter of one of the said *William Whelling's* Pieces which was Cutt off and Stolen, and

A

that

Workers destroyed the fabrics of employers who resisted the combinations (proto-trade unions). This 1747 proclamation supported the suppression of combinations. (NAI)

G. II. R.

BY THE

LORD LIEUTENANT and COUNCIL

OF

IRELAND,

A

PROCLAMATION.

BEDFORD.

 HEREAS We have received Information upon Oath, That on *Monday* the Twelfth of this Inftant, *December*; *Thomas Afhworth*, late of *Donnybrooke*, in the County of the City of *Dublin*, Linen-Stamper and Paper-Printer, was moft barbaroufly and inhumanly Murdered on the High Road from the City of *Dublin* to *Donnybrooke*, aforefaid; having received feveral Slugs or Bullets on the Left Side of his Head and Face, from the Difcharge of a Blunderbufs, or Piftol, from fome Perfon or Perfons unknown.

WE, the Lord Lieutenant and Council, having a juft Abhorrence of fo Deteftable a Crime, and being defirous that due Encouragement may be given for Difcovering, Apprehending and Convicting the Perfon or Perfons guilty of the faid Murder, Do, by this Our Proclamation, Publifh and Declare, that if any Perfon or Perfons, fhall, within three Kalendar Months, from the Date of this Our Proclamation, Take and Apprehend all, or any of the Perfons concerned in the faid Murder, fo as they be Convicted thereof, the Perfon or Perfons fo Taking and Apprehending, fhall Receive as a Reward, the Sum of One Hundred Pounds for the firft Perfon who fhall be fo Taken, Apprehended and Convicted; and the Sum of Fifty Pounds for each of the other Perfons who fhall be Taken, Apprehended and Convicted of the faid Murder.

AND

Thomas Ashworth, described as a paper printer, was murdered in 1757 by fabric furnishers opposed to the introduction of wallpaper. (NAI)

Stoneybatter. They were well armed, and carried their victim into the Liberties to exact their revenge. He was, however, rescued by local residents in Meath Street.[11]

There was an ever-increasing use of products that were amenable to mass production. These drew the ire of traditional craftsmen, who retained the domestic scale of work. There was violent opposition to innovations such as wallpaper that reduced the demand for fabric furnishings. In 1757 a paper printer named Thomas Ashworth was killed near his home on the Donnybrook road. That was just one of a long series of incidents in which workers wrecked the premises of wallpaper producers. In the late 1760s offenders were publicly whipped after an attack on a house in Anglesea Street destroyed a large stock of paper. Wallpaper was especially amenable to factory production, and by 1800 the city's largest firms had chosen that option.[12]

Agitation within the silk industry brought a significant advance of work practices during the 1740s. Yet their overall progress was checked by the wider changes going on. Units of production were growing, and there was a shift away from family-based workshops. During the 1750s about a thousand textile workers were employed by Benjamin and Joseph Houghton in premises that included their factory at Cork Street. The Houghtons produced both cotton and linen, as well as blends called cotton unions. They persistently paid below the rates agreed by the guild, and as a result sometimes needed army protection.[13]

Aggrieved workers campaigned against innovation. They resisted the importation of English machinery that threatened their livelihood and ransacked factories where these machines were set up. They singled out places where the new apparatus had the greatest impact on jobs – for example, where ribbons were turned out much faster. This is what happened in 1764 when workers broke into the house of James Harding at Wormwood Gate. Harding had replaced several winders with an imported machine to speed up his production of wool and flax cords. These men wrecked his new machine and beat up his wife. It is clear that the government was alarmed by this attack on innovation. It offered a reward of £40 for each offender, causing the attackers to go into hiding.[14]

Many workers took exception to women taking their places, and accepting lower wages and poorer conditions. In the mid-1760s journeymen silk weavers ejected some four hundred women from their looms. This violence against female textile workers went as far as murder. In 1767 a cotton spinner named Elinor Ringley was taken to a field near James Street where she was brutally killed.[15]

The move towards factory production came at a time of greater competition with English centres. Masters were expanding their control over the materials and simultaneously reducing wages. There was a neglect of the traditional craft skills.

BY THE

LORDS JUSTICES and COUNCIL

OF

IRELAND,

A

PROCLAMATION.

SHANNON. JN. PONSONBY.

HEREAS We have received Information on Oath, That *James Harding* has for several Years past followed the Trade of Card-making in the City of *Dublin*, for the Manufactory of Wool and Flax, and that some Time in the Month of *February* last, the said *James Harding*, at a considerable Expence, procured an Engine from *England*, for managing the Wire and holding the Leather used in making Wool and Flax Cards with Exactness and Dispatch, which saved the Labour of many Men: And whereas We have also received Information on Oath, That on the Night of the Twenty ninth Day of *March* last, *Nicholas Rorke, Thomas Ward, John Wilkinson, Edward Harris,* and *Patrick Norton,* and several other Evil-minded Journeymen of the Card-making Trade, to the Number of Fourteen and upwards, armed with Pistols, Hangers, and other Weapons, broke into the House of the said *James Harding* at *Wormwood-Gate* in the said City of *Dublin,* and forcibly tore down the said Engine, and burned or otherwise destroyed the same, and broke Part of the said *Harding*'s House, cut and abused the said *James Harding*'s Wife, in such a Manner that she has been since under the Care of a Physician and (most Part of the Time) two Surgeons, who are of Opinion she will never recover the proper Use of her right Arm: And whereas the several Persons concerned in and guilty of the said Offence have absconded and concealed themselves, so as they cannot be apprehended and taken:

WE,

In 1764 a large reward was offered for the arrest of men who broke up the machinery imported by James Harding to replace several cord winders. (NAI)

Widespread cheating allowed apprentices to qualify too early as journeymen. Employers brought in new apprentices and journeymen willing to work under inferior conditions. These changes caused some workers to take strike action.

There was better organisation amongst the combinations during the 1760s. They were networking with allies in London and sharing information on tactics. One letter sent by seventeen workers in Dublin to their London comrades related how 'Mr Armstrong, Young Webster, Baltiboys, Kennedy, etc, makes it their business at unreasonable hours to go armed with blunderbusses, pistols, swords and cutlasses, heading the army and watch, and lodging whom they think proper in Newgate.' Groups of journeymen emigrated to London, where Irish weavers became prominent in the agitation that was already well established.[16]

Other workers followed the example of the weavers, including the tailors, printers, shoemakers, bakers, coopers and tanners. These combinations used violence to pursue their claims, but the butchers gained a particular notoriety. In the early 1780s they attempted to restrict jobs to native Dubliners. This ban on outsiders was supported by the weavers, hosiers and coopers. The shoemakers saw these strangers as unlawful men who were fair game for a thrashing, and some victims ended up in the Liffey. The lone surviving foreign butcher at the Smithfield Market was threatened with severe punishment; he was the last of six Englishmen after all his mates had been banished.[17]

Several attempts were made to stamp out these proto-unions. In 1780 a group of thirty-seven master skinners was jailed for combining together. In 1794

A drover leading cattle to slaughter beside St Patrick's cathedral, c. 1795. The butcher is waiting with his long knife. (From James Malton, *A Picturesque and Descriptive View of the City of Dublin*, 1799) (NGI)

TARRING and FEATHERING
The Reward of the Enemies of Ireland

An episode of industrial strife in the Liberties when tar and feathers were applied to a victim. (*Walker's Hibernian Magazine,* July 1794) (Board of Trinity College, Dublin)

fifteen journeymen were arrested for attacking shoemakers who had opposed the combinations. Large rewards were posted for offenders – the sums ranged from £40 to £1,000. Any informer was offered a pardon along with the reward. When the authorities turned up the heat, the workers tried new methods to defend themselves. Some episodes took on the signs of a guerrilla war. The sheriffs and craft-masters ransacked workers' homes. Taverns used by journeymen were raided, and any conniving publican was pilloried at the Tholsel. In 1770 an ambush on journeymen tailors unearthed records of their organisation and methods. It also revealed a defence fund that supported members against prosecutions.[18]

During the 1770s the workers hired men to attack offending employers; these militants were known as 'Lighthorsemen'. They tarred and feathered victims, and destroyed their property. Some journeymen persuaded them to drown a troublesome ribbon weaver, while others used them to thrash a master printer who was too obstinate. This violence continued over the following two decades, bringing great unrest to the weavers, tailors and sawyers.[19]

In 1780 officialdom turned to new methods. The Combination Act (19 & 20 Geo. iii, c.19 [Ire.]) was the most notable legal instrument employed to thwart the workers. In the same year the Volunteers set up in response to the American Revolution offered rewards for the discovery of troublemaking workers. Like earlier initiatives this campaign had mixed results, but the harassment went on. Each Easter the journeymen tailors gathered in the Liberties to promote the interests of their trade. In 1789 this meeting took place in a house off High Street. When the occasion became boisterous the police used the opportunity to attack the delegates. Local residents sided with the tailors and together they fought off the officialdom. The police returned armed with muskets and bayonets, but two of their men were killed in the counter-attack. This period of unrest involved the tailors and carpenters along with others, such as the sugar bakers and the skinners. Two weavers and two sawyers ended up on the scaffold in 1790.

Any success achieved by the combinations was qualified by the impact it had on the women who were displaced. Stark divisions were created between male and female workers. These women were compelled to make demands on any charitable institutions that might offer them support. By 1800 females made up the great majority of inmates at the House of Industry.[20]

Industrial violence

As the tide of fashion ebbed and flowed it had enormous repercussions for households in the clothing trade. There were campaigns to support Irish manufactures, and these began as early as 1703 when parliament promoted the use of native products such as furniture and clothing. In 1720 Jonathan Swift published a pamphlet for the same reason. Just like fashion itself, these initiatives were fickle and transient. People with real wealth wanted to show it off by wearing the latest creations from London and Paris. At the same time unemployed workers were not willing to suffer in silence. This was made clear in the 1750s when the taste for exotic oriental goods spread from London to Dublin. A surge in imported fabrics could be very damaging, and it generated great unrest. The corporation set up a special fund to prosecute agitators who destroyed imported garments. Weavers, tailors and tanners were to the fore, and fought against the importation of clothing and footwear. Bakers, coopers and construction workers also got involved. Hunger spurred these confrontations, and food riots were part of the ferment. In crisis years the lord mayor was forced to intervene and prohibit the export of certain foods. In 1764 a well-armed group of forty people seized a consignment of bacon from a vessel at George's Quay.

BY THE

LORDS JUSTICES and COUNCIL

OF

IRELAND,

A

PROCLAMATION.

BOWES, C. DROGHEDA. J[N]. PONSONBY.

 HEREAS WE have received Information upon Oath, That on *Wednesday* the Eleventh Day of *March* Instant, about Half an Hour after Seven of the Clock in the Evening, a Number of unknown Persons, about Thirty or Forty, riotously went on board the Ship The *Happy Return* of *Arundel* (whereof *Peter Friendly* is Master) at her Moorings on *George*'s *Quay* in the City of *Dublin*, in a forceable Manner, armed with Cutlasses and other Weapons, and broke open the Hatches of said Ship, and compelled the People on Board to strike a Light for them, and entered into the Hold of said Ship, and carried away a very considerable Quantity of Bacon, Part of the Cargo with which the said Vessel was laden, and also cut and damaged the Rigging and Decks of the said Ship.

NOW

This proclamation relates to a desperate attack on a ship laden with bacon by hungry people seeking food, 1767. (NAI)

Compensation was paid to merchants whose stores were raided by the hungry workers. In 1767 the corporation paid £500 for imported wheat, and sold it at Thomas Street Market.[21]

Building workers reacted violently when English tradesmen were employed on construction projects. These newcomers had to accept the established rules and subscribe to the combinations. Distressed weavers and tailors became more agitated during the closing decades of the century. After the closure of two large factories in the crisis year of 1793 an estimated five thousand employees roamed the streets. They spread out from the Liberties and were followed by their families. They raided warehouses and stores, and seized food from hucksters. This violence prompted the closure of shops in Thomas Street, Dame Street and St Stephen's Green.

According to William Drennan, a city doctor, the Liberties' weavers were distraught. They raided bakeries, flour stores and potato sheds. Food shops were looted and provision carts were hijacked. In 1796 a crowd of over three thousand people seized a consignment of potatoes on the quays. The raids went on throughout the 1790s, and the tension rose when millers and merchants hoarded food.[22]

Assaults on merchants

> Great cry and little wool – is now become
> the plague and proverb of the weaver's loom.
> No wool to work on, neither weft nor warp,
> Their pockets empty and their stomachs sharp,
> Ladies, relieve the weavers, or they die.
>
> Thomas Sheridan, 1721[23]

The vice-regal court had plenty of big spenders, and its influence trickled down the social ladder. It was a good source of employment where quality clothing and provisions could be supplied. However, the Castle could not be relied on for continuous remuneration. The support for Irish-made clothing gained momentum during the 1730s when greater efforts were made to persuade wealthy women to wear locally produced garments. Some gentlemen's clubs refused to toast any woman who wore French lace. The workers' efforts turned to the boycott of imports, and violence crept into the agenda. Importers of cotton and woollen drapery had their premises ransacked, and the offending goods were burned in the streets. The lord mayor warned that such attacks would be severely punished. Some weavers were arrested when they tethered their victims and led them in a procession through the town. Following the destruction of a woollen warehouse at Usher's Quay in 1771 a reward of £20 was offered by city merchants. In a related incident gunfire was exchanged when Liberties weavers attacked a draper's house in Grafton Street. During the constitutional agitation of the 1780s the Volunteers were encouraged to wear Irish clothes. Unemployed weavers supported these actions, and crowded the streets when high society was gathering for fancy balls. Carriages were stopped to check whether the occupants were wearing Irish clothes. Guards were consequently placed on all approaches to Rotunda balls.[24]

> If the ladies of Ireland would please to wear stuff,
> The trades men of Dublin would shortly be up,
> But those foreign dresses the ladies does wear,
> Which leaves our poor tradesmen in grief and despair.
>
> Anon., 'The Ladies Dress, or the Downfall of the Stay-makers', *c.* 1790[25]

Agitation against imports was stepped up in the 1790s. Armed men attacked any man wearing nankeen (Nanking cotton) waistcoats and breeches, as well as any women dressed in muslin coats. Women wearing English gowns had acid thrown over them, and those wearing Spanish shoes had their footwear slashed. Tailors using imported fabrics were tarred and feathered.[26] These campaigns took on a political hue during the 1780s when some of the violence was promoted by the underground movement of the United Irishmen. According to the Castle informer Francis Higgins, almost forty per cent of Dublin rebels who surrendered during the 1798 uprising were textile workers. This direct action followed a pattern already established elsewhere. Notable targets for London workers were lace from Europe and cotton from India.[27] In the 1750s Cork weavers opposed imports of cotton garments, and in the 1780s unemployed textile workers in that city blocked the import of woollen goods; they also held up the use of new machinery.[28] The similarity in tactics is an indication of networking between the workers' organisations. The irony is that each city was busy defending its own patch.

Sectarian division

> Rioters and ruffians of every kind render it impossible for many to pass through the streets at night without insult or assault.
>
> *Hibernian Journal*, 13 September 1780

The best-known Dublin factions were the Liberty Boys and Ormond Boys. The first of these was formed by Protestant weavers south of the river, while the latter (their opponents) mainly comprised Catholic butchers from the north quays. These two groups waged war over seven decades. The Liffey formed both a physical and a symbolic barrier between them, and pitched battles, with the use of meat hooks and long knives, were fought out along the quays. Many of the bloodiest encounters lasted a few days, ending in fatalities. Commercial life was halted while the trouble lasted. These occasions revealed the absence of a reliable police force, and the parish watch remained cowering in the background. Violence could die down for a few years, only to be revived by some perceived slight. In 1748 a truce was announced and details of the settlement were even published in the newspapers. Just as before, it proved futile, and the violence went on for another four decades.[29]

Accounts of violence associated with Dublin's Orange faction are quite scarce. In 1802 riots followed the commemoration of the Battle of the Boyne on the twelfth of July. This trouble began after some young men parading with Orange sashes were harassed and insulted. These aggrieved individuals then ventured out with firearms to seek retaliation. Further injury was prevented by the arrival of the Castle Guard.[30]

Religious repression became a public spectacle, and entire crowds were arrested for Sabbath-breaking. In 1772 two hundred revellers were detained in St John's parish during a single night. William Forbes, the lord mayor for 1766, demolished a ball alley in Aungier Street after local residents blamed it for offensive behaviour and property damage.[31]

The army and the chalking acts

> Whereas divers profligate and evil disposed persons have of late with knives or other offensive weapons cut and stabbed, or with pistols have wounded or attempted to wound, by firing, shooting, and discharging the same, many of his majesty's subjects either with an attempt to murder, rob, or maim, or merely with a wanton and wicked intent to disable or disfigure them.
>
> 17 & 18 Geo. III, c.11 [Ire.] (1777–78)

The proximity of the barracks to the Ormond Market generated considerable trouble because soldiers were used to enforce the Sabbath. The troops suppressed sporting activity along the quays, and there was violent retaliation when they visited riverside taverns and brothels. These factions were well established by the 1750s. Contests between the butchers and the soldiers grew at an alarming rate during the following decades. When the butchers had the advantage of surprise, their long knives could overcome muskets and bayonets. During the 1770s and '80s a few hundred soldiers were permanently disabled by the practice known as 'houghing', which crippled the victims by cutting the sinews of their legs; many of them died of their wounds. One episode in 1774 lasted more than a fortnight. It was sparked by an attack on soldiers bowling at Oxmantown Green. These men hobbled home in a desperate state. Four of the butchers were caught, but were soon released when their friends bribed the constable. When the assailants celebrated with a boastful rampage, soldiers went to the Ormond Market to cut and maim innocent people in an imitation of the butchers' foul deeds. More bloodletting occurred over the following days. At least twenty-four troops were left crippled, and the episode was so severe that the soldiers were confined to barracks for a while.[32]

There was a similar episode the following year. Soldiers were crippled near the Ormond Market and their comrades sought revenge. The search party ransacked meat stalls, destroying all the produce they could find. Some soldiers were arrested, but their comrades set them free. Severe houghing episodes broke out during 1777–78 and again in 1780–81, continuing off and on until the mid-1780s. Substantial rewards and even hanging did not deter the offenders. As a result the elite Castle Guard was used to patrol the vicinity of the Ormond Market. After the episode of 1774 ordinary soldiers made public appearances in pairs and were well armed.[33]

Conflict between the soldiers and the parish watch intensified over the following years. Both sides competed in extortion from the brothels. Bands of army officers known as 'marauding bucks' attacked the watch. There was great concern at the spectacle of Dublin's agencies of law and order fighting each other: 'winking at the licentiousness of soldiers is a sure prognostic of an intention of either introducing or confirming despotism.'[34]

During the early 1780s the pattern of violence changed. The Volunteers assumed a role in policing, and this brought them into confrontation with the army. Soldiers assaulted Volunteers who blocked their criminal activities. Some of these attacks resulted in the deaths of innocent passers-by. In 1788 forty soldiers were caught red-handed when they stole liquor from dram shops in Copper Alley. In order to distract the Volunteers they turned on innocent pedestrians, stabbing them with their bayonets.[35]

Political feuding

> The profession of knocking-down, buffing, maiming, abusing, etc, spreadeth very largely, the professors whereof have lately extended their infernal dominions to Temple-Bar, Fleet-street, and other places, to the great terror of helpless women, children and cripples.
>
> *Faulkner's Dublin Journal*, 20 January 1750

Political celebrations brought the factions out onto the streets. Anniversaries such as the king's birthday or May Day were very divisive. There were fatalities when the army intervened to remove maypoles and other symbols. When a new viceroy arrived in the city or a new university provost was declared, revellers ran through the streets ordering householders to light candles in their windows. They shouted 'Lights, lights!' and smashed the windows of any house that did not comply. In 1795 the college students created mayhem when neighbours were slow to honour their new provost. In response, a contrary mob attacked the local press gangs. Two houses were gutted, with the contents destroyed in a bonfire. In November 1805 two nights' illuminations were demanded to celebrate Nelson's victory at Trafalgar, and those deemed less than enthusiastic had their windows broken. Groups opposed to these celebrations were just as likely to smash the windows of families that did light up. There was even more violence when these two groups came face to face.[36]

As the factions multiplied it was harder to identify their actual grievances. For a brief period in 1750 the Liberty Boys and the Ormond Boys joined together in opposition to both the army and the parish watch. Some obscure groups that behaved violently, such as the Cross Lane Boys and

An IRISH CHEROKEE.

Marauding thugs troubled all parts of the city. The man in this case is well dressed. (*Walker's Hibernian Magazine*, April 1792) (UCD)

Newmarket Boys, were probably pursuing agendas related to their employment, while others, such as the Pinkindindies, were merely malevolent boyos. This latter group was active during the 1780s; it comprised about twenty young men who attacked innocent passers-by. They stabbed women with the exposed tips of short swords, forcing them to part with valuables. They also extorted payments from private houses by removing lamp brackets and railings.[37] During the 1790s political agitators were inspired by the French Revolution. At least a dozen of these covert groups were active in the city. Some of them were very small and only identified by the name of the public house where they gathered. The spread of these organisations was facilitated by the custom of workshops keeping 'outdoor' apprentices, a practice that reduced supervision.[38]

Violent factions such as these were also seen in Cork. Severe clashes between the weavers and the butchers began in the late 1720s, and the growth of workers' combinations increased tension. Illuminations led to rioting and throughout the 1760s violence followed the May-bush celebrations. References to the houghing of soldiers largely coincide with the Dublin pattern.[39]

A fear of republican sedition followed the French Revolution. Several policemen were killed when rioting accompanied the 1790 election, and the cost of damage to property exceeded £70,000. It was believed that some troops and parish watchmen were siding with the rebels.[40] Rumours of an army mutiny spread in 1795, inspired by soldiers drinking in rebel taverns along Barrack Street. The cavalry patrolled the streets, intent on breaking up public gatherings. Agitation by 'those new fashioned pests, called Croppies' accelerated up to the 1798 uprising, and when the rebellion came there was widespread sectarian violence. Fear prompted some families to depart for England, leaving their houses vacant.[41]

The rising in Dublin was suppressed by the yeomanry posted at Smithfield, at Newmarket, the river crossings and at the city approaches. Terrorist tactics were used, such as hanging rebels beside the main bridges. Dublin insurgents participated in the rising outside of the city, notably in Wicklow and Wexford; as we have seen, many were weavers, with a notable proportion coming from the Liberties.[42] The city was slow to recover from the trauma of the uprising. A decade later John Gamble vividly recalled 'when every house was a barrack, every public building a prison, and every street a Golgotha, or a shambles, on the lamp posts of which some wretched fellow creature was daily suspended, who, while his limbs quivered in the agonies of death, was the subject of brutal joke and unfeeling exultation'.[43]

D'Olier Street (left) and Westmoreland Street, radiating southwards from the new Carlisle Bridge, were splendid streetscapes created by the Wide Streets Commission. (Henry Brocas)

11

Development Control and Infrastructural Provision

Whereas the inhabitants of the city of Dublin have not of late been sufficiently supplied with water, which hath been occasioned by the great increase of the inhabitants of the said city, and the insufficiency of the works formerly constructed to supply such a number.

15 & 16 Geo. III, c.24 [Ire.] (1775–76)

Water shortages

Eighteenth-century Dubliners relied on a decrepit, medieval water system. This was the culvert that ran down from the southern foothills into the old heart of the city. Water was constantly disappearing from the timber pipes and pollution had become a serious problem by the 1720s. Effluent from brewers, millers, tanners and bleach greens was usually to blame. As early as 1719 tucking mills were fouling the main supply with urine, soap and other unwholesome matter. Other sources of pollution were equally unsavoury. In 1755 the supply was diverted away from the rotting corpses at the workhouse cemetery. Throughout the 1770s the Liberties' supply was seriously polluted:

Many persons throw in, wash, dip, scour, beat, and steep, within the said water course, linen, woollen, cloths, yarn, flax, tape, manufactures of linen, cotton, coloured with dye stuffs, skins, garbage, and commit several other nuisances to corrupt and foul said water.

19 & 20 Geo. III, c.13 [Ire.], cl.xxii (1779–80)

Brooking's 1728 city map included a view of the Basin beside James' Street. This was the first of three reservoirs built during the Georgian era. They were totally inadequate. As late as 1770 only twenty per cent of the population had a mains supply, and that was intermittent. The Basin was bone dry when the English traveller Richard Twiss saw it in 1775.[1] Up to the 1830s wealthy residents turned to hawkers selling water door-to-door. Houses within the affluent squares had basement areas where a large butt could be installed. A trade also built up in the sale of water stolen from the public system. Various remedies were tried by the city council, and these included buying private water rights, a process that began during the 1740s. The corporation purchased mills on the River Liffey in order to divert the flow. These purchases included a large mill at Islandbridge. Later, the corporation turned to the new Grand Canal, and financial assistance was given to extend the waterway as far as the Basin. This new source came on-stream in 1777.[2]

Another extension came in 1787. This served the area within the Circular Road, but a decade later it was inadequate. The corporation sought to extend supplies from the waterways. In 1806 the Grand Canal was used to feed a reservoir on the south side at Portobello, and in 1814 the Royal Canal was feeding a third reservoir, on the north side at Blessington Street. Other initiatives included the provision of street fountains to serve poor people who had no other supply. This venture brought further controversy. An inordinate number of fountains were erected for the exclusive Sackville Mall. By far the most expensive fountain was erected in Merrion Square, where the Rutland fountain cost £2,000, along with a further £20,000 spent on statues to decorate it.

A domestic water cistern of the Georgian era in a basement at Gardiner Street. This is a rare survival.

The Rutland fountain was erected in Merrion Square. Named after the viceroy, it was designed to impress the wealthy new residents. (NLI)

Complaints about the water shortage persisted, even after the installation of cast-iron pipes began in the 1790s; that work went on into the 1820s and beyond. Corporation workers rang a bell to alert householders when the supply was actually present in the mains. Initiatives were taken to shift sources of pollution further away. Legislation compelled river mills to move out as far as Templeogue, and in 1740 stringent controls were placed on bleach greens within five miles of the city. In some cases industrialists were forced to lodge a security bond to guarantee against pollution.[3]

✳ ✳ ✳ ✳ ✳

Dublin was slow to learn the terrible lesson from London's Great Fire of 1666, and it was only in the following century that rudimentary fire engines came into use. The first picture of one operating in the city appeared in 1711. This contraption was sold by John Oates, who carried on a trade in such machinery. These were simple vehicles carrying a twin-handled pump attached to a cistern that was filled up with buckets of water. Improvement of the fire brigade was held back

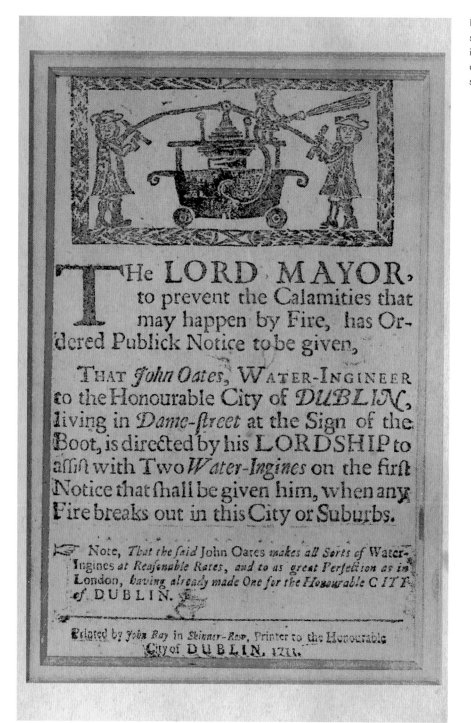

Basic fire engines such as this device introduced in 1711 could hardly quell a serious outbreak. (DCC)

by the absence of a reliable water supply. There were frequent outbreaks of fire, especially where old timber-built structures huddled together. Haystacks, timber yards and workshops presented a particular hazard. In 1757 a Thomas Street sugar factory valued at over £5,000 was destroyed by fire.[4]

Insights into this topic survive in the diary of a parish constable working near St Patrick's cathedral during the 1720s. He described the combustion of a tallow-chandler's workshop in Vicar Street and how it destroyed two adjoining houses. Several houses in St Nicholas Street were ruined by the inferno that erupted from a druggist's workshop; the culprit in that case had been boiling turpentine. In a third example the damage arose from a drinks warehouse in Temple Bar; the flaming liquid flowed down the narrow streets to the Liffey, and the blaze on the waterfront was so intense that ships had to weigh anchor and escape.[5]

Crime was associated with fire outbreaks. In 1789 an extensive fire at the new Custom House drew a large crowd of onlookers; pickpockets reaped a reward from the confusion as many purses and handkerchiefs were stolen. Episodes such as this explain why the work was left to the parish watch. An act of 1719 charged each parish with providing its own fire engine, and this led to the construction of fire stations. In 1738 St Brigid's parish paid £3 for a building to house its engine.

Private fire insurance reached Dublin during the 1720s, and this was another service that highlighted urban priorities. Insurance companies had fire engines, but they only served their own clients: only those premises displaying the company's distinctive fire mark got assistance when a blaze broke out. In the public sector it was affluent parishes that made most progress. The watchmen of St Anne's acquired an improved type of machine in the mid-1760s, and these men were paid a salary of £4 for firefighting. Over time the benefit of cooperation with adjoining parishes was taken into account. By the 1820s St Anne's was making payments to 'foreign' firemen who came into its area to fight outbreaks.[6]

Sewerage facilities

> So where the sew'rs thro' broken channels glide,
> And stagnant filth coagulates the tide,
> Lur'd by the stench unnumber'd flies resort,
> And wanton circling, mix in various sport.
>
> Anon., The Upper Gallery, 1733[7]

Affluent households disposed of sewage by emptying their chamber pots into either a cesspit or cesspool. Others merely threw the contents out onto the street. Such casual disposal of ordure was, of course, prohibited, and offenders could be heavily fined. Some streets had gutters called kennels that served as open sewers, carrying effluent down the centre of the carriageway. Poorer quarters retained a casual attitude, and certain localities accumulated 'cart loads of filth, the dirt of boghouses, the offals of slaughter houses'.[8] The unreliable water supply held back advances in sanitary engineering. In 1782 the *Hibernian Journal* advertised water closets made at number 7 Cope Street; these were claimed to be the first in Ireland. Although water closets are mentioned in corporation records as early as 1811, they remained scarce until water supplies became more dependable five decades later. In theory it was easy for occupiers to install a sewer connection, and in 1782 the Wide Streets Commission laid down clear guidelines for its enterprise at Dame Street:

> That the taker of each lot shall build vaults to the front of his holding fifteen feet in depth from the front line, the crown of the vaults to be twenty four inches at least under the level of the fill, as set forth in the Plan no.3 and shall also build a sewer opposite to his lot of stone and mortar, or brick and mortar, three feet wide in the clear and three feet high to the springing of the arch, the crown of the

A chamber pot (made in Westerwald, Germany, c. 1710) recently retrieved from a Georgian cesspit. (Courtesy of Franc Myles)

arch twelve inches high from the springing, the crown of the arch to be in the clear ten feet seven inches under the top of the sill, as set out in the Plan no.3.[9]

Dame Street acquired one of the first conventional sewers, and the WSC spent several decades getting it to work properly. From the 1760s through to the 1780s a terrible stench lingered about the place. Notoriety followed the malodour because this street dominated the ceremonial route connecting the Castle with Parliament House. In 1785 occupants of new buildings lodged complaints, but it was the gathering of parliament at College Green that spurred the WSC into action. It decided to eradicate the stench by upgrading the entire project. Priority was given to laying an entirely new sewer through Dame Street to College Green, with all the offensive contents diverted down through Anglesea Street into the Liffey. This work was timed to avoid any disturbance of parliament. In order to prevent a repeat of previous problems, the contractor William Pemberton had to lodge a security bond to the value of £300. Despite these good intentions there was to be no redemption for Dame Street. Pipes backed up where little account was taken of gravity, and it was claimed that thirty thousand residents had to suffer the nuisance.[10]

In the decade after the Union a great proportion of the city remained without sewers, and cesspits were still in use during the Regency. In Westmoreland Street and Sackville Street raw sewage was removed through openings made in the street. It lay there day after day, to the great annoyance of the public, until a heavy downpour carried it away.[11]

Road conditions and public transport

> Whereas the publick pavements are in many places of the said city very much out of repair, and in several places raised to such a height, especially before the new buildings, that carriages, coaches, or horses, cannot with safety pass the same … and great quantities of coal-ashes, dirt and other filth of late have been and are daily thrown into the streets, lanes, and alleys …
>
> 4 Geo I, c.11 [Ire.], cl.i (1717)

Growing traffic was a challenge to the narrow, medieval carriageways. As late as the 1780s important streets such as Skinners' Row were just 5 metres wide; it also had shopfronts and cellars jutting out on either side, leaving only 3.5 metres for vehicles. These were terrible places for pedestrians. At Skinners' Row the footpath was just 0.3 metres wide and in poor condition. As public disquiet grew, so did the search for someone to blame. As early as the 1680s the pavers were demanding that their work had to be restricted to guild members, and during the eighteenth century the shoddy construction was blamed on labourers who replaced the qualified craftsmen.[12]

One reason for the poor condition of highways was the theft of the gravel topping. Property developers stole this material to lay driveways, and farmers used it to scour milk churns – they dumped their farmyard dung on the highway and then, pretending to remove it, took the gravel instead. The Howth road had a notorious reputation for this abuse, and residents of the North Strand resented how they were deprived of a healthy airing.

Politicians criticised the state of the streets. During the winter of 1784–85 Sir John Blaquiere MP blamed bad roads for bringing commercial life to a halt. He rebuked the authorities for allowing congealed snow and dirt to build up until accidents were caused. Some months later John Beresford MP and Luke Gardiner MP claimed the ruinous state of the approach roads was a disgrace to the city. In 1790 the Lord Chancellor claimed the way to the Linen Hall was impassable. Hely Dutton (1802) also condemned the approaches; crumbling footpaths on the Donnybrook road and North Strand forced pedestrians to wade ankle-deep through mud and water.[13]

There were great numbers of shop signs jutting out from sloping roofs. A substantial proportion of Dubliners were illiterate, and they relied on these visual aids to identify business places. An attempt was made in 1763 to compel businesses to attach signs flat to the front of their shops, but this failed. Reform did not come until the mid-1770s, and that was two decades after the good example set by London. The removal of such impediments made it easier to drive about, and rich households bought vehicles to carry them around in comfort. During 1785 there were twenty-three new carriages registered, and the addresses of buyers reflected the social gradient. These purchasers lived in Marlborough Street (two), Holles Street (two), Dorset Street (two), Granby Row (two), Ranelagh Road (two), Grafton Street, Sackville Street, Ely Place, Anne Street, Jervis Street, Denmark Street, Hume Street, Merrion Square, Molesworth Street, Dawson Street, Gloucester Street, Peter's Row and Clontarf Road.[14]

Visitors were impressed by the amount of public transport. They thought hackneys were more common than in London, and the same was said of sedan chairs. Much of this business, however, was generated by the state of the streets.

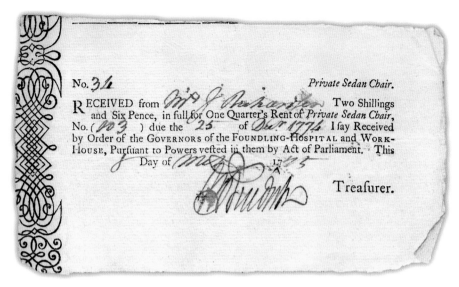

A sedan-chair licence issued to Mrs J. Richardson, 1775. This mode of transport suited wealthy women. (DCC)

No. 34   *Private Sedan Chair.*

RECEIVED from *Mrs J. Richardson* Two Shillings and Six Pence, in full for One Quarter's Rent of *Private Sedan Chair*, No. (103) due the 25 of *Decr 1774* I say Received by Order of the GOVERNORS of the FOUNDLING-HOSPITAL and WORK-HOUSE, Pursuant to Powers vested in them by Act of Parliament. This Day of *March* 1775

Treasurer.

By the early 1730s there were about two hundred hackney coaches for hire, along with an equal number of sedans. The hackneys grew from 150 to 300 during the period 1707–71, while sedan chairs went from 80 to 400. Regulations for public vehicles were introduced in 1793. They specified the maximum number for each type of vehicle and also controlled the public parking spaces.

Public transport found plenty of customers as the city expanded, but there was not much improvement in the quality of the service. The dirty interiors, hard seats and broken windows inspired a literary response: 'As so many respectable folks are in the habit of hiring a Jowlt for the purpose of "taking the air", never defeat their innocent intentions by glazing your windows – a thorough blast ventilates a vehicle, refreshes the passengers, and disperses those fusty vapours so very sickening to weak stomachs.'[15]

✳ ✳ ✳ ✳ ✳

All drivers of publick carriages are to keep the gutters or middle of the streets through which they pass, upon their left hand, and if they are obliged by the stopping of carriages, or any other accident, to change their side, they are, as soon as possible, to return to it again.

Faulkner's Dublin Journal, 5 November 1748

Two-way traffic was introduced in 1748, but the law was widely ignored. Parliament still agonised over non-compliance by road users five decades later.

This system advocated right-hand driving, as can be observed in contemporary prints. The authorities were slow to provide signposts and milestones. The Paving Board was subjected to constant criticism; pedestrians were always complaining about the condition of sidewalks. Street lighting was weak and was absent from poorer districts. It was hard to raise taxes in the Liberties, and residents were therefore denied services.[16]

St Anne's parish had 140 street lamps in 1755, and this number kept on increasing until it reached 173 in 1779. St Anne's secured this service through an annual agreement. The contractor got a fee for each light, so the deal grew more attractive as the number increased. During the 1750s the payment per lamp was fifteen shillings, but this increased as well; it doubled within a few years. The arrangement became more businesslike, and in 1775 we find the first undertaker with the '& Co.' appellation. Yet St Anne's was exceptional. In the early 1780s only three per cent of city houses had a private lamp, although the number rose quickly over the following decade. According to the *Hibernian Journal* the total expanded from 2,247 to 10,666 in the period 1782–86.[17]

The Paving Board gave priority to opulent streets. In 1784 the Duke of Leinster acknowledged that areas occupied by the nobility were well maintained while the main streets and trading areas were neglected. In 1806 one supervisor admitted that the board had 'one standard for settling their ideas of those terms as applied to Merrion-square, and another as applied to Thomas-street'. There was a strong reaction to the Paving Board fining householders who neglected footpaths in front of their houses when the general public could not cross the streets without wading through muck. The board conceded that neglect left footpaths slippery but denied any blame because its function merely related to the carriageways; it continued to prosecute property owners who failed to obey the law by sweeping their footpaths every day.[18]

Market regulation

Food production was poorly regulated. As early as 1724 St Michan's parish prosecuted butchers for slaughtering cattle directly outside the church. Offal was thrown out of slaughterhouses under the cover of darkness, and pigs gathered to feed on the gory entrails; it created the most intolerable stench imaginable. During the 1770s the Ormond Market was described as a receptacle for blood and guts, giving off an unbearable stink. Newhall Market was impassable due to the mound of carcases blocking the street; dead sheep and lambs were left bleeding on the pavement. Neighbours were offended when beggars attracted by the free food defecated in the streets. During the 1780s the open sewer running from Newhall down through Cook Street was constantly clogged by gory offal. During the summer the rotten blood turned green, and the smell was so offensive that local residents threatened to evacuate their homes. Waste at the Clarendon Market formed 'a hillock of the offals of vegetables, the carcases of half a dozen dead dogs, and a quantity of guts of other animals'. Rotting garbage at the Castle Market made good food go bad, and the neighbours protested that the slaughtering of pigs made sleep impossible. By the 1840s as many as ten thousand animals were reportedly being slaughtered each week at the markets.[19]

Conditions were just as bad at the fish markets. There was a long-standing nuisance at the Pill Lane Market (adjoining the Ormond Market). When it was finally demolished in 1829 the local residents applauded the lord mayor. In his response he recalled how the mounds of offal had blocked local traffic, making it virtually impossible to conduct business.[20]

Street cleaning and sanitation

> Here, on one side, extends a length of street,
> Where dirt-bespattered cars and coaches meet.
> On t'other, in the ditches lazy flood,
> Dead cats and dogs lie bloated, drenched in mud.
>
> Thomas Newburgh, 1758[21]

The city scavengers were supposed to remove dirt from the streets, including offal from slaughterhouses and ordure from cesspits. They appeared in Hamilton's *Cries of Dublin* using birch brooms and shovels, and wearing aprons and ankle-gaiters. It was a primitive system that relied on depots in the backstreets to store the waste. Their dunghills accumulated throughout the Liberties and down along the docks. The scavengers got a reputation for negligence, dragging their carts around carelessly. Passers-by had to avoid being struck by the foul-smelling contents. During the 1770s it was widely believed that Dublin had the dirtiest streets in Europe. In 1771 a survey of St Anne's parish revealed how neglected the streets were. Dawson Street and Clarendon Street were totally disregarded, and there were broken pavements to the front of exclusive properties such as Kildare House and Powerscourt House. Schoolhouse Lane was full of rubbish, Clarendon Market was an offensive nuisance, and all the stable lanes from Kildare Street to Nassau Street contained substantial dunghills.[22]

By the early 1790s smelly pavements disfigured the riverside area. Sporadic efforts were made to clean the new Carlisle Bridge, but half the houses in Fleet Lane were seen as repositories for pestilent filth. The neglect of the Liberties prompted householders in Meath Street to take on the task themselves. They supplied some purpose-built carts, and the same thing happened in St Michan's parish.[23] However, these were exceptions and most of the Liberties received no attention:

> Into the backyard of each house, frequently not 10 feet deep, is flung from the window of each apartment the ordure and filth of its numerous inhabitants, from whence it is seldom removed, that I have seen it nearly on a level with the windows of the first floor, and the moisture that, after heavy rains flows from this heap, having frequently no sewer to carry it off, runs into the street by the entry leading to the staircase.[24]

Scavangers

Two street sweepers celebrate the discovery of a large coin. (Hugh Douglas Hamilton, 1760) (Private collection)

Comparisons with other cities

Similar conditions prevailed in other urban centres. As late as 1805 Cork's public sewers were blocked and mounds of manure formed a serious traffic hazard. One of the least dangerous highways was likened to a muddy canal. The paving of North Main Street with flagstones began in 1763, and street lighting was also announced. Progress was slow, however, and residents continued to provide their own lamps. Four decades later the condition of North Main Street was described as alarming.[25]

During the 1760s the streets of Liverpool were narrow and dirty. Old cobbles and flags collapsed under the growing volume of traffic, and projecting cellars were a hazard for pedestrians. A substantial proportion of the streets were paved by 1795, although some remained unimproved into the 1820s. As late as 1842 some important streets had no sewers. A 1775 account stated that Manchester's streets were no better than a common dunghill, and the churchyards were profaned by the dumping of ordure. A year later Manchester got an improvement act, but even in the 1800s sewers and paving lagged behind new development. Edinburgh likewise was a smelly place; each night at 10 p.m. the town guard beat his drum warning residents to return home, but this was taken as a signal for residents to empty their chamber pots out onto the streets. A reliable water supply did not arrive until the 1820s.[26]

Reform came earlier to London. Improvement acts for Westminster and the City were passed in 1762 and 1766 respectively. The Westminster Act was a turning point because cambered carriageways were created, replacing rounded pebbles with flags. Gutters were laid along both edges and raised footpaths were installed. The law provided for the removal of balconies, uncovered cellars and projecting shop signs. The infamous Fleet Ditch was culverted. The London Building Act of 1774 served to regulate speculative housing construction. It identified four distinct building categories, ranging from the two-storey fourth-rate house up to the premier four-storey house occupying a plot of 84 square metres. In his 1780s satire *Bon Ton*, David Garrick asserted London's streets were so well paved that hackney passengers fell asleep. They had to attach strings to their hands for the coachman to pull in order to wake them on arrival at their destination. Between 1785 and 1800 some 211 paving and improvement acts were passed for English cities and towns.[27]

Reformers were alarmed by the slums of Paris. Early improvements closed overcrowded cemeteries, covering up foul drains, removing slaughterhouses and moving hospitals out to healthier surroundings. Better paving was introduced in 1782 when large granite flags started replacing cobbles. A ban was imposed on new streets less than 9 metres wide. Later advances added more bridges, along with better water supplies, public lighting and street numbering. The city's obsession with the rising tide of ordure continued until a collective effort at proper sewerage emerged in 1826.[28]

Legal remedies

> Why brothels, soap manufactories, slaughter-houses, glass-houses, and lime-kilns, distilleries, etc, are suffered to exist in the midst of a crowded population I shall not presume to enquire.
>
> Revd James Whitelaw, 1805[29]

Dublin's development control operated through statutes, covenants in property leases and injunctions at common law. Statutes were the main instruments but were selectively applied. For example, prosecutions for pollution by industrialists were pursued in tandem with incentives for decentralisation. Substantial grants were offered to cotton factories willing to move at least 10 miles from the city. We have noted the example of the aptly named Prosperous in County Kildare. Other schemes emerged in north County Dublin at Malahide and Balbriggan, and in west County Wicklow at Stratford-on-Slaney.[30]

There was widespread corruption in the building industry, and fatalities followed the frequent collapse of brick-built houses. Building sites extended out onto the sidewalk, and pedestrians regularly died from falling into unlit excavations. Jerry-building forced the government to bring in regulations during the 1720s. These initiatives brought progress because, amongst other things, they regulated the size of building bricks.[31]

> Many a hard working citizen, whose lungs will not permit him to sleep in the smoke and fogs of Dublin, is necessitated to take some small house in the environs to fly to when his shop is shut.
>
> *Hibernian Journal*, 28 January 1778

Urban expansion created a demand for all sorts of building materials, and factories set up wherever the entrepreneurs saw fit. Brick-making was regarded as a health hazard, and by the 1770s this was conceded by parliament. A new law prohibited the baking of bricks within two miles of the city lamps. Soon afterwards the same approach was applied to the limekilns of the building industry: they were banned within the area of the public lamps. Three years later an amending act reinforced this prohibition.[32]

Glass factories were singled out for suppression. Residents of North Strand claimed 'the health of many has been much injured, and the lives of several weakly persons lost' due to the smoke and dust of local glassworks. An act of 1784 banished these offenders to three quarters of a mile beyond the Circular Road; the only exception permitted was down along the quays, where there were fewer people to complain. In order to disperse the smoke and fumes, factory chimneys had to be 50 feet high. In 1791 Lord Clonmel cited brewing and candle manufacturing amongst the worst polluters, together with lime burning and glass factories. Warburton, Whitelaw and Walsh in their *History of the City of Dublin* (1818) were aghast at the dirty industries crowded together in the Liberties.

Houses had to make way for slaughterhouses, dairies, soap factories, distilleries, lime kilns and glass factories.[33]

Clearing pollution was expensive. In 1787 £2,000 was paid by the Wide Streets Commission for the removal of glassworks from Abbey Street. These factories were demolished to facilitate development linking Drogheda Street with Mabbot Street. As the city spread beyond the Circular Road, conflicts with bad neighbours continued. In 1786 there was widespread interest in an injunction brought against a proposed glass factory at Ballybough. As it turned out, the application failed because the industry did not yet exist.[34]

Wide streets and turnpikes

> Our grand streets are wide and commodious,
> And nobody constantly using them,
> Our thoroughfares narrow and odious,
> Where thousands stand daily abusing them.
>
> Anon., Paddy's Return, late eighteenth century[35]

> The wheel-cars follow each other in a long line like a flock of wild geese, with a nasty kind of teazing and jingling noise that is unsufferable.
>
> John Gamble, 1811[36]

Georgian Dublin was fortunate in having the Wide Streets Commission. The WSC was a planning agency involved in land use and urban design. It laid out new streets, beginning in the late 1750s with Parliament Street, a spacious thoroughfare linking the Castle with the last Liffey crossing at Essex Bridge. Its most important schemes were carried out during the 1780s and 1790s, and included the new central business district formed by Lower Sackville Street, Westmoreland Street, D'Olier Street and Dame Street.

The WSC completed the quays and riverside streets, opening up both sides of the Liffey. Its work was innovative in terms of architecture and engineering. Majestic brick terraces were complemented with flagstone pavements that encouraged pedestrian circulation. Developers who acquired plots in Westmoreland Street in 1799 were obliged to construct a sidewalk almost 4 metres wide. Restrictions were placed on inappropriate land use. In North Frederick Street the building leases prohibited brewing, soap boiling, silversmithing, pewtering and blacksmithing.[37]

Dublin badly needed the coordinating role of the WSC. Landlords such as the Gardiners and Fitzwilliams acted with some disregard to integration of their infrastructure with that of neighbouring estates. Yet the WSC was hardly a planning authority in the modern sense. It did not have enough power to regulate land use across the city, and it could not restrain urban sprawl. Nor did it have the power to halt the dereliction of the south-west, and it could not direct waste disposal. Rather the WSC was one of several agencies acting simultaneously but not in unison. Many development initiatives were left to other bodies. The ring road formed by the North and South Circular Roads was created by a turnpike trust. All the main commercial approaches to the city became toll roads, and after this process began in 1729 it went on for over a century. The corporation regarded the road-development agencies as agents of the large estates and opponents of the mercantile interest. In 1778 the corporation requested parliament to abolish all the turnpike trusts.[38]

Despite the corporation's reservations, the WSC had considerable influence on public opinion. Interest in town planning was stimulated by the novelty and symmetry of Parliament Street. Commentators realised that these initiatives could lead further, and early in 1769 *The Freeman's Journal* outlined the possibilities. Philadelphia was cited as a role model; it was regarded as a city where beauty was derived from a well-devised plan. It had very regular streets, and prominent sites were reserved for the most significant buildings.

Some desirable projects were put forward for Dublin. Amongst the options

D'Olier Street (left) and Westmoreland Street, radiating southwards from the new Carlisle Bridge, were splendid streetscapes created by the Wide Streets Commission. (Henry Brocas)

Dame Street, as
enhanced by the Wide
Streets Commission.
This image reflected the
great public interest in
the commission's work.
(J. Charles, *Modern
Map of the Roads of
Ireland*, 1814)

was a new Liffey crossing combined with relocation of the Custom House. These initiatives were bound to be controversial because they would move commerce further away from the old heart of the city. They were opposed by the merchants of the medieval quarter, who argued that eastward expansion had already gone too far; public institutions such as parliament and the university were so far out they could not contribute to the city.[39]

Margaret Leeson, the doyen of Dublin madams. She is depicted as Diana the huntress. (Pompeo Batoni, c. 1772) (NGI)

12

Prostitution

How oft she broke her marriage vows,
In kindness to maintain a spouse;
Till swains unwholesome spoiled the trade,
For now the surgeon must be paid.

Jonathan Swift, Philis, or the Progress of Love, 1719

WOMEN WERE EXCLUDED FROM THE public world of politics, religion and the professions. The guilds barred them from all the skilled crafts. They had no place in the armed forces. In legal terms married women were the possession of their husbands.

The most notable outlet for female workers was domestic service, and there was a rapid expansion within this part of the workforce. Nevertheless, domestic service presented a serious challenge. Cultural differences caused friction, and many females arriving from the countryside laboured under two handicaps: they were Catholics and they spoke Irish.[1]

Ambiguity and immorality

Young females in genteel households were vulnerable to sexual exploitation. This theme is widespread in the contemporary literature. From the 1760s onwards some women

271

in domestic service were willing to take a chance on alternatives such as the emerging factories, but opportunities in that sphere could easily be exaggerated.

Unemployed females claimed the vagaries of ladies' fashions left hundreds of dressmaking colleagues in a desperate state. They had to choose between hunger and the sex trade because men had taken a thousand women's jobs in the shops, and they were now restricted to servitude, starvation or prostitution. One sixteen-year-old described the absence of employment for females such as herself: those jobs monopolised by men included hairdressing, stay-making, shoemaking and midwifery as well as the teaching of music, dance, writing and foreign languages. As the century closed the House of Industry blamed the severe reduction in female employment for the great influx of streetwalkers it saw at its doors.[2]

The plight of women was reflected in the extent of prostitution during the second half of the eighteenth century. There were frequent accounts of passers-by offended by the streetwalkers' behaviour, but the consistency of reports about wailing, screaming and shrieking suggests utter desperation. Deprivation led to depravation, and the sex trade grew quickly because the supply and demand met one another. A reliable market was generated by the large barracks and the busy port. Custom also came from young workers who were forced to remain unmarried, and these included workshop apprentices. Alcohol and sex were the most popular indulgences offered by the city, and they were usually found together.[3]

No social class had a monopoly on conjugal infidelity, and ambivalence about sexual morality allowed considerable latitude to courtesans and prostitutes. Women working at the upper end of the market found clients at the Rotunda concerts, in the theatres, on the Circular Road and at army exercises in Phoenix Park.[4] One of the clearest manifestations of this business was in the theatre, where it was the female performers who were blamed. During the 1740s Thomas Sheridan denounced the regime at the Smock Alley Theatre. He felt it was far too easy for young gallants to have their way with the female players; some only had to produce a shilling while others only needed a swagger and an oak sapling. At the Crow Street Playhouse the apartment of the impresario Richard Daly was reputed to serve as a brothel in the morning and a gambling den in the evening. Daly served as procurer for Francis Higgins, the 'Sham Squire'; Higgins allegedly formed intrigues with the pirouette dancers and the ladies of the ballet.[5]

As the city grew, so did the opportunities. Enterprising prostitutes travelled about in carriages, sitting behind large windows that displayed them to the clients. During the summer months these market leaders worked the seaside resorts of Clontarf, Sandymount, Irishtown and Blackrock. Public ambivalence could be measured in various ways. A man identified only as Mr D. held an annual ball for prostitutes at his house in Bridge Street; it attracted women from Francis Street, Cook Street, Essex Street and Copper Alley. It was a great success and in 1792 there were about 250 revellers.[6] Clients at the upper end of the market held more discreet gatherings. A gentleman known as Squire Crupper hosted fandangos at his Whitehall villa on the north side; these evenings drew the most select prostitutes from the city:

> Peg Plunket shall honor my board at Whitehall,
> And Buxom Joan Driscoll, shall lead up the ball.[7]

The doyenne of Dublin madams, Margaret Leeson (nee Plunket), was part of one such high-class outing arranged in 1791 to the home of Captain Southwell in the southern foothills of Rathfarnham. The female contingent included some of the first-rate 'impures' – namely Groves, Beresford, O'Brien, Mrs Bennis and old Mrs Sterling.[8] These gatherings imitated London's Cyprian balls that brought together the nobility and their courtesans; one of those get-togethers in the Argyle Rooms attracted more than a thousand guests. Critical comment increased as the spectacles of 'vamped up impudence' expanded. The presence of prostitutes in St Stephen's Green greatly offended respectable women promenading on the Beaux Walk.[9]

Workplaces

> Of the nocturnal street-walkers, that infest the more opulent parts of the city, a very large proportion issues from the Liberty.
>
> Revd James Whitelaw, 1805[10]

These women did not occupy a distinct quarter of the kind found in some European cities. It was more like the London lifestyle, where they lived alongside their clients. Alleyways provided retreats between the Castle and the Liffey. Copper Alley, Fishamble Street and Essex Street were favourite haunts. The trade followed the customers, and as early as the 1720s the residents of St Mary's parish were resisting the arrival of offensive bawdy houses. Respectable visitors deserted the resort at Irishtown when 'Mother' Brooks brought her prostitutes there in the 1790s.[11]

The conventions and constraints of city life made customers available to the women. Workshop apprentices were normally forbidden to marry, and this predicament attracted intercourse with prostitutes.[12] Women working in the Temple Bar area gained proximity to the university, where the male students and most of their teachers were supposed to be celibate. In the same way, contingents of streetwalkers settled beside the barracks and were supported by the soldiers. Women soliciting at the lowest level were mainly found along the quays, a work area that expanded eastwards with each passing decade. The poorest women emerged only after dark, when their tattered clothes were not so easily seen. Much of the activity remained in the Temple Bar area, between Dame Street and the Liffey.[13] (See appendix three for a list of brothels operating in the period 1747–1800).

Attempts were made to conceal the sex trade from busybodies. The most frequent cover used was the public house selling alcohol, but other venues operated as washhouses or bagnios:

> Mother B-n's Bagnio in Fishamble Street – the Munster Bagnio in Smock Alley, the Dublin Bagnio on the Blind Quay, the Royal Bagnio on Essex Quay, – Mother M-y's Bagnio in Anglesea Street, with above fifty others on the Blind Quay, and different parts of the city of less repute, but equally notorious.
>
> *Hibernian Journal*, 6 May 1776

In 1777 the *Hibernian Journal* called for the closure of all brothels operating as bagnios, and the anonymous author of *Hibernia Curiosa* (1782) warned visitors to the city that these bagnios were dangerous places. When police reform was mooted in 1786, one of the urgent tasks was suppression of scandalous washhouses. Some other venues that attracted attention used fronts such as milliners' shops. One Fishamble Street brothel operated ostensibly as a china shop, while another at Stafford Street appeared more like a hotel. A notorious place in St Stephen's Street operated as the London Coffee House.[14] Bagnios began to decline as cheap hotels became more common towards the end of the century. In 1793 *The Freeman's Journal* revealed a new format resembling a haberdasher's shop where partitions were installed to allow the women to work in cubicles. At one such place on Aston Quay shop assistants and apprentices traded stolen goods for favours.[15]

One surviving record of brothel activity around 1740 described a venue on George's Quay: this was a tavern called the Rose and Crown in which 'every man worth a shilling might have a pretty woman while it lasted'. The bawd entertained a parlour full of drunken sailors who spent all their money on the women and the wine. The writer was an army captain, and he boasted of further adventures in brothels at Fishamble Street and Liffey Street. He ended up, however, in Newmarket Prison.[16]

Whenever prostitution was repressed the women turned to new tactics. In the winter of 1788–89 the Temple Bar streetwalkers were soliciting in three or four public houses beside their lodgings. Every back alley in the vicinity of Fishamble Street, Copper Alley and Smock Alley reputedly contained bawdy houses. For clients in the lowest brothels the hazards were physical as well as moral. Desperation drove some women into the houses being demolished by the Wide Streets Commission, sometimes with fatal consequences. It was reported in 1791 that certain Copper Alley brothels were likely to collapse into the street; their crumbling walls leaned out several feet over the foundations. One dive at the corner of Trinity Street and Andrew Street was leaning out so far from the adjoining houses that the women would have abandoned it if they had 'half the sagacity attributed to rats'.[17]

The scale of the sex trade

'Nor gin nor purl will I receive',
(She answer'd, with a frown)
'You'll surely give what others give?
Come – give me half-a-crown.'

Edward Walsh, Rapture!, 1793[18]

Any account of the number of women engaged in prostitution must remain conjectural. In 1776 a writer to the *Hibernian Journal* stated there were seventy-four brothels in the city, but this would appear to be a substantial underestimation. A decade later the same newspaper cited three hundred brothels with alcohol licences, as well as innumerable others with no licence. Some streets acquired clusters of brothels; the upper end of Dorset Street allegedly had eleven. The number of women arrested might also suggest the scale of the trade. For example, seventeen soliciting females were detained in a single raid on Copper Alley in September 1788. A few nights later watchmen rounded up thirty-two women around St Stephen's Green. More dramatically, about 150 prostitutes were apprehended in forty-eight hours during July 1799 in the Rotunda and St Stephen's Green areas.[19]

It was claimed that Dublin had at least twenty thousand women who were either beggars, prostitutes or mere layabouts. By 1794 institutions like the Magdalen Asylum took in about forty-five females each year. In 1813 a new Magdalen refuge was announced, and it was claimed to be urgently needed. The thousands of prostitutes could not be fitted into the two hundred spaces available, yet the intake doubled by 1821. Other indications of the scale of the business were found along the money trail. In 1794 the pimp of Margaret O'Brien (of Longford Street and Blackrock) absconded with £600 of her earnings. Margaret Leeson retired in 1792 and moved into a new house on the Blackrock road that cost £600. Elizabeth McClean, one of the city's most successful madams, had a dowry of £4,000 when she got married in 1798. A brothel business was offered for sale in 1796 for £1,000 plus four guineas per week.[20]

Recruiting methods

> Believe me, my fair-one, thy bloom was designed
> To bless some young lover, gay, sprightly and kind,
> Who always has ready a treasure of joys,
> Whose friendship ne'er slackens, whose love never cloys.
>
> Mr Marchant, 1770[21]

Women came to prostitution from several different avenues. Many of them were seduced in the classic pattern depicted by William Hogarth in *A Harlot's Progress*. One woman explained how young females coming from the country were met with feigned concern and offered housekeeping jobs. A significant proportion of procuring women had spent their own lives in the business.[22] Men deceived these females by assuming guises such as wealthy merchants or fashionable beaux. Some dancing masters turned out to be pimps, and there was anxiety that boarding schools were being used to recruit girls. Literature was blamed as well, and pornographic novels were credited with swelling the ranks of the willing females as well as those willing to pay for sex. Private theatricals had become popular within wealthy households, and these were now condemned for the same reason.[23]

Women were often pushed into the sex trade by sheer force. During the 1780s and 1790s residents of Thomas Street were alarmed by the shrieks of females dragged indoors to be ravished. It was easy for culprits to evade detection in the darkness that marked the Liberties after nightfall. Women were usually recruited locally, but from time to time exotic newcomers were brought in from other places; Belfast and Liverpool were notable sources. Some females were very young. There were many reports of girls aged about fourteen, and towards the end of the century they were getting even younger. In 1788 *The Freeman's Journal* reported on a twelve-year-old, and two years later the same newspaper referred to girls aged ten or eleven. These cases reflected the growing fear of contracting venereal disease.[24]

Disturbance and violence

> Their riots and clamours at the dead of night are terrifying and alarming; and their brawling blasphemies, execrations and obscenities, at more early hours, are shocking.
>
> *The Freeman's Journal*, 6 July 1790

Brothels attracted violence. It was the death of a customer in a Smock Alley dive that sparked off large-scale riots in May 1768. That crowd wrecked numerous local brothels; over several days they broke up premises in Fishamble Street, Blind Quay, Anglesea Street and Sycamore Alley. Six agitators were killed at an Arran Street brothel when the roof caved in. These clashes had serious consequences for females who got caught up in the violence: 'This ought to be a lesson to all unhappy women to be on their guard, as they have suffered so much on this occasion: most of them being destitute of money, friends or other means to support them.'[25]

A curfew was imposed but the rioters were too numerous to control. The trouble spread south as far as Ringsend, Irishtown and Donnybrook. Terrified prostitutes fled into the surrounding countryside during that summer. They were seen wandering through the fields in a dazed state, trying to survive by eating wild berries and flowers, and drinking milk from cows. This unrest continued during the following years, and city crowds reacted violently to the seduction of any young female. A woman was killed in 1771 for enticing a young girl from The Coombe to join her. In 1774 young men wrecked a brothel in Anglesea Street after a girl was taken in there. A similar incident occurred in College Street a year later, and the place was demolished by neighbours. During Easter 1791 a large crowd rioted when a young girl was bundled into the Ross Lane brothel of Mrs Marlow. That premises was destroyed; when the police tried to intervene they were driven back by a barrage of bricks and stones.[26]

In 1781 a Temple Bar brothel keeper was arrested for the death of a working woman. Later that year a seventeen-year-old girl was killed for refusing to work in a dive in Little Booter Lane. A crowd attacked the building, breaking all the windows, and these people were proceeding to demolish it when the sheriff intervened. The owner, Anne McDonagh, had a bad reputation and before long was in trouble again for blinding one of her workers.[27]

Later in the same year there was serious rioting at a brothel in Fleet Lane. It began as a faction fight when butchers from the Fleet Market seriously injured a band of soldiers. Army comrades wreaked revenge on the butchers and ransacked the brothel. This melee drew a large gathering, and a crowd estimated at five thousand stormed every brothel in Fleet Lane. The police were driven off by a shower of missiles before the rioters moved on to attack two brothels at Crown Alley. A cavalry detachment was called in, followed by more soldiers. They succeeded in driving back the crowd, but the rioters returned next morning. Further trouble erupted in December 1792 when a crowd described as rough apprentices and idle ruffians attacked a Church Lane brothel. They broke all the windows and wrecked the furniture before the army arrived. Soon afterwards there was a riot at the Trinity Street brothel of 'Mother' Brooks. It was started by apprentices who would not pay the women. When they were prevented from leaving they destroyed the furniture, while the crowd outside proceeded to break the windows.[28]

Violence between the butchers and the army was part of a wider agenda of extortion: they competed in grafting from the bawdy houses around Dame Street and College Green. In September 1793 a riot began when sailors challenged the graft by local butchers at a Hawkins Street brothel. The butchers chased the sailors with long knives and meat hooks. One householder who gave sanctuary to the sailors was threatened with the total destruction of his property. He responded by seriously injuring one of the butchers, striking him with his sword. In another episode, brothels in Exchequer Street were badly damaged when the prostitutes fought off an attack by butchers. An apprentice butcher was thrown out the window onto the street below.[29]

A serious episode in 1795 lasted two months, and the main targets were brothels used by press gangs. Notorious venues in Strand Street were attacked, but the violence spread across into Liffey Street and Abbey Street. The fittings of one building were burned outside in a bonfire. Days later a crowd of almost four hundred people attacked brothels in Trinity Street, Cope Street, Fleet Street and Townsend Street. In Ship Street the occupants of The Thatched Cabin had to flee when it was ransacked. Violence returned a few days later, and soldiers dispersed well-armed rioters who gathered outside the brothels. A building in

Wood Street was severely damaged. When the troops tried to seize six of the offenders they met with a firm response. A magistrate was seriously injured by a missile. These attacks drove the Dame Street streetwalkers into a state of hysteria. The troops secured a brief respite, but violence returned a month later. Brothels were wrecked, along with the hideouts of press gangs.[30]

Public outrage grew, but the violence continued. A riot erupted when a prostitute was killed at a brothel in Kennedy's Lane. The crowd tried to demolish the building, but the sheriff was able to intervene. Weeks later the rioters returned following allegations that a misfortunate girl was forced to work there. They smashed the interior, but the sheriff was able to save the place from demolition.[31]

The impact of the barracks

Barrack Street was the bargain basement of the sex market. Soldiers kept their 'doxies' there, and the area developed a distinctive culture. Venereal disease was rampant. There was great concern at the barracks that prostitutes seduced the sentries. Madams followed military manoeuvres. They operated at campsites outside the city, and followed the army when it went abroad. In 1795 seven Barrack Street women accompanied the 87th Regiment to the Netherlands. Bawds established an active trade at Loughlinstown when that south Dublin camp was set up in the 1790s in response to the threat of a French invasion. At

The Lock Hospital treated women afflicted with syphilis. In 1792 it took over this Townsend Street building after it had been vacated by the Hospital for Incurables. (From *Dublin Magazine*, April 1764)

its peak during the summer of 1795 it held about four thousand soldiers. 'Mother' Brooks was one of the city's sex merchants doing business there.[32]

Dublin and London compared

> Dublin strongly resembles London, of which it is a beautiful copy.
>
> John Gamble, 1811[33]

London's Lock Hospital opened in 1746, with Dublin's equivalent following under a decade later. Dublin's Magdalen refuge (1766) came eight years after that of London. According to Randolph Trumbach, London normally had three thousand prostitutes during the 1760s and 1770s. Its Magdalen Asylum (1758) admitted over 2,500 reforming females in its first three decades. Trumbach found that London's mid-Georgian prostitutes started work at the age of fifteen, and their working life spanned a decade. In 1817 a House of Commons inquiry found most of them were aged between eighteen and twenty-two, and that they worked for just two or three years. While milliners' shops were used as fronts, taverns were the most common form of bawdy house. Trumbach considered over half of the women soliciting between Charing Cross and Fleet Street had previously been milliners.

Women's participation in the London sex trade kept pace with the rapid population growth. The 1817 inquiry found that three parishes (out of about 160) contained two thousand prostitutes. These were, however, atypical East End parishes where the streetwalkers comprised over three per cent of the population. Paris in the 1770s contained about twenty thousand prostitutes. This would equate to a participation rate of about 3.3 per cent of the population. Based on these figures it might be suggested that the scale of London's vice trade was about three times greater than Dublin's. However, when population is taken into account the Irish capital may have had more prostitutes per capita.[34]

Squatters in a disused church (Lord Portlester's Chapel, St Audeon's), 1820s. (George Petrie, *c.* 1828) (NGI)

13

Aftermath

Farewell the time – farewell the day!
When Dublin, though not great, was gay …
Her buildings, to the town confin'd,
Were warmer kept, and better lin'd …

J.J. Stockdale, 1812[1]

URBANISATION FOUND IT DIFFICULT TO cope with the victims of its success. As Dublin's population grew, so did the poverty. Too many aspects of administration were left to the parishes, and some of these places had too little income. Overcrowding reached alarming proportions during the Regency, and it was parishes such as St Brigid's and St Catherine's that suffered the worst congestion. In Wood Street a dozen dwellings had 304 occupants. Nearby in Bull Alley there were sixty-eight residents in a single house, with one room containing fifteen women who had fallen on hard times.[2]

Fashion and amenity faded away where the streets were dominated by people determined to partake in the fight for food. Pigs continued to roam the streets, and passers-by were appalled to see animals intended for human consumption foraging in the sewers and dunghills. A spectacle was formed by unemployed weavers, the mad and the depressed, hobbling ex-servicemen and blind beggars. People had an abiding terror

This image of Dame Street's post-Union decline offers a strong contrast with the grandeur seen in Malton's 1790s print. (George Petrie, 1821) (UCD)

of picking up some awful illness from them. The Lock Hospital pleaded for assistance because it could not cope with the increase in venereal patients.[3]

The official response to this turmoil was excessive, increasing unrest rather than containing it. Affluent residents sought more pleasant surroundings where the parish officers were better organised. Early nineteenth-century Dublin grew more polarised, horizontally by class and vertically by religion. As the winding medieval streets declined, the airy squares and broad streets of suburbia were rising. Green fields lured those seeking more separate surroundings where a fine villa might proclaim their arrival.

While these changes were gradual, they were relentless. The price paid for city living continued to rise. Urban dwellers were more involved in the retail trade, consuming more items from shops. They were forced to pay taxes on goods of all sorts, and this burden fell most heavily on middle-income households. However, there was no mass exodus, and efforts were made to stem the flow from the city, if only to protect property values. By the end of the Georgian era the aristocratic streets and genteel houses formed just a small proportion of the total. Most of

This model illustrates the forces that influenced the direction of urban expansion.

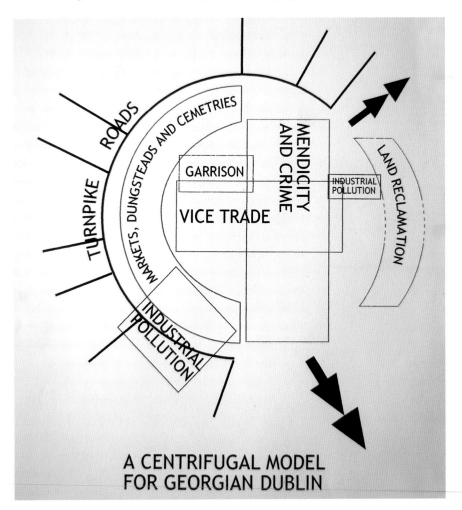

A CENTRIFUGAL MODEL FOR GEORGIAN DUBLIN

the rest had declined so far that they were being compared to the London parish of St Giles, where the poorest Irish emigrants had settled.[4]

> With regard to the people in the Liberty, they are in the most pitiable, wretched and famishing condition.

> Francis Higgins, 1800[5]

Those people who most needed the support of the community were left behind by those who might be able to help them. Although civic administration and policing were gradually reformed in the course of the nineteenth century, problems of housing and health continued to scar the face of the city. The flight of affluent households to the suburbs offered further proof of the city's inability to tackle its growing disorders. Foul, congested slums and airy seaside villas became the strongly contrasting emblems of that Victorian disconnection which was to survive for over a century. Dublin was divided as never before.

Appendix 1:

Dublin Diaries

Two surviving diaries reveal details of everyday life in the Georgian capital. They were both written by middle-class individuals. One of them records aspects of a household in Peter Street during the 1750s and 1760s. This was the family of a government official that occupied a relatively spacious house. There were seven hearths for which £1 5s tax was paid in 1754. They had domestic servants and the daughters received private education from a tutor. This family favoured the south side as they also had a country house in Milltown and took day trips to Harold's Cross and Templeogue for the fresh air. In 1761 they ventured further south, going into County Wicklow, where they visited Bray, Tinnehinch and Powerscourt House. There were nights at the city theatres at Crow Street and Smock Alley, as well as outings to the gardens at the Rotunda Hospital and Marlborough Green. In 1764 a visit was made to Ranelagh Gardens to support a charity entertainment.

Throughout the 1750s and 1760s this family professed allegiance to the status quo. They listened to debates in Parliament House, attended balls at the Castle, and were to be seen at the military exercises in Phoenix Park. In 1761 they watched the fireworks display at St Stephen's Green celebrating the coronation of King George III. An orthodox reading habit was reflected in the books they bought or borrowed from the lending library; there was great attention paid to religious topics and moral formation.

Source: H.F. Berry, 'Notes from the diary of a Dublin lady in the reign of George II', *Journal of the Royal Society of Antiquaries of Ireland*, vol. viii. part ii, 5th series (1898), pp. 141–54

A later diary was kept by a young man for a two-year period after the Union in 1801. This writer lived on the north side and was twenty-one years old. He had spent his first two decades at Eccles Street, but moved to Gardiner Street in 1801. This new home pleased him very much because the back rooms gave fine views over Dublin Bay. He found it genteel and healthful, and it was fitted up in the latest fashion.

On Sundays this young man drove out to Monkstown to visit a family named Miller. His hosts lived in a house called Prospect and he greatly admired its location and layout. It was a superb building decorated in the very best taste. It stood on 5 hectares, commanding a prospect of the sea and the mountains. Even on wet days it was a much more enjoyable place than the city. He was familiar with the prevailing ethos of moral reform because he knew the philanthropist Samuel Rosborough, a man he compared to the social reformer John Howard. Dean Walter Kirwan, the celebrity preacher, was also known to him, but he predicted that his dramatic admonitions would ultimately have little effect.

Theatre outings were part of his social calendar, but the regular appearance in the select boxes of celebrity madam Sally McClean caused him unease; on one occasion she even turned up in the same box as himself, along with a bevy of her working women and a parcel of soldier clients.

Our diarist suspected corruption in the Wide Street Commissioners – it promoted the rise of the eastern side of the city and used public money to support its own advance. He saw severe corruption at the Customs House; all ranks were accused of extortion from the merchants – how else could an official on £50 a year support a lifestyle where he 'entertains company at an elegant table – rolls in a curricle and pair, and has his villa and winter residence?'

This account also refers to the spread of new housing into the countryside; the area rising southwards on the foothills at Rathfarnham was thickly dotted with villas. Blackrock possessed all the gossip that made it a successful watering place; even during Sunday service one could hear the latest scandal spreading in loud whispers along the pews.

Source: Journal kept by a young man in Dublin from February 1801 to May 1803, RIA ms. 24.K.14–15

Appendix 2:

An Inventory of Hanging Shop Signs in the 1750s and 1760s
(including the trade concerned)

The Half Moon and Seven Stars, Francis Street (poplin)

The Salmon, Francis Street (poplin)

The Cock, High Street (shoes)

The Churn, Plunket Street (bacon)

The Plough, Queen Street (mending china)

The Golden Peruke, Essex Street (shirts)

The Cheshire Cheese, Bride's Alley (bellows)

Tea Tub, Goat's Alley, off Stephen Street (milliner)

Eagle and Child, Little Butter Lane (Drury Street) (chimney sweep)

Merry Shepherd, Clarendon Market (firewood)

Barber's Pole, St Nicholas Gate (caps)

Spread Eagle, Combe (stay maker)

Hen and Chickens, Cole's Alley, Castle Street (stay maker)

Old Sot's Hole, beside Essex Bridge (chop house)

Bull's Head, Smithfield (tavern)

Three Candlesticks, North King Street (tavern)

Bear, Smithfield (tavern)

Blue Leg, High Street (tavern)

George and the Dragon, Brown Street (tavern)

Red Lion, Bachelor's Walk (tavern)

Rose Tavern, Castle Street (tavern)

Brethern, or *Swaddling House*, Butter Lane (Bishop Street) (clear starcher)

Dove and Pendant, Castle Street (aprons)

Bunch of Keys, York Street (kettles)

Three Cats, Aston Quay (coal)

King's Arm and Two Bibles, Dame Street (stationery)

Royal Peruke, High Street (shoes)

Green Tree, Francis Street (draper)

Lambeck's Head, Castle Street (glover)

Horse Shoe, Thomas Street (bellows)

Munster King, Aston's Quay (coal)

Shuttle, Stephen Street (haberdasher)

Angel, Aungier Street (carpenter)

Three Black Birds, Francis Street (house painter)

Dial, Capel Street (caps)

Bee Hive, Bride Street (chintz)

Ship, Cornmarket (linen)

Red Lion, Cutpurse Row (roofing)

Draper's Head, Chequer Lane (wainscoting)

Sun, Upper Church Street (tea)

Windmill, George's Lane (flour)

Golden Stocking, Castle Street (stockings)

Source: H.F. Berry, 'Notes from the diary of a Dublin lady in the reign of George II', *Journal of the Royal Society of Antiquaries of Ireland*, vol. 8, pt 2, 5th series (1898), p. 150

Appendix 3:

Brothels Operating in Eighteenth-century Dublin (with identifiable proprietors and recorded dates of activity)

Name	Street	Year	Notes
Madam B—	Trinity Street	1791[1]	
'Mother' B—	Fishamble Street	1776[2]	
Norah Beatty, alias Mrs Marlow	Ross Lane (Bride Street)	1791	(riot at premises in which some prostitutes, including Catherine Neale, were assaulted)[3]
Miss Boyd	Longford Street	c. 1780[4]	
Mrs Brazen	Aston's Quay	1793[5]	(disguised as haberdashery shop; Lord — met his 'doxies' there)
'Mother' Brooks	Trinity Street, Irishtown and Lehaunstown army camp	1792–95	(operating at Irishtown during summer season in 1792 and reputed to have been already thirty years in business; riots at her Trinity Street premises in November 1793 and June 1795 (young man killed in latter episode); fire caused severe damage there in July 1794; set up brothel at Lehaunstown army camp in June 1795)[6]
Mary Browne	Prince's Street (nr Sir John Rogerson's Quay)	1751	(convicted of brothel keeping and sentenced to be carted through the street; on account of her great popularity and police connivance she was allowed to conceal herself on the floor of the cart)[7]
— Burns	Swift's Row (Jervis Street)	1791	(jailed for severely injuring a customer)[8]
Mrs C—	Fleet Street	1788	(premises set up above an academy; reputed to be the most infamous of the soliciting women)[9]
Elizabeth Crummers	Sycamore Alley	1798	(tried along with six of her working women for robbing a customer)[10]
Mr and Mrs Cullen	Joseph's Lane (South Great George's Street)	1777	(a riot occurred when they were pilloried for brothel keeping)[11]

Name	Street	Year	Notes
Mrs Davis	Fishamble Street	1792	(disguised as a china shop; severe damage caused to premises when four bucks pushed a blind horse into it)[12]
Mrs Digges	Capel Street	1791	(two riots occurred at this premises in 1791)[13]
Margaret Flood	Copper Alley	1747	(whipped through the streets for brothel keeping)[14]
Mrs Grant (née Connor)	Stafford Street	1791–92	(disguised as a hotel, was reputed to have a monopoly of the fashionable customers; recruited women in Liverpool)[15]
Alice Grew	Vicar Street	1717[16]	
Miss Groves and Miss Evans	Longford Street	1792	(Groves was severely injured when she refused entry to two bucks)[17]
Catherine Halfpenny	Marshall Alley (Fishamble Street)	1768[18]	
— Jones	Exchequer Street (Clarendon Street junction)	1778	(scene of rioting in autumn 1778)[19]
— Keenan	Barley Fields (Frederick Street North)	1791	(during a riot all the furniture was removed and burned in the street)[20]
Mrs Dorcas Kelly	Copper Alley	1788	(was executed after five male corpses were found in her brothel)[21]
Mrs Kelly	Ross Lane (Bride Street)	1778	(man severely wounded there resisting an extortion attempt by soldiers)[22]
'Mother' Kelsey	Ellis's Quay	1779[23]	
Margaret Leary (alias Mary Roche, alias Smallman)	Fleet Street	1791	(operated two brothels in Fleet Street; sentenced to a year in jail and pilloried twice for possession of stolen property)[24]
Margaret Leeson	Drogheda (O'Connell) Street, Pitt (Balfe) Street	1765–85	(Drogheda Street premises ransacked by a mob in early 1779)[25]
Thomas Leonard	Winetavern Street	1770	(pilloried at the Tholsel for brothel keeping)[26]

Name	Street	Year	Notes
'Mother' Lloyd	Capel Street	1796	(rumours in March 1796 that she had been murdered, whereas she had fled for debt)[27]
Marie Lewellin	Blackmoor Yard (Anglesea Street)	1788	(scene of the infamous rape of Mary Neil, aged thirteen, by Lord Carhampton; Lewellin was sentenced to death)[28]
Catherine Locker	Essex Street	1766	(pilloried at the Tholsel for brothel keeping)[29]
Julian Long	nr Christchurch	1765[30]	
Mrs Lovett	Bow Lane (Longford Street)	1791[31]	
'Mother' M—y	Anglesea Street	1776	(disguised as bagnio)[32]
Mrs Maher	Essex Street	1796	(sentenced to transportation for robbing a customer)[33]
Ann Martin	nr Temple Bar	1758[34]	
John Mc Cartney	King's Head Court (Exchequer Street)	1796[35]	
Elizabeth McClean	Eustace Street, Barrack Street, Sandymount	1795–98	(amongst most successful madams, at one time controlling sixteen women; army personnel prominent amongst her clientele; she operated a summer business at Sandymount)[36]
Anne McDonagh	Little Booter's Lane	1781–82	(particularly disorderly; premises ransacked in October 1781 after the killing of a thirteen-year-old Belfast girl who had refused to work there; another riot in summer 1782 when McDonagh blinded one of her workers)[37]
Margaret Molloy	Crane Lane	1780s	(operated from premises of Francis Higgins, popularly known as the 'Sham Squire')[38]
Moll Moore	Capel Street	1791–96	(premises damaged in 1791 riot; she served jail sentence for stabbing one of her workers: following her release in March 1796 she was rearrested and jailed for brothel keeping)[39]

Name	Street	Year	Notes
Margaret O'Brien	Longford Street, Blackrock	1791–96	(operated a summer business at Blackrock)[40]
Bridget Orde (alias West, alias Featherstone)	Great Britain Street	1791[41]	
Mrs Pluck	King's Head Court (corner of Dame Street/South Great George's Street)	1795	(formerly a street trader)[42]
Mrs Porter	King's Head Court (corner of Dame Street/South Great George's Street)	1795[43]	
— Prendergast (alias McLaughlin)	Temple Street	1776	(accused of murder)[44]
Ms R—	Fownes Street	1779[45]	
Alice Rice	Essex Street	1766	(pilloried at the Tholsel for brothel keeping)[46]
Mrs Reilly	St Mary's Parish	1795	(jailed for robbery of a customer)[47]
Philip Reilly and Catherine Smith	White Lyon Court, nr Little Strand Street	1736[48]	
Maria Roberts	Abbey Street	1792[49]	
Mrs Robinson	Stafford Street, Monmouth Street	1792[50]	
— Scully	South Great George's Street	1796[51]	
Mr Simpson	Crown Alley	1791	(premises damaged in serious rioting)[52]
Ms Truly	Kennedy's Lane	1795-96	(riot after dead prostitute discovered in premises in December 1795; building damaged in two January 1796 riots after allegation that female passer-by had been forced into prostitution there)[53]
Mrs W—	Irishtown	1796	(operated a summer business at Irishtown)[54]
Kitty Waistcoat	Luke Street	1774[55]	

Name	Street	Year	Notes
Mrs West (née A—)	Capel Street	*c.* 1780[56]	
Margaret Whittle (alias Porter)	Mark Street	*c.* 1780[57]	

BROTHELS[+] 1747–1800

[+]with identifiable dates, addresses and proprietors

Appendix 4:

Lock Hospital Admissions, Townsend Street, Dublin, 1792–1835

Year	Admitted	Discharged	Died	Treatment duration (in weeks)	Outpatients
1792	274*	142*			
1793	1,013	981	15*	7	1,124*
1794	992*	938	13	9	1,886
1795	1,389	1,264	30	8	1,552
1796	1,696	1,630	40	7	931
1797	1,651	1,589	26	7	828
1798	1,525	1,467	36	7	1,223
1799	1,681	1,569	38	7	1,310
1800	1,538	1,452	48	8	1,630
1801	1,810	1,680	38	7	3,026
1802	1,806	1,713	39	7	3,546
1803	1,738	1,679	35	7	4,183
1804	1,558	1,450	47	8	5,136
1805	1,363	1,223	34	9	6,170
1806*	593*	521*	19*		3,114*
1807	1,374*				5,350*
1808–09					
1810	1,290*				5,438*
1811	340*	342*	9*		
1812	1,430	1,365	58	10	
1813	1,646	1,538	65	9	5,286*
1814	1,666	1,590	61	9	
1815	1,586	1,488	59	10	
1816	1,586	1,531	51	9	4,954*
1817	1,670	1,580	43	9	

Year	Admitted	Discharged	Died	Treatment duration (in weeks)	Outpatients
1818	1,888	1,783	44	8	
1819	1,773	1,713	44	8	5,099*
1820	593	585	8		
1821	813	804	9		
1822	775	757	18		
1823	673	663	8		
1824	677	522	5		
1825	681	694	18	11	
1826	636	646	17	12	
1827	684	695	7	11	
1828	816	836	11	10	
1829	744*	718*	24*	10	
1830	677	704	12	12	
1831	688	703	11	11	
1832	757	764	16	9	
1833	698	700	15	11	
1834	781	800	18	10	
1835	861	894	14	8	

*Incomplete or unreliable

Source: Dublin Lock Hospital minute books, held at library of Royal College of Physicians, Dublin

Appendix 5:

Dublin Foundling Hospital Petitions for Retrieval of Children (abridged excerpts from the records)

1   Rose Trench; seduced whilst in the service of the Duchess of Richmond, praying to have her child restored.

2   Bridget Kearney; this girl travelled 100 miles on foot in order that she might herself place her child safely in the Hospital cradle and she travelled back the same distance.

3   Mary Clarendon; pleading for her child and showing quarrels between her husband and herself arising from the child's desertion.

4   Catherine Kelly; her child was sent to the Hospital without the knowledge of the parents.

5   Anne Keown; the request was made by the parents of her seducer. Their hearts were softened by the loss of their son.

6   Hannah Carroll; gross deception was practised to get the infant into the Hospital.

7   Bridget M'Cullogh; a rich Protestant seduced his poor Catholic servant and then sent her child to the Foundling Hospital against her will.

8   Debb Doran; her child had been forcibly torn from her.

9   Catherine Carolan; her child was forcibly abstracted from her.

10 'Arthur Wellington' (two letters, both unsigned, in a lady's handwriting); the parents (per Wodsworth) were of gentle birth. The first letter expressed solicitude about the infant and the second explained the circumstances under which she had been compelled by the 'family' to place the boy in the Hospital and under which she sought to regain him.

11 Hessy Harte; in remorse, owning her child.

12 'Kelly's child'; direct cross-swearing as to its paternity.

13 'Mary Ward's child'; a case of forcible abduction.

14 'Mary Donney's child'; relating the misery of the mother at parting with her child.

15 'Mary Kane's child'; revealing the evil deeds of a rich man.

16 'Anne M'Cloughry's child'; the infant was taken away by her seducer and then abandoned by him.

17 'Lettie Spires' child'; a petition made jointly with the child's grandfather.

18 'John Smith'; with a fictitious signature and cunning address, requesting information about a child named Mary Whitehead but carefully evading having the infant returned to him.

19 Ally Byrne; married the father of her child and got it back.
20 Mary Kelly; relating her misery and her efforts to regain the infant.

Source: William Dudley Wodsworth, *A Brief History of the Ancient Foundling Hospital of Dublin, from the Year 1702* (Dublin, 1876)

Appendix 6:

St Patrick's Hospital Admissions, 1757–1807

Title	Surname	Personal names	Date of admission	County	Town	Occupation	Notes
	Gill	Robert	1757				
	Mc Ewen	John	1757				
	Brabazon	Edward	1757				
	Wran	Thomas	1757				
	Kelly	William	1757				
	Mc Mullin	Henry	1757				
	Mahoney	Margaret	1757				
	Murry	Anne	1757				
	Crofts	Sarah	1757				
	Mc Owen	Judith	1757				
	Wheatley	?	1758				son of George Wheatley
	Gill	?	1761			apothecary	
	Burke	Hubert	1769				son of Mary Burke, widow
	Balmer	Sarah	1769				
	Wade	Thomas	1769	Dublin	Finglas		son of James Wade of Cardiff's Bridge, Dublin
	Dunn	Collum	1769	Dublin	Dublin	farmer (formerly)	
	Pike	Ann	1769				
Mrs	Corrigan	?	1769	Dublin	Dublin		wife of John Corrigan, chaiseman, of Capel Street, Dublin
	Oates	John	1770				

Title	Surname	Personal names	Date of admission	County	Town	Occupation	Notes
	Swinburne	Thomas	1770				killed a man in a fit of madness
Mrs	Sherlock	?	1770				
	Philpot	William	1770				
	Gordon	Joseph	1770				
Mrs	Cathrens	Jane	1770				
	Guest	Thomas	1770				
	Wight	Rice	1770	Limerick			son of Revd Williamson Wight. He was not admitted in 1770 having been examined and not found to be an idiot
	Brennan	James	1770	Westmeath	Raharnodah [Raharney?]		murdered his father with a candlestick in a fit of madness
	Maquay (alias mc quay)	Mary	1770				aunt of George Maquay, merchant
	Bryan	Dennis	1770				
	Ross	Margaret	1771				
	Leedham	Francis	1771				
	Byrne	Mary	1771	Dublin			recommended by St James' parish
	?	?	1771	Dublin	Dublin		'a male idiot now lying destitute of friends in the market house on Thomas Street'
	Clarke	Elizabeth	1771				

Title	Surname	Personal names	Date of admission	County	Town	Occupation	Notes
	Malone	Frances	1771				
Mrs	Egan	Ann	1771	Cork	Charleville		daughter of Revd Carbery Egan (Church of Ireland)
	?	?	1771	Tyrone	Cappagh		
Mrs	Fox	Ann	1771				wife of Hugh Fox
	Silk	Elizabeth	1771				
Mrs	Cuffe	?	1772				wife of Ambrose Cuffe
Revd	Fleming	Josiah	1772			Church of Ireland curate in the diocese of Clogher	
	Campbell	Martha	1772				
	Gray	Brice	1772				
	Fitzgerald	James	1772				
	Walsh	Richard	1772				son of Revd Canon Philip Walsh (Church of Ireland)
	Hill	Catherine	c. 1772				
	Baily	Darcy	1773				
	Magauran	Nathaniel	1774				
	Hutchinson	John	1774				
	Courtney	John Cooke	1774				
	Wybrants	Elizabeth	c. 1774				
	Whyte	Elizabeth	1775				
	Hitchcock	John	1775				son of Mrs Dorothy Hitchcock, widow
	?	Margery	1776	Tyrone			

Title	Surname	Personal names	Date of admission	County	Town	Occupation	Notes
	Kelly	John	1776	Dublin			late of College Green Lower
	Laban	William	1777				
Revd	Stewart	?	1777			priest – Church of Ireland?	
	Carlisle	William	1777			tradesman – recommended by Mrs Forde, a benefactor of the hospital	
Mrs	Mc Claghry	Medicis	1777				wife of a trooper – recommended by Mr Corbet
	Lamb	William	1778				son of William Lamb, late vicar of Saint Patrick's cathedral (a Church of Ireland priest?)
Mrs	Barret	?	1778	Louth	Drogheda		wife of an innkeeper – recommended by the mayor and corporation of Drogheda
	Walsh	Richard	1778				
	Green	Sheppy	1779			merchant	
	Walsh	Michael	1779				
	Kane	Laurence	1779				
	Archbold	George	c. 1779				
	Walsh	Richard	1780	Dublin	Dublin		recommended by St Audoen's parish
Mrs	Young	Elizabeth	1780	Dublin	Dublin		wife of Baptist Young – recommended by St Michan's parish

Title	Surname	Personal names	Date of admission	County	Town	Occupation	Notes
	Farrell	Catherine	1780	Louth	Drogheda		recommended by the parish and mayor of Drogheda
	Murray	Thady	1780	Kildare	Leixlip		recommended by the parish of Leixlip
Miss	Hervey	?	c. 1780				sister of another patient Miss Julia Hervey
	Sherlock	William	c. 1780	Dublin	Dublin	clothier, of Francis Street, Dublin	
	King	Ann	1781				
	Green	Mary Ann	1782				
	Grange	Anthony	1782				recommended by the bishop of Cork, the archdeacon of Dublin and others
	(b)		1783				one of twelve lunatics from the House of Industry and the Bridewell
	(i)		1783				one of twelve lunatics from the House of Industry and the Bridewell
	(g)		1783				one of twelve lunatics from the House of Industry and the Bridewell
	(f)		1783				one of twelve lunatics from the House of Industry and the Bridewell

Title	Surname	Personal names	Date of admission	County	Town	Occupation	Notes
	(e)		1783				one of twelve lunatics from the House of Industry and the Bridewell
	(k)		1783				one of twelve lunatics from the House of Industry and the Bridewell
	(c)		1783				one of twelve lunatics from the House of Industry and the Bridewell
	Cahill	Andrew	1783				
	(d)		1783				one of twelve lunatics from the House of Industry and the Bridewell
	(l)		1783				one of twelve lunatics from the House of Industry and the Bridewell
	Drinan	?	1783				recommended by Lord Belmore
	(a)		1783				one of twelve lunatics from the House of Industry and the Bridewell
	Mc Nabb	Patrick	1783	Dublin	Dublin		recommended by St Mark's parish
	(h)		1783				one of twelve lunatics from the House of Industry and the Bridewell

Title	Surname	Personal names	Date of admission	County	Town	Occupation	Notes
	Willican	George	1783	Dublin	Dublin		recommended by St Peter's parish
Miss	Cary	Winifred	1783	Roscommon	Elphin		recommended by the parish of Elphin
Miss	Maddock	Elizabeth Ann	1783	Dublin	Dublin		daughter of Ben Maddock, hatter
Miss	Williams	Ann	1783				daughter of Henry Williams, brewer
	Deane	Garret	1783	Dublin	Dublin		of Saint Audoen's parish; recommended by Mr Foster
	?	?	1783				recommended by Revd Dr Dealtry
	O'Brien	?	1783	Wicklow			
	(j)		1783				one of twelve lunatics from the House of Industry and the Bridewell
	Richardson	Joseph	1783				
Miss	Chatham	Elizabeth	1783				
	Beckett	William	1783				
	Boyle	Mary	1783				
	Brennan	Edward	1783				
	Skelton	William	1783				
	Collins	Luke	1783				recommended by Right Hon. John Foster
	Hudson	Francis	1783	Dublin	Dublin		of Saint Audoen's parish
	Brett	Elizabeth	1783				

Title	Surname	Personal names	Date of admission	County	Town	Occupation	Notes
	?	?	1783				a lunatic at the House of Industry
	?	?	1783				a lunatic at the House of Industry
Revd	Brady	Anthony	1783				Roman Catholic priest
	?	?	1783				a lunatic at the House of Industry
	?	?	1783				a lunatic at the House of Industry
	Glindon	Martin	1783	Dublin	Dublin		of St James' parish
	Sampson	Robert	1783				
	Law	John	c. 1783				
	Black	Ann	c. 1783				
	Taylor	Amelia	c. 1783				
	Fox	James	1784	Dublin	Dublin		recommended by St Catherine's parish
	Mc kee	John	1784				
	Driscol	Catherine	1784	Dublin	Dublin		recommended by St Michael's parish
	Comerford	Margaret	1784				
	Mc manus	Elizabeth	1784	Cavan	Belturbet		recommended by provost of Belturbet
	Whyte	William	1784				
	Ryder	John	1784				
	Nilan	Jane	1784				

Title	Surname	Personal names	Date of admission	County	Town	Occupation	Notes
	Egan	Catherine	1784	Dublin	Dublin		recommended by St Mary's parish
Mrs	Stewart	?	1784				a widow
	Brown	Richard	1784				
	Gill	Patrick	1784				
	Haggerty	George	1784	Dublin	Dublin		recommended by St Andrew's parish
	Hunter	Samuel	1784				
	Mc crenor	Hugh	1784				
	(iii)		1784				one of three male pauper lunatics from the Bridewell
	(ii)		1784				one of three male pauper lunatics from the Bridewell
	(i)		1784				one of three male pauper lunatics from the Bridewell
	Murphy	George	1784				recommended by Revd Dr Hastings
	Huband	Elinor	1784				
Miss	Boyle	Mary	1784	Dublin	Dublin		daughter of Pat Boyle, tailor – recommended by St Michan's parish
	?	?	1784				recommended by Dr Ratcliff
	Sheridan	James	1784				
	Mc Cready	Hugh	1784				

Title	Surname	Personal names	Date of admission	County	Town	Occupation	Notes
Revd	Oliver	?	c. 1784			priest – Church of Ireland?	
	Mussin	Catherine	1785	Dublin	Dublin		recommended by St James' parish
Revd	Oliver	?	1785			priest – Church of Ireland?	
	?	?	1785				'an insane woman recommended by Sir Hopton Scott'
	Driden	James	1785	Dublin	Dublin		recommended by St Peter's parish
	Sweeny	William	1785				
	Costello	Eleanor	1785				recommended by the parish of St Nicholas Without
	Hughes	Elizabeth	1785	Dublin	Dublin		recommended by St James' parish
	Dawson	Thomas	1785	Dublin	Chapelizod		recommended by the parish of Chapelizod
	Newin	Ann	1785	Dublin	Dublin		recommended by the parish of St Nicholas Within
	Bennett	Susannah	1785	Carlow	Carlow		recommended by the parish of Carlow
	Grange	Lucinda	1785	Dublin	Dublin		recommended by St Mark's parish
	Archbold	Elizabeth	1785	Dublin	Dublin		recommended by St Thomas' parish

Title	Surname	Personal names	Date of admission	County	Town	Occupation	Notes
	Cruise	Catherine	1785	Dublin	Dublin		recommended by St Werburgh's parish
	?	?	1785				recommended by the archbishop of Dublin
	Logan	John	1785	Dublin	Dublin		recommended by St Peter's parish
	Clifford	?	1785				
	Mc quillan	Daniel	1785				
	Hannally	Hugh	c. 1785				
	Hill	Anne	c. 1785				
	Duggan	Mary	1786				
	Harrison	William	1786				
	(ii)		1786				one of the female patients recommended by the bishop of Cloyne
	(i)		1786				one of the female patients recommended by the bishop of Cloyne
	Hannally	Hugh	1786				
	Earl	Anne	1786	Dublin	Dublin		of St James' parish
	Sadler	William	1786	Dublin	Dublin		recommended by St Andrew's parish
	Rudd	Hanna	1786				recommended by Revd Dean of Limerick
	Murphy	Mary	1786				

Title	Surname	Personal names	Date of admission	County	Town	Occupation	Notes
	Heaphy	Margaret	1786				
	Butler	Susannah	1786				
	Wilkinson	William	1786				
	Shea	Patrick	1786				
Revd	Oliver	?	1786				priest – Church of Ireland?
	Newin	Anne	1786	Dublin	Dublin		
	Arnold	Richard	1786				
	Finletter	Martha	1787				
	Nowlan	Catherine	1787	Dublin	Dublin		
	Cooper	Margaret	1787	Monaghan	Donagh		recommended by the parish of Donagh
Miss	Ringwood	Catherine	1787				
	Eccles	Thomas	1787				only ten years old
	Heyd	Owen	1787				
	Kathrens	George	1787	Dublin	Dublin		recommended by St Michael's parish
	Courtney	John Cooke	1787				
	Bolton	James	1788				
	Byrne	John	1788				
	Jackson	Charles	1788				
	Blanchfield	John	1788				
	Adamson	John	1788				
	Maclune	David	1788				
	Worthington	Richard	1788	Dublin	Dublin		recommended by St Peter's parish

Title	Surname	Personal names	Date of admission	County	Town	Occupation	Notes
	Howard	Mary	1788				recommended by Revd Dr Walsh and the churchwardens of his parish
	Burke	Thomas	1788				recommended by the Provost and Fellows of Trinity College Dublin
	Swift	John	1788	Dublin			recommended by St Peter's parish
	Sweeny	Elizabeth	1788				
	Smyth	Thomas	1788				
	Kathrens	Murray	c. 1788				husband of Mrs Elizabeth Kathrens
	Perrin	William	1789				
	Wincherly	John	1789				
	Bellew	Patrick	1789				recommended by the parish of Callan
	Butler	Elizabeth	1789				recommended by the archbishop of Dublin
	Jonquier	James	1789				
	Murphy	Lucy	1789				
	Neill	Elinor	1789				
	Mahon	Elizabeth	1789				
	Proctor	Elizabeth	1789				
	Bennet	Frances	1789				
	Reilly	Catherine	1789				
	Carey	Michael	1789				recommended by Revd Sands

Title	Surname	Personal names	Date of admission	County	Town	Occupation	Notes
	Fay	Mary	1789				
	Neill	John	1789				recommended by the bishop of Ossory
	Flanagan	Mary	1789				
	Richy	Elizabeth	1789				
	Wilkins	Joshua	1789				
	Mc kiernan	Owen	1789				
	Callaghan	Michael	1789	Dublin	Dublin		recommended by St Thomas' parish
	Neilan	James	1789				
	Kirwan	James	1789				
	Lisnard	Elizabeth	1790				
	Stephens	Ann	1790				recommended by the bishop of Ferns
	Marlay	Charles	1790	Dublin			recommended by the parish of Clontarf
Mr	?	?	1790				recommended by Revd Montgomery of Roscommon
Mrs	Coe	?	1790				wife of Joshua Coe – recommended by Revd Harpur
	Carr	Daniel	1790				
	Kathrens	George	1790	Dublin			recommended by St Michael's parish
	Mc lean	Mary	1790				
	O'leary	Rebecca	1790				
	Reilly	Elizabeth	1790				

Title	Surname	Personal names	Date of admission	County	Town	Occupation	Notes
	Mussan	Catherine	1790				
	Johnston	Catherine	1790				
	Reilly	Samuel	1790				
	O'keefe	John	1790				
	Murphy	William	1790				
	Stephens	Thomas	1790				
	Ross	Thomas	1790				
	Fitzpatrick	James	1790				
	O'leary	Mary	1791				
	Benton	Deborah	1791				
	Knight	James	1791				
	Booth	John	1792	Kildare			recommended by the parish of Clane
Mr	Sullivan	?	1792				son of Daniel Sullivan
Mr	Collins	?	1792				son of Mary Collins
	Malone	Bridget	1792				
Mr	Healy	?	1792	Dublin			husband of Elizabeth Healy – recommended by St Mary's parish
Mr	Duff	?	1792				son of Catherine Duff
	Archbold	Margaret	1792				
	Hoey	Patrick	1792				
	Collins	Elizabeth	1792				
Revd	Martin	Eugene	1792			priest	
	Gray	Margaret	1792	Dublin			recommended by the curate of St Paul's parish

Title	Surname	Personal names	Date of admission	County	Town	Occupation	Notes
	Dunbar	David	1792				
	Ferrier	?	1792				
Miss	Hervey	Julia	1792				sister of another patient Miss Hervey 'who has been many years a boarder'
	Rivers	Catherine	1792				
Mr	Hinckley	?	1792				
	Kelly	Judith	1792				
	Maffett	Sarah	1792				recommended by the Duchess of Leinster
	Smith	Thomas	c. 1792				
	Maguire	Eleanor	1793				
	Murray	Henry	1793				
	White	Ann	1793				
	Coady	Margaret	1793				
	Byrne	Ellen	1793				
	Donnellan	Ann	1793				
	Sweeny	Mary	1793	Dublin			recommended by St John's parish
	Roberts	Catherine	1793				
	Ginsela (or kinsella?)	Ann	1793	Dublin			recommended by St John's parish
	Cartwright	Francis	1793				
	Kennedy	Samuel	1793				
	Sherry	George	1793				
	St john	James	1793				
	Hill	Francis	1793				

Title	Surname	Personal names	Date of admission	County	Town	Occupation	Notes
	Ferguson	William	1793				
	Reilly	Thomas	1793				
	Myers	William	1793	Dublin			recommended by St Mark's parish
	Waters	Thomas	1793				
	Rilson	Robert	1793				
	Murphy	Mary	1793	Dublin			recommended by St Ann's parish
	Cahill	Catherine	1793				daughter of James Cahill – recommended by St Catherine's parish
Mr	Sheppey	?	1793				recommended by the Marquess of Waterford
	O'leary	Rebecca	1793				
Mrs	Markey	?	c. 1793				
	Dillon	Charlotte	1794				recommended by St Peter's parish
	Dunn	John	1794				
	Day	Robert	1794				
	Duff	Catherine	1794				
	Bewley	Mary	1794				
	Long	Thomas	1794				
	Kelly	Judith	1794				
	Plant	Rachel	1794				
	Voakes	Trophia	1794				
	Muldowny	Loughlin	1794				

Title	Surname	Personal names	Date of admission	County	Town	Occupation	Notes
	Hughes	Elizabeth	1794	Leitrim	Drumsna		recommended by the parish of Drumsna
	Smith	Thomas	1794				
	Malone	Patrick	1794				
	Boulger	Ann	1794				
	Mc Daniel	Margaret	c. 1794				
	Marshall	William Blaney	1795				
	Woods	Bridget	1795				
	Digby	Richard	1795				
	Handy	Christopher	1795				
	Flood	Owen	1795				
Mrs	Ewing	?	1795				wife of John Ewing
Mrs	Herbert	?	1795				wife of Joseph Herbert
	Jesson	Robert	1795	Dublin			recommended by St Andrew's parish
	O'Brien	John	1795				
	Dillon	Ann	1795				
	Codd	Elinor	1795				
	Foley	Ann	1795				
	Finny	Robert	1795				
	Poland	?	1795				daughter of George Poland
	Fagan	Mary	1795	Dublin			of St Mark's parish
	Starkey	William	1795	Down	Kilcliff		
	Vaughan	Fergus	1795				
	Lacy	Mary	1795				

Title	Surname	Personal names	Date of admission	County	Town	Occupation	Notes
	Byrne	James	1795				
	Freeman	Elizabeth	1795				
	Grant	Margaret	1795				
	Gartland	John	1795				
	Hughes	Catherine	1795				
	Mills	Thomas	1795				
	Hughes	Patrick	1795				
	Carr	Mark	1795	Longford	Granard		
	Fleming	George	1796	Meath	Clonard		recommended by the parish of Clonard
	Mc auley	John	1796				
	Murphy	Margaret	1796				
	Morris	Bell	1796				
	Maunsell	Standish	1796				
	Hamilton	Mathew	1796				
Mrs	Ward	?	1796	Tyrone	Strabane		wife of John Ward, innkeeper
	Fitzgerald	James	1796				
	Kerr	Mark	1796				
	Fay	Bridget	1796				
	Dunn	Sarah	1796				
	Braddell	Frances	1796				
	Cotton	Barbara	1796				
	Molloy	Patrick	1796				
	Cumings	Harriet	1796				
	Strong	Mary Ann	1796				
	Dempsey	Catherine	1796				
	Murphy	John	c. 1796				

Title	Surname	Personal names	Date of admission	County	Town	Occupation	Notes
	Elliot	John	1797				
	Price	John	1797				recommended by Revd Dr Paul
	Woods	Jane	1797	Down	Newry		recommended by the parish of Newry
	Bradshaw	John	1797				
	Colossi	Mary Ann	1797				
	Russell	John	1797	Dublin	Clontarf		recommended by the parish of Clontarf
	Foran	Elinor	1797				
	Fitzwilliams	Ann	1798	Dublin	Blackrock		
	Dowdall	Mary	1798				
Revd	Rice	?	1798			priest – Church of Ireland?	
	Logan	John	1798				
Mrs	Carragher	?	1798				wife of Arthur Carragher
	Murphy	Joseph	1798				
	Gifford	Elinor	1799				
	Jones	Francis	1799	Dublin	North Strand		
	Fleming	Elizabeth	1799				
	Kearney	John	1799	Dublin	Dublin		of St Werburgh's parish
	Porter	Ann	1799				
	Brien	Darby	1799				
	Hughes	Ann	1799				
	Field	Esther	1799				

Title	Surname	Personal names	Date of admission	County	Town	Occupation	Notes
	?	?	1799			apprentice of the widow Walsh	
	?	?	1799				'the object recommended by the Rt Hon the Speaker'
	Kennedy	Thomas	1799				
	Kearney	Robert	1799				
	Horner	Samuel	1799				
	Wood	?	1799	Dublin	Dublin		'an inhabitant of the Deanery of St Patrick's Cathedral'
	Cullian	Mary	1800				
Mrs	Gregg	?	1800	Dublin	Dublin		wife of William Gregg of St James' Street
	Neville	Edward	1800	Dublin	Dublin		of St Peter's parish
	Campbell	Ann	1800	Dublin	Dublin		of St Andrew's parish
	Blundel	Michael	1800	Roscommon	Elphin		
	Gibson	Alexander	1800	Cavan	Cootehill		
	?	?	1800				'the patient claimed to be admitted into the hospital by Lord Tullamore'
	Gilmor	John	1800				
	Lyons	Jane	1800	Dublin	Dublin		of St Catherine's parish

Title	Surname	Personal names	Date of admission	County	Town	Occupation	Notes
Mrs	Morgan	?	1800				wife of John Morgan
	Cuby	Stephen	1800	Louth	Dundalk		
Mrs	Quinlan	?	1800				wife of Daniel Quinlan
	Kildillon	Elizabeth	1800				recommended by the inspector general of prisons in Ireland
	Ryder	Frederick	1800	Dublin	Dublin		
	Swords	Esther	1800				
Mrs	Phair	?	1800				wife of John Phair
	Collinson	Robert	1800				
	Tydd	?	1800				
	?	?	1800				'an idiot in the Magdalen Asylum'
Revd	Ross	Samuel	1800	Derry		priest (Presbyterian minister)	
	Benham	Esther	1800	Down	Bryansford		
	Conolly	Peter	c. 1800				
	Monk	Catherine	1801	Dublin	Dublin		of St Mark's parish
	Kelly	John	1801	Fermanagh	Enniskillen		
	Gilmore	William	1801	Sligo			
	Bowen	Ann	1801				
	Hughes	James	1801			student at Trinity College, Dublin	

Title	Surname	Personal names	Date of admission	County	Town	Occupation	Notes
	Callaghan	James	1801				
	Mc clean	Mary	1801				
	Bowen	Catherine	1801	Mayo	Hollymount		
	Dillon	Thomas	1801	Dublin	Rathcoole		
	Houston	Elizabeth	1801	Dublin	Dublin		of Abbey Street
	Reay (alias Brown)	Maryanne	1801	Donegal			
	Conolly	Peter	1801				
	Hughes	James	1801	Dublin	Dublin		of St Michael's parish
	Pelligrini	Alphonso	1802				
	Maw	Castleton, jnr	1802	Wexford	Gorey		son of Castleton Maw, surgeon
	Cary	Charles	1802	Leitrim	Carrick on Shannon		
	Rose	Eliza	1802	Dublin	Dublin		of St Peter's parish
	Wilson	William	1802				
	Norton	Catherine	1802				
	Mc clean	Robert	1802				
	Coyle	James	1802				
	Taaffe	William	1802				
	Cuiset (or Cuisset)	Ann	1802				
	Tandy	Ann	1802				
	Hutchinson	George	1802				
	Dwyer	Catherine	1803				'an incurable who was a servant in the hospital and lost her health'

Title	Surname	Personal names	Date of admission	County	Town	Occupation	Notes
	Douglas	Sarah	1803				
	Glenan	Bridgett	1803				
	Harford	Bridget	1803	Dublin	Dublin		of St Andrew's parish
Mrs	Knowlas	Susana	1803	Meath	Duleek		wife of William Knowlas
	Hufford	Catherine	1803	Waterford			
Mrs	Allen	Ann	1803	Dublin	Dublin		wife of John Allen of St Michan's parish
Miss	Hamilton	Ann	1804	Leitrim	Manor-hamilton		
	Porterfield	James	1804				
	Baird	Moses	1804	Donegal	Donaghmore		
	O'neil	Butthen	1804	Dublin	Dublin		of Usher's Quay
	Headen	Francis	1804	Roscommon	Frenchpark		
	Garvy	Elenor	1804				
	Mc brinn	Christian	1804				
	Mc connel	William	1804				
	Reilly	James	1804	Meath	Kilsykre		son of Edward Reilly, schoolmaster
	Ogle	Thomas	1804	Dublin	Dublin		of St Catherine's parish
	Hutchinson	William	1804	Kilkenny	Mountgale, Kilkenny		
	Lestrange	William	1804	Offaly	Daingean		
Mrs	Lane	?	1804	Dublin	Dublin		wife of Peter Lane of St Ann's parish

Title	Surname	Personal names	Date of admission	County	Town	Occupation	Notes
Mrs	Horan	?	1804	Kildare	Kilcullen		wife of John Horan of Blackhall
	[Name illegible - ends in -on]		1804				
	Magher	Ann	1804				
	Warmingham	Thomas	1804				
	Hughes	Patrick	1804	Tyrone	Strabane		
	Madden	Walter	1804	Dublin	Dublin		son of Thomas Madden of Little Mary's Lane, Dublin
	Arthurs	Walter	1804	Laois	Cool-banagher		
	Giordani	Thomas	1804	Dublin			son of Tommaso Giordani, 'teacher of music' (also a well-known composer); his father was a prominent composer in Dublin and was organist at the Pro-Cathedral
Mr	Harrison	?	c. 1804				brother of Jervis Harrison
	Farrell	Catherine	1805				
	O'brien	Michael	1805				
	Leister	Christopher	1805				
Mrs	Graham	Elenor	1805	Dublin	Dublin		wife of William Graha, shoemaker, of the Coal Quay

Title	Surname	Personal names	Date of admission	County	Town	Occupation	Notes
Miss	Moore	?	1805				daughter of Sarah Moore, widow
	Green	John	1805				
Miss	Flanaghan	?	1805	Dublin			daughter of Catherine Flanaghan
	Bickerton	Jane	1805	Down	Donaghadee		
	Hughes	?	1805				
	Cheshire	Mary	1805	Louth	Drogheda		
	Dempsey	Garrett	1805	Dublin	Dublin		son of Mary Dempsey, a poor widow of St James' parish
Mrs	Foley	Ann	1805				wife of Redmond Foley
	Goff (or Gough)	George	1805			musician	
	Mooney	Micheál	1805				
	Rudd	Ann	1805			governess	
	Milliken	John	1805			ensign	
	Emerson	Sophia	1805				'a poor young woman, apparently insane, calling herself by the name of Sophia Emerson'
	Rudd	Ann	1806				
	Ray	Hannah	1806				
	Tandy	John	1806				
	Headon	Peter	1806				

Title	Surname	Personal names	Date of admission	County	Town	Occupation	Notes
Mrs	Hyde	?	1806				wife of John A. Hyde
	Litton	Sarah	1806				
	Graham	John	1806				
	O'connor	Mary	1806				
	Kearney	Mary	1806				
	White	Robert	1806				
	Fitzgerald	Catherine	1806				
	Johnson	Elizabeth	1806				
Miss	Dowdall	Margaret	1806				daughter of Ann Dowdall
	Barclay	Barnes	1806				
	Skelly	James	1806				
	Keating	Patrick	1806				
	Coote	?	1806				
	Mills	Ann	1806				
	Molloy	Richard	1806				
	Hayes	Charlotte	1806				
	Hyland	Ann	1806				
Revd	Richardson	Henry	1806			priest (presumably Church of Ireland)	
	Dempsey	Mary (or Maria)	1806				

Bibliography

Manuscript Sources

Blackrock Association, minute book (1782–99) (NLI ms. 84)

Bolton mss. (NLI ms. 15926), Return of watch for St Paul's parish, 25 March 1782–25 March 1784

[British army], *Dublin Garrison Order Book (1812–19)*, Pakenham Mahon Papers (NLI ms. 9475)

____, *Instructions to Corps Doing Duty in the Garrison of Dublin* (Dublin, 1838)

Journal kept by a young man in Dublin from February 1801 to May 1803 (RIA ms. 24.K. 14–15)

[Newgate Prison], A register containing medical instructions and prescriptions (Newgate Gaol, 1813–15) (NLI ms. 16, 256)

St Patrick's Hospital, Dublin, records

Westmoreland Lock Hospital, Dublin, records

[British] Public Record Office, Home Office records .O.100 (correspondence, Ireland)

Contemporary Works and Pamphlets

Anon., *A Compendium of the Laws of Forestalling, Engrossing, and Regrating, etc.* (Dublin, 1800)

____, *Animadversions on the Street Robberies in Dublin* (Dublin, 1765)

____, *A Month's Tour in North Wales, Dublin and its Environs* (London, 1781)

____, *A Report from the Committee Appointed to Enquire into the State and Management of the Fund of the Work-house of the City of Dublin* (Dublin, 1758)

____, *A Report Upon Certain Charitable Establishments in the City of Dublin* (Dublin, 1809)

____, *Arguments in Proof of the Necessity and Practicability of Suppressing Street Begging in the City of Dublin* (Dublin, 1817)

____, *A View of the Present State of Ireland* (Dublin, 1780)

____, *Institution for Administering Medical Aid to the Sick Poor* (Dublin, 1812)

____, *Ireland in 1831: Letters on the State of Ireland* (London, 1831)

____, *Hibernia Curiosa: A Letter from a Gentleman in Dublin, to his Friend at Dover in Kent* (2nd edn, London, 1782)

____, *Methods Proposed for Regulating the Poor* (Dublin, 1724)

____, *Observations on the House of Industry, Dublin* (Dublin, 1818)

____, *Previous Promises Inconsistent with a Free Parliament* (Dublin, 1760)

____, *Proceedings of the Corporation Instituted for the Relief of the Poor* (Dublin, 1774)

____, *Reasons For and Against the Removal of the Market-House* (Dublin, 1768)

____, *Remarks on the Principle of a Bill Now Pending in Parliament for the Establishment of Turnpikes Round the City of Dublin* (Dublin, 1786)

____, *Report of the Commissioners Appointed to Enquire into the Conduct and Management of the Corporation for Paving, Cleansing, and Lighting the Streets of Dublin* (Dublin, 1806)

_____, *Rules, Orders, and Bye-laws, Made by His Majesty's Commissioners of Police, for the District of the Metropolis* (Dublin, 1793)

_____, *Scheme for the Proportion which the Protestants of Ireland May Probably Bear to the Papists, etc.* (Dublin? 1732)

_____, *Sketches of Ireland Sixty Years Ago* (Dublin, 1847)

_____, *The Case of the Stage in Ireland: Containing the Reasons For and Against a Bill for Limiting the Number of Theatres in the City of Dublin* (Dublin, 1758)

_____, *The Metropolis* (2nd edn, Dublin, 1805)

_____, *Third Report of the Committee of the Dublin Female Penitentiary* (Dublin, 1816)

Archer, Joseph, *Statistical Survey of the County Dublin* (Dublin, 1801)

Boulter, Hugh, *Letters Written by his Excellency Hugh Boulter D.D.* (London, 1770), 2 vols.

Bowden, Charles Topham, *A Tour Through Ireland* (Dublin, 1791)

Brooke, Robert, *A Letter from Mr. Brooke to an Honourable Member of the House of Commons* (Dublin, 1786)

Carpenter, Andrew (ed.), *Verse in English from Eighteenth-century Ireland* (Cork, 1998)

Cromwell, Thomas, *Excursions Through Ireland* (London, 1820), 2 vols.

Day, The Hon. Mr. Justice, *A Charge Delivered to the Grand Juries of the City and County of Dublin, 23 January 1810* (Dublin, 1830)

Delany, Mary, *Letters from Georgian Ireland: The Correspondence of Mary Delany, 1731–68*, ed. Angelique Day (Belfast, 1991)

de Latocnaye, A., *A Frenchman's Walk Through Ireland, 1796–7*, trans. John Stevenson (Dublin, 1917)

Dutton, Hely, *Observations on Mr. Archer's Statistical Survey of the County of Dublin* (Dublin, 1802)

Farrell, Isaac, *Suggestions on the Dublin Improvements* (Dublin, 1841)

Faulkner, George, *Prince of Dublin Printers: The Letters of George Faulkner*, ed. Robert E. Ward (Lexington, KY, 1972)

Ferrar, John, *A View of Ancient and Modern Dublin* (Dublin, 1796)

Emily, Duchess of Leinster, *Correspondence of Emily, Duchess of Leinster (1731–1814)*, ed. Brian Fitzgerald (Dublin, 1957), 3 vols.

Foster, Edward, *A Letter to Sydenham Singleton Esq. on the Present State of the Insane Poor in the Kingdom* (Dublin, 1777)

Fry, Elizabeth and Joseph John Gurney, *Report Addressed to the Marquess Wellesley, Lord Lieutenant of Ireland* (London, 1827)

Gamble, John, *Sketches of History, Politics and Manners Taken in Dublin, and the North of Ireland, in the Autumn of 1810* (London, 1811), reproduced in John Gamble, *Society and Manners in Early Nineteenth-century Ireland*, ed. Breandán Mac Suibhne (Dublin, 2011)

_____, *Views of Society and Manners in the North of Ireland in a Series of Letters Written in the Year 1818* (London, 1819), reproduced in John Gamble, *Society and Manners in Early Nineteenth-century Ireland*, ed. Breandán Mac Suibhne (Dublin, 2011)

Geoghegan, Edward, *Observations on the Necessity of Regulating the Medical Profession* (Dublin, 1795)

Gilbert, John T. and R.M. Gilbert (eds), *Calendar of Ancient Records of Dublin* (Dublin, 1889–1944), 19 vols.

Hamilton, Hugh Douglas, *The Cries of Dublin: Drawn from the Life by Hugh Douglas Hamilton, 1760*, ed. William Laffan (Dublin, 2003)

House of Industry, *An Account of the Proceedings of the Governors of the House of Industry in Dublin* (Dublin, 1801)

Jeffreys, Nathaniel, *An Englishman's Descriptive Account of Dublin* (London, 1810)

Leeson, Margaret, *Memoirs of Mrs Margaret Leeson* (Dublin, 1795–97, reprinted, Dublin, 1995)

Lewis, R., *The Dublin Guide* (Dublin, 1787)

Lloyd, Edward, *A Description of the City of Dublin* (London, 1732)

Luckombe, Philip, *A Tour Through Ireland* (Dublin, 1789)

M'Gregor, John, *New Picture of Dublin* (Dublin, 1821)

Malton, James, *A Picturesque and Descriptive View of the City of Dublin* (Dublin, 1799)

O'Keefe, John, *Recollections of the Life of John O'Keefe* (London, 1826)

Pool, Robert and John Cash, *Views of the Most Remarkable Public Buildings, Monuments and other Edifices in the City of Dublin* (Dublin, 1780)

Rosborough, Samuel, *Observations on the State of the Poor of the Metropolis* (Dublin, 1801)

Rutty, Dr John, *An Essay Towards a Natural History of the County of Dublin* (Dublin, 1757)

Taylor, George and Andrew Skinner, *Maps of the Roads of Ireland* (London, 1778; repr. Shannon, Co. Clare, 1969)

Tuckey, Francis H., *The County and City of Cork Remembrancer* (Cork, 1837; repr. Cork, 1980)

Tuomy, Martin, *A Treatise on the Principal Diseases of Dublin* (Dublin, 1810)

Twiss, Richard, *A Tour in Ireland in 1775* (Dublin, 1776)

Wakefield, Edward, *An Account of Ireland, Statistical and Political* (London, 1812)

Warburton, J., Revd J. Whitelaw and Revd R. Walsh, *History of the City of Dublin* (London, 1818)

Watson, Samuel, *The Gentleman's and Citizen's Almanac for Dublin* (Dublin, various dates)

Whaley, Buck, *Buck Whaley's Memoirs*, ed. Sir Edward Sullivan (London, 1906)

Whitelaw, Revd James, *An Essay on the Population of Dublin, Being the Result of an Actual Survey Taken in 1798, etc.* (Dublin, 1805)

Young, Arthur, *A Tour in Ireland 1776–1779* (London edn 1892, repr. Shannon, 1970)

Parliamentary Proceedings and Statutes

The parliamentary register or histories of the proceedings and debates of the House of Commons of Ireland

6 Geo. I, c.15 [Ire] (1719)

10 Geo. I, c.3 [Ire] (1723)

3 Geo. II, c.19 [Ire] (1729)

1 Geo. III, c.10 [Ire] (1760)

1 Geo. III, c.14 [Ire] (1760)

3 Geo. III, c.21 [Ire] (1763)

3 Geo. III, c.27 [Ire] (1763)

3 Geo. III, c.28 [Ire] (1763)

3 Geo. III, c.36 [Ire] (1763)

5 Geo. III, c.16 [Ire] (1765)
11 Geo. III, c.16 [Ire] (1771)
11 & 12 Geo. III, c.13 [Ire] (1771–72)
11 & 12 Geo. III, c.22 [Ire] (1771–72)
11 & 12 Geo. III, c.27 [Ire] (1771–72)
13 & 14 Geo. III, c.22 [Ire] (1773–74)
15 & 16 Geo. III, c.24 [Ire] (1775–76)
15 & 16 Geo. III, c.34 [Ire] (1775–76)
17 & 18 Geo. III, c.11 [Ire] (1777–78)
17 & 18 Geo. III, c.38 [Ire] (1777–78)
9 & 20 Geo. III, c.13 [Ire] (1779–80)
23 & 24 Geo. III, c.35 [Ire] (1783–84)
25 Geo. III, c.43 [Ire] (1785)
26 Geo. III, c.32 [Ire] (1786)
26 Geo. III, c.61 [Ire] (1786)
26 Geo. III, c.86 [Ire] (1786)
27 Geo. III, c.38 [Ire] (1787)
28 Geo. III, c.50 [Ire] (1788)

Newspapers and Periodicals
Dublin Chronicle
Dublin Evening Post
Dublin Historical Record (journal of the Old Dublin Society)
Eighteenth-century Ireland (journal of the Eighteenth-century Ireland Society)
Faulkner's Dublin Journal
Freeman's Journal
Journal of the Royal Society of the Antiquaries of Ireland
Journal of the Cork Historical and Archaeological Society
Walker's Hibernian Magazine

Books and Journals

Aalen, F.H.A. and Kevin Whelan (eds), *Dublin City and County: From Prehistory to the Present* (Dublin, 1992)

Ashworth, William, *The Genesis of Modern British Town Planning* (London, 1968)

Baigent, Elizabeth, 'Economy and society in eighteenth-century English towns: Bristol in the 1770s', in Dietrich Denecke and Gareth Shaw (eds), *Urban Historical Geography: Recent Progress in Britain and Germany* (Cambridge, 1988)

Bannon, Michael J. (ed.), *A Hundred Years of Irish Planning: The Emergence of Irish Planning, 1880–1920* (Dublin, 1985)

Bannon, Michael J. (ed.), *Planning: The Irish Experience, 1920–1988* (Dublin, 1989)

Barnard, Toby, *Making the Grand Figure: Lives and Possessions in Ireland, 1641–1770* (New Haven, CT and London, 2004)

Bell, Colin and Rose, *City Fathers: The Early History of Town Planning in Britain* (London, 1969)

Berry, F.H., 'Notes from the diary of a Dublin Lady in the reign of George II', *Journal of the Royal Society of the Antiquaries of Ireland*, vol. xxviii (1898)

Best, Edith M., 'St Paul's parish, Dublin', *Journal of the Royal Society of the Antiquaries of Ireland*, vol. civ (1974)

Blacker, Revd B.H., *Brief Sketches of the Parishes of Booterstown and Donnybrook* (Dublin, 1874)

Borsay, Peter (ed.), *The Eighteenth-century Town: A Reader in English Urban History, 1688–1820* (London, 1990)

Boydell, Brian, *A Dublin Musical Calendar, 1700–1760* (Dublin, 1988)

____, *Rotunda Music in Eighteenth-century Dublin* (Dublin, 1992)

Brady, Joseph and Anngret Simms (eds), *Dublin Through Space and Time* (Dublin, 2001)

Briggs, Asa, *The Age of Improvement, 1783–1867* (London, 1969)

Buer, M.C., *Health, Wealth, and Population in the Early Days of the Industrial Revolution* (London, 1926)

Bunce, Michael, *The Countryside Ideal: Anglo-American Images of Landscape* (London, 1994)

Burke, Nuala T., 'A hidden Church? The structure of Catholic Dublin in the mid-eighteenth century', *Archivium Hibernicum*, vol. xxxii (1974)

____, 'An early modern Dublin suburb: the estate of Francis Aungier, Earl of Longford', *Irish Geography*, vol. vi, no.4 (1972)

____, 'Dublin, 1600–1800: a study in urban morphogenesis' (unpublished PhD thesis, Trinity College, Dublin, 1973)

Butel, P. and L.M. Cullen (eds), *Cities and Merchants: French and Irish Perspectives on Urban Development, 1500–1900* (Dublin, 1986)

Carey, Tim, *Mountjoy: The Story of a Prison* (Cork, 2000)

Casey, Christine, 'The Dublin domestic formula', in Christine Casey (ed.), *The Eighteenth-century Dublin Town House* (Dublin, 2010)

____ (ed.), *The Eighteenth-century Dublin Town House* (Dublin, 2010)

Chalklin, C.W., *The Provincial Towns of Georgian England: A Study of the Building Process, 1740–1820* (London, 1974)

Clark, Peter (ed.), *The Cambridge Urban History of Britain* (Cambridge, 2000), vol. 2

____ and R.A. Houston, 'Culture and leisure, 1700–1840', in Peter Clark (ed.), *The Cambridge Urban History of Britain* (Cambridge, 2000), vol. 2

Collins, James, *Life in Old Dublin* (Dublin, 1913)

Connolly, S.J., 'Albion's fatal twigs: justice and law in the eighteenth century', in Rosalind Mitchison and Peter Roebuck (eds), *Economy and Society in Scotland and Ireland, 1500–1939* (Edinburgh, 1988)

Corbin, Alain, *The Foul and the Fragrant Odour and the French Social Imagination (Le Miasme et la Jonquille)* (Paris, 1982; English trans. New York, 1986)

Corcoran, Michael, *Our Good Health: A History of Dublin's Water and Drainage* (Dublin, 2005)

Cosgrave, Dillon, *North Dublin* (Dublin, 1909; repr. Dublin, 1977)

Costello, Vandra, 'Public space for display and promenade in Georgian Dublin', in Gillian O'Brien and Finola O'Kane (eds), *Georgian Dublin* (Dublin, 2008)

Craig, Maurice [James] (ed.), *The Legacy of Swift: A Bi-centenary Record of St. Patrick's Hospital* (Dublin, 1948)

____, *Dublin, 1660–1860: A Social and Architectural History* (London, 1957; repr. Dublin, 1969)

____, *The Architecture of Ireland from the Earliest Times to 1880* (Dublin, 1982)

____, *The Volunteer Earl, Being the Life and Times of James Caulfeild First Earl of Charlemont* (London, 1948)

Cruikshank, Dan, *The Secret History of Georgian London: How the Wages of Sin Shaped the Capital* (London, 2009)

Cullen, L. [Louis] M., *An Economic History of Ireland Since 1660* (London, 1972)

____, *Princes and Pirates: The Dublin Chamber of Commerce, 1783–1983* (Dublin, 1983)

____, 'Catholic social classes under the Penal Laws', in T.P. Power and Kevin Whelan (eds), *Endurance and Emergence: Catholics in Ireland in the Eighteenth Century* (Dublin, 1990)

____, 'The growth of Dublin, 1600–1900: character and heritage', in F.H.A. Aalen and Kevin Whelan (eds), *Dublin City and County: From Prehistory to Present* (Dublin, 1992)

Cummins, N. Marshall, *Some Chapters of Cork Medical History* (Cork, 1957)

Curran, C.P., *Dublin Decorative Plasterwork of the Seventeenth and Eighteenth Centuries* (London, 1967)

____, *The Rotunda Hospital, its Architects and Craftsmen* (Dublin, 1946)

de Vries, Jan, *European Urbanisation, 1500–1800* (London, 1984)

____, 'Problems in the measurement, description, and analysis of historical urbanization', in A.D. van der Woude, Akira Hayami and Jan de Vries (eds), *Urbanisation in History: A Process of Dynamic Interactions* (Oxford, 1990)

Dickson, David, 'Catholics and trade in eighteenth-century Ireland: an old debate revisited', in T.P. Power and Kevin Whelan (eds), *Endurance and Emergence: Catholics in Ireland in the Eighteenth Century* (Dublin, 1990)

____, *Dublin: The Making of the Capital City* (London, 2014)

____, 'In search of the old Irish Poor Law', in Rosalind Mitchison and Peter Roebuck (eds), *Economy and Society in Scotland and Ireland, 1500–1939* (Edinburgh, 1988)

____, 'Large-scale developers and the growth of eighteenth-century Irish cities', in P. Butel and L.M. Cullen (eds), *Cities and Merchants: French and Irish Perspectives on Urban Development, 1500–1900* (Dublin, 1986)

____, 'The demographic implications of Dublin's growth, 1650–1850', in Richard Lawton and Robert Lee (eds), *Urban Population Development in Western Europe from the Late-eighteenth to the Early-twentieth Century* (Liverpool, 1989)

____, 'The place of Dublin in the eighteenth-century Irish economy', in J.M. Devine and David Dickson (eds), *Ireland and Scotland, 1600–1850: Parallels and Contrasts in Economic and Social Development* (Edinburgh, 1983)

____ (ed.), *The Gorgeous Mask: Dublin, 1700–1850* (Dublin, 1987)

Duffy, Hugo, *James Gandon and His Times* (Kinsale, Co. Cork, 1999)

Dunleavy, Mairéad, *Dublin Barracks: A Brief History of Collins Barracks, Dublin* (Dublin, 2002)

____, *Pomp and Poverty: A History of the Silk Industry in Ireland* (New Haven, CT and London, 2011)

Earle, Peter, *A City Full of People: Men and Women in London, 1650–1750* (London, 1994)

____, *The Making of the English Middle Class: Business, Society and Family Life in London, 1660–1730* (London, 1991)

Fagan, Patrick, 'The population of Dublin in the eighteenth century with particular reference to the proportion of Protestants and Catholics', in *Eighteenth-century Ireland*, vol. vi (1991)

____, *The Second City: Portrait of Dublin, 1700–1760* (Dublin, 1986)

Fitzpatrick, Wm. J., *Curious Family History, or Ireland Before the Union* (6th edn, Dublin, 1870)

Foster, Sarah, 'An honourable station in respect of commerce, as well as constitutional liberty': retailing, consumption and economic nationalism in Dublin, 1720–85', in Gillian O'Brien and Finola O'Kane (eds), *Georgian Dublin* (Dublin, 2008)

French, C.E.F., 'William Burton Conyngham (1733–1796)', *Journal of the Royal Society of the Antiquaries of Ireland*, vol. cxv (1985)

Garnham, Neal, 'How violent was eighteenth-century Ireland?', *Irish Historical Studies*, vol. xxx, no. 119 (May 1997)

____, 'The short career of Paul Farrell: a brief consideration of law enforcement in eighteenth-century Dublin', *Eighteenth-century Ireland*, vol. xi (1996)

____, *The Courts, Crime and the Criminal Law in Ireland, 1692–1760* (Dublin, 1996)

Gilbert, J.T., *A History of the City of Dublin* (Dublin, 1861)

Gillespie, Elgy (ed.), *The Liberties of Dublin* (Dublin, 1973)

Girouard, Mark, *Cities and People: A Social and Architectural History* (London, 1986)

Glin, The Knight of, 'A directory of the Dublin furniture trade, 1752–1800', in Agnes Bernelle (ed.), *Decantations: A Tribute to Maurice Craig* (Dublin, 1992)

Gough, Michael, 'The Dublin Wide Street Commissioners (1758–1851): an early modern planning authority', *Pleanáil: Journal of the Irish Planning Institute*, no. 11 (1992–93)

Graham, B.J. and L.J. Proudfoot (eds), *A Historical Geography of Ireland* (London, 1993)

Greene, John, 'The repertory of Dublin theatres, 1720–45', *Eighteenth-century Ireland*, vol. 2 (1987)

Griffith, Lisa-Marie, 'Mobility and mayors: merchant utilization of the position of lord mayor, 1760–1800', in Gillian O'Brien and Finola O'Kane (eds), *Georgian Dublin* (Dublin, 2008)

Hall, Thomas, *Planning Europe's Capital Cities* (London, 1997)

Hand, Tony, 'Supplying stone for the Dublin house', in Christine Casey (ed.), *The Eighteenth-century Dublin Town House* (Dublin, 2010)

Handcock, William Donville, *The History and Antiquities of Tallaght in the County of Dublin* (Dublin, 1876; repr. Dublin, 1991)

Harrison, Wilmot, *Memorable Dublin Houses* (Dublin, 1890; repr. Dublin, 1971)

Harvey, John, *Dublin: A Study in Environment* (London, 1949)

Henry, Brian, *Dublin Hanged: Crime, Law Enforcement and Punishment in Late Eighteenth-century Dublin* (Dublin, 1994)

Herlihy, Jim, *The Dublin Metropolitan Police* (Dublin, 2001)

Hill, Bridget, *Servants: English Domestics in the Eighteenth Century* (Oxford, 1996)

Hill, Jacqueline, *From Patriots to Unionists: Dublin Civic Politics and Irish Protestant Patriotism, 1660–1840* (Oxford, 1997)

____, 'Religion, trade and politics in Dublin, 1798–1848', in P. Butel and L.M. Cullen (eds), *Cities and Merchants: French and Irish Perspectives on Urban Development, 1500–1900* (Dublin, 1986)

____, 'The politics of Dublin Corporation, 1760–'92', in David Dickson, Dáire Keogh and Kevin Whelan (eds), *The United Irishmen: Republicanism, Radicalism and Rebellion* (Dublin, 1993)

____, 'The shaping of Dublin government in the long eighteenth century', in Peter Clark and Raymond Gillespie (eds), *Two Capitals: London and Dublin, 1500–1840* (Oxford, 2001)

Hogan, Ita Margaret, *Anglo-Irish Music, 1780–1830* (Cork, 1966)

Hohenberg, Paul M. and Lynn Hollen Lees, *The Making of Urban Europe, 1000–1950* (London, 1985)

Jones, Colin, *Paris: Biography of a City* (London, 2006)

Joyce, Weston St John, *The Neighbourhood of Dublin* (Dublin, 1939)

Kavanagh, Ann C., *John Fitzgibbon, Earl of Clare: Protestant Reaction and English Authority in Late Eighteenth-century Ireland* (Dublin, 1997)

Kelly, James, 'Infanticide in eighteenth-century Ireland', *Irish Economic and Social History*, vol. xix (1992)

____, *The Liberty and Ormond Boys: Factional Riot in Eighteenth-century Dublin* (Dublin, 2005)

Kennedy, Máire, *French Books in Eighteenth-century Ireland* (Oxford, 2001)

Kinane, Vincent, 'Printer's apprentices in 18th- and 19th-century Dublin', *Linen Hall Review*, vol. 10, no. 1 (summer 1993)

Landers, John, *Death and the Metropolis: Studies in the Demographic History of London, 1670–1830* (Cambridge, 1993)

Lawton, Richard and Robert Lee (eds), *Urban Population Development in Western Europe from the Late Eighteenth to the Early Twentieth Century* (Liverpool, 1989)

Lennon, Colm and John Montague (eds), *John Rocque's Dublin: A Guide to the Georgian City* (Dublin, 2010)

____, *Irish Historic Atlas, No. 19, Dublin, Part II, 1610 to 1756* (Dublin, 2008)

Loeber, Ralph, Hugh Campbell, Livia Hurley, John Montague and Ellen Rowley, *Art and Architecture of Ireland: Vol. IV, Architecture, 1600–2000* (Dublin, 2014)

Longfield, Ada K., 'History of the Irish linen and cotton printing industry in the 18th century', *Journal of the Royal Society of the Antiquaries of Ireland*, vol. lxvii (1937)

M'Cready, Revd C.T., *Dublin Street Names, Dated and Explained* (Dublin, 1892)

Maguire, J.B., 'Dublin Castle: three centuries of development', *Journal of the Royal Society of the Antiquaries of Ireland*, vol. cxv. (1985)

Malcolm, Elizabeth, *Swift's Hospital: A History of St. Patrick's Hospital, Dublin, 1746–1989* (Dublin, 1989)

Mangan, Michelle, 'A comparison of the experiences of Dublin city and Limerick city during the cholera epidemic of 1832', in Gillian O'Brien and Finola O'Kane (eds),

Georgian Dublin (Dublin, 2008)

Maxwell, Constantia, *Dublin Under the Georges, 1714–1830* (London, 1956)

McCabe, Desmond, *St Stephen's Green, Dublin, 1660–1875* (Dublin, 2011)

McCarthy, Patricia, 'From parlours to pastries: inventories and the eighteenth-century Dublin interior', in Christine Casey (ed.), *The Eighteenth-century Dublin Town House* (Dublin, 2010)

McCracken, J.L., *The Irish Parliament in the Eighteenth Century* (Dundalk, 1971)

____, 'The political structure, 1714–60', in T.W. Moody and W.E. Vaughan (eds), *A New History of Ireland*, vol. 4 (Oxford, 1986)

____, 'The social structure and social life, 1714–1760', in T.W. Moody and W.E. Vaughan (eds), *A New History of Ireland*, vol. 4 (Oxford, 1986)

McCullough, Niall, 'The Dublin house', in Christine Casey (ed.), *The Eighteenth-century Dublin Town House* (Dublin, 2010)

McDowell, R.B., 'Ireland in 1800', in T.W. Moody and W.E. Vaughan (eds), *A New History of Ireland*, vol. 4 (Oxford, 1986)

____, *Ireland in the Age of Imperialism and Revolution, 1760–1801* (Oxford, 1979)

____, *Social Life in Ireland, 1800–45* (Dublin, 1957; repr. Dublin, 1963)

McLynn, Frank, *Crime and Punishment in Eighteenth-century England* (London, 1989)

McParland, Edward, 'James Gandon and the Royal Exchange competition, 1768–69', *Journal of the Royal Society of the Antiquaries of Ireland*, vol. cii, pt i (1972)

____, 'Strategy in the planning of Dublin, 1750–1800', in P. Butel and L.M. Cullen (eds), *Cities and Merchants: French and Irish Perspectives on Urban Development, 1500–1900* (Dublin, 1986)

____, 'The Wide Street Commissioners: their importance for Dublin architecture in the late 18th early 19th century', *Quarterly Bulletin of the Irish Georgian Society*, vol. xv, no. i (Jan.–Mar. 1972)

Milne, Kenneth, *The Dublin Liberties, 1600–1850* (Dublin, 2009)

Mooney, Tighearnan and Fiona White, 'The gentry's winter season', in David Dickson (ed.), *The Gorgeous Mask: Dublin, 1700–1850* (Dublin, 1987)

Moylan, Thomas King, 'Vagabonds and sturdy beggars, iii', *Dublin Historical Record*, vol. i, no. 3 (September 1938)

Mumford, Lewis, *The City in History* (London, 1961)

Munter, Robert, *A Dictionary of the Print Trade in Ireland, 1550–1775* (New York, 1988)

Murphy, Seán, 'The Dublin anti-union riot of 3 December 1759', in Gerard O'Brien (ed.), *Parliament, Politics and People: Essays in Eighteenth-century History* (Dublin, 1989)

Musgrave, Clifford, *Life in Brighton* (London, 1970)

'Nemo', *A Brief Record of the Female Orphan House, North Circular Road, Dublin from 1790 to 1890* (Dublin, 1893)

Ní Sheaghdha, Nessa, 'Irish scholars and scribes in eighteenth-century Dublin', *Eighteenth-century Ireland*, vol. 4 (1989)

Nicholls, George, *A History of the Irish Poor Law* (London, 1856)

O'Brien, Gerard, 'Scotland, Ireland, and the antithesis of Enlightenment', in S.J. Connolly, R.A. Houston and R.J. Morris (eds), *Conflict, Identity and Economic Development: Ireland and Scotland, 1600–1939* (Preston, 1995)

_____ (ed.), *Parliament, Politics and People: Essays in Eighteenth-century History* (Dublin, 1989)

O'Brien, Gillian, "'What can possess you to go to Ireland?": visitors' perceptions of Dublin, 1800–1830', in Gillian O'Brien and Finola O'Kane (eds), *Georgian Dublin* (Dublin, 2008)

_____ and Finola O'Kane (eds), *Georgian Dublin* (Dublin, 2008)

O'Carroll, Joseph, 'Contemporary attitudes towards the homeless poor 1725–1775', in David Dickson (ed.), *The Gorgeous Mask: Dublin, 1700–1850* (Dublin, 1987)

O'Cathain, Diarmaid, 'John Fergus MD: eighteenth-century doctor, book collector and Irish Scholar', *Journal of the Royal Society of the Antiquaries of Ireland*, vol. cxviii (1988)

Ó Cionnaith, Finnian, *Mapping, Measurement and Metropolis: How Land Surveyors Shaped Eighteenth-Century Dublin* (Dublin, 2012)

O'Connell, Maurice R., 'Class conflict in a pre-industrial society: Dublin in 1780', *Irish Ecclesiastical Record*, vol. ciii (1965)

O'Connor, Stephen, 'The Volunteers of Dublin, 1778–84: a short study of urban volunteering', in Gillian O'Brien and Finola O'Kane (eds), *Georgian Dublin* (Dublin, 2008)

Ó Gráda, Cormac, *Ireland: A New Economic History, 1780–1939* (Oxford, 1994)

O'Kane, Finola, 'The appearance of a continuing city': Dublin's Georgian suburbia', in Gillian O'Brien and Finola O'Kane (eds), *Georgian Dublin* (Dublin, 2008)

_____, 'The Fitzwilliam family's development of Merrion Square', in Christine Casey (ed.), *The Eighteenth-century Dublin Town House* (Dublin, 2010)

O'Neill, Timothy P., 'Fever and public health in pre-Famine Ireland', *Journal of the Royal Society of the Antiquaries of Ireland*, vol. ciii (1973)

Ó Snodaigh, Pádraig, 'Some police and military aspects of the Irish Volunteers', *Irish Sword*, vol. xiii (1977–79)

_____, *The Irish Volunteers, 1715–1793: A List of the Units* (Dublin, 1995)

O'Sullivan, William, *The Economic History of Cork City From the Earliest Times to the Act of Union* (Cork, 1937)

Ogborn, Miles, 'This most lawless space: the geography of the Fleet and the making of Lord Hardwicke's Marriage Act of 1753', *New Formations*, no. 37 (spring 1999)

Osborough, W.N., *Law and the Emergence of Modern Dublin* (Dublin, 1996)

Picard, Liza, *Dr Johnson's London: Everyday Life in London, 1740–1770* (London, 2001)

Pollard, Mary, *Dublin's Trade in Books, 1550–1800* (Oxford, 1989)

Porter, Roy, *London: A Social History* (London, 1994)

_____, *Madmen: A Social History of Madhouses, Mad-Doctors & Lunatics* (Stroud, Gloucestershire, 2004)

Prunty, Jacinta, *Dublin Slums, 1800–1925: A Study in Urban Geography* (Dublin, 1998)

Robins, Joseph, *The Lost Children: A Study of Charity Children in Ireland, 1700–1900* (Dublin, 1980)

Roche, Daniel, *The People of Paris: An Essay in Popular Culture in the 18th Century (le Peuple de Paris)*, trans. Marie Evans (Leamington Spa, 1987)

Roundtree, Susan, 'Brick in the eighteenth-century Dublin town house', in Christine Casey (ed.), *The Eighteenth-century Dublin Town House* (Dublin, 2010)

Rude, George, *Hanovarian London, 1714–1808* (London, 1971)

Rynne, Colin, *Industrial Ireland, 1750–1930: An Archaeology* (Cork, 2006)

Sheldon, Esther K., *Thomas Sheridan of Smock-Alley* (Princeton, NJ, 1967)

Sheridan, Edel, 'Designing the capital city: Dublin *c.* 1660–1810', in Joseph Brady and Anngret Simms (eds), *Dublin Through Space and Time* (Dublin, 2001).

_____, 'Living in the capital city: Dublin in the eighteenth century', in Joseph Brady and Anngret Simms (eds), *Dublin Through Space and Time* (Dublin, 2001)

Shoemaker, Robert B., 'The London "mob" in the early eighteenth century', in Peter Borsay (ed.), *The Eighteenth-century Town: A Reader in English Urban History, 1688–1820* (London, 1990)

Sjoberg, Gideon, *The Preindustrial City: Past and Present* (New York, 1966)

Skinner, David, *Wallpaper in Ireland, 1700–1900* (Tralee, 2014)

Smith Morris, Eleanor, *British Town Planning and Urban Design* (Harlow, Essex, 1997)

Smyth, James, 'Dublin's political underground in the 1790s', in Gerard O'Brien (ed.), *Parliament, Politics and People: Essays in Eighteenth-century History* (Dublin, 1989)

Stafford-Johnson, J., 'The Dublin Penny Post 1773–1840', *Dublin Historical Record*, vol. 4, no. 3 (March–May 1942)

Starr, J.P., 'The enforcing of law and order in eighteenth-century Ireland' (unpublished PhD thesis, Trinity College, Dublin, 1968)

Stevens, Julie Anne, 'Views of Georgian Dublin: perspectives of the city', in Gillian O'Brien and Finola O'Kane (eds), *Georgian Dublin* (Dublin, 2008)

Swift, John, *History of the Dublin Bakers and Others* (Dublin, 1948)

Swift, Jonathan, *Verses on the Death of Dr. Swift* (Dublin, 1731)

Thompson, E.P., 'The moral economy of the English crowd in the eighteenth century', *Past and Present*, no. 50 (February 1971)

Trumbach, Randolph, *Sex and the Gender Revolution*, vol. 1 (Chicago, 1998)

Turpin, John, 'The School of Ornament of the Dublin Society in the 18th century', *Journal of the Royal Society of the Antiquaries of Ireland*, vol. cxvi (1986)

Twomey, Brendan, 'Financing speculative property development in early eighteenth-century Dublin', in Christine Casey (ed.), *The Eighteenth-century Dublin Town House* (Dublin, 2010)

Walsh, J.J., *Industrial Dublin Since 1698, and the Silk Industry in Dublin* (Dublin, 1913)

_____, *Opera in Dublin, 1705–1797* (Dublin, 1973)

Whelan, Irene, *The Bible War in Ireland: The 'Second Reformation' and the Polarization of Protestant–Catholic Relations, 1800–1840* (Dublin, 2005)

White, R.J., *Life in Regency England* (London, 1963)

Wise, Sarah, *The Italian Boy: Murder and Grave-robbery in 1830s London* (London, 2004)

Young, Canon E.J., 'A Dublin slaughter house nuisance of 1723', *Dublin Historical Record*, vol. 5, no. 2 (December 1942–February 1943)

Youngson, A.J., *The Making of Classical Edinburgh, 1750–1840* (Edinburgh, 1966)

Notes and References

Abbreviations

BPP, HC   British Parliamentary Papers, House of Commons
HMC   Historical Manuscripts Commission
NAI   National Archives of Ireland
NGI   National Gallery of Ireland
NLI   National Library of Ireland
Parl. Reg. Ire. Parliamentary Register or Histories of the Proceedings and Debates of the
                 House of Commons of Ireland
RIA   Royal Irish Academy

Chapter 1: Urbanisation in Georgian Dublin

1   Ronald Grimsley, 'Rousseau's Paris', in Paul Fritz and David Williams (eds), *City and Society in the 18th Century* (Toronto, 1973), p. 8.

2   Anon., *Scheme of the Proportions which the Protestants of Ireland May Probably Bear to the Papists* (1732), p. 3 (claims a thirty-nine per cent increase in city houses in the period 1718–32); David Dickson, *Dublin: The Making of the Capital City* (London, 2014), pp. 124ff.

3   Cormac Ó Gráda, Economics Department, University College, Dublin, personal communication, January 2014.

4   Anon., *A Month's Tour in North Wales, Dublin and its Environs* (London, 1781), p. 76; [Fitzwilliam Estates] *Survey by Jonathan Barker* (1762) (NAI ref. 2011/3/1); John Greene, *Map of Bow Bridge c. 1700*, Dublin City Library and Archive, reproduced in Finnian Ó Cionnaith, *Mapping, Measurement and Metropolis: How Land Surveyors Shaped Eighteenth-century Dublin* (Dublin, 2012), p. 176.

5   M. Pollard, *Dublin's Trade in Books, 1550–1800* (Oxford, 1989), pp. 30ff, 130.

6   [George Faulkner], *Prince of Dublin Printers: The Letters of George Faulkner*, ed. Robert E. Ward (Lexington, KY, 1972); Robert Munter, *A Dictionary of the Print Trade in Ireland, 1550–1775* (New York, 1988); Dickson, *Dublin*; A.R. Humphries, *The Augustan World: Life and Letters In Eighteenth-century England* (London, 1954), p. 95.

7   Charles F. Mullett, 'Community and communications', in Fritz and Williams (eds), *City and Society*, p. 80.

8   Toby Barnard, *Irish Protestants: Ascents and Descents, 1641–1770* (Dublin, 2004), p. 339.

9   Gerard O'Brien, 'Scotland, Ireland, and the antithesis of Enlightenment', in S.J. Connolly, R.A. Houston and R.J. Morris (eds), *Conflict, Identity and Economic Development: Ireland and Scotland, 1600–1939* (Preston, 1995), pp. 125ff.

10   Samuel Madden, *Letter to the Dublin Society, on the Improving Their Fund, and the Manufactures, Tillage, etc. in Ireland* (Dublin, 1739), pp. 28ff; [Royal Dublin Society], *Proceedings on the Petitions of Sundry Manufacturers and Others and the Disposition of the Sum of Ten Thousand Pounds, Committed to their Determination, by Order of the Right Honourable and Honourable the Knights, Citizens and Burgesses in Parliament Assembled, Session 1761 and 1762* (Dublin, various dates), pp. 22, 33, 42, 50.

11 David Dickson, 'The place of Dublin in the eighteenth-century Irish economy', in J.M. Devine and David Dickson (eds), *Ireland and Scotland, 1600–1850: Parallels and Contrasts in Economic and Social Development* (Edinburgh, 1983), p. 185; A.J. Youngson, *The Making of Classical Edinburgh, 1750–1840* (Edinburgh, 1966), p. 193.

12 John Carr, *The Stranger in Ireland* (London, 1806), p. 56.

13 Arthur Dobson, *William Hogarth* (London, 1898), pp. 238ff, 284ff.

14 Hugh Douglas Hamilton, *The Cries of Dublin*, ed. William Laffan (Dublin, 2003).

15 Marcellus Laroon, *The Cryes of London* (London, 1687, and later reprints).

16 *Faulkner's Dublin Journal*, 17 June 1750; *Belfast News-Letter*, 17 March 1789; H.J. Berry, 'Notes from the diary of a Dublin lady in the reign of George II', *Journal of the Royal Society of the Antiquaries of Ireland*, vol. 8, pt 2, 5th series, pp. 145ff.

17 Nuala Burke, 'A hidden Church? The structure of Catholic Dublin in the mid-eighteenth century', *Archivium Hibernicum*, vol. 32 (1974), pp. 81ff.

18 John James McGregor, *New Picture of Dublin* (Dublin, 1821), p. 130; Timothy P. O'Neill, 'Irish trade banners', in Caoimhín Ó Danachair (ed.), *Folk & Farm: Essays in Honour of A.T. Lucas* (Dublin, 1976), p. 178.

19 Vic Gatrell, *City of Laughter: Sex and Satire in Eighteenth-century London* (London, 2006), p. 239.

20 St John's parish, Dublin, Vestry Account Books, 9 December 1724; St Anne's parish, Dublin, Vestry Proceedings, 16 February 1781.

21 Wm. J. Fitzpatrick, *Curious Family History, or Ireland Before the Union* (6th edn., Dublin, 1870), p. 88.

22 *Faulkner's Dublin Journal*, 5 July, 2 August 1770; John Gamble, *Sketches of History, Politics and Manners Taken in Dublin, and the North of Ireland, in the Autumn of 1810* (London, 1811), reproduced in John Gamble, *Society and Manners in Early Nineteenth-century Ireland*, ed. Breandán Mac Suibhne (Dublin, 2011), p. 45.

23 J. Warburton, Revd J. Whitelaw and Revd R. Walsh, *History of the City of Dublin* (London, 1818), vol. 2, p. 1036; Karl Von Hailbronner (1836?), in Eoin Bourke (ed.), *'Poor Green Erin': German Travel Writers' Narratives on Ireland from Before the 1798 Rising to the Great Famine* (Frankfurt, 2012), p. 261; Knut Jongbohn Clement (1839), in Bourke (ed.), *'Poor Green Erin'*, pp. 261ff; Jakob Venedey (1843), in Bourke (ed.), *'Poor Green Erin'*, p. 424.

24 Edward MacLysaght, *Irish Life in the Seventeenth Century* (Dublin, 1979), p. 199.

25 Wide Streets Commission, Dublin, Minutes (Gilbert Library, Pearse Street, Dublin 2), vol. 1, 4 August 1761.

26 Mairéad Dunlevy, 'Samuel Madden and the scheme for the encouragement of useful manufactures', in Agnes Bernelle (ed.), *Decantations: A Tribute to Maurice Craig* (Dublin, 1992), pp. 22ff.

27 BPP, HC, 1810 (193), *Eighth Report from the Commissioners of the Board of Education in Ireland. Foundling Hospital*, p. 10; BPP, HC, 1801 (16), House of Industry, Dublin, Account of the Governors for the Year Ending 25 March 1800, p. 131; Warburton et al., *History of the City of Dublin*, vol. 1, p. 111.

28 Dickson, *Dublin*, p. 177.

29 2 Geo. I, c.17, cl.5 [Ire.] (1715); this part of the Whitelaw census was reproduced in Patrick Fagan, 'The population of Dublin in the eighteenth century with particular reference to

the proportions of Protestants and Catholics', *Eighteenth-century Ireland*, vol. 6 (1991), p. 155.

30   Peter Earle, *A City Full of People: Men and Women in London, 1650–1750* (London, 1994), pp. 39ff, 42ff; Bridget Hill, *Servants: English Domestics in the Eighteenth Century* (Oxford, 1996), pp. 32ff; The Knight of Glin, 'A directory of the Dublin furniture trade, 1752–1800', in Agnes Bernelle (ed.), *Decantations: A Tribute to Maurice Craig* (Dublin, 1992), pp. 50–9.

31   David Skinner, *Wallpaper in Ireland, 1700–1900* (Tralee, 2014), pp. 20ff, 95.

32   Karl Gottlob Kuttner, 'Briefe uber Ireland' (Leipzig, 1785), in Eoin Bourke (ed.), *'Poor Green Erin': German Travel Writers' Narratives on Ireland from Before the 1798 Rising to the Great Famine* (Frankfurt, 2012), pp. 33ff.

33   David Skinner, 'Flocks, flowers and follies: some recently discovered Irish wallpapers of the eighteenth century', *Irish Architectural and Decorative Studies* (journal of the Irish Georgian Society), vol. 6. (2003), p. 19; Christine Casey (ed.), *The Eighteenth-century Dublin Town House* (Dublin, 2010).

34   *Faulkner's Dublin Journal*, 28 May, 12 June, 17 July 1744.

35   Tighearnan Mooney and Fiona White, 'The gentry's winter season', in David Dickson (ed.), *The Gorgeous Mask: Dublin, 1700–1850* (Dublin, 1987), pp. 2ff.

36   Jerry White, *London in the Eighteenth Century: A Great and Monstrous Thing* (London, 2012), p. 153.

37   Casey (ed.), *Eighteenth-century Dublin Town House*; James Francis Goodwin, *Ireland in the Empire, 1688–1770* (Cambridge, MA, 1973), p. 141.

38   Robert W. Malcolmson, *Popular Recreations in English Society, 1700–1850* (Cambridge, 1973), p. 34.

39   Edward Lloyd, *A Description of the City of Dublin* (London, 1732), p. 12.

40   T.C. Bernard, '"Grand metropolis" or "the anus of the world"? The cultural life of eighteenth-century Dublin', in Peter Clark and Raymond Gillespie (eds), *Two Capitals: London and Dublin, 1500–1840* (Oxford, 2001), p. 200; R.F. Foster, *Modern Ireland, 1600–1972* (London, 1988), p. 185; Louis M. Cullen, 'The growth of Dublin, 1600–1900: character and heritage', in F.H.A. Aalen and Kevin Whelan (eds), *Dublin City and County: From Prehistory to Present* (Dublin, 1992), p. 252.

41   Arthur Young, *A Tour in Ireland, 1776–1779* (4th edn., London 1892; repr. Shannon, Co. Clare, 1970), vol. 1, pp. 18ff.

42   Maire Kennedy, *French Books in Eighteenth-century Ireland* (Oxford, 2001), pp. 107, 164.

43   Gerard O'Brien, 'Scotland, Ireland, and the antithesis of the Enlightenment', in Connolly et al. (eds), *Conflict, Identity and Economic Development*, p. 133.

44   [Irish Government], proclamation dated 8 July 1718 (Dublin, 1718); *Freeman's Journal*, 4 June 1768; Anon., *Scheme of the Proportions*, p. 3; Fagan, 'The population of Dublin', pp. 125ff; David Dickson, 'The demographic implications of Dublin's growth, 1650–1850', in Richard Lawton and Robert Lee (eds), *Urban Population Development in Western Europe from the Late-Eighteenth to the Early-Twentieth Century* (Liverpool, 1989), p. 180.

45   Peter Borsay, 'London, 1660–1800: A distinctive culture?', in Peter Clark and Raymond Gillespie (eds), *Two Capitals: London and Dublin, 1500–1840* (Oxford, 2001), p. 175.

46   T.J. Walsh, *Opera in Dublin, 1705–1797: The Social Scene* (Dublin, 1973), pp. 9, 23, 25.

47   Peter Hall, *Cities in Civilization: Culture, Innovation and Public Order* (London, 1998), p. 711.

48   Hanns Gross, *Rome in the Age of the Enlightenment* (Cambridge, 1990), pp. 17, 325.

49   Eleanor Smith Morris, *British Town Planning and Urban Design* (Harlow, Essex 1997), pp. 16ff; Vic Gatrell, *The First Bohemians: Life and Art in London's Golden Age* (London, 2013), pp. 9ff.

50   Robert Pool and John Cash, *Views of the Most Remarkable Public Buildings, Monuments and Other Edifices in the City of Dublin* (Dublin, 1780); Grimsley, 'Rousseau's Paris', p. 9.

51   Nicholas Phillipson, 'Towards a definition of the Scottish Enlightenment', in Fritz and Williams (eds), *City and Society*, p. 126.

52   Roger Emerson, 'The Enlightenment and social structures', in Fritz and Williams (eds), *City and Society*, pp. 104ff.

53   Maurice James Craig, *The Volunteer Earl* (London, 1948), p. 103.

54   *Freeman's Journal*, 17 March, 24 April, 5 May 1789; Patrick Fagan, *Catholics in a Protestant Country: The Papist Constituency in Eighteenth-century Dublin* (Dublin, 1998), p. 17; Dickson, 'Place of Dublin', p. 186; J.L. McCracken, 'The political structure, 1714–60', in T.W. Moody and W.E. Vaughan (eds), *A New History of Ireland* (Oxford, 1986), vol. 4, pp. 57ff.

55   www.excavations.ie; Dublin 2002:0578, Smithfield, Dublin.

56   *Dublin Chronicle*, 31 July 1788, quoted in Finnian Ó Cionnaith, *Mapping, Measurement and Metropolis: How Land Surveyors Shaped Eighteenth-century Dublin* (Dublin, 2012), p. 183.

57   Sir F.D. Mackinnon, 'The law and the lawyers', in A.S. Turberville (ed.), *Johnson's England: An Account of the People and Manners of His Age* (Oxford, 1933), vol. 2, p. 289.

58   Douglas Hay, 'Authority and the criminal law', in Douglas Hay, Peter Linebaugh, John. G. Rule, E.P. Thompson and Cal Winslow (eds), *Albion's Fatal Tree: Crime and Society in Early Eighteenth-century England* (London, 1977), pp. 17ff.

59   James Walvin, *English Urban Life, 1776–1851* (London, 1984), p. 36; Alain Corbin, *The Foul and the Fragrant Odour and the French Social Imagination* [*Le Miasme et La Jonquille* (Paris, 1982)] (English trans. New York, 1986), pp. 102, 165; Daniel Roche, *The People of Paris: An Essay in Popular Culture in the 18th Century* [*Le Peuple de Paris*], trans. Marie Evans (Leamington Spa, 1987), pp. 33–4, 49–50, 70; Youngson, *Making of Classical Edinburgh*, p. 227.

Chapter 2: Conflict and Confrontation

1   Edward Wakefield, *An Account of Ireland, Statistical and Political* (London, 1812), vol. 1, p. 737.

2   Peter Earle, *The Making of the English Middle Class: Business, Society and Family Life in London, 1660–1730* (London, 1991), p. 327.

3   Emily Cockayne, *Hubbub: Filth, Noise and Stench in England, 1600–1770* (New Haven, CT and London, 2007), pp. 72ff; Pamela Sharpe, 'Population and society, 1700–1840', in Peter Clark (ed.), *The Cambridge Urban History of Britain* (Cambridge, 2000), pp. ii, 521.

4   St Anne's parish, Dublin, Vestry Proceedings, 17 April 1759, 28 October 1761.

5   W.J.R. Wallace (ed.), *The Vestry Records of the Parishes of St Bride, St Michael Le Pole and St Stephen, Dublin, 1662–1742* (Dublin, 2011), p. 206; St Anne's parish, Dublin, Vestry Proceedings, 19 April 1808.

6   Anon., *Journal of a Tour, etc., Performed in August 1804* (London, 1806), p. 36; Vincent Kinane, 'Printer's apprentices in 18th- and 19th-century Dublin', *Linen Hall Review*, vol. 10, no. 1 (summer 1993), p. 11.

7   Maria Edgeworth, *The Absentee* (London, 1812; repr. London, 1976), p. 165; Anon., *The State of County Infirmaries in Ireland, and Hints Thrown Out for Their Improvement* (Dublin, 1805), p. 5; Dr Brian Boydell, 'Music', in Ian Campbell Ross (ed.), *Public Virtue, Public Love: The Early Years of the Dublin Lying-in Hospital* (Dublin, 1986), p. 120.

8   Earle, *Making of the English Middle Class*, p. 13.

9   Pádraig Ó Fágáin, *Éigse na hIarmhí* (Dublin, 1985), p. 142; Tim Hitchcock, *Down and Out in Eighteenth-century London* (London and New York, 2004), p. 6; White, *London in the Eighteenth Century*, p. 157.

10 BPP, HC, 1835 (369) xxxii [32], *Poor Law Commissioners Enquiry*, pt i, appendix A, supplement, p. 61.

11 Samuel Rosborough, *Observations on the State of the Poor of the Metropolis* (Dublin, 1801), p. 11.

12 Mary E. Daly, 'Social structure of the Dublin working class, 1871–1911', *Irish Historical Studies*, vol. 23 (1982–83), p. 123.

13 St Anne's parish, Dublin, Vestry Proceedings, 16 February, 24 July 1781.

14 Wide Streets Commission, Dublin, Minutes, vol. 2, 30 June 1766, vol. 5, 19 July 1784, 21 May 1785, vol. 7, 19 October 1787, 13 March 1789, vol. 11, 13 July, 26 October 1792, vol. 13, 8 May 1795, vol. 14, 4 May 1798; Finnian Ó Cionnnaith, *Mapping, Measurement and Metropolis: How Land Surveyors Shaped Eighteenth-century Dublin* (Dublin, 2012), p. 30.

15 Richard Annesley MP, 9 November 1782, in *Parl. Reg. Ire.* (2nd edn, Dublin, 1784), vol. 1, p. 326.

16 [Buck Whaley], *Buck Whaley's Memoirs*, ed. Sir Edward Sullivan (London, 1906), pp. 332ff.

17 Edward Willes, *The Letters of Lord Chief Baron Edward Willes to the Earl of Warwick, 1757–62*, ed. James Kelly (Aberystwyth, 1990), p. 97 (there was great expense associated with the parliamentary season in Dublin as Irish households kept almost twice as many servants as noble or wealthy English families did); Revd James Whitelaw, *An Essay on the Population of Dublin* (Dublin, 1805), p. 5; Anon., *Journal of a Tour in Ireland*, p. 20; Constantia Maxwell, *Dublin Under the Georges, 1714–1830* (London, 1956), p. 85.

18 *Hibernian Journal*, 23 January 1784, 23 September 1785; *Dublin Evening Post*, 14 July 1787, *Freeman's Journal*, 4 September 1788.

19 *Hibernian Journal*, 14 September 1778: 'Every vice and folly of the rich and great is reflected with all the additional deformity that brutality of manners can give them. If rich wines and sumptuous living affect the fortunes of the great, a general drunkenness precludes the poor from the comforts of life. If families are rendered miserable by the gallantries of the unprincipled rake, rapes attended with circumstances too shocking to repeat, are daily committed by the more abandoned clown.'

20 *Faulkner's Dublin Journal*, 11 September 1750; *Hibernian Journal*, 13 May 1776.

21 *Freeman's Journal*, 26 August 1790, 18 April 1793.

22 *Dublin Evening Post*, 15 May 1787; *Freeman's Journal*, 12 June 1792.

23 *Faulkner's Dublin Journal*, 11 November 1752, 12 August 1773; *Hibernian Journal*, 25 August 1783.

24 *Hibernian Journal*, 14 April 1777; *Freeman's Journal*, 29 January 1788.

25 *Freeman's Journal*, 30 August 1794.

26 *Freeman's Journal*, 6 March 1788; Gamble, *Sketches of History*, reproduced in Gamble, *Society and Manners*, p. 76.

27 *Hibernian Journal*, 27 May 1776, 21 March 1777; *Freeman's Journal*, 29 January, 3 July 1788; *Freeman's Journal*, 29 April, 9, 11 September 1788, 4 June, 14 November 1789, 4 December 1798, 2 July 1799.

28 Isaac Bickerstaaf, *Stephen's Green: A Rhapsody* (Dublin, 1763), p. 6.

29 Anon., *To the Honourable House of Commons, etc. the Humble Petition of the Footmen In and About the City of Dublin* (Dublin, 1732).

30 *Hibernian Journal*, 27 February 1782.

31 John T. Gilbert and R.M. Gilbert (eds), *Calendar of Ancient Records of Dublin* (Dublin, 1889–1944), vol. 14, pp. 276, 310, 324, vol. 15, p. 391; *Freeman's Journal*, 26 August 1790, 27 November 1792; Bickerstaaf, *Stephen's Green*, p. 6.

32 Gilbert and Gilbert (eds), *Calendar of Ancient Records of Dublin*, vol. 13, p. 37; *Freeman's Journal*, 27 June 1789, 26 August 1790, 5 June 1794.

33 *Dublin Satirist*, November 1809.

34 [William Drennan], *The Drennan Letters*, ed. D.A. Chart (Belfast, 1931), pp. 57, 161, 237.

35 'A Real Paddy' [Pierce Egan], *Real Life in Ireland* (London, 1821; repr. London, 1904), p. 32.

36 White, *London in the Eighteenth Century*, p. 447.

37 Anon., *Four Letters Originally Written in French, Relating to the Kingdom of Ireland* (Dublin, 1739), p. 27; Anon., *A View of the Present State of Ireland* (Dublin, 1780), p. 38; James Malton, *A Picturesque and Descriptive View of the City of Dublin* (Dublin, 1799; repr. Dublin, 1981); 10 Geo. III, c.3 [Ire.] (1723), cl.17; *Hibernian Journal*, 10 April 1786; *Dublin Evening Post*, 12 December 1787; *Freeman's Journal*, 21 October 1792.

38 Young, *Tour in Ireland*, vol. 1, p. 21; A. de Latocnaye, *A Frenchman's Walk Through Ireland, 1796–7*, trans. John Stevenson (Dublin, 1917), p. 17.

39 Anon., *Arguments in Proof of the Necessity and Practicability of Suppressing Street Begging in the City of Dublin* (Dublin, 1817), p. 3.

40 Anon., *Proceedings of the Corporation Instituted for the Relief of the Poor* (Dublin, 1774), pp. 19ff; Rosborough, *Observations*, p. 33; Anon., *Arguments in Proof* [...] *in the City of Dublin*, p. 7; Anon., *Observations on the House of Industry, Dublin* (Dublin, 1818), p. 1; Anon., *A Month's Tour in North Wales, Dublin and its Environs* (London, 1781), p. 103; Gamble, *Sketches of History*, reproduced in Gamble, *Society and Manners*, p. 44; *Faulkner's Dublin Journal*, 27 July 1769; *Hibernian Journal*, 27 January 1778, 19 May, 25 August 1786; *Freeman's Journal*, 27 July 1769, 22 May, 26 July 1788, 4 May 1793, 12 January, 26 April, 28 May 1796.

41 Hamilton, *Cries of Dublin*, pl. 22, 41, 58; *Freeman's Journal*, 11 June 1771; Anon., *The Characteristic Phantasmagoria* (Dublin, *c.* 1810), pp. 17ff.

42 Joseph Archer, *Statistical Survey of the County Dublin* (Dublin, 1801), p. 139.

43 BPP, HC, 1810 (193), *Eighth Report from the Commissioners of the Board of Education, in Ireland. Foundling Hospital*, appendix 10, p. 34.

44 Anon., *Methods Proposed for Regulating the Poor* (Dublin, 1724), p. 6; Dr William Drennan to Mrs McTier, 23 April 1798; Carr (ed.), *Drennan Letters*, p. 272; *Faulkner's Dublin Journal*, 11 September 1750, 15 April 1755, 26 April 1768; *Dublin Evening Post*, 24 May 1787; *Freeman's Journal*, 26 July 1788, 5 May 1796, 23 September 1797.

45 Johann Wilhelm, Baron von Archenholz, *A Picture of England, Containing a Description*

of the Laws, Customs and Manners of England (Dublin, 1791), p. 73, cited in Richard Schwartz, *Daily Life in Johnson's London* (Madison, WI, 1983), p. 40.

46   Mary Alcock, 'The Chimney-sweeper's Complaint' (1798), in Andrew Carpenter (ed.), *Verse in English from Eighteenth-century Ireland* (Cork, 1998), p. 538.

47   *Freeman's Journal*, 16 June, 29 September 1789; Warburton et al., *History of the City of Dublin*, vol. 2, p. 891; *Report of the Select Committee of the House of Commons on Chimney Sweeps 1817*, in Strathearn Gordon and T.G.B. Cocks (eds), *A People's Conscience* (London, 1952), p. 76; N. Marshall Cummins, *Some Chapters of Cork Medical History* (Cork, 1957), p. 71.

48   *Faulkner's Dublin Journal*, 10 October 1750; *Freeman's Journal*, 1 May 1792.

49   *Hibernian Journal*, 12 March 1783, 23 September 1785; *Freeman's Journal*, 11 July 1795; Whitley Stokes, *Projects for Re-establishing the Internal Peace and Tranquility of Ireland* (Dublin, 1799), p. 34.

Chapter 3: Municipal Government

1   Anon., *Dublin: A Satirical Essay, in Five Books: Book 1* (Dublin, 1788), p. 3.

2   St Anne's parish, Dublin, Vestry Proceedings, 15 July 1767, 20 February 1773.

3   Ibid., 16 February, 24 July 1781.

4   23 Geo. II, c.19 [Ire.] (1749); 17 & 18 Geo. III, c.47 [Ire.] (1777–78); St Anne's parish, Dublin, Vestry Proceedings, 21 October 1763, 22 February 1765.

5   *Hibernian Journal*, 13 August 1784.

6   *Freeman's Journal*, 21 May, 13 October 1789.

7   Warburton et al., *History of the City of Dublin*, vol. 2, p. 1063; BPP, HC, 1823, *Select Committee on Dublin Taxation 1822*, pp. 4ff, 12ff, 19; Jacqueline Hill, *From Patriots to Unionists: Dublin Civic Politics and Irish Protestant Patriotism, 1660–1840* (Oxford, 1997), p. 356.

8   St Anne's parish, Dublin, Vestry Proceedings, various dates 1775–1840; J.T. Gilbert, *A History of the City of Dublin* (Dublin, 1861), vol. 1, p. 341; Desmond McCabe, *St Stephen's Green, Dublin, 1660–1875* (Dublin, 2011), p. 111.

9   Anon., *Plan of St George's Dispensary for Administering Advice and Medicines to the Poor, etc.* (Dublin, 1801), pp. 15ff.

10   St Anne's parish, Dublin, Vestry Proceedings, 7 April 1761, 14 September, 1773; Edith M. Best, 'St Paul's parish, Dublin', *Journal of the Royal Society of the Antiquaries of Ireland*, vol. 14 (1974), p. 22.

11   Gilbert and Gilbert (eds), *Calendar of Ancient Records of Dublin*, vol. 10, pp. 242, 281, vol. 11, pp. 172, 356, 364, 403, vol. 12, pp. 17, 68, 128ff, 186, 262, vol. 13, p. 226.

12   Anon., *Animadversions on the Street Robberies in Dublin, etc.* (Dublin, 1765), pp. 2ff.

13   St Anne's parish, Dublin, Vestry Proceedings, 27 April 1762, 18 April, 21 October 1763, 22 February 1765, 14 October 1773, 20 July 1786, 7 April 1795.

14   St Thomas' parish, Dublin, Directors of the Watch Minute Book, 1750 (NAI ref. M/4961); Best, 'St Paul's parish, Dublin', p. 17.

15   3 Geo. II, c.15 [Ire.] (1729); Neal Garnham, *The Courts, Crime and the Criminal Law in Ireland, 1692–1760* (Dublin, 1996), pp. 80ff; idem, 'The short career of Paul Farrell: a brief consideration of law enforcement in eighteenth-century Dublin', *Eighteenth-century Ireland*, vol. 11 (1996), p. 49.

16 James Kelly (ed.), *Proceedings of the Irish House of Lords, 1771–1800* (Dublin, 2008), vol. 1, pp. 165ff, vol. 2, p. 491.

17 Gilbert and Gilbert (eds), *Calendar of Ancient Records of Dublin*, vol. 11, p. 171, vol. 12, p. 301, vol. 13, pp. 118, 187.

18 Anon., *An Intercepted Letter from J.T. Esq., Writer at Canton, to his Friend in Dublin, Ireland* (2nd edn, Dublin, 1804), p. 9.

19 Warburton et al., *History of the City of Dublin*, vol. 2, p. 1063; 33 Geo. III, c.16 [Ire.]; *Belfast News-Letter*, 31 March 1789; R.B. McDowell, 'Ireland in 1800', in Moody and Vaughan (eds), *New History of Ireland*, vol. 4, pp. 705ff; Hill, *From Patriots to Unionists*, pp. 43, 79, 91, 162ff.

20 Warburton et al., *History of the City of Dublin*, vol. 1, p. 535, vol. 2, pp. 1033ff, 1067.

21 Twenty-one groups formed by the nineteen parishes and two Liberties contingents; *Faulkner's Dublin Journal*, 18 November 1746, 3 October 1747, 8 October 1748, 20 February 1750, 20 March 1753; Gilbert and Gilbert (eds), *Calendar of Ancient Records of Dublin*, vol. 15, p. 459.

22 Gilbert and Gilbert (eds), *Calendar of Ancient Records of Dublin*, vol. 11, pp. 385, 414.

23 Kelly (ed.), *Proceedings of the Irish House of Lords*, vol. 3, p. 28.

Chapter 4: Trends in the Pattern of Growth

1 Rosborough, *Observations*, p. 42.

2 Nuala T. Burke, 'Dublin, 1600–1800: A study in urban morphogenesis' (PhD thesis, Trinity College, Dublin, 1972).

3 Revd John Anketell, 'Description of Sunday Evening Spent in a Coffee-house in the City of Dublin', in idem, *Poems on Several Subjects* (Dublin, 1793), p. 132.

4 11 & 12 Geo. III, c.13 [Ire.].

5 26 Geo. III, c.86 [Ire.].

6 Nathaniel Jeffreys, *An Englishman's Descriptive Account of Dublin* (London, 1810), p. 85.

7 *Freeman's Journal*, 11 February 1769.

8 The minutes of the Wide Streets Commission (50 vols.) are held in Dublin City Council's Gilbert Library, Pearse Street, Dublin 2.

9 Wide Streets Commission, Dublin, Minutes, vol. 5, 28 February 1785.

10 Ibid., 16 June 1772; Gilbert, *History of the City of Dublin*, vol. 1, p. 305.

11 Wide Streets Commission, Dublin, Minutes, vol. 2, 25 May 1778.

12 Ibid., 15, 17 April 1779; vol. 4, 26 September 1783.

13 Ibid., 9, 27 August, 16, 20 September, 11 November 1779.

14 Ibid., vol. 1, 24 July 1762.

15 John Winstanley, 'A Thought in the Pleasant Grove at Cabragh', in idem, *Poems* (Dublin, 1742).

16 Gilbert and Gilbert (eds), *Calendar of Ancient Records of Dublin*, vol. 13, p. 315; James Kelly, 'Scarcity and poor relief in eighteenth-century Ireland; the subsistence crisis of 1782–4', *Irish Historical Studies*, vol. 27. no. 109 (May 1992), pp. 40ff, 56ff.

17 Hely Dutton, *Observations on Mr Archer's Statistical Survey of the County of Dublin* (Dublin, 1802), p. 13.

18 *Jones' Sentimental and Masonic Magazine*, June 1795.

19 George Cheyne, *An Essay of Health and Long Life* (4th edn, Dublin, 1725), p. 52; [Jonathan Swift], *The Correspondence of Jonathan Swift*, ed. Harold Williams (Oxford, 1964), vol. 1, p. 62, vol. 4, pp. 169, 268; Jonathan Swift, *Collected Works*, ed. George Faulkner, vol. 17, quoted in Manning Robertson, *Dun Laoghaire: The History, Scenery and Development of the District* (Dublin, 1930), p. 19; Laetitia Pilkington, *Memoirs of Laetitia Pilkington* (Dublin and London, 1748–54; repr. Athens, GA, 1997), vol. 1, p. 18; John Ferrar, *A View of Ancient and Modern Dublin* (Dublin, 1796), p. 75.

20 Cheyne, *Essay of Health and Long Life*, p. 4; Sir Michael Creagh, *Seasonable Advice to the Magistrates and Chief Inhabitants of the City of Dublin* (Dublin, 1727), p. 5.

21 Dr Richard Russell, *A Dissertation on the Use of Sea-water in the Diseases of the Glands* (Dublin, 1752); *Faulkner's Dublin Journal*, 17–21 July 1753; Clifford Musgrave, *Life in Brighton* (London, 1970), pp. 50ff; Colin and Rose Bell, *City Fathers: The Early History of Town Planning in Britain* (London, 1969), p. 125.

22 Maurice James Craig, *The Volunteer Earl* (London, 1948), p. 125.

23 John Smith, *The Curiosities of Common Water* (Dublin, 1725); James Nelson, *An Essay on the Government of Children* (Dublin, 1763); John Gifford, *A Short Account of Fixed Air and its Medicinal Virtues when Combined with Water* (Dublin, 1776); Anon., *A Report of the Cases Relieved and Cured in the Baths Appropriated for the Reception of the Poor* (Dublin, 1777); Anon., *Observations on the Efficacy of Cold Bathing, in the Cure of Nervous, Bilious, Scrophalous and Other Chronic Diseases* (Dublin, 1786); Michael Ryan, *An Enquiry into the Nature, Causes and Cure of the Consumption of the Lungs* (Dublin, 1787).

24 Francis Elrington Ball, *Howth and its Owners* (Dublin, 1917), p. 130.

25 John Rutty, *The Argument of Sulphur or no Sulphur in Waters Discussed* (Dublin, 1762), p. 94.

26 [Duchess of Leinster], *Correspondence of Emily, Duchess of Leinster*, vol. 1 (Dublin, 1949), pp. 228, 251, 322, vol. 2. (Dublin, 1953), p. 234, vol. 3 (Dublin, 1957), p. 147.

27 *Hibernian Journal*, 21 May 1783, 20 November 1786; *Freeman's Journal*, 7 June 1790, 12 July 1796; Abraham Bosquet, *Howth: A Descriptive Poem* (Dublin, 1787); Anon., 'The Flesh Brush', in Anon., *The West Briton, Being a Collection of Poems on Various Subjects* (2nd edn, Dublin, 1800):

> The Goddess felt a little cold,
> And shudder'd from a sudden shock,
> As from a dipping at Blackrock.

28 Anon., 'A Petition to the Ladies of Dublin from Dunlary Written by the Old Washwomen' (Dublin, *c.* 1720), in Andrew Carpenter (ed.), *Verse in English from Eighteenth-century Ireland* (Cork, 1998), p. 101.

29 Edward Baynard MD, *Health, a Poem, Showing how to Procure, Preserve and Restore it* (Dublin, 1721), p. 29.

30 *Faulkner's Dublin Journal*, 28 February 1743, 12 February 1744, 12 April 1746, 21 February 1747, 17 March 1750; Charles Smith, 'Kilmacud, County Dublin', in Paul Connolly, Dennis A. Cronin and Brian Ó Dálaigh (eds), *Irish Townlands: Studies in Local History* (Dublin, 1998), p. 191.

31 Charles Lucas, *An Essay on Waters* (London, 1756); *Hibernian Journal*, 30 June, 9 July 1783.

32 *Hibernian Journal*, 20 November 1786; Ferrar, *View of Ancient and Modern Dublin*, p. 75; William Patterson MD, *An Analytical View* (Dublin, 1800), p. xxxviii.

33 J.J. Stockdale, *Petticoat Loose* (4th edn, London, 1812), p. 54.

34 'A Real Paddy' [Pierce Egan], *Real Life in Ireland*, p. 35.

35 The Strand formed part of the road leading out to Clontarf and over time was absorbed by urban expansion. Its name and function were replaced by Beresford Place and Amiens Street.

36 *Flying Post*, 15 September 1709; Lloyd, *Description of the City of Dublin*, p. 14; Anon., *Chivalrie, No Trifle, – or the Knight and His Lady* (Dublin, 1746), p. 6; William Philips, *St Stephen's Green* [play] (Dublin, 1700):
[Marina]: Oh, tis such a comfort! When my husband is in a dogged humour, to call for my glass chariot and take the air on the Strand.

37 Lloyd, *Description of the City of Dublin*, p. 14; Anon., *A Short and Easy Method of Reducing the Exhorbitant Pride and Arrogance, of the City of Dublin* (Dublin, 1748), p. 31; Anon., *The Life and Uncommon Adventures of Capt. Dudley Bradstreet* (Dublin, 1760), pp. 70ff; Edward Willes, *The Letters of Lord Chief Baron Edward Willes to the Earl of Warwick, 1757–62*, ed. James Kelly (Aberystwyth, 1990), p. 21; Faulkner, *Prince of Dublin Printers*, p. 78; Carr, *Stranger in Ireland*, p. 31; Erin I. Bishop, *The World of Mary O'Connell, 1778–1836* (Dublin, 1999), p. 14.

38 J.G. Zimmermann, *Solitude* (1784–86; English trans. London, 1798); Michael Bunce, *The Countryside Ideal: Anglo-American Images of Landscape* (London, 1994), p. 26; Gerald Finlay, 'The encapsulated landscape: an aspect of Gilpin's picturesque', in Fritz and Williams (eds), *City and Society*, p. 193.

39 Mary Delany, *Letters From Georgian Ireland: The Correspondence of Mary Delany, 1731–68*, ed. Angelique Day (Belfast, 1991), p. 165.

40 R.J. White, *Life in Regency England* (London, 1963), p. 129.

41 Charles Morris, 'Country and town' (*c.* 1798), in Roger Lonsdale (ed.), *The New Oxford Book of Eighteenth-century Verse* (Oxford, 1987): see also George Crabbe, *The Village: Book 1* (1783), in ibid.:

    … few amid the rural tribe have time
    To number syllables and play with rhyme

    …

    Can poets soothe you, when you pine for bread
    By winding myrtles round your ruined shed?

42 *Hibernian Journal*, 21 May 1783; *Dublin Chronicle*, 15 May 1788; *Freeman's Journal*, 27, 31 May, 19 August 1788, 21 May, 4 June, 24 September 1789, 24 May, 10 June 1794, 5 July 1796, 10 August 1798; Lady Louisa Connolly to Countess of Kildare, 28 August, 8, 10 October 1776, in [Duchess of Leinster], *Correspondence of Emily, Duchess of Leinster*, vol. 3, pp. 219, 230, 232.

43 *Freeman's Journal*, 18 June 1791, 4 May 1793.

44 *Hibernian Journal*, 30 June 1783, 16 October 1786; *Freeman's Journal*, 15 January, 9 August 1788; *Dublin Chronicle*, 2 November 1790, quoted in Revd B.H. Blacker, *Brief Sketches of the Parishes of Booterstown and Donnybrook* (Dublin, 1874), p. 427; Archer, *Statistical Survey*, p. 89.

45 *Faulkner's Dublin Journal*, 20 December 1766, 28 January 1769; J. Stafford-Johnson, 'The Dublin Penny Post 1773–1840', *Dublin Historical Record*, vol. 4, no. 3 (March 1942), pp. 81ff.

46 'A Real Paddy' [Pierce Egan], *Real Life in Ireland*, p. 42.

47 *Freeman's Journal*, 14, 31 May, 12 July 1791, 12 May 1792; Ferrar, *View of Ancient and Modern Dublin*, p. 80; John Gamble, *Views of Society and Manners in the North of Ireland in a Series of Letters Written in the Year 1818* (London, 1819), reproduced in John Gamble, *Society and Manners in Early Nineteenth-century Ireland*, ed. Breandán Mac Suibhne (Dublin, 2011), p. 474: 'We shut our eyes to the crowd of people in jaunting cars, singles, and coaches that every moment passed us, but we could not altogether shut our ears.'

48 Dutton, *Observations*, p. 146.

49 *Faulkner's Dublin Journal*, 2 September 1760.

50 Anon., *Previous Promises Inconsistent with a Free Parliament* (Dublin, 1760), p. 30.

51 *Faulkner's Dublin Journal*, 2 April 1771; *Hibernian Journal*, 25 August, 24 September 1783, 19 October 1785; *Freeman's Journal*, 17 January, 24 April 1789, 31 May, 22 December 1791.

52 *Freeman's Journal*, 2, 12 August 1788; Anon., *An Admirer of General, or Useful, and Necessary Improvements. Letters Addressed to Parliament* (Dublin, 1786), appendix, p. 203.

53 Anon., *The Economist, Showing in a Variety of Estimates, from Fourscore Pounds a Year to Upwards of £800 how Completely and Genteely a Family May Live with Frugality for a Little Money* (Dublin, c. 1775), p. 11; Anon., *Reports of the Committee of St Mary's Parish on Local Taxation* (Dublin, 1823), p. 28.

54 Dr John Rutty, *An Essay Towards a Natural History of the County of Dublin* (Dublin, 1757), p. 75; John O'Keefe, *Recollections of the Life of John O'Keefe* (London, 1826), p. 26.

55 Mary Delany, 'A View of Part of ye Little Grove of Evergreens at Delville with ye Country Beyond it and Bay of Dublin 1744' (NGI, ref. no. 2722 [22]), reproduced in Mark Laird and Alicia Weisberg-Roberts (eds), *Mrs Delany and Her Circle* (New Haven, CT and London, 2009), p. 127; *Freeman's Journal*, 26–28 June 1788; [Fitzwilliam Estate], 'Survey by Jonathan Barker 1762' (NAI ref. no. 2011/3/1); Anon., 'View of the Hill of Howth, Ireland's Eye and Lambay, Taken from Killmacud, 1788' (NGI, ref. no. 11756); John Henry Campbell, 'Ringsend and Irishtown from the Grand Canal, Dublin' (1809) (NGI, ref. no. 3970).

56 St Anne's parish, Dublin, Vestry Proceedings, 16 April 1795, 18 October 1797, 30 December 1799, 18 November 1807; Ferrar, *View of Ancient and Modern Dublin*, p. 127.

57 *Faulkner's Dublin Journal*, 13 July 1799.

58 BPP, HC, 1823, *Report of the Select Committee on Dublin Taxation*, 1822, p. 4.

59 Wide Streets Commission, Dublin, Minutes, vol. 13, 30 January 1795, 16, 23 November 1795, vol. 14, 7 April 1797, 26 January 1798.

60 Jacqueline R. Hill, 'Religion, trade and politics in Dublin, 1798–1848', in P. Butel and L.M. Cullen (eds), *Cities and Merchants: French and Irish Perspectives on Urban Development, 1500–1900* (Dublin, 1986), p. 250; David Dickson, 'Large-scale developers and the growth of eighteenth-century Irish cities', in Butel and Cullen (eds), *Cities and Merchants*, p. 212.

61 BPP, HC, 1820 (84), *Report of the Commissioners Appointed by the Lord Lieutenant of Ireland to Inspect the House of Industry*, appendix, p. 15.

62 Carr, *Stranger in Ireland*, p. 52; Carr (ed.), *Drennan Letters*, pp. 321ff, 345; Gamble, *Sketches of History*, reproduced in Gamble, *Society and Manners*, pp. 28, 73.

63 Maria Edgeworth, *The Absentee* (1812, repr. London, 1975), p. 164.

64 *Hibernian Journal*, 4 June 1784; *Freeman's Journal*, 24 August 1790 ('All speculations in building have been, for some time past, directed to the vicinity of the New Custom House, and streets are now, where six months past were fields').

65 *Faulkner's Dublin Journal*, 16 June 1761, 24 May 1763, 20 January 1774; *Hibernian Journal*, 11 October 1780, 12 March 1781, 25 August 1783; St Anne's parish, Dublin, Vestry Proceedings, 24 January 1781.

66 *Belfast News-Letter*, 9 June 1789; *Hibernian Journal*, 7 May 1784; *Freeman's Journal*, 26 June, 2 October 1788; Ferrar, *View of Ancient and Modern Dublin*, p. 74.

67 J.C. Curwen, *Observations on the State of Ireland* (London, 1818), vol. 2, p. 109.

68 Gilbert and Gilbert (eds), *Calendar of Ancient Records of Dublin*, vol. 11, pp. 44, 80, 148, 224, 299, 351, 402, 444.

69 Ada K. Longfield, 'History of the Irish linen and cotton printing industry in the 18th century', *Journal of the Royal Society of the Antiquaries of Ireland*, vol. 67 (1937), p. 56; Dickson, 'Place of Dublin', pp. 179ff; Dickson, 'Large-scale developers', p. 113.

70 *Faulkner's Dublin Journal*, 19 May 1767, 29 July 1769, 7 August 1770; see sheet no. 2 of John Rocque's 1756 Dublin city map.

71 11 Geo. III, c.16 [Ire.] cl.1, 3 (1771); Revd Charles Barry, *Plan of Rathmines School* (4th edn, Dublin, 1795), p. 17; Journal kept by a young man in Dublin from February 1801 to May 1803 (RIA ms. 24.K.14–15), p. 5 (October 1801).

72 John Swift, *History of the Dublin Bakers and Others* (Dublin, 1948); L.M. Cullen, *Princes and Pirates: The Dublin Chamber of Commerce, 1783–1983* (Dublin, 1983), pp. 16ff.

73 Mairéad Dunlevy, *Pomp and Poverty: A History of the Silk Industry in Ireland* (New Haven, CT and London, 2011), pp. 5, 47ff, 67, 73.

74 Ibid., p. 104.

75 *Faulkner's Dublin Journal*, 7 February 1771.

76 Thomas Newburgh, 'The Beau Walk, in Stephen's Green', in Andrew Carpenter (ed.), *Verse in English from Eighteenth-century Ireland* (Cork, 1998), p. 319.

77 'An Heroic Epistle to Richard Twiss' (1771), quoted in Fitzpatrick, *Curious Family History*, p. 92.

78 *Faulkner's Dublin Journal*, 17 June 1750; *Hibernian Journal*, 16 May 1781; Gilbert and Gilbert (eds), *Calendar of Ancient Records of Dublin*, vol. 10, p. 21, vol. 11, p. 362, vol. 13, p. 365; McCabe, *St Stephen's Green*, p. 110.

79 Warburton et al., *History of the City of Dublin*, vol. 2, p. 768.

80 15 & 16 Geo. III, c.20 [Ire.] (1775–76).

81 Sheet no. 4 of John Rocque's 1756 city map.

82 Gilbert and Gilbert (eds), *Calendar of Ancient Records of Dublin*, vol. 9, p. 63, vol. 11, p. 374, vol. 11, pp. 412, 441; *Hibernian Journal*, 1, 17, 31 January, 7, 9 February, 2 August 1776, 3 January 1777; *Faulkner's Dublin Journal*, 21 October 1769, 16 July 1771, 15 February 1774; Anon., *Reasons For and Against the Removal of the Market-house* (Dublin, 1768), pp. 8ff; Canon E.J. Young, 'St. Michan's parish in the eighteenth century', *Dublin Historical Record*, vol. 3, no. 1 (September 1940), p. 3.

83 Gilbert and Gilbert (eds), *Calendar of Ancient Records of Dublin*, vol. 12, pp. 49, 371, 415ff, vol. 13, p. 156, vol. 14, pp. 168ff.

84   Ibid., vol. 10, pp. 359ff, vol. 11, pp. 115, 389, vol. 13, pp. 224, 373, vol. 14, pp. 13, 168ff; Anon., *Journal of a Tour in Ireland*, p.9.

85   Gilbert and Gilbert (eds), *Calendar of Ancient Records of Dublin*, vol. 14, pp. 92, 107, 139, 154.

86   Ibid., vol. 7, p. 31; Dutton, *Observations*, p. 158.

87   Bosquet, *Howth: Descriptive Poem*, p. 13.

88   *Freeman's Journal*, 31 May 1791.

89   Anon., *Journal of a Tour in Ireland*, p. 8.

90   E. Jane Whately, *Life and Correspondence of Richard Whately DD, Late Archbishop of Dublin* (2nd edn, London, 1868), p. 69.

91   Lewis Mumford, *The City in History* (London, 1961), p. 437.

92   Dickson, *Dublin*, p. 290; Peter Pearson, *Between the Mountains and the Sea: Dún Laoghaire–Rathdown County* (Dublin, 1998), pp. 92ff; Diarmuid Ó Gráda, 'The Historical Geography of Dún Laoghaire' (unpublished BA dissertation, University College, Dublin, 1968).

93   Anon., *Sketches of Ireland Sixty Years Ago* (Dublin, 1847), p. 54: 'Of this famous and flourishing community nothing remains at the present day but large houses, with stone fronts and architectural ornaments, in ruins, in remote and obscure streets.'

94   *Freeman's Journal*, 31 May 1791; Nathaniel Jeffries, *An Englishman's Descriptive Account of Dublin* (London, 1808), p. 80; Anon., *Journal of a Tour Through Several of the Southern Counties of Ireland* (London, 1809), p. 1; Anon., *Institution for Administering Medical Aid to the Sick Poor* (Dublin, 1812), p. 15.

95   David Dickson, 'Death of a capital? Dublin and the consequences of Union', in Peter Clark and Raymond Gillespie (eds), *Two Capitals: London and Dublin, 1500–1840* (Oxford, 2001), p. 118.

Chapter 5: Crime and the Failure of the Legal System

1   James Buchan, *Capital of the Mind: How Edinburgh Changed the World* (Edinburgh, 2007), p. 320.

2   Hanns Gross, *Rome in the Age of the Enlightenment* (Cambridge, 1990), pp. 215ff.

3   Anon., *The Parish Guttlers: Or the Humours of a Select Vestry* (Dublin, 1725), pp. 18ff.

4   Brian Henry, *Dublin Hanged: Crime, Law Enforcement and Punishment in Late Eighteenth-century Dublin* (Dublin, 1994), pp. 173ff; Neal Garnham, 'How violent was eighteenth-century Ireland?', *Irish Historical Studies*, vol. 30, no. 119 (May 1997); James Kelly, *The Liberty and Ormond Boys* (2005); J.M. Beattie, *Crime and the Courts in England, 1660–1800* (Oxford, 1986), pp. 74ff, 135.

5   *Faulkner's Dublin Journal*, 21 May 1754, 8 January, 23 July 1760, 28 December 1773; *Hibernian Journal*, 19 March 1777, 17 November 1780.

6   St Thomas' parish, Dublin, Vestry Record Books, various dates including 25 September 1770 and 25 September 1775.

7   Anon., *Animadversions on the Street Robberies in Dublin*, pp. 2ff, 11; St John's parish, Dublin, Vestry Account Books, various dates; *Faulkner's Dublin Journal*, 13 July 1756, 6 August, 10, 14 September, 21 December 1765; *Dublin Evening Post*, 9 August 1787; *Freeman's Journal*, 7 November 1789; Garnham, *Courts, Crime and the Criminal Law in Ireland*, p. 30.

8   *Faulkner's Dublin Journal*, 16 February 1769.

9   Ibid., 17 March 1753, 22 January, 3 August, 3 September 1754, 6, 27 April 1756; *Freeman's Journal*, 25 February 1779; *Hibernian Journal*, 11 October, 6 December 1780, 1 January 1781, 27 February 1782.

10 St Thomas' parish, Dublin, Vestry Record Books, 12 October, 6 November, 1771.

11 *Freeman's Journal*, 23 January, 10 June 1790.

12 Anon., *Observations on the State and Condition of the Poor, Under the Institution for their Relief, in the City of Dublin* (Dublin, 1775), pp. 9ff; Warburton et al., *History of the City of Dublin*, vol. 1, p. 618; *Faulkner's Dublin Journal*, 18 April 1775; *Hibernian Journal*, 27 December 1780, 27 June, 15 October 1781, 14 August 1782, 19 November 1783, 25 February, 6 April 1785; *Freeman's Journal*, 7 August 1779, 22 May 1788, 3, 5, 21 May 1791, 12 November 1795.

13 [St Paul's Parish, Dublin], Bolton mss., Return of Watch for St Paul's Parish, 25 March 1782–25 March 1784 (NLI ms. 15926).

14 Peter Clark and Raymond Gillespie (eds), *Two Capitals: London and Dublin, 1500–1840* (Oxford, 2001), p. 4; Neal Garnham, 'Police and public order in eighteenth-century Dublin', in Clark and Gillespie (eds), *Two Capitals*, p. 83.

15 *Faulkner's Dublin Journal*, 31 May 1757, 16 February 1769, 5 April, 2 August 1770; *Hibernian Journal*, 19 September 1777, 20 September 1780, 1 April, 19 October 1785; *Dublin Evening Post*, 3, 31 May, 1, 20 September 1787; *Freeman's Journal*, 10, 22 January, 3 April, 24 May, 12 June, 5, 19 July, 11, 18 October 1788, 15 August, 24, 29 September, 13 October 1789, 4 March, 1 April, 10 June 1790, 4 December 1791, 28 August, 20 December 1792.

16 *Hibernian Journal*, 27 May 1776, 21 March 1777, 23 April 1783, 23 June 1784; *Freeman's Journal*, 6 July 1779, 4 June 1789, 18 September 1794.

17 *Faulkner's Dublin Journal*, 11 September 1750, 23 December 1752, 11 January 1755, 3, 31 December 1757, 1 July 1773, 30 September 1778; *Hibernian Journal*, 24 March 1777; *Dublin Evening Post*, 15 September 1787; *Freeman's Journal*, 6 July 1779, 29 August 1795, 3 May, 16 August 1796.

18 *Faulkner's Dublin Journal*, 4 August 1753; *Hibernian Journal*, 29 September 1783; *Freeman's Journal*, 11 September 1788, 1 December 1789, 25 June 1795.

19 Anon., *Sketches of Ireland Sixty Years Ago* (Dublin, 1847), p. 80.

20 *Hibernian Journal*, 5 April, 8 September 1780, 31 March, 27 August 1782.

21 *Hibernian Journal*, 22 December 1780, 25 May, 26 September, 1, 3, 5, 15 October, 12 December 1781.

22 St Anne's parish, Dublin, Vestry Proceedings, 15, 20 October 1777.

23 *Hibernian Journal*, 25 August 1783; St Anne's parish, Dublin, Vestry Proceedings, 17 August 1784; Beattie, *Crime and the Courts in England*, p. 48.

24 *Parl. Reg. Ire.*, vol. 9, pp. 397–8, cited in Henry, *Dublin Hanged*, p. 148.

25 *Hibernian Journal*, 23 August, 2 October 1786; *Dublin Evening Post*, 24 May, 7 July 1787; *Freeman's Journal*, 9, 11 October 1788; R. Lewis, *The Dublin Guide* (Dublin, 1787), p. 105; Kelly (ed.), *Proceedings of the Irish House of Lords*, vol. 1, p. 530; J.P. Starr, 'The enforcing of law and order in eighteenth-century Ireland' (unpublished PhD thesis, Trinity College, Dublin, 1968), pp. 161ff; R.B. McDowell, *Ireland in the Age of Imperialism and Revolution, 1760–1801* (Oxford, 1979), p. 67; Henry, *Dublin Hanged*, pp. 137ff; Hill, *From Patriots to Unionists*, p. 184.

26 *Freeman's Journal*, 27 June, 31 December 1789, 1 May 1792, 19 February 1795; Charles Topham Bowden, *A Tour Through Ireland* (Dublin, 1791), p. 16; Starr, 'Enforcing of law and order in eighteenth-century Ireland', p. 185.

27 *Freeman's Journal*, 3 March, 21 May 1791, 17 January 1795; Bowden, *Tour Through Ireland*, p. 15; [Francis Higgins], *Revolutionary Dublin, 1795–1801: The Letters of Francis Higgins to Dublin Castle*, ed. Thomas Bartlett (Dublin, 2004), p. 99; Ferrar, *View of Ancient and Modern Dublin*, p. 70.

28 *Freeman's Journal*, 12 November 1796, 7 February, 12, 21 October 1797, 15 February 1798; Starr, 'Enforcing of law and order in eighteenth-century Ireland', pp. 167ff; Henry, *Dublin Hanged*, pp. 151ff.

29 *Freeman's Journal*, 28 May, 30 July 1796, 12 January, 11, 14, 16 February, 30 March, 26 August, 12 September 1797, 26, 29 May 1798, 15 January 1799.

30 McGregor, *New Picture of Dublin*, p. 74; *Faulkner's Dublin Journal*, 19 December 1772; *Freeman's Journal*, 4 December 1779, 5 July 1788, 21 May 1789, 14 April 1792, 2 September 1794.

31 *Faulkner's Dublin Journal*, 12 February, 22 October 1757; *Freeman's Journal*, 31 May, 12 June, 19, 26 July, 27, 30 September, 9 October, 11 November 1788, 7, 17 November 1789; *Hibernian Journal*, 9 July, 3 November 1784; Anon., *Animadversions on the Street Robberies in Dublin*, p. 10.

32 Anon., *An Essay Towards a Method of Speedily Manning a Fleet* (Dublin, 1755), p. 13; *Hibernian Journal*, 1, 17, 31 January, 7, 9 February, 2 August 1776, 3 January 1777, 16 December 1778, 23 October 1779, 8 January 1781, 19 September 1783; *Freeman's Journal*, 24 March 1772, 23 February 1779, 2 September 1794, 19, 26 March, 16 May 1795.

33 *Hibernian Journal*, 25 August, 10, 17 September, 8 October 1783, 23 January 1784; *Freeman's Journal*, 2, 7 December 1790, 15 January 1793; Anon., *Four Letters Originally Written in French, Relating to the Kingdom of Ireland* (Dublin, 1739), p. 26.

34 BPP, HC, 1823, *Select Committee on Dublin Taxation, 1822*, pp. 4ff, 12ff, 19.

35 William Blackstone, *Commentaries on the Laws of England*, vol. 1, p. 406 (Oxford, 1765; repr. London, 1966); J. Duncan Craig, *Real Pictures of Clerical Life in Ireland* (London, 1875), p. 35; Derek Jarrett, *England in the Age of Hogarth* (London, 1974), p. 48; *Faulkner's Dublin Journal*, 9 October 1770, 20 February 1772; *Hibernian Journal*, 19 September 1777, 11 October 1780; *Freeman's Journal*, 22 July 1779, 16 April 1790.

36 *Faulkner's Dublin Journal*, 30 March 1756, 6 December 1768, 6, 24 December 1770; *Hibernian Journal*, 17 January 1777, 11 October 1780, 31 May, 21 August, 2 September 1782; *Freeman's Journal*, 22 April 1779, 29 July 1790, 14 April 1791, 9 December 1794, 19 February 1795; Francis. H. Tuckey, *The County and City of Cork Remembrancer* (Cork, 1837; repr. Cork, 1980), pp. 156ff, 187, 203ff, 214, 255.

37 *Faulkner's Dublin Journal*, 12 January 1771; *Hibernian Journal*, 15, 22 November 1776, 17 January 1777; *Freeman's Journal*, 14, 16, 18 July, 13, 18 August, 3, 27 October 1795.

38 *Faulkner's Dublin Journal*, 16 March 1756, 12 February, 22 October 1757, 28 October 1773, 4 January, 11 August 1774; *Hibernian Journal*, 25 March 1777, 25 March 1778, 3 November 1784; *Freeman's Journal*, 3 June, 16 December 1788, 31 December 1789; 1 Geo. III, c.10 [Ire.] (1706); 3 Geo. III, c.27 [Ire.] (1763); Anon., *A Compendium of the Laws of Forestalling, Engrossing, and Regrating* (Dublin, 1800).

39   John Winstanley, *Two Tippling Friends Turn'd Cooks, or the Roasting of a Cat*, in idem, *Poems*; *Freeman's Journal*, 6, 10 July 1790, 25 June 1799.

40   *Faulkner's Dublin Journal*, 29 October 1751 ('Five in six of our sex, who are so unhappy as to lose their virtue, are first undone for want of some business to employ their time and thoughts'); *Freeman's Journal*, 24 January 1774, 12 January, 6 April 1790, 15 November 1792; Joseph Robins, *The Lost Children: A Study of Charity Children in Ireland, 1700–1900* (Dublin, 1980), p. 12; Henry, *Dublin Hanged*, p. 37; James Kelly, 'Infanticide in eighteenth-century Ireland', *Irish Economic and Social History*, vol. 19 (1992), pp. 5ff.

41   Carr (ed.), *Drennan Letters*, appendix, p. 403; *Faulkner's Dublin Journal*, 1, 4 September 1750, 16 April 1751, 21 August 1752, 11 August 1753, 8 October 1757; *Hibernian Journal*, 25, 27 April, 6 June, 14 November 1781, 19 September 1783, 13 May 1785; *Dublin Evening Post*, 19 May 1787; *Freeman's Journal*, 31 January 1788, 14 June 1791.

42   *Faulkner's Dublin Journal*, 8 June 1765, 9 August 1768; *Hibernian Journal*, 27 April 1781, 19 September 1783; *Freeman's Journal*, 3, 10, 13 June 1794.

43   *Hibernian Journal*, 7, 24 March 1777, 3 January 1783, 23 August 1784, 14 January 1785; *Freeman's Journal*, 10 August 1788, 10 January 1789, 22 March 1796; Henry, *Dublin Hanged*, p. 173; V.A.C. Gatrell, *The Hanging Tree: Execution and the English People, 1770–1868* (Oxford, 1994), p. 7.

44   Frank McLynn, *Crime and Punishment in Eighteenth-century England* (London, 1989), p. 264.

45   *Hibernian Journal*, 6 July 1785.

46   *Faulkner's Dublin Journal*, 8 January 1760, 16 April 1767, 14, 24 October 1769, 26 September 1772, 9, 25 March, 9 November 1773; *Hibernian Journal*, 13 October 1777; *Freeman's Journal*, 10 October 1789.

47   *Faulkner's Dublin Journal*, 25 March, 21 September 1773, 24 September, 11 October 1774; *Hibernian Journal*, 22 April, 28 July 1776, 13, 27 October, 22 December 1777; *Freeman's Journal*, 17 October, 16 December 1797, 21 March 1799.

48   *Hibernian Journal*, 22 April, 5 July 1776.

49   Francis Wheately, *The Dublin Volunteers in College Green, 4th November, 1779* (NGI, cat. no. 125); Pádraig Ó Snodaigh, *The Irish Volunteers, 1715–1793: A List of the Units* (Dublin, 1995), pp. 35ff; *Hibernian Journal*, 6, 22, 27 December 1780, 26 September, 5, 30 November, 12 December 1781, 16 January 1782.

50   Maurice James Craig, *The Volunteer Earl* (London, 1948), pp. 199ff.

51   *Belfast News-Letter*, 13 January 1789; *Hibernian Journal*, 1, 10, 24 January, 12 March, 25 May, 26 August, 26 September, 1, 3, 5, 15 October, 5 November, 12 December 1781, 9, 16 January, 18 March, 13 September 1782, 10 September 1783, 5 January, 7 August 1784.

52   Blackrock Association, Minute Book (1782–99) (NLI, ms. 84); *Hibernian Journal*, 20 October 1784; *Dublin Evening Post*, 15 November 1787; *Freeman's Journal*, 29 January 1788, 7 August 1790, 24 January 1799.

Chapter 6: Public Health

1   Dr John Rutty, *A Chronological History of the Weather and Seasons, and of the Prevailing Diseases in Dublin* (Dublin, 1770), p. 339 (Rutty's so-called summer cholera was a seasonal bilious disorder rather than the deadly Asian cholera, which did not reach Ireland until the 1830s).

2   BPP, HC, 1835 (369), xxxii [33], *Appendix to First Report of Poor Law Commissioners*, pt i, appendix B, p. 449.

3   John Smith, *The Curiosities of Common Water* (8th edn, Dublin, 1725), p. 22; C. Lucas, *An Essay on Waters* (London, 1756), pt 1, p. 163.

4   Edward Barry MD, *A Treatise on a Consumption of the Lungs* (Dublin, 1726), p. 50; *Hibernian Journal*, 5 November 1781; John Brennan MD, *Essay on Child-bed Fever* (Dublin, 1813), p. 13; Thomas Mills MD, *An Essay on the Utility of Blood-letting in Fever* (Dublin, 1812).

5   *Belfast News-Letter*, 27 October 1789.

6   O'Donel T.D. Browne, *The Rotunda Hospital, 1745–1945* (Edinburgh, 1947), p. 107.

7   William Turton MD, *Some Observations on Consumption* (Dublin, 1813), pp. 50, 82ff; Henry Kennedy MD, *A Few Observations on the Natural Effect of Fever, to Which the Poor of Dublin are Liable* (Dublin, 1801), pp. 6ff; Martin Tuomy MD, *A Treatise on the Principal Diseases of Dublin* (Dublin, 1810), p. 116.

8   Rosborough, *Observations*, p. 42.

9   *Freeman's Journal*, 4 January 1791.

10   *Faulkner's Dublin Journal*, 13 July 1769; *Hibernian Journal*, 27 September 1780, 28 August 1783; *Dublin Evening Post*, 7 July 1787; Thomas Davies, *Memoirs of the Life of David Garrick Esq.* (Dublin, 1780), vol. 1, p. 43.

11   *Faulkner's Dublin Journal*, 17 June 1749, 9 August 1760, 25 July 1761.

12   Anon., *A Report Upon Certain Charitable Establishments in the City of Dublin* (Dublin, 1809), p. 50; Archer, *Statistical Survey*, p. 138; *Faulkner's Dublin Journal*, 10 August 1745.

13   *Faulkner's Dublin Journal*, 21 May 1754; Kelly (ed.), *Proceedings of the Irish House of Lords*, vol. 1, p. 543, vol. 2, p. 483.

14   *Faulkner's Dublin Journal*, 1 September 1744, 11 September 1750, 29 May 1753, 1 June 1754, 30 October 1756, 16 February 1775; *Dublin Evening Post*, 19 July, 18 September 1787; *Freeman's Journal*, 3 July 1788, 1 December 1789, 25 September 1792; Rosborough, *Observations*, p. 20; Warburton et al., *History of the City of Dublin*, vol. 2, pp. 1128, 1342; Gilbert, *History of the City of Dublin*, vol. 2, p. 21.

15   Sheet no. 4, John Rocque's 1756 city map; 4 Geo. I, c.11 [Ire.] cl.4 (1717); 6 Geo. I, c.15 [Ire.] cl.3 (1719); 3 Geo. II, c.13 [Ire.] cl.3 (1729); 26 Geo. III, c.61 [Ire.] cl.110 (1786); *Faulkner's Dublin Journal*, 26 June 1762, 4 June 1768; *Dublin Evening Post*, 9 June 1787; *Freeman's Journal*, 29 January 1788; Anon., *An Intercepted Letter from J.T. Esq, Writer at Canton, to his Friend in Dublin, Ireland* (2nd edn, Dublin, 1804), p. 3; Revd C.T. M'Cready, *Dublin Street Names, Dated and Explained* (Dublin, 1892).

16   *Faulkner's Dublin Journal*, 13 February 1753, 3 May 1763, 13 October 1770, 2 April 1771, 20 January 1777, 13 March 1778; *Hibernian Journal*, 17 February 1783; *Freeman's Journal*, 31 May 1788, 27 August 1818; Rosborough, *Observations*, p. 42; Henry Ibbeken MD, *A Treatise on Rheumatism* (Dublin, 1797), p. 61; Carr, *Stranger in Ireland*, p. 31; Anon., *Journal of a Tour in Ireland*, p. 8.

17   Gamble, *Views of Society*, reproduced in Gamble, *Society and Manners*, p. 477.

18   *Faulkner's Dublin Journal*, 31 March 1772.

19   Ibid., 20 November 1750, 11 November 1752, 18 February, 4 March 1766; *Hibernian Journal*, 22 September 1780.

20   Anon., *A Report from the Committee Appointed to Enquire into the State and Management*

of the Fund of the Work-house of the City of Dublin (Dublin, 1758), p. 4; Gilbert and Gilbert (eds), *Calendar of Ancient Records of Dublin*, vol. 10, p. 175.

21 *Freeman's Journal*, 4 August, 17 November 1789.

22 Anon., *State of County Infirmaries in Ireland Considered*, p. 27; Anon., *Report of the Association for the Suppression of Mendicity in Dublin for the Year 1818* (Dublin, 1818), p. 10; McGregor, *New Picture of Dublin*, p. 228; Archer, *Statistical Survey*, p. 138; BPP, HC, 1820 (84), *Report of the Commissioners Appointed by the Lord Lieutenant of Ireland to Inspect the House of Industry*, appendix, p. 15; E. Evans, 'History of Dublin hospitals and infirmaries from 1118 till the present time, no. xxv: Fever Hospital and House of Recovery, Cork Street', *Irish Builder*, no. 39 (1897), pp. 181–3.

23 *Parl. Reg. Ire.*, 1792, appendix, p. 12; Westmoreland Lock Hospital, Minute Books, vol. 1, September 1804; Anon., *Report Upon Certain Charitable Establishments*, appendix, p. 17; Anon., *General Rules, By-laws, and Regulations for the House of Industry* (Dublin, 1813), p. 7.

24 Molyneux Asylum for Blind Females, Dublin, Minute Books, various dates.

25 Kelly (ed.), *Proceedings of the Irish House of Lords*, vol. 2, p. 491.

26 *Hibernian Journal*, 13 May 1776; *Freeman's Journal*, 28 August 1794; Anon., *Advice and Directions to Hackney Coachmen* (Dublin, 1809), p. 1; Gilbert, *History of the City of Dublin*, vol. 2, p. 21.

27 *Faulkner's Dublin Journal*, 19 September 1752, 6 August 1754, 23 August 1757, 16 September 1758, 22 February 1766, 13 January 1767, 27 May 1775; *Hibernian Journal*, 1 May 1776, 27 September 1780, 27 September 1790; Rosborough, *Observations*, p. 29; Anon., *Report Upon Certain Charitable Establishments*, p. 53.

28 *Faulkner's Dublin Journal*, 16 September 1758; *Hibernian Journal*, 27 September 1780; *Freeman's Journal*, 29 May 1788; 11 & 12 Geo. III c.11 [Ire.] (1772); 25 Geo. III, c.43 [Ire.] (1785); 26 Geo. III, c.32 [Ire.] (1786); 27 Geo. III, c.38 [Ire.] cl.2 (1787); Anon., *Report Upon Certain Charitable Establishments*, p. 53.

29 Richard Twiss, *A Tour in Ireland in 1775* (Dublin, 1776), p. 30; Anon., *Journal of a Tour in Ireland*, p. 13; Anon., *Ireland in 1831: Letters on the State of Ireland* (London, 1831), p. 8.

30 Wakefield, *Account of Ireland*, vol. 1, p. 735; Warburton et al., *History of the City of Dublin*, vol. 1, p. 446; Carr, *Stranger in Ireland*, p. 488.

31 *Hibernian Journal*, 23 April 1783; *Dublin Evening Post*, 27 December 1787; *Freeman's Journal*, 27 March, 3 April 1788, 5 May 1796, 16 September 1797; *Parl. Reg. Ire.* (1785), vol. 4, p. 211; Warburton et al., *History of the City of Dublin*, vol. 1, p. 446.

32 *Freeman's Journal*, 5, 11, 14, 19, 28 May, 14 June 1791.

33 Jonathan Swift, *Verses on the Death of Dr. Swift* (Dublin, 1731).

34 Hanns Gross, *Rome in the Age of the Enlightenment* (Cambridge, 1990), p. 210.

35 William Hogarth, pl. 8, *The Rake's Progress* (London, 1735).

36 St Patrick's Hospital, Dublin, Record Books; Elizabeth Malcolm, *Swift's Hospital: A History of St Patrick's Hospital, Dublin, 1746–1989* (Dublin, 1989).

37 BPP, HC, 1835 (369) xxxii [32], *Poor Law Commissioners Enquiry*, pp. 418ff.

38 McGregor, *New Picture of Dublin*, pp. 283ff.

39 BPP, HC, 1835 (369) xxxii [32], *Poor Law Commissioners Enquiry*, p. 450.

40 Ibid., pp. 70ff, 81, 95ff, 357; [Irish Government], proclamation dated 29 October 1844 (NAI ref. no. 463).

41 Topham Bowden, *Tour Through Ireland*, p. 24.

42 Best, 'St Paul's Parish, Dublin', pp. 20ff.

43 St Anne's parish, Dublin, Vestry Proceedings, 21 March 1761.

44 11 & 12 Geo. III, c.22 [Ire.] (1771–72); Warburton's *Ireland*, vol. 1, p. 509.

45 Dutton, *Observations*, p. 107.

46 Gamble, *Views of Society*, reproduced in Gamble, *Society and Manners*, p. 46; Wakefield, *Account of Ireland*, vol. 2, p. 792.

47 *Faulkner's Dublin Journal*, 20 November 1750, 28 June 1770; *Freeman's Journal*, 20 May 1796, 20 May 1797; Dutton, *Observations*, pp. 13, 107; William J. Fitzpatrick, *History of the Dublin Catholic Cemeteries* (Dublin, 1900), p. 5; Dr John Fleetwood, *The Irish Body Snatchers: A History of Body Snatching in Ireland* (Dublin, 1988); W.N. Osborough, *Law and the Emergence of Modern Dublin* (Dublin, 1996), p. 166.

48 Carmel Connell, *Glasnevin Cemetery, Dublin, 1832–1900* (Dublin, 2004).

49 Thomas Laqueur, 'The places of the dead in modernity', in Colin Jones and Drar Wahrman (eds), *The Age of Cultural Revolutions: Britain and France, 1750–1820* (London, 2002), p. 17; Fitzpatrick, *History of the Dublin Catholic Cemeteries*, pp. 14 ff.

50 17 Geo. II, c.5 [Ire.] (1743); *Faulkner's Dublin Journal*, 21 May 1757; *Dublin Evening Post*, 28 August, 6 November 1787; *Freeman's Journal*, 12 July 1788, 26 December 1789.

51 *Faulkner's Dublin Journal*, 24 August 1769, 10 August 1771, 21 April, 11 August, 8 October 1774; *Hibernian Journal*, 26 January 1776, 5 October 1778, 23 April 1783; *Freeman's Journal*, 7 March 1799; Warburton's *Ireland*, vol. 1, p. 1 (print entitled *St. Patrick's Cathedral from the North*), vol. 2, p. 1070; Malton, *View of the City of Dublin*, pl. 2; Canon E.J. Young, 'A Dublin slaughter house nuisance of 1723', *Dublin Historical Record*, vol. 5, no. 2 (December 1942), pp. 75ff.

52 26 Geo. III, c.61 [Ire.] cl.115 (1786); *Faulkner's Dublin Journal*, 21 April 1774; *Freeman's Journal*, 9 October 1788, 16 June 1789, 16 November 1793, 31 October, 17 November 1795, 8 September 1796; Starr, 'Enforcing of law and order in eighteenth-century Ireland', p. 98.

53 *Faulkner's Dublin Journal*, 31 May, 14 June 1763, 16 August 1765; Malton, *View of the City of Dublin*, pls 1, 2, 23; Pool and Cash, *Views of […] the City of Dublin*, title page; Joseph Tudor, *This Perspective View, of the Illuminations and Fireworks, to be Exhibited at St Stephens's Green, at Dublin* [artwork], *Universal Magazine*, April 1749; Tuckey, *County and City of Cork Remembrancer*, pp. 223, 227.

54 *Faulkner's Dublin Journal*, 5 February, 8 April 1760, 4 June 1768; Gilbert and Gilbert (eds), *Calendar of Ancient Records of Dublin*, vol. 10, p. 49; 26 Geo. III, c.61 [Ire.] (1786); Anon., *A Diary of the Weather and Winds for 19 Years Commencing with AD 1716 and Concluding with 1734*, ms, Gilbert Collection, Dublin City Libraries; Gatrell, *First Bohemians*, p. 28.

55 *Hibernian Journal*, 28 September 1785; *Freeman's Journal*, 19 August 1788, 15 January 1789 (Musaeus, 'The Progress of Beauty'):

> At length when for years on the flags she has strayed,
> Her blood all polluted, her system decayed,
> On straw, at some bunter's, she gives up her breath,
> Or in some filthy kennel arrested by death.

56 Twiss, *Tour in Ireland*, p. 49.

57 *Hibernian Journal*, 25 September 1778; *Freeman's Journal*, 7 October 1779.

58 McGregor, *New Picture of Dublin*, p. 250; William Dudley Wodsworth, *A Brief History of the Ancient Foundling Hospital of Dublin, From the Year 1702* (Dublin, 1876), p. 11; Joseph Robins, *The Lost Children: A Study of Charity Children in Ireland, 1700–1900* (Dublin, 1980), p. 32.

59 *Faulkner's Dublin Journal*, 2 August 1746 (Dr John Profily cures all poor VD patients recommended by their parish church warden), 22 March 1755 ('Gowlands Great Specifick requires no confinement but may be taken, and the cure accomplished, without the knowledge of the nearest friend'); Anon., *An Easy and Infallible Cure for Several Diseases* (Dublin, *c.* 1750), p. 39; Thomas Gataker, *A Letter to a Surgeon* (London, *c.* 1754), pp. 18ff; John Wade, *Pharmacoepia Pauperum: Containing a Collection of Cheap and Efficacious Medicines* (Dublin, 1768); Samuel Watson, *The Gentleman's and Citizen's Almanac for 1777* (Dublin, 1777), p. 88; *Faulkner's Dublin Journal*, 22 March 1755, 30 January 1768; Westmoreland Lock Hospital, Record Books; *Freeman's Journal*, 14 November 1789, 5 October 1793; 1 Geo. III, c.14 [Ire.] (1760); John Gay, *The Harlot's Progress* (London, 1739):

> No wicked whores shall have good luck,
> Who follow their own wills;
> But purg'd shall be to skin and bone,
> With mercury and pills.

60 Anon., *The Trifling Age* (Dublin, *c.* 1784), p. 2.

61 John Watson, *The Gentleman and Citizen's Almanac for 1766* (Dublin, 1766), p. 73; *Faulkner's Dublin Journal*, 23 May 1758; *Freeman's Journal*, 28 February 1763.

62 *Freeman's Journal*, 17 March, 5, 19 June 1792.

63 *Parl. Reg. Ire.*, 1787, vol. 2, appendix dxlic [639], appendix dxxxiv [534].

64 Stephen Dickson, *A Letter to His Medical Brethren* (Dublin, *c.* 1795).

65 Warburton et al., *History of the City of Dublin*, vol. 2, p. 774; A Register Containing Medical Instructions and Prescriptions (Newgate Prison, 1813–15) (NLI ms. 16, 256); Westmoreland Lock Hospital, Record Books, vol. 1, 4 March, 13 April 1820, Report to Lord Lieutenant, October 1829, Memorial of Hospital Governors to the Lord Lieutenant, 3 February 1838.

66 'A Real Paddy' [Pierce Egan], *Real Life in Ireland*, p. 108.

67 3 Geo. III, c.28 [Ire.] cl.6, 7 (1763); 5 Geo. III, c.16 [Ire.] (1765); 17 & 18 Geo. III, c.28 [Ire.] cl.1 (1777–78); *Hibernian Journal*, 7 July 1784; McGregor, *New Picture of Dublin*, p. 168.

68 Kelly (ed.), *Proceedings of the Irish House of Lords*, vol. 1, pp. 178ff, 206ff, vol. 2, p. 347; *Hibernian Journal*, 8 November 1786; *Freeman's Journal*, 11 March 1788.

69 Thomas King Moylan, 'Vagabonds and sturdy beggars, pt 3', *Dublin Historical Record*, vol. 1, no. 3 (September 1938), p. 68.

70 *Hibernian Journal*, 6 July 1785; *Freeman's Journal*, 1 April 1790; Kennedy, *A Few Observations on the Nature and Effect of Fever*, p. 14; Mr Justice Day, *A Charge Delivered to the Grand Juries of the City and County of Dublin, 23 January 1810* (Dublin, 1830), p. 19.

71 Kelly (ed.), *Proceedings of the Irish House of Lords*, vol. 1, p. 179; *Hibernian Journal*, 16 October 1776, 16 October 1780.

72 Pool and Cash, *Views of [...] the City of Dublin*, pp. 55ff; *Freeman's Journal*, 11 August 1791.

73 Gilbert and Gilbert (eds), *Calendar of Ancient Records of Dublin*, vol. 13, p. 373, vol. 14, p. 173, vol. 15, pp. 509ff; *Freeman's Journal*, 6 August 1789; Elizabeth Fry and Joseph John

Gurney, *Report addressed to the Marquess Wellesley, Lord Lieutenant of Ireland* (London, 1827), pp. 28ff; McGregor, *New Picture of Dublin*, p. 173.

74 Anon., *State of County Infirmaries in Ireland Considered*, pp. 31ff; Molyneux Asylum for Blind Females, minute books, 14 May 1816.

75 Anon., *First Part of the Report of the Sub-committee of the Society for Promoting the Comforts of the Poor* (Dublin, 1800), pp. 9ff.

76 Archer, *Statistical Survey*, p. 140; Thomas Willis, *Facts Connected with the Social and Sanitary Condition of the Working Classes in the City of Dublin* (Dublin, 1845; repr. Dublin, 2002), p. 82.

Chapter 7: Responses to Deprivation

1 Anon., *The Parish Guttlers: Or the Humours of a Select Vestry* (Dublin, 1725).

2 *Faulkner's Dublin Journal*, 13 October 1747.

3 Sir Michael Creagh, *Seasonable Advice to the Magistrates and Chief Inhabitants of the City of Dublin* (Dublin, 1727), p. 4.

4 10 Geo. I, c.3 [Ire.]; David Dickson, 'The state of Ireland before 1798', in Cathal Póirtéir (ed.), *The Great Irish Rebellion of 1798* (Cork, 1998), p. 17.

5 Anon., *The Vestry Records of the Parishes of St Bride, St Michael Le Pole and St Stephen, Dublin, 1662–1742*, ed. W.J.R. Wallace (Dublin, 2011), pp. 249ff; Warburton et al., *History of the City of Dublin*, vol. 2, p. 739.

6 *Freeman's Journal*, 28 February 1764, 18 November 1769; BPP, HC, 1820 (84), *Report of the Commissioners Appointed by the Lord Lieutenant of Ireland to Inspect the House of Industry*, appendix, p. 14; Rosborough, *Observations*, p. 20.

7 St Anne's parish, Dublin, Vestry Proceedings, 9 October 1792; St Peter's parish, *Resolutions and Regulations of the Committee for Managing the Charitable Trust* (Dublin, 1813); Anon., *Proceedings of the Corporation Instituted for the Relief of the Poor* (Dublin, 1774), pp. 10ff; John Binns, *Recollections of the Life of John Binns* (Philadelphia, 1856), p. 28.

8 *Faulkner's Dublin Journal*, 15 February, 3 May, 9, 26 July 1757.

9 St Anne's parish, Dublin, Vestry Proceedings, 15 July 1767.

10 *Faulkner's Dublin Journal*, 13 October 1747, 27 January, 10 February 1750, 5 August 1769; *Dublin Evening Post*, 13 December 1787.

11 Warburton et al., *History of the City of Dublin*, vol. 2, p. 768.

12 Anon., *The Case of the Foundlings of the City of Dublin* (Dublin, *c.* 1730), p. 4; *Faulkner's Dublin Journal*, 13 October 1747; 13 & 14 Geo. III, c.17 [Ire.] (1773–74); 15 & 16 Geo. III, c.25 [Ire.] (1775–76); Archer, *Statistical Survey*, p. 127; McGregor, *New Picture of Dublin*, p. 249; Joseph O'Carroll, 'Contemporary attitudes towards the homeless poor, 1725–1775', in David Dickson (ed.), *The Gorgeous Mask: Dublin 1700–1850* (Dublin, 1987), p. 70; Mary Hayden, 'Charity children in 18th-century Dublin', *Dublin Historical Record*, vol. 5, no. 3 (March 1943), pp. 94ff; Joseph Robins, *The Lost Children: A Study of Charity Children in Ireland, 1700–1900* (Dublin, 1980), pp. 8ff, 12ff.

13 23 Geo. III, c.11 [Ire.] cl.9; Kenneth Milne, *The Irish Charter Schools, 1730–1830* (Dublin, 1997); Helena Kelleher Kahn, 'Objects of raging detestation; the Charter Schools', *History Ireland*, vol. 19, no. 2 (March/April 2011), pp. 25ff.

14 Anon., *Plan and Regulations of the Society for Promoting the Comforts of the Poor* (Dublin, 1799).

15 This section draws mainly on the work of William Dudley Wodsworth, *A Brief History of the Ancient Foundling Hospital of Dublin, From the Year 1702* (Dublin, 1876). This is a neglected source and its reliability is suggested by the role of Wodsworth as assistant secretary of the Local Government Board (Ireland), together with his publication for HMSO of a digest of the sanitary laws in force in Ireland.

16 *Freeman's Journal*, 31 May 1796.

17 Wodsworth, *Brief History of the Ancient Foundling Hospital*, p. 46.

18 Anon., *Third Report of the Committee of the Dublin Female Penitentiary* (Dublin, 1816), pp. 58ff, 65ff.

19 Kelly (ed.), *Proceedings of the Irish House of Lords*, vol. 3, p. 171; N. Marshall Cummins, *Some Chapters of Cork Medical History* (Cork, 1957), p. 59.

20 Wakefield, *Account of Ireland*, vol. 2, 427ff; Warburton et al., *History of the City of Dublin*, vol. 1, pp. 590ff.

21 11+12 Geo. III, c.11 [Ire.] 13+14 Geo. III, c.46 [Ire.]; Hamilton, *Cries of Dublin*, pl. 35.

22 Henry Ellis to William Knox, 10 November 1773, HMC, vol. vi, 1901, Knox mss.

23 *Faulkner's Dublin Journal*, 8 May 1744; 23 Geo. III, c.11 [Ire.] (1749) cl.10; *Dublin Magazine*, April 1762; Archer, *Statistical Survey*, p. 1210; Helen Burke, *The Royal Hospital Donnybrook: A Heritage of Caring, 1743–1993* (Dublin, 1993).

24 *Faulkner's Dublin Journal*, 1 September 1744; Warburton et al., *History of the City of Dublin*, vol. 2, p. 728.

25 BPP, HC, 1835 (369) xxxii [32], *Appendix to the First Report of Poor Law Commissioners*, pt i, appendix B, 444ff.

26 *Faulkner's Dublin Journal*, 23 July 1745, 18 November 1746, 9 May, 17 June 1749, 30 October, 2 November 1756; *Hibernian Journal*, 24 June 1778, 7 May 1781, 25 November 1782, 11 June 1783, 23 January 1784; *Freeman's Journal*, 25 February 1779, 27 July 1790, 1 January, 21 May, 9 June 1791, 5 June 1794, 16 May 1795, 5 May 1796; Anon., *Arguments in Proof* […] *in the City of Dublin*, p. 5; Archer, *Statistical Survey*, p. 126; McGregor, *New Picture of Dublin*, pp. 273ff; Starr, 'Enforcing of law and order in eighteenth-century Ireland', p. 135.

27 St Anne's parish, Dublin, Vestry Proceedings, 17 June 1762, 15 July 1767, 29 September 1774, 2 January 1775, January 1799, 5 November 1805.

28 11 & 12 Geo. III, c.30 [Ire.] (1772); Rosborough, *Observations*, p. 41; Warburton et al., *History of the City of Dublin*, vol. 1, p. 622.

29 11 & 12 Geo. III, c.46 [Ire.] (1773–74).

30 *Faulkner's Dublin Journal*, 29 October 1768, 20 May 1773; *Dublin Evening Post*, 11 December 1787; *Belfast News-Letter*, 22 December 1789; *Freeman's Journal*, 5 September 1793, 3 April 1794, 16 May 1795; Rosborough, *Observations*, pp. 7ff; Gamble, *Views of Society*, reproduced in Gamble, *Society and Manners*, p. 77.

31 *Freeman's Journal*, 22 December 1789, 5 June 1794; [House of Industry], *An Account of Industry in Dublin* (Dublin, 1801), pp. 26ff.

32 [House of Industry], *An Account of the Proceedings of the Acting Governors of the House of Industry* (Dublin, 1798), pp. 4, 20; Anon., *The Ninth and Tenth Reports of the Society for*

Bettering the Condition and Increasing the Comforts of the Poor (Dublin, 1800), pp. 100ff; BPP, HC, 1820 (84), *Report of the Commissioners Appointed by the Lord Lieutenant of Ireland to Inspect the House of Industry*, appendix, pp. 3ff, 14; BPP, HC, 1821 (587), *House of Industry, Dublin, Letters from Charles Grant, Chief Secretary to the Lord Lieutenant, to the Commissioners of the House of Industry, 1 February 1820*, pp. 2ff; *Belfast News-Letter*, 3 May 1789; Archer, *Statistical Survey*, p. 126.

33 Pool and Cash, *Views of [...] the City of Dublin*, pp. 22ff; [Faulkner], *Prince of Dublin Printers*, p. 120; R. Lewis, *The Dublin Guide* (Dublin, 1787), pp. 155ff.

34 *Hibernian Journal*, 28 January 1778, 14 August 1782; 11+12 Geo. III, c.30 [Ire.]; Tuckey, *County and City of Cork Remembrancer*, p. 175.

35 *Hibernian Journal*, 9, 11, 16 February 1778, 5 May 1780, 30 June 1786; *Freeman's Journal*, 15 March 1788, 29 August 1793.

36 13 & 14 Geo. III, c.46 [Ire.]; Anon., *Proceedings of the Corporation Instituted for the Relief of the Poor* (Dublin, 1774), p. 7; Anon., *Observations on the House of Industry*, p. 1; *Dublin Evening Post*, 13 December 1787.

37 [House of Industry], *Account of the Proceedings of the Governors of the House of Industry*, pp. 26ff.

38 Henry Kennedy MD, *A Few Remarks on the Affairs of the House of Industry at Dublin* (Dublin, 1799).

39 [House of Industry], *Account of Industry in Dublin*, pp. 32ff; George Barnes, *Strictures on 'An Account of the Proceedings of the Acting Governors of the House of Industry'* (Dublin, 1798); Anon., *The Ninth and Tenth Reports of the Society for Bettering the Condition and Increasing the Comforts of the Poor* (Dublin, 1800), p. 106; Anon., *Journal of a Tour in Ireland*, p. 11; Warburton et al., *History of the City of Dublin*, vol. 1, p. 631; McGregor, *New Picture of Dublin*, pp. 173, 273ff.

40 Rosborough, *Observations*, p. 9; *Hibernian Journal*, 14 April 1777, 11 June 1783, 30 June, 24 July 1786; *Freeman's Journal*, 6 July 1779, 28 February, 15 March 1788, 26 August, 16 October 1790, 9 June 1791, 2 February, 25 September, 20 October 1792.

41 *Faulkner's Dublin Journal*, 10 October 1752, 20 March, 24 April 1753; 25 July 1761, *Hibernian Journal*, 12 March 1783.

42 Revd William Magee, *A Sermon Preached Before the Association for Discountenancing Vice, and Promoting the Practice of Religion and Virtue* (Dublin, 1796).

43 *Four Letters Originally Written in French, Relating to the Kingdom of Ireland* (Dublin, 1739), p. 26 ('Numerous poor tradesmen, who for want of bread, do sometimes gather in a tumultuous manner'); *Faulkner's Dublin Journal*, 21 May 1754 ('Witness the great numbers of poor peoples who are forced to other countries, and journeymen weavers and others, who are begging in our streets for want of business').

44 *Faulkner's Dublin Journal*, 3 May 1757; Knut Jongbohn Clement, quoted in Bourke (ed.), *'Poor Green Erin'*, p. 261.

45 Gilbert and Gilbert (eds), *Calendar of Ancient Records of Dublin*, vol. 12, p. 105, *Hibernian Journal*, 12 May 1783, 5 January 1785.

46 Robert Brooke, *A Letter from Mr Brooke to an Honourable Member of the House of Commons* (Dublin, 1786); Lord Mountmorres, 17 December 1783, in Kelly (ed.), *Proceedings of the Irish House of Lords*, vol. 1, p. 167; *Hibernian Journal*, 9 May, 15 December 1783.

47   *Hibernian Journal*, 3 July 1786; *Dublin Evening Post*, 16, 21 June 1787; *Freeman's Journal*, 4 June 1789; Carr (ed.), *Drennan Letters*, p. 158.

48   *Some Account of the Origin and Plan of an Association Formed for the Establishment of a House of Recovery, Fever Hospital, etc.* (Dublin, 1801), p. 28.

49   *Hibernian Journal*, 15 December 1783; *Freeman's Journal*, 5 September 1793, 3 April 1794, 28 May 1795; Carr (ed.), *Drennan Letters*, p. 162 (*c.* May 1793).

50   St Anne's parish, Dublin, Vestry Proceedings, 10 December 1800, 11 April 1836; David Dickson, 'In search of the old Irish poor law', in Rosalind Mitchison and Peter Roebuck (eds), *Economy and Society in Scotland and Ireland, 1500–1939* (Edinburgh, 1998).

51   Anon., *Cutchacutchoo, or the Jostling of the Innocents* (Dublin, 1805), p. 11.

52   *Hibernian Journal*, 15 October 1781, 24 October 1783, 7 January, 28 September 1785; *Freeman's Journal*, 26 September, 10 October 1795; R. Lewis, *The Dublin Guide* (Dublin, 1787), p. 46; [Lock Penitentiary], *Selection of Hymns, Used in the Chapel of the Lock Penitentiary, Dorset-Street* (Dublin, 1799).

53   *Faulkner's Dublin Journal*, 22 March 1763, 2 June 1767, 30 January 1768; *Freeman's Journal*, 11 May, 24 August 1790, 24 March 1792; Anon., *Thoughts on the Misery of a Numerous Class of Females: Particularly Addressed to Those of Their Own Sex, Whom God has Entrusted with Affluence* (Dublin, 1793); McGregor, *New Picture of Dublin*, pp. 264ff; Edward Geoghegan, *Observations on the Necessity of Regulating the Medical Professions* (Dublin, 1795); Tuomy, *Treatise on the Principal Diseases of Dublin*, p. 350.

54   McGregor, *New Picture of Dublin*, pp. 265ff; Ferrar, *View of Ancient and Modern Dublin*, p. 61; *Freeman's Journal*, 11 February 1794; Anon., *A New Edition of the Tract, Which Gave Origin to the Institution of the Lock Penitentiary* (Dublin, 1805); Warburton et al., *History of the City of Dublin*, vol. 2, p. 697; Archer, *Statistical Survey*, p. 125.

55   Anon., *Report Upon Certain Charitable Establishments*, p. 11; McGregor, *New Picture of Dublin*, pp. 264ff.

56   'Nemo', *A Brief Record of the Female Orphan House, North Circular Road, Dublin from 1790 to 1890* (Dublin, 1893), pp. 6–21; *Hibernian Journal*, 24 March 1783, 8 February, 29 November 1786; *Dublin Evening Post*, 7 July 1787; *Freeman's Journal*, 11 November 1788, 24 August 1790, 8 January 1791, 21 October 1794.

Chapter 8: The Interface of Criminality and Immorality

1   *Hibernian Journal*, 28 March 1785; *Dublin Evening Post*, 18 September 1787 (a woman working in a Crown Alley brothel emptied a chamber pot over a passer-by; she charged him with assault after he had taken revenge); Derek Jarrett, *England in the Age of Hogarth* (London, 1974), p. 155.

2   *Freeman's Journal*, 16 August 1788, 24 August 1791, 19 July 1792, 31 May 1796; *Hibernian Journal*, 3 November 1784, 7 January, 31 October, 12 November, 19 December 1785, 21 June 1786, 12, 19 August, 4 September 1788, 25 May, 12 June 1790, 22 January, 28 May 1791, 30 June, 10 May 1792, 14 September 1797.

3   *Freeman's Journal*, 1 September 1789, 9 January 1790 (the crowd did not interfere when a Bride Street prostitute attempted to rob an old man's watch after he refused payment), 29 August, 22 October 1795, 29 March, 14, 16 April, 26 May 1796, 11 November 1798; *Dublin Evening Post*, 15 September 1787; *Freeman's Journal*, 10 January 1788 (streetwalkers stole

cloaks, aprons and caps in Parliament Street and Essex Gate), 22 January 1788 (prostitutes seized the garments of a dressmaker in Cope Street), 20 March 1788 (a prostitute stole the cloak of a well-dressed woman in Mary's Lane), 3 April 1788 (a prostitute stole the cloak and jewels of a woman in Marlborough Street), 15 August 1789 (two prostitutes enticed a country girl into their High Street cellar, where they stole her clothes), 5 July 1791, 31 December 1795 (a girl enticed into a Crane Lane brothel was gravely abused and robbed of her cloak), 21 November 1798 (soliciting women at St Stephen's Green stole women's garments).

4   *Freeman's Journal*, 1 May 1788 (an armed gang from Stoneybatter abducted prostitutes from Essex Street and Crane Lane for the Mayday festival), 29 July 1788 (a prostitute who attacked an innocent passer-by at Arran Quay was tied up by the mob and thrown into the Liffey), 16 August 1788, 3 November 1789, 21 June, 6 November 1791 (a sailor was drowned by two prostitutes who threw him into the Liffey at George's Quay), 29 October 1793, 6 October, 5 November, 22 December 1796, 27 June 1797; Edward Foster MD, *A Letter to Sydenham Singleton Esq. on the Present State of the Insane Poor in the Kingdom* (Dublin, 1777), p. 8.

5   Anon., *The Trifling Age* (Dublin, *c.* 1784), p. 2; *Hibernian Journal*, 11 October 1780; *Freeman's Journal*, 11 May 1790, 14 May, 14 July 1796.

6   [Whaley], *Buck Whaley's Memoirs*, pp. 33ff.

7   *Faulkner's Dublin Journal*, 13 September 1770; *Hibernian Journal*, 31 October 1785.

8   *Freeman's Journal*, 15 August 1795.

9   *Hibernian Journal*, 25 September 1780; *Freeman's Journal*, 23 November 1790, 11 June 1791.

10 *Hibernian Journal*, 28 December 1785, 4 January 1789; *Freeman's Journal*, 5, 8 July 1788, 24 September 1789, 12 October 1790, 21 April 1795.

11 *Freeman's Journal*, 6 April, 6 July 1790.

12 Ibid., 24 May 1792.

13 Ibid., 24 April 1779, 18 July, 4 August 1783, 28 May, 20 December 1791, 21 February, 16 March 1797; *Dublin Evening Post*, 5 May, 2 August, 15 September 1787.

14 *Hibernian Journal*, 25 February, 6 April 1785, 4, 6 October 1786; *Dublin Evening Post*, 15 September 1787; *Freeman's Journal*, 6 July, 26 August 1790, 28 May, 11 August 1791, 5 May 1798.

15 Anon., *The Spirit of Irish Wit* (London, 1812), p. 138; Fitzpatrick, *Ireland Before the Union*, pp. 60, 129 (p. 60 re. Francis Higgins, the 'Sham Squire', *c.* 1790: 'The flashman introduced him to the convenient matron, whom he seldom failed to lay under contribution – the price of protecting her in her profession'); *Hibernian Journal*, 29 March 1776; *Freeman's Journal*, 28 May, 16 July 1796, 7 February 1797.

16 Anon., *The Gentleman, an Heroic Poem* (Dublin, 1747); [British army], *Dublin Garrison Order Book* (1812–19), Pakenham Mahon Papers (NLI, ms 9475); [British army], *Instructions to Corps Doing Duty in the Garrison of Dublin* (Dublin, 1838), pp. 21ff; *Hibernian Journal*, 2 April 1777, 23 October, 16 December 1778, 12 May 1780, 7 December 1781; *Freeman's Journal*, 16 October, 23 September 1779, 23 July 1791, 2 September 1794, 9 May 1795.

17 *Freeman's Journal*, 24 January 1791; Gilbert, *History of the City of Dublin*, vol. 2, pp. 13, 113, 165.

18 Fitztpatrick, *Curious Family History*, p. 71.

19   *Report of the Select Committee of the (British) House of Commons 1817*, in StRathearn Gordon and J.G.B. Cocks, *A People's Conscience* (London, 1952), pp. 43ff.

20   *Faulkner's Dublin Journal*, 20 February 1750, 11 March 1769, 2, 26 January 1771; *Hibernian Journal*, 2 August 1776, 10 May, 27 October, 3 November 1784; *Freeman's Journal*, 1 September 1789, 10 August 1797.

21   *Hibernian Journal*, 24 March 1777, 19 August 1778, 28 November 1785; *Freeman's Journal*, 11, 19 May 1791, 27 June 1793.

22   BPP, HC, 1812, *Papers Relating to the Police of Dublin: Memorial Presented to the Lord Lieutenant by Certain Citizens of Dublin, 7 April 1812*, pp. 2ff; BPP, HC, 1812, *Copy of a Memorial Presented to his Grace Duke of Richmond and Lennox, Lord Lieutenant, 21 April 1812*, p. 9.

23   *Faulkner's Dublin Journal*, 14 May, 5 October, 23 November 1765, 8 March 1766, 4, 21 August 1770, 5 September 1772; *Freeman's Journal*, 14, 21 July 1796.

24   *Hibernian Journal*, 5 November 1781, 24 July, 9 September 1782; *Freeman's Journal*, 21 February 1797, 6, 11 July 1799.

Chapter 9: Public Opinion and the Prevailing Ethos

1   Much of this section has been informed by Wakefield, *Account of Ireland*; Warburton et al., *History of the City of Dublin*; McGregor, *New Picture of Dublin*; Beattie, *Crime and the Courts in England*; Malcolmson, *Popular Recreations in English Society*; Keith Thomas, *Man and the Natural World: Changing Attitudes in England, 1500–1800* (London, 1983); Robert B. Shoemaker, *Gender in English Society, 1650–1850: The Emergence of Separate Spheres?* (London, 1998); Gatrell, *City of Laughter*; Irene Whelan, *The Bible War in Ireland: The 'Second Reformation' and the Polarization of Protestant–Catholic Relations, 1800–1840* (Dublin, 2005).

2   *Hibernian Journal*, 14, 28 September 1778; Tuomy, *Treatise on the Principal Diseases of Dublin*, p. 84.

3   James Kelly, *'That Damn'd Thing Called Honour': Duelling In Ireland, 1570–1860* (Cork, 1995).

4   Beattie, *Crime and the Courts in England*, pp. 460ff, 623.

5   *Belfast News-Letter*, 14 July 1789.

6   *Faulkner's Dublin Journal*, 29 May 1750, 12 April 1766.

7   Ibid., 29 May 1750, 24 May 1763, 12 April 1766, 13 June 1769, 31 August 1771, 19 September 1772, 19 June 1773; *Hibernian Journal*, 25 February 1785; *Freeman's Journal*, 13, 17, 22, 31 July 1779, 7 October 1788, 22 September 1789, 27 August 1793; *Dublin Chronicle*, 8 July 1788.

8   *Faulkner's Dublin Journal*, 12 June 1744, 20 August 1750, 16 October 1762, 21 June 1763, 2 August 1770, 15 February, 19 April 1774; *Hibernian Journal*, 10 February 1782, 3 November 1784; *Dublin Evening Post*, 5 May 1787; *Freeman's Journal*, 19 February, 12 July 1788, 26 December 1789.

9   *Freeman's Journal*, 16 August 1770.

10   Dr Achmet, *The Theory and Uses of Baths* (Dublin, 1772); Anon., *Report of the Cases Relieved and Cured*; *Faulkner's Dublin Journal*, 22 May 1750, 23 April 1771, 7 January, 18 April 1775; *Hibernian Journal*, 6 May 1776, 5 February, 5 November 1780.

11   Revd Thomas McDonnell, *The Eighth Commandment Considered in its Full Extent: And Particularly, as Applicable to the Present Reigning Spirit of Gaming* (Dublin, 1760), p. 29.

12   3 Geo. III, c.21 [Ire.] (1763), cl.xi, xv; 3 Geo. III, c.28 [Ire.] (1763), preamble; 5 Geo. III, c.16 [Ire.] (1765), cl.22.

13   *Faulkner's Dublin Journal*, 12 April 1766; *Freeman's Journal*, 15 October 1768, 31 August, 3 September 1771, 30 May, 2 June, 19 September 1772, 15 February 1774.

14   *Freeman's Journal*, 19 September 1772, 13, 20, 31 July 1779, 26 December 1789, 18 April 1793; Gamble, *Sketches of History*, reproduced in Gamble, *Society and Manners*, p. 46.

15   J.B., Journeyman Weaver, *A Letter to the Inhabitants of Dublin, and the Liberty* (Dublin, 1759), p. 8.

16   White, *London in the Eighteenth Century*, p. 435.

17   Stanley Sadie (ed.), *The New Grove Dictionary of Music and Musicians* (2nd edn, New York, 2001), vol. 18, p. 516; Don Michael Randel (ed.), *The Harvard Dictionary of Music* (4th edn, Cambridge, MA, 2003), p. 594.

18   Thomas Bowdler, *The Family Shakespeare, in Ten Volumes, in which Nothing is Added to the Original Text, but those Words and Expressions are Omitted which Cannot be Read Aloud in a Family* (London, 1818), 10 vols.

19   *Freeman's Journal*, 19 October 1771; *Hibernian Journal*, 5 September 1777, 7 September 1778; David Hempton and Myrtle Hill, *Evangelical Protestantism in Ulster Society* (London and New York, 1992), pp. 8ff.

20   Letter (unsigned) from a lady at Lucan Bridge to Mrs Bayliss, London, 11 April 1808, HMC, 13, appendix, vol. 3, ms 10, pp. 590–3; Shoemaker, *Gender in English Society*, p. 88; Patricia McCarthy, 'Vails and travails; how Lord Kildare kept his household in order', *Irish Architectural and Decorative Studies*, journal of the Irish Georgian Society, vol. 6 (2003), pp. 132, 136; White, *London in the Eighteenth Century*, p. 233.

21   'A Physician', *The Toilet-assistant* (Dublin, 1777), pp. 75ff.

22   Shoemaker, *Gender in English Society*, pp. 32ff.

23   *Freeman's Journal*, 8 February 1770; Wakefield, *Account of Ireland*, vol. 2, p. 783; McCabe, *St Stephen's Green*, pp. 167, 191ff.

24   *Freeman's Journal*, 28 August 1790.

25   Anon., *The Grand Masquerade, or the Devil in Dublin* (Dublin, 1810), p. 10; Anon., *The Characteristic Phantasmagoria, or the Satirical Exhibition of the Most Conspicuous Individuals who Now Figure in the Irish Metropolis* (Dublin, 1810), pp. 10ff.

26   [Lock Penitentiary], *Selection of Hymns*, hymns 1, 7, 12, 13, 31, 40.

27   *Freeman's Journal*, 13 January, 3, 14, 22 November, 3 December 1789, 17 April 1792; Beattie, *Crime and the Courts in England*, p. 569; White, *London in the Eighteenth Century*, p. 471.

28   Revd Feijoo, *The Multitude of Holydays Detrimental to the Publick, and not Advantageous to Religion (a Translation by James Tilson for the Benefit of Irish R. Catholic Clergy)* (Dublin, 1760), p. 10.

29   Warburton et al., *History of the City of Dublin*, vol. 2, p. 868.

30   Binns, *Recollections of the Life of John Binns*, pp. 29ff; Wakefield, *Account of Ireland*, vol. 2, pp. 788ff.

31   McGregor, *New Picture of Dublin*, p. 279; Molyneux Asylum for Blind Females, Dublin, Minute Books, 14 May 1816.

32 Anon., *A Letter to His Excellency Earl Camden, etc.* (Dublin, 1795), p. 11; Warburton et al., *History of the City of Dublin*, vol. 2, pp. 677, 887; Whelan, *Bible War in Ireland*, p. 56.

33 Warburton et al., *History of the City of Dublin*, vol. 2, pp. 885ff; McGregor, *New Picture of Dublin*, pp. 231ff; Hempton and Hill, *Evangelical Protestantism in Ulster Society*, pp. 82ff.

34 Wakefield, *Account of Ireland*, vol. 1, p. 738.

35 McGregor, *New Picture of Dublin*, p. 311.

36 Thomas Shillitoe, *Caution and Warning to the Inhabitants of Great Britain* (3rd edn, London, 1799), p. 4.

37 Anon., *Animadversions on the Street Robberies in Dublin*, p. 11; *Belfast News-Letter*, 23 June 1789.

38 Anon., *Observations on the Pernicious Consequences of the Excessive Use of Spirituous Liquors* (Dublin, 1788), p. 15; Beattie, *Crime and the Courts in England*, pp. 497ff.

39 St Anne's parish, Dublin, Vestry Proceedings, 25 March 1788, 11 September 1792, January 1799, 5 November 1805, 17 February 1809, 23 December 1828.

40 *Hibernian Journal*, 7 March 1777; *Freeman's Journal*, 9, 11 November 1797; Beattie, *Crime and the Courts in England*, p. 544.

41 *Faulkner's Dublin Journal*, 16 April 1771; *Dublin Evening Post*, 6 November 1787; *Freeman's Journal*, 25 July 1789, 6 July 1790.

42 *Hibernian Journal*, 19 October 1785, 15 December 1786; *Freeman's Journal*, 16 August 1788.

43 James Orr, 'The Execution' (1798), in Andrew Carpenter (ed.), *Verse in English from Eighteenth-century Ireland* (Cork, 1998), p. 551.

44 Carr, *Stranger in Ireland*, pp. 118ff; *Hibernian Journal*, 23 July 1777, 21 May 1784, 27 July 1785; *Freeman's Journal*, 24 July 1779, 26 January 1788, 7 September, 10 November 1789, 30 November 1791, 27 October, 20 December 1792.

45 *Hibernian Journal*, 15 May 1786; *Freeman's Journal*, 26 January 1788, 21 May 1789.

46 [Lord Lieutenant], proclamation dated 20th March 1767 (NAI ref. no. 189).

47 *Hibernian Journal*, 8 January 1776, 27 October 1780; *Freeman's Journal*, 24 November 1789; Fleetwood, *Irish Body Snatchers*, p. 34.

48 R. Lewis, *The Dublin Guide* (Dublin, 1787), p. 46.

49 *Hibernian Journal*, 7 July, 25 August 1783, 10 May 1784, 23 March, 6 July 1785, 5 July, 15 December 1786; *Freeman's Journal*, 28 July 1789, 3, 5 May 1791.

50 *Hibernian Journal*, 10 October 1777.

51 Ibid., 21 December 1778; *Freeman's Journal*, 4 August 1792; Best, 'St Paul's parish, Dublin', p. 24; Pollard, *Dublin's Trade in Books*, p. 21.

52 [The Society for Increasing the Comforts of the Poor], *The Ninth and Tenth Reports of the Society for Bettering the Condition and Increasing the Comforts of the Poor* (Dublin, 1800), p. 104.

53 Warburton et al., *History of the City of Dublin*, vol. 2, p. 1060; Henry Heaney, 'Ireland's penitentiary, 1820–1831: an experiment that failed', *Studia Hibernica*, no. 14 (1974), pp. 28, 36.

54 Revd William Magee, *A Sermon Preached Before the Association for Discountenancing Vice* (Dublin, 1796), p. 32; [The Society for Increasing the Comforts of the Poor], *First, Second, Ninth and Tenth Reports of the Society for Promoting the Comforts of the Poor, etc.* (Dublin, 1800); Warburton et al., *History of the City of Dublin*, vol. 2, p. 1036.

Chapter 10: Factions and Combinations

1   2 Geo. I, c.17 [Ire.] cls.5, 11 (1715).

2   *Freeman's Journal*, 26 October 1771; Anon., *Institution for Administering Medical Aid to the Sick Poor*, p. 12; Binns, *Recollections of the Life of John Binns*, p. 24.

3   Binns, *Recollections of the Life of John Binns*, p, 24; Vincent Kinane, 'Printers' apprentices in 18th- and 19th-century Dublin', *Linen Hall Review*, vol. 10, no. 1 (summer 1993), p. 11.

4   Finnian Ó Cionnaith, *Mapping, Measurement and Metropolis: How Land Surveyors Shaped Eighteenth-century Dublin* (Dublin, 2012), pp. 20, 25, 182.

5   John J. Webb, *The Guilds of Dublin* (Dublin, 1929; repr. New York, 1970), p. 138.

6   Kinane, 'Printers' apprentices in 18th- and 19th-century Dublin', pp. 11ff.

7   Madden, *Letter to the Dublin Society*, pp. 28ff; [Royal Dublin Society], *Proceedings on the Petitions of Sundry Manufacturers and Others and the Disposition of the Sum of Ten Thousand Pounds, Committed to their Determination, by Order of the Right Honourable and Honourable the Knights, Citizens and Burgesses in Parliament Assembled, Session 1761 and 1762* (Dublin, various dates), pp. 22, 33, 42, 50; Carr, *Stranger in Ireland*, p. 151.

8   *Belfast News-Letter*, 17 February 1789; Conor Lucey, '"In very good business"; Andrew Callnan's house-decorating practice, 1790–1804', *Journal of the Royal Society of the Antiquaries of Ireland*, vol. 137 (2007), p. 119.

9   Webb, *Guilds of Dublin*, pp. 133, 195, 202, 241ff, 278ff; Jacqueline Hill, 'Artisans, sectarianism and politics in dublin, 1829–49', *Saothar*, vol. 7 (1981), pp. 15ff; Knight of Glin, 'A directory of the Dublin furniture trade', p. 48.

10   Kelly (ed.), *Proceedings of the Irish House of Lords*, vol. 2, pp. 284ff; Webb, *Guilds of Dublin*, p. 243; Mel Doyle, 'The Dublin guilds and journeymen's clubs', *Saothar*, vol. 7 (1977), pp. 8ff.

11   [Lord Lieutenant], proclamation dated 4 November 1747 (1747) (NAI ref. 134); *Faulkner's Dublin Journal*, 26 June, 6 July 1762, 16 August 1763, 7 September 1765, 18 September 1770 (a weaver was killed for working below the minimum wage), 2, 4 October 1770 (a group of journeymen silk weavers who attacked a master craftsman were repulsed, and two of them were killed).

12   [Lord Lieutenant], proclamation dated 19 December 1757 (NAI ref. 166); *Faulkner's Dublin Journal*, 1, 6 July 1769; Skinner, *Wallpaper in Ireland*, p. 95.

13   Dunleavy, *Pomp and Poverty*, pp. 78ff.

14   [Lord Lieutenant], proclamation dated 22 June 1764 (1764) (NAI ref. 184); *Hibernian Journal*, 15 October 1781.

15   [House of Industry], *Account of the Proceedings of the Governors of the House of Industry*, p. 26; [Lord Lieutenant], proclamation dated 10 April 1767 (NAI ref. 191).

16   *Calendar of Home Office Papers* (1766–69), no. 1317, 20 October 1769; Dunleavy, *Pomp and Poverty*, pp. 48, 51ff, 73.

17   *Faulkner's Dublin Journal*, 7 September 1765, 12 December 1767, 10 March, 17 April 1770, 19, 26 October 1773; *Hibernian Journal*, 5 March 1780, 15 October 1781; *Freeman's Journal*, 11, 14, 24 April 1789, 19 June, 6 July 1790, 13, 18 December 1794; Gilbert and Gilbert (eds), *Calendar of Ancient Records of Dublin*, vol. 12, pp. 28, 43, 67ff; HMC Rep 13, App III, ms 4182.

18   *Faulkner's Dublin Journal*, 25 January, 3 March, 17 April 1770.

19   *Faulkner's Dublin Journal*, 14, 19 October 1773, 14 April 1774, 21 March 1775; Brian Henry, 'Industrial violence, combinations and the law in late eighteenth-century Dublin', *Soathar*, vol. 18 (1993), p. 25.

20   *Freeman's Journal*, 11, 14, 24 April 1789, 6 July 1790; *Belfast News-Letter*, 14 April 1789; Henry, *Dublin Hanged*, p. 181; [House of Industry], *Account of the Proceedings of the Governors of the House of Industry*, pp. 26ff.

21   Gilbert and Gilbert (eds), *Calendar of Ancient Records of Dublin*, vol. 10, pp. 130, 134, 217, 296, 338, 382, vol. 11, pp. 161, 340, 345, 366, vol. 12, pp. 28, 43, 67ff, 137.

22   *Dublin Evening Post*, 17 July 1787; *Freeman's Journal*, 11 September 1788, 3, 7 May 1793, 8 April, 3 May 1794, 30 May 1795, 12 January 1796; Dr Wm Drennan to Saml McTier, 8 May 1793, Carr (ed.), *Drennan Letters*, p. 161; [Higgins], *Revolutionary Dublin*, pp. 113ff, 283, 289.

23   Thomas Sheridan, 'A prologue spoken by Mr Elrington at the Theatre Royal in Dublin on behalf of the distressed weavers', in Patrick Fagan (ed.), *A Georgian Celebration: Irish Poets of the Eighteenth Century* (Dublin, 1989), p. 165.

24   *Faulkner's Dublin Journal*, 30 May 1771, 12, 21 August 1773, 16 August 1774; *Hibernian Journal*, 18 March 1782; *Freeman's Journal*, 14 April, 5 May 1789; Max Von Boehn, *Modes and Manners* [*Die Möde* (Berlin, 1914)], trans. Joan Joshua (London, 1935), vol. 4, p. 194.

25   Anon., 'The Ladies Dress, or the Downfall of the Stay-makers' (*c.* 1790), in Andrew Carpenter (ed.), *Verse in English from Eighteenth-century Ireland* (Cork, 1998), p. 516.

26   *Hibernian Journal*, 18 March, 16 May, 11 June, 9 July 1783, 10 May, 23 June 1784; *Freeman's Journal*, 22 August 1793; Kuttner, *Briefe uber Ireland*, pp. 36ff; J.D. Herbert, *Irish Varieties for the Last Fifty Years* (London, 1836), p. 86.

27   Kelly (ed.), *Proceedings of the Irish House of Lords*, vol. 1, p. 530, vol. 2, p. 588; Robert B. Shoemaker, 'The London "mob" in the early eighteenth century', in Peter Borsay (ed.), *The Eighteenth-century Town: A Reader in English Urban History, 1688–1820* (London, 1990); Von Boehn, *Modes and Manners*, vol. 4, p. 197; [Higgins], *Revolutionary Dublin*, pp. 148, 371.

28   Tuckey, *County and City of Cork Remembrancer*, pp. 136, 143, 162, 176, 188, 198, 244; C.G. Doran, 'Some unpublished records of Cork, part 2', *Journal of the Cork Historical and Archaeological Society*, vol. 2 (January 1893), p. 111; William O'Sullivan, *The Economic History of Cork from the Earliest Times to the Act of Union* (Cork, 1937), pp. 215ff.

29   *Faulkner's Dublin Journal*, 17 March 1750, 28 September 1751, 11 August, 15 September 1764, 13 December 1768, 25 February, 22 June 1769, 30 November 1773; *Freeman's Journal*, 8 May 1790.

30   Journal kept by a young man in Dublin from February 1801 to May 1802 (RIA ms. 24.K.14–15), 12 July 1802.

31   *Faulkner's Dublin Journal*, 3, 10 February 1753, 5 August 1769, 16 August 1770, 30 May, 19 September 1772, 11, 5 October 1773, 19 April, 19 May, 11 June 1774; *Freeman's Journal*, 13, 22, 31 July 1779, 20 May, 12 July 1788, 5 November 1794; *Dublin Evening Post*, 5, 15 May 1787; *Hibernian Journal*, 14, 30 November, 5 December 1781, 10 February 1782, 3 November 1784; *Dublin Chronicle*, 8 July 1788; Gilbert and Gilbert (eds), *Calendar of Ancient Records of Dublin*, vol. 11, p. 328; Hill, *From Patriots to Unionists*, p. 80.

32   *Faulkner's Dublin Journal*, 17 March 1750, 3, 10 February 1753, 11 August, 8 September 1764,

28 September 1770, 6 January, 1, 3, 8, 10, 20 September 1774, 10, 31 January, 7 February, 25 March 1775; *Hibernian Journal*, 10 October, 3, 31 December 1777, 13 February 1778, 1 September 1780, 5 March 1781, 28 August 1782, 31 March 1783, 20 February, 28 May 1784; Gilbert and Gilbert (eds), *Calendar of Ancient Records of Dublin*, vol. 12, pp. 345, 347ff; Twiss, *Tour in Ireland*, p. 60.

33 *Faulkner's Dublin Journal*, 6 January, 10 September, 8, 20, 22 October, 8 November 1774, 10, 31 January, 2, 7, 9, 16 February, 4, 7, 25 March 1775; *Hibernian Journal*, 10 October, 3, 31 December 1777, 13 February, 16 December 1778, 1, 11, 13 September, 9, 30 October 1780, 5 March 1781, 28 August, 13 September 1782, 31 March, 23 August, 3 November 1783, 20 February, 2 May 1784, 18 April, 21 June 1785; the 'chalking' acts were temporary statutes introduced in 1774 and continued in 1777–78, 1779–80 and 1783–84 – for example, 17 & 18 Geo. III, c.11 [Ire.] (1777–78).

34 *Freeman's Journal*, 23, 25 February, 4, 30 March 1779; *Hibernian Journal*, 14 September 1778, 24 March 1780.

35 *Parl. Reg. Ire.*, vol. 4, p. 294; *Hibernian Journal*, 6, 22, 27 December 1780, 1, 24 January 1781, 2 September 1785, 3 May 1786; *Freeman's Journal*, 31 May, 3 June 1788.

36 *Hibernian Journal*, 4 July 1781, 4 May 1785, 5 May 1786; *Freeman's Journal*, 1 May 1788, 31 January, 2 April 1795; H.O.100/34, report of Lord Lieutenant, July 1792; Sir John Blaquiere to John Beresford, Dublin, 30 January 1795, in William Beresford (ed.), *The Correspondence of the Right Hon. John Beresford* (London, 1854), vol. 2, p. 65; Dr William Drennan to Mrs McTier, *c.* January 1799, Dr Drennan to Mrs McTier, 10 November 1805, Carr (ed.), *Drennan Letters*, pp. 288, 350.

37 *Hibernian Journal*, 13 March 1776, 27 December 1780, 12 March, 15 October, 12 December 1781, 17 December 1784; Herbert, *Irish Varieties for the Last Fifty Years*, pp. 77ff.

38 Kevin Whelan, *The Tree of Liberty: Radicalism, Catholicism and the Construction of Irish Identity, 1760–1830* (Cork, 1996), p. 77.

39 Tuckey, *County and City of Cork Remembrancer*, pp. 128, 132, 138, 141, 154, 162, 168ff, 178, 181, 183, 198; John Fitzgerald, 'Ms. Commonplace Book' [1 August 1784]', *Journal of the Cork Historical and Archaeological Society*, vol. 9. no. 58 (April 1903), p. 127.

40 *Freeman's Journal*, 11, 13 May 1790, 21 April 1798 ('The green and yellow colours from having been the banners of sedition are now become the distinctive badges of those wretched females who draw subsistence from "infamous notoriety"'); James Kelly, *The Liberties and Ormond Boys: Factional Riot in Eighteenth-century Dublin* (Dublin, 2005), pp. 34ff.

41 *Freeman's Journal*, 25, 27 August 1795, 5, 12, 21 April, 16 June, 4 December 1798, 7 March 1799.

42 Tommy Graham, 'Dublin's role in the 1798 rebellion', in Cathal Póirtéir (ed.), *The Great Irish Rebellion of 1798* (Cork, 1998), pp. 55ff.

43 Gamble, *Sketches of History*, reproduced in Gamble, *Society and Manners*, p. 58.

Chapter 11: Development Control and Infrastructural Provision

1 John Crawford to Robt Molesworth, 23 July 1710, HMC, viii. 8, 1913 (Clements mss); Twiss, *Tour in Ireland*, p. 22.

2 Gilbert and Gilbert (eds), *Calendar of Ancient Records of Dublin*, vol. 4, p. 34; 15 & 16 Geo. III, c.24 [Ire.] (1775–76), preamble.

3   Gilbert and Gilbert (eds), *Calendar of Ancient Records of Dublin*, vol. 9, pp. 63ff ('the filth and stench that comes from the buck houses of the several bleachers'), vol. 10, pp. 29, 175, vol. 11, p. 236, vol. 14, pp. 21, 33, 233, 252, vol. 15, pp. 12, 87, 110, 120, 148, 189, 264, 291, 427; 6 Geo. I, c.16 [Ire.] (1740); 15 & 16 Geo. III, c.24 [Ire.] (1775–76); 19 & 20 Geo. III, c.13 [Ire.] (1779–80); 26 Geo. III, c.61 [Ire.] (1786); 28 Geo. III, c.50 [Ire.] (1788); *Hibernian Journal*, 3 August 1781; Carr, *Stranger in Ireland*, p. 53; *Dublin Evening Post*, 23 October 1787; *Freeman's Journal*, 17 January 1795.

4   *Faulkner's Dublin Journal*, 13 October 1753, 19 March 1757, 10 April 1764; St Anne's parish, Dublin, Vestry Proceedings, 1 May 1764.

5   Anon., *A Diary of the Weather and Winds for 19 Years Commencing with AD 1716 and Concluding with 1734* (anon. ms, Gilbert Collection), 18 August 1723, 10 September 1728, 5 May 1729.

6   St Anne's parish, Dublin, Vestry Proceedings, 1 May 1764, 2 May 1765, 12 April 1830; [St Brigid's parish, Dublin], *The Vestry Records of the Parishes of St Bride, St Michael le Pole and St Stephen, Dublin, 1662–1742*, ed. W.J.R. Wallace (Dublin, 2011), pp. 253, 289; 6 Geo. I, c.8 [Ire.] (1719); Best, 'St Paul's parish, Dublin', p. 18; Tom Geraghty and Trevor Whitehead, *The Dublin Fire Brigade* (Dublin, 2004), pp. 2ff; *Belfast News-Letter*, 24 November 1789.

7   Andrew Carpenter (ed.), *Verse in English from Eighteenth-century Ireland* (Cork, 1998), p. 245.

8   *Faulkner's Dublin Journal*, 29 May 1753, 1 June 1754; *Hibernian Journal*, 20 January 1777.

9   Gilbert and Gilbert (eds), *Calendar of Ancient Records of Dublin*, vol. 16, p. 260; *Hibernian Journal*, 6 February 1782; Wide Streets Commission, Dublin, Minutes, vol. 3, 22 January 1781, vol. 4, 21 June 1782, 30 April 1784.

10   Wide Streets Commission, Dublin, Minutes, vol. 6, 26 August, 17 October, 21, 25 November 1785, 8 May, 9, 19 June 1786, vol. 7, 20 October 1786, vol. 8, 18 March 1788, vol. 9, 30 October 1789; *Faulkner's Dublin Journal*, 24 May 1763; *Dublin Evening Post*, 1 September 1787.

11   Anon., *Report of the Commissioners Appointed to Enquire into the Conduct and Management of the Corporation for Paving, Cleansing, and Lighting the Streets of Dublin* (Dublin, 1806), p. 8; Warburton et al., *History of the City of Dublin*, vol. 2, pp. 1076ff; Isaac Farrell, *Suggestions on the Dublin Improvements* (Dublin, 1841), p. 12.

12   Gilbert, *History of the City of Dublin*, vol. 1, p. 182; Webb, *Guilds of Dublin*, p. 218.

13   *Faulkner's Dublin Journal*, 30 April 1751, 1, 22 November 1755, 1 May, 3 July, 7 August, 2 November 1756, 30 June 1759, 23 June 1761, 1 November 1763, 10 January, 31 March 1764, 2 September 1769, 19 June 1773; *Parl. Reg. Ire.* (2nd edn, 1784), vol. 2, p. 362, vol. 3, p. 145; Kelly (ed.), *Proceedings of the Irish House of Lords*, vol. 2, pp. 163, 491; Dutton, *Observations*, p. 147.

14   *Faulkner's Dublin Journal*, 21 June 1763; Pool and Cash, *Views of […] the City of Dublin*, p. 16; *Parl. Reg. Ire.*, 1787, pt 2, appendix dvi [506].

15   Lloyd, *Description of the City of Dublin*, p. 3; Anon., *Rules, Orders, and Bye-laws, Made by His Majesty's Commissioners of Police, for the District of the Metropolis* (Dublin, 1793); George Nicholls, *A History of the Irish Poor Law* (London, 1856), p. 49; Anon., *Advice and Directions to Hackney Coachmen*, p. 24.

16   *Faulkner's Dublin Journal*, 8 October, 5 November 1748, 12 July, 19 August, 17 October

1760, 23 June 1761, 18 September 1762, 6 March, 7 April, 21 August 1764, 28 October 1766; *Freeman's Journal*, 23 September 1788; Kelly (ed.), *Proceedings of the Irish House of Lords*, vol. 2, p. 491; 13 & 14 Geo. III, c.22 [Ire.] (1773/4); 15 Geo. III, c.11 [Ire.] (1775); Dutton, *Observations*, p. 136.

17 *Faulkner's Dublin Journal*, 20 January 1756, 27 March 1764, 13 December 1770; *Hibernian Journal*, 9 February 1784, 1 February 1786; *Dublin Evening Post*, 31 May 1787; *Freeman's Journal*, 15 March 1788, 17 November 1789; St Anne's parish, Dublin, Vestry Proceedings, various dates.

18 Anon., *Remarks on the Principle of a Bill now Pending in Parliament for the Establishment of Turnpikes Round the City of Dublin* (Dublin, 1786), p. 27; Kelly (ed.), *Proceedings of the Irish House of Lords*, vol. 1, p. 209; Anon., *Report of the Commissioners Appointed to Enquire into […] the Streets of Dublin*, p. 6; *Dublin Satirist*, November 1809, p. 2; *Freeman's Journal*, 21 December 1793, 15 January 1795.

19 Gilbert and Gilbert (eds), *Calendar of Ancient Records of Dublin*, vol. 10, p. 5, vol. 13, p. 377; *Faulkner's Dublin Journal*, 10 June 1775; *Hibernian Journal*, 13 August 1784, 31 May, 6 September, 10 November 1786; *Freeman's Journal*, 12 January, 7 September 1790, 18 October 1794, 29 August 1797; Anon., *Report of the Commissioners Appointed to Enquire into […] the Streets of Dublin*, p. 8; Young, 'A Dublin slaughter house nuisance', pp. 75ff.

20 Anon., *Address by the Inhabitants of Pill Lane to the Lord Mayor Jacob West and his Reply* (NLI ms. 8280); Joseph Tickell, *Scientific and Sanitary Argument etc.* (Dublin, 1848), p. 18.

21 Newburgh, 'The Beau Walk, in Stephen's Green', in Carpenter (ed.), *Verse in English*, p. 319.

22 Gilbert and Gilbert (eds), *Calendar of Ancient Records of Dublin*, vol. 9, pp. 52, 66, 150, 229; Hamilton, *Cries of Dublin*, pl. 42; *Hibernian Journal*, 28 January, 17 November 1780, 23 April 1783, 12 March 1784, 3 January 1785; St Anne's parish, Dublin, Vestry Proceedings, 25 July 1771.

23 Gilbert and Gilbert (eds), *Calendar of Ancient Records of Dublin*, vol. 12, pp. 252, 281; *Faulkner's Dublin Journal*, 1 October 1772; *Freeman's Journal*, 9 September 1791; Young, 'St. Michan's parish in the eighteenth century', p. 4.

24 Whitelaw, *Essay on the Population of Dublin*, p. 50.

25 Tuckey, *County and City of Cork Remembrancer*, pp. 140ff, 149–50, 165–6, 226 (citing *Cork Mercantile Chronicle*, 3 April 1805), 244; O'Sullivan, *Economic History of Cork*, pp. 138ff.

26 M.C. Buer, *Health, Wealth, and Population in the Early Days of the Industrial Revolution* (London, 1926), pp. 82ff; C.W. Chalklin, *The Provincial Towns of Georgian England: A Study of the Building Process, 1740–1820* (London, 1974), pp. 148ff; Youngson, *Making of Classical Edinburgh*, pp. 240ff; Cockayne, *Hubbub*, p. 248.

27 Ferrar, *View of Ancient and Modern Dublin*, p. 35; David Garrick, *Bon Ton: Or High Life Above Stairs* (London, 1785); Anon., 'Between a Contractor and his Wife' (1775), in Roger Lonsdale (ed.), *The New Oxford Book of Eighteenth-century Verse* (Oxford, 1987); George Rudé, *Hanovarian London, 1714–1808* (London, 1971), p. 136; Roy Porter, *London: A Social History* (London, 1994), pp. 104, 125; Buer, *Health, Wealth, and Population*, pp. 82ff.

28 Corbin, *Foul and the Fragrant Odour*, pp. 90ff; Roche, *People of Paris*, pp. 16, 32, 101, 157.

29 Whitelaw, *Essay on the Population of Dublin*.

30 *Parl. Reg. Ire.* (1785), vol. 4, p. 260; J.J. Webb, *Industrial Dublin Since 1698 and the Silk*

Industry in Dublin (Dublin, 1913), p. 70; L.M. Cullen, An Economic History of Ireland Since 1660 (London, 1972), pp. 93ff; Cormac Ó Gráda, Ireland: A New Economic History, 1780–1939 (Oxford, 1994), pp. 275ff; Young, 'A Dublin slaughter house nuisance', pp. 75ff.

31 3 Geo. II, c.19 [Ire.] cl.11, 12 (1729); Faulkner's Dublin Journal, 18 February, 4 March 1766.

32 11 Geo. III, c.6 [Ire.] (1771), 11 & 12 Geo. III, c.27 [Ire.] (1772); 15 & 16 Geo. III, c.34 [Ire.] (1775–76).

33 Freeman's Journal, 21 August 1779; 23 & 24 Geo. III, c.35 [Ire.] (1783–74); Parl. Reg. Ire. (2nd edn, 1784), vol. 2, p. 98; Kelly (ed.), Proceedings of the Irish House of Lords, vol. 2, p. 238; Warburton et al., History of the City of Dublin, vol. 1, p. 446.

34 Hibernian Journal, 10 November 1786; BPP, HC, 1828, p. xxii. Wide Streets Commission (Dublin), Accounts and Papers, nos. 6, 10.

35 Herbert, Irish Varieties for the Last Fifty Years, p. 217.

36 Gamble, Sketches of History, reproduced in Gamble, Society and Manners, p. 41.

37 Carr, Stranger in Ireland, p. 137.

38 3 Geo. II, c.19 [Ire.] (1729), 3 Geo. III, c.36 [Ire.] (1763); Gilbert and Gilbert (eds), Calendar of Ancient Records of Dublin, vol. 12, p. 538.

39 Freeman's Journal, 17, 28 January, 11, 18, 28 February, 7 March 1769.

Chapter 12: Prostitution

1 Pádraig Ó Fágáin, Éigse na hIarmhí (Dublin, 1985), p. 142.

2 Faulkner's Dublin Journal, 29 October 1751; Freeman's Journal, 5 June 1794, 14 July 1796; [House of Industry], Account of the Proceedings of the Governors of the House of Industry, pp. 26ff.

3 R. Lewis, The Dublin Guide (Dublin, 1787), pp. 50ff ('Our sight was constantly struck with objects disgraceful to human nature; with wretched strumpets, tricked out in tawdry apparel, or covered with tattered weeds; and where our ears were continually assaulted with vociferations that would startle deafness, and appal blasphemy'); Hibernian Journal, 3 January 1781 (prostitutes 'wound the ears of delicacy, by the vilest effusions of lewdness and excretion'), 4 February 1784 (the noise created by soliciting women in Essex Street was grossly offensive and they should be kept indoors), 3 November 1784 (the whores infesting every corner of the city 'proclaim aloud the profligacy of the times'), 2 August 1787 ('The screams, the blasphemies, and the execrations of those miscreants, wound the ear of every passenger'), 15 September 1787 (soliciting women filled the main streets with the most horrid blasphemies); Freeman's Journal, 20 December 1791 ('the alarming riots, loud shrieks, noisy wranglings and horrid oaths and blasphemies of the miscreants'), 5 July 1791 (swarms of women are soliciting throughout the city, with vile, abusive language), 17 October 1795 (the watch seized several streetwalkers who were causing a disturbance 'with loud screams, and infamous howlings').

4 Journal kept by a young man in Dublin from February 1801 to May 1803 (RIA ms 24.K. 14–15), 19 February 1801, 8 March 1803; Anon., The Tricks of the Town Laid Open (Dublin, c. 1754), p. 11; Anon., Dublin Satirist, November 1809, pp. 25ff; Anon., Dublin, a Satirical Essay etc., Book 1 (Dublin, 1788) ('On seeing Bright Delia, a prostitute in her carriage': 'Virtue on pattens o'er the kennel strides,/ And vice triumphant in her chariot rides'); Freeman's Journal, 15 January 1789 ('The progress of beauty': 'On the Circular-road the

high Phaeton see,/ The delicate hunter, gilt coach vis-a-vis …'); *Freeman's Journal*, 3 October 1789 ('On seeing a young and beautiful Courtesan, in a very splendid equipage': 'No fear, remorse, or guilt she feels/ But drags them at her chariot heels,/ Amidst the blaze of day'); Anon., *The Metropolis* (2nd edn, Dublin, 1805), p. 30:

> But who comes here to set the world agaze,
> Fawn-colour'd liv'ries, and curvetting greys,
> In hue, her chariot with the topaz vies,
> What splendid Countess blazes on my eyes?
> – No countess, but a queen, whose Paphian reign
> Extends o'er love and folly – Queen Maclean.

5 Anon., *The Case of the Stage in Ireland: Containing the Reasons For and Against a Bill for Limiting the Number of Theatres in the City of Dublin* (Dublin, 1758); Anon., *An Answer to the Memoirs of Mrs Billington* (London, 1792), p. 53.

6 *Freeman's Journal*, 18, 28 August 1790, 7 January 1792, 29 August 1793, 4 August, 6 October 1796, 18 April, 23 September 1797; Gilbert, *History of the City of Dublin*, vol. 2, p. 79; Fitzpatrick, *Curious Family History*, p. 77.

7 Margaret Leeson, *Memoirs of Mrs Margaret Leeson* (Dublin, 1795–97; repr. Dublin 1995), vol. 3, p. 211.

8 Ibid., p. 169.

9 *Hibernian Journal*, 5 September 1777, 7 September 1778 (prostitutes should be refused admission to concerts and Rotunda balls – 'a dozen public prostitutes mixing indiscriminately with ladies of family and fortune'); *Freeman's Journal*, 29 May 1788; *Dublin Evening Post*, 19 July 1787; Anon., *Female Honour* (Dublin, 1742), p. 8 ('There lies our female honour, 'tis the shame/ Of vice that hurts us – Whore! the odious name'); *Walker's Hibernian Magazine,* November/December 1771 (in their quarters the women 'lie crowded together, mad with intemperance, ghastly with famine, nauseous with filth, and noisome with disease'); ibid., May 1775 ('the present amazing increase of wretched prostitutes'); Thomas Burke, *English Night-life* (2nd edn, London, 1943), p. 76.

10 Whitelaw, *Essay on the Population of Dublin*, p. 64.

11 St Mary's parish, Vestry Book, 6 March 1722, cited in Starr, 'Enforcing of law and order in eighteenth-century Ireland', p. 113; Tony Henderson, *Disorderly Women in Eighteenth-century London: Prostitution and Control in the Metropolis, 1730–1830* (London, 1999), p. 45.

12 *Hibernian Journal*, 3 September 1777; Soame Jenyns, 'The Modern Fine Lady' (1751), in Roger Lonsdale (ed.), *The New Oxford Book of Eighteenth-century Verse* (Oxford, 1987), p. 459:

> The fribbling beau, the rough unwieldy clown,
> The ruddy templar newly on the town,
> Th' Hibernian captain of gigantic make,
> The brimful parson and th'exhausted rake.

13 Anon., *Clarissa: Or, the Courtezan* (Dublin, 1749), p. 4: 'Thronging whores with rough attention pour/ From off the quays, the bridge, the streets around'; *Hibernian Journal*, 24 October 1783, 9 February, 8 August, 16 November, 19 December 1785 (the residents of Essex Street and Crampton Court should organise themselves to eject 'the swarms of prostitutes and bullies'), 6 October 1786; *Dublin Evening Post*, 5 May, 20 September 1787;

Freeman's Journal, 12, 17 July, 19 August 1788, 5 September, 7 November 1789, 11, 25 May, 10 July, 19 August 1790 (much younger women have joined the very large numbers soliciting in Dame Street, Trinity Street and College Green), 10, 28 May, 7, 21 July 1792, 7 March 1795, 12 July 1796, 28 April 1798.

14   *Hibernian Journal*, 31 March 1777, 3 January 1781, 6 September 1786; *Freeman's Journal*, 7 July, 18 October 1791, 28 February, 29 March 1792; *Hibernia Curiosa, A Letter from a Gentleman in Dublin, to his Friend at Dover in Kent* (2nd edn, London, 1782), p. 20.

15   *Freeman's Journal*, 27 June, 4, 11, 14, 16, 18, 23 July, 1, 18 August, 1 September, 3 October 1795.

16   Anon., *The Life and Uncommon Adventures of Capt. Dudley Bradstreet* (Dublin, 1760).

17   *Hibernian Journal*, 16 March 1785; *Freeman's Journal*, 18 October, 1 November 1788, 22 December 1791, 17 November 1796.

18   Carpenter (ed.), *Verse in English*, p. 490.

19   *Hibernian Journal*, 2 August 1776, 20 November 1778, 14 November, 7 December 1781 (soldiers set free sixty prostitutes from the House of Industry), 7, 31 October, 28 November 1785; *Freeman's Journal*, 27, 30 September, 18 October 1788, 6 July 1799.

20   *Freeman's Journal*, 22 December 1789, 23 August 1791, 20 March 1793, 28 October 1794, 14 April, 4 August 1796, 5 July 1798; Leeson, *Memoirs of Mrs Margaret Leeson*; Anon., *Four Letters in Answer to an Address to the Committee of the Dublin Female Penitentiary* (Dublin, 1813), pp. 12ff; 'A Real Paddy' [Pierce Egan], *Real Life in Ireland*, p. 54 (commemorated Elizabeth McClean in a ballad entitled 'Dublin Nuisances or Down with the Watch': 'Sure Sally is a sad slut,/ What would the jade be a'ter?').

21   Mr Marchant, 'The Old Bawd's Lure to a Country Girl on Her First Arrival in Town', in Anon., *The Muses Choice* (4th edn, Dublin, 1770), p. 157.

22   *Hibernian Journal*, 24 July 1786; Anon., *The Satirical Ambulator, by Peeping Tim, for the Year 1791* (Dublin, 1791), p. 26 ('When wither'd punk lost beauty mourns,/ From whore to bawd she surely turns …'); William Hogarth, *A Harlot's Progress* (London, 1731); Austin Dobson, *William Hogarth* (London, 1898), p. 169 (refers to the 1739 Dublin reprint, with Hogarth's prints, of Joseph Gay's *The Lure of Venus: Or a Harlot's Progress. An Heroical Poem*).

23   *Freeman's Journal*, 14 May 1791, 21 April 1795, 21, 31 May, 15 September 1796; Anon., *The Tricks of the Town Laid Open* (Dublin, *c*. 1754), p. 28.

24   *Freeman's Journal*, 3 July, 23 September 1788, 13 January 1789, 11 May 1790, 1 January 1791 (a young woman was forced into a Stafford Street brothel by five men, including three sedan-chair porters hired for the purpose), 8 September 1791, 11 July, 25 August 1795 (an old woman who kept a fruit stall at the Essex Street/Parliament Street corner was hanged for complicity in the rape of a young girl).

25   *Faulkner's Dublin Journal*, 10, 14, 17, 21 May 1768.

26   Ibid., 14 May, 23 August, 1 December 1768 (a Fishamble Street brothel keeper, Catherine Halpenny, was killed in a riot).

27   Ibid., 23 May 1771, 11 October, 2 September 1775; *Freeman's Journal*, 23 April, 28 July, 2 August 1791.

28   *Freeman's Journal*, 26 November 1793, 5 July 1794, 16 June 1796.

29   Ibid., 23 July 1791, 1 December 1792, 21 September, 26 November 1793, 23 September 1794.

30   Ibid., 11, 14 July, 27 October 1795.

31   Ibid., 14, 18, 23 July, 13, 18 August, 12 December 1795, 12 January 1796.

32   *Faulkner's Dublin Journal*, 3 February 1753; *Freeman's Journal*, 1 October 1789, 19 April 1794,
      19 March, 16 June, 4 July 1795, 12 July 1796; Ferrar, *View of Ancient and Modern Dublin*, p.
      127; Anon., *Report Upon Certain Charitable Establishments*, p. 4; Anon., 'A Much Admired
      Song Call'd Tied My Toes to the Bed' (Dublin?, undated ballad sheet):

                  When I first came to Dublin I view'd Barrack Street
                  I was a hearty young fellow and smart on my feet
                  I met with a girl call'd Bessey Maclane
                  She brough me to a lodgin call'd sweet Dirty Lane.

      'The Humours of Donnybrook Fair', in Hugh Shields (ed.), *Old Dublin Songs* (Dublin,
      1988): 'Barrack Street rangers, the known ones and strangers,/And many that no one can
      tell how they live'; 'The Dublin Jack of All Trades' in ibid.: 'In Barrack Street I lost my
      wife,/ I'm glad I ne'er could find her.'

33   Gamble, *Sketches of History*, reproduced in Gamble, *Society and Manners*, p. 22.

34   A.D. Harvey, *Sex in Georgian England: Attitudes and Prejudices from the 1720s to the
      1820s* (London, 1994), pp. 101ff; Randolph Trumbach, 'Modern prostitution and gender
      in Fanny Hill: libertine and domesticated fantasy', in G.S. Rousseau and Roy Porter
      (eds), *Sexual Underworlds of the Enlightenment* (Manchester, 1987), pp. 79ff; Randolph
      Trumbach, 'Sex, gender, and sexual identity in modern culture: male sodomy and female
      prostitution in Enlightenment London', in John C. Fout (ed.), *Forbidden History: The
      State, Society, and the Regulation of Sexuality in Modern Europe* (Chicago, 1992), pp.
      99ff; Susan Staves, 'British seduced maidens', *Eighteenth-century Studies*, no. 2 (winter
      1980–81), p. 134; *Report of the Select Committee of the House of Commons 1817*, in Strathearn
      Gordon and J.G.B. Cocks, *A People's Conscience* (London, 1952), pp. 53, 79ff; Colin Jones,
      Paris: Biography of a City (London, 2006), pp. 236ff.

Chapter 13: Aftermath

1   J.J. Stockdale, *Petticoat Loose* (4th edn, London, 1812), p. 55.

2   Anon., *The Picture of Dublin* (4th edn, Dublin, 1813), p. 57.

3   *Faulkner's Dublin Journal*, 10 August 1745, 4 September 1756, 6 July 1779, 10 July, 20
     December 1790, 21 April, 20 September 1796, 4 December 1798, 2 July 1799; *Freeman's
     Journal*, 11 November 1788, 2 September 1794, 31 October 1795, 3 January 1799;
     Westmoreland Lock Hospital, Record Books; Anon., *Arguments in Proof* [...] *in the City
     of Dublin*, pp. 6ff; W. Harty MB, 'Review of an historic sketch of the causes, progress,
     extent and mortality of the contagious fever', *Dublin Magazine*, vol 2, no. 8 (August 1820),
     p. 134.

4   Leitch Ritchie, *Ireland Picturesque and Romantic* (London, 1831), vol. 1, p. 13.

5   [Higgins], *Revolutionary Dublin*, p. 293.

Appendix 3: Brothels Operating in Eighteenth-century Dublin

1   *Freeman's Journal*, 30 November 1791.

2   *Hibernian Journal*, 6 May 1776.

3   *Freeman's Journal*, 23 April, 28 July, 2 August 1791.

4   Leeson, *Memoirs of Mrs Margaret Leeson*, vol. 3.

5   *Freeman's Journal*, 5 October 1793.

6   Ibid., 7 July 1792, 26 November 1793, 5 July 1794, 16 June 1795.

7   *Faulkner's Dublin Journal*, 18 May 1751; Pilkington, *Memoirs of Laetitia Pilkington*, vol. 1.

8   *Freeman's Journal*, 7 May 1791.

9   Ibid., 17–19 July 1788.

10 Ibid., 11 November 1798.

11 *Hibernian Journal*, 10 October 1777.

12 *Freeman's Journal*, 28 February 1792.

13 Ibid., 11 May, 11 June 1791.

14 *Faulkner's Dublin Journal*, 31 October 1747.

15 *Freeman's Journal*, 8 September 1791, 29 March 1792; Leeson, *Memoirs of Mrs Margaret Leeson*, vol. 3.

16 David Fleming, 'Public attitudes to prostitution in eighteenth-century Ireland', *Irish Economic and Social History*, vol. 32 (2005), p. 4.

17 *Freeman's Journal*, 24 April 1792.

18 *Faulkner's Dublin Journal*, 1 December 1768.

19 *Hibernian Journal*, 17 August 1778.

20 *Freeman's Journal*, 2 August 1791.

21 Ibid., 16 August 1788; Gilbert, *History of the City of Dublin*, vol. 1, p. 94.

22 *Hibernian Journal*, 23 October 1778.

23 *Freeman's Journal*, 2 March 1779.

24 Ibid., 8, 22 January 1791.

25 Leeson, *Memoirs of Mrs Margaret Leeson*, vol. 1, p. iii; *Freeman's Journal*, 23 February 1779; 'A Real Paddy' [Pierce Egan], *Real Life in Ireland*, p. 48.

26 *Faulkner's Dublin Journal*, 3 March 1770.

27 *Freeman's Journal*, 31 March 1796.

28 Ibid., 5 July, 14 August, 16 December 1788, 7 July 1789; Archbold Hamilton Rowan, *A Brief Investigation of the Sufferings of John, Anne and Mary Neil* (Dublin, 1788).

29 *Faulkner's Dublin Journal*, 4 November 1766.

30 Ibid., 11 November 1765.

31 *Freeman's Journal*, 4 September 1791.

32 *Hibernian Journal*, 6 May 1776.

33 *Freeman's Journal*, 14 April 1796.

34 Fleming, 'Public attitudes to prostitution', p. 10.

35 *Freeman's Journal*, 26 May, 22 December 1796.

36 Ibid., 1 August 1795, 9, 28 April, 14 May, 28 July, 4 August 1796, 5 July 1798; Anon., *Dublin Journal, 1801–3* (RIA Ms. 24k), pp. 14ff; Hugh Shields (ed.), *Old Dublin Songs* (Dublin, 1988), pp. 57ff.

37 *Hibernian Journal*, 15 October 1781, 8, 24 July, 14 August 1782.

38 Fitzpatrick, *Curious Family History*, p. 100.

39 *Freeman's Journal*, 11 May 1791, 31 March 1796; Leeson's *Memoirs*, iii.

40 *Freeman's Journal*, 23 August 1791, 20 March 1793, 28 October 1794, 4 August 1796.

41 Ibid., 8 September 1791; Leeson, *Memoirs of Mrs Margaret Leeson*, vol. 3.

42 *Freeman's Journal*, 10 December 1795.

43 Ibid., 5 December 1795.

44 *Hibernian Journal*, 5 July 1776.

45 *Freeman's Journal*, 11 February 1779.

46 *Faulkner's Dublin Journal*, 2 December 1766.

47 *Freeman's Journal*, 24 October 1795.

48 Fleming, 'Public attitudes to prostitution', p. 14.

49 *Freeman's Journal*, 27 October 1795.

50 Ibid., 27, 31 March 1792; Leeson, *Memoirs of Mrs Margaret Leeson*, vol. 3.

51 *Freeman's Journal*, 16 April 1796.

52 Ibid., 23 July 1791.

53 Ibid., 12 December 1795, 10, 14 January 1796.

54 Ibid., 4 August 1796.

55 *Faulkner's Dublin Journal*, 13, 24 September 1774.

56 Leeson, *Memoirs of Mrs Margaret Leeson*, vol. 3.

57 Ibid.

Index

Note: illustrations are indicated by page numbers in bold.

commerce 2, 3–4, 16–18, 110, 269; *see* also retail trade
Common Council 73–4
communications 16–17, 99
Connolly, Thomas 138
constables 49, 72, 126, 127, 133, 165, 204; *see* also parish watch; police
construction work 155, 246, 266
Cook Street 11, 263, 273
Cooley, Thomas 32, 74
Coombe, the 111, 213, 277
Cope Street 200, 258, 278
Copper Alley 102, 200, 249, 273, 275
Cork 33, 61, 138, 165, 247, 251, 264
Cork Hill 21, 206, 213
Cork Street Fever Hospital 156, 157, 173, 187
Cornmarket 85
corporal punishment 125, 129, 134, 183, 184, 210, 211, 229, 230, 234, 240
Corrigan, Joseph 60
corruption 72, 123, 126, 132, 191, 192, 204, 206–7, 249, 290
cotton 21, 111, 240, 247, 266
countryside 93, 96–7, 103–5, **103, 104**, 290
Court of King's Bench 73
courts *see* ecclesiastical courts; law courts
Covent Garden 32
craftsmen 17–20, 23, 26, 234–47
Creagh, Sir Michael 90, 176–9
Cries of Dublin (Hamilton) **7**, 9, **20, 48, 52,** 60, **62, 68,** 157, 186, 263
crime 15, 50–52, 53, 71, 109, 120, 123–45, 199–205, 210–11, 220–21, 226–31, 257
crimpers 138
Cross Lane Boys 250
Crow Street theatre 24, 234, 272, 289
Crumlin 213
Curwen, J.C. 109
Custom House 32, 116, **117**, 257, 269, 290
customs duties 2

Dalkey 101, 144
Daly, Richard 272
Dame Street 6, 85–9, 102, 129, 140, 192, 200, 207, 246, 258–9, 267, **269**, 278, 279, **284**
Dargle valley 55–8
Dawson, Joshua 79
Dawson estate 79–80
Dawson Street 45, 79, 226, 263
Deacon, John 229
death penalty 40, 125, 127, 129, 139, 140–41, 211, 221, 226, 227–9, 244
debtors' prisons 58–9, 152, 170, 171, 204

Defoe, Daniel 6, 43
Delany, Mary 96–7, 104
Denny, Lady Arabella 221
Dexter, James 171
Dirty Lane 115, 152, **153**, 237
disability 160, 189, 191; *see also* blindness
dissection 229
distilleries 77, 111, 267
Dixon, Joshua 207
Dr Steevens' Hospital 169
dogs 165, 171
D'Olier Street **252**, 267, **268**
domestic life **10**, 20–21, 97, 216–17
domestic servants **19**, 20, 28, 37, 50–52, 132, 138, 183, 206, 210, 214, 217, 234, 271–2, 289
Donnybrook 102, 103, 105, 111, 218, 277
Donnybrook Fair 218, **219**
Donnybrook road 141, 167, 240, 260
Dorset Street 70, 106–7, 154, 195, 200, 275
Drennan, William 55, 61, 108, 194, 246
drinking 72, 123, 132, 152, **158**, 158–9, **159**, 171, 192, 200, 204, **205**, 209, **210**, 213, 214, 224, 226, 272; *see also* public houses; whiskey
Drumcondra 58, 111, 213
Dublin Castle **3**, 6, **34**, 35, 44, 86, 106, 130, 132, 192, 206, 216, 218, 259, 289
Dublin Chronicle xii, 37
Dublin Corporation 12, 37, 65, 69–70, 71–5, 81, 90, 116, 132, 134, 166, 189, 191, 193, 246, 254, 255, 268
Dublin Female Penitentiary 195
Dublin Philosophical Society 7
duels 210
Dún Laoghaire *see* Dunleary
Duncan, William: map of Dublin 119–20
Dunghill Lane 115, 152, **153**
dunghills 90, 115, 116, 150, 151–5, **153**, 203, 237, 263, 264
Dunleary 90, 92, 94, 101, 103, **119**, 119–20, **120**
Dunlevy, Mairéad 111
Dutton, Hely 163, 164, 260
dysentry 147, 151

Eccles Street 70, 289
ecclesiastical courts 12, 233
Edgeworth, Maria 46, 108
Edgeworth, Robert 211
Edinburgh 8, 27, 34, 41, 123, 265
education 8–9, 26, 60, 182–3, 186, 188, 210, 231, 276, 289
Education Society **225**
Egan, Pierce 58, 94, 100, 169–70
Ellis, Henry 187

Mobile Library Service
Unit 1
The Square Industrial Complex
Tallaght, Dublin 24
Ph: 4597834